Trade, Inflation, and the Dollar

Trade, Inflation, and the Dollar

Thibaut de Saint Phalle

NEW YORK OXFORD
OXFORD UNIVERSITY PRESS
1981

Library of Congress Cataloging in Publication Data

De Saint Phalle, Thibaut.
Trade, inflation, and the dollar.
Bibliography: p.
Includes index.
1. United States—Commerce. 2. International finance. 3. Balance of payments—United States. 4. International economic relations. I. Title.
HF3031.D44 332'.042 81-2456
ISBN 0-19-502970-4 AACR2

Printing (last digit): 98765432
Printed in the United States of America

To Mariana,

without whose patience, support,
and active participation,
this book would never have been written.

"What is the use of a book," thought Alice, "without pictures or conversation."

Alice's Adventures in Wonderland

Acknowledgments

This book would not have been written if Walter Sauer, who served as an official of the Export-Import Bank almost continuously from 1935 until his death in 1980, had not urged me to write it and reviewed each chapter. Walter made government his life work. He was the greatest public servant I have known. The Bank was his life and he inspired all who knew him. He was most patient with my innate distrust in a democracy of solutions imposed by government.

So many people helped in making this book possible. As research assistants I was fortunate to obtain help from Georgetown students in economics: Peter Cohen, Gary Kearns, Jeanie Newman, and Helen Walsh. Jorge Lamas in the European Division of Eximbank helped me to understand and translate some very complicated trade tables. David Morse, Robert Krieble, David O'D. Kennedy, Robert Hefner, F. M. Hunt, William Shipman, Lionel Olmer, and many other wise men read various chapters and provided their comments. My secretary and assistant Lita Henley typed and pasted, read and corrected for hours outside her normal duties. Theodora McGill and her library staff at Exim put in many hours of extra time finding materials for me. Fred Sujat, one of Exim's bright lawyers, provided additional research and helped with the intricacies of the copyright office. Finally, two friends guided and helped to sharpen my thinking: Nasrollah Fatemi, my friend and colleague from academia, and above all, Adlai Stevenson, Senator from Illinois, who supervised Eximbank activity in his capacity as Chairman of the Subcommittee on International Finance of the Senate Committee on Banking, Currency and Urban Affairs, and spent many hours convincing me that government policies were the compromise of the possible.

Contents

Trade, Inflation, and the Dollar

Introduction

The writing of a book follows a tortuous path at best. This book started from one idea, born several years ago, turned into something else as a result of job experience in Washington, and finally became a study of complex international economic relationships, not a study done from the viewpoint of an economist or from the perspective of standard economic thinking, but a sort of distillation of one man's experience and observations over many years, in many countries, involved actively in many endeavors.

The origins of the book go back to 1975. I set out to write a study of international banking with two friends—Dr. Zuhair Mikdashi, professor of banking at Lausanne University, writer of numerous books on energy and development, and advisor to Arab government; and Dr. Nasrollah Fatemi, dean emeritus of the graduate school of international studies at Fairleigh Dickinson University in New Jersey, and close friend and colleague, with whom I had collaborated on two earlier books.* Our purpose was to write a book on the development of international private commercial banking and its role in the development of national economies.

Fatemi was to trace the development of the U.S. banking system, I was to do the growth of private international and Eurocurrency banking (a subject I was teaching at the Center for Education in International Management in Geneva, Switzerland), and Mikdashi was to supply the analysis of the new development banks in the Arab countries and their coming role as key participants in international banking. As it happens in many such ambitious projects, events caught up with the participants before the research could be completed. In my case, I came back to the United States and accepted, in 1977, an appointment as one of the five full-time directors of the Export-Import Bank of the United States, a position that has led to the writing of this book on international trade in the context of U.S. economic policy.

*"*The Dollar Crisis,*" (Fairleigh Dickinson University Press, 1963); *Multinational Corporation* (A. S. Barnes, 1976).

Unfortunately, aside from five years in the U.S. Navy in World War II, much of it spent in remote parts of China, and a few years of part-time activity thereafter in Vietnam (then Indochina), coming to the Bank was my first experience in the federal political process. As soon as I came to Washington, a number of perceptions became apparent. The first was that I was totally unaccustomed to executive-branch collective decisionmaking. The second was that I found in the Congress of the United States a number of remarkable men and women who were truly concerned with the problems affecting the country but unfortunately had little time to reflect on the solutions because of constant pressure to legislate in all directions.*

As a former financial lawyer my credibility with the Congress was not automatic, as an investment banker, not much better. But I found to my surprise that as a former professor of international law and finance in a respected institution, I was considered to be intelligent, unbiased, and experienced: in other words, a man whose judgment a congressman could trust. I decided that I had better live up to this role and learn enough about the role of what is called the Ex-Im Bank to be able to answer questions about its function, relevance, and the degree of funding that might be appropriate at a period when budgetary restraints had become a necessity.

This book, then, is the result of an effort to think through a complex international problem, and then explain it in simple, understandable terms. I hope that some key legislators may find the time to read it. Members of Congress, and particularly senators, can apply a much longer time-frame to the solution of major problems than can the elected officials or appointees within the executive branch of government, whose period in office is so short that any considerations of long-range planning tend to be seen as irrelevant.

This is particularly true of economic or budgetary matters. An incoming administration is essentially governed by its predecessor's budget for its first year in office and only can attempt to review and modify a second year's budget already submitted to the Congress by the previous administration. Any major modifications made can be expected to bring about spending results in the third year, when the administration in power is already preparing to face a new election the following November. The

* Business executives have long since learned that, as they reach the top jobs in their companies, they must spend less and less time on details. In Congress, the opposite has been true. As individual congressmen reach leadership positions, they get more and more staff members who make sure that their bosses have more details than ever to learn about.

tendency thus is to react to events, rather than to plan ahead, and to demand almost instantaneous solutions to problems when such solutions, to be worthwhile, may require years of gradual economic adjustment before they can become truly effective.

Inflation is one such problem, the development of new policies on trade is another, monetary policy is certainly a third. We lack in the United States a system of shadow cabinets that would permit those who may one day have to serve in high appointive office to follow the great political and economic problems of the day well in advance of the time when they have to act upon them. Perhaps in time the political parties will substitute "think tanks" such as the Brookings Institution, the Georgetown Center for Strategic and International Studies, or the American Enterprise Institute, to perform this function of analysis for them.

This was then the third perception: that it was helpful for certain individuals within an administration (whose responsibilities did not require them to be constantly participating in day-to-day actions requiring immediate attention) to be reflecting on the governmental function to which they were assigned, determining its relevance, and preparing in-depth analyses of its efficacy.

To reflect on the function and relevance of the Bank, it was necessary to reflect on the nature of international trade, to examine why it was that Americans had become such poor traders after the magnificent start, to examine the present components of the American balance of payments and to ask why we had boxed ourselves into so bad a position with respect to imported oil. From there, thinking progressed to the nature of the monetary relationships that determined whether the country's goods could be sold competitively abroad, to the Bretton Woods monetary system that the United States had been so responsible for creating at the end of World War II and which had worked so well during the difficult postwar period. This led to thinking of how later presidents had destroyed this system, and how they had substituted a new system (or nonsystem), permitting each nation—and particularly the United States—to carry on its own domestic economic policies without regard for the effect of their actions on the economies of other countries.

This brought me to the nature of inflation and to the manner in which it was exported from the United States to other nations; how new liquidity was created throughout the world by U.S. government policies, ultimately resulting in the growth of the U.S. federal debt to $1 trillion; how this steady increase in world liquidity funded first the rebuilding of plants in Europe and Japan and then the industrialization of such countries as

Brazil, Mexico, South Korea, and Taiwan among others. This new liquidity, internationally referred to as the Eurodollar market, enabled the industrialized world to weather, through recycling, the oil crises of 1973–74 and 1979–80. I also observe how trade increased as technology spread to the countries under Communist rule, as well as to the developing countries. This change meant that trade would gradually force governments, both East and South, to permit the development of societies where the consumer would at last be given an opportunity to raise his standard of living to approach that of the West.

At this point, I thought the concept of the book was completed and the future clear. The world would gradually become like the United States, Western Europe, or Japan, societies in which the role of government would be contained and individuals allowed to develop their creative talents and exchange the goods they produced, with gradually decreasing government constraints. Alas, the Tokyo Round on international trade made clear how pervasive was the system of nontariff trade barriers. The growth of protectionism in the United States and elsewhere now threatens the free exchange of goods, and a new dilemma confronts the United States: how do we rebuild our own industrial plant to produce better and cheaper goods so that we can compete more successfully in the international marketplace?

When the book was finished a friend, president of a very successful high-technology company, who had read it chapter by chapter came to Washington and said: "It is incomplete. We are losing our productivity advantage and we are ceasing to be competitive in many industries not only overseas but in our own home markets." I then analyzed a number of capital goods industries and found to my surprise that he was indeed correct for reasons that appeared to vary from industry to industry. And so chapter 10 was written and first published separately* as a way of flagging this particular problem—related to the rest of the book but going beyond the immediate question of trade.

This book is not to be read as an economic treatise. Rather, it is a reflection of my own experience of forty years spent in international business: as a lawyer, a business executive, an investment banker, a doctor of troubled companies, a teacher, author, and finally, briefly, a government official. I call it an "entrepreneurial view" because I very strongly believe that economic relationships can best be handled—if not fully

*See, *U.S. Productivity and Competitiveness in International Trade,* The Center for Strategic and International Studies Significant Issues Series, Vol. II, No. 12 (Washington D.C. 1980).

understood—by individuals engaging in thousands of individual transactions rather than by economic planners. Economists are essential to governments, as accountants are essential to businessmen, because they can tell us where we have been and why we have come from there to here. But the future can only be charted by individual creativity and the acceptance of risk.

1
The U.S. Balance of Payments

To understand the complex international economic relationships that are the subject of this book, one must clearly understand the precise meaning of certain terms. The first of these terms is the "balance of payments." Commentators often confuse the "balance of payments" with the term "balance of trade." While the error is understandable, the two terms are not interchangeable.

In part the confusion comes from the fact that both are properly measured in monetary terms. In any year in which the United States has exports of goods greater in dollar value than the dollar value of the goods it has imported, it is said to have a positive balance of trade. The balance-of-payments ledger, on the other hand, represents a much broader picture—the overall money movement between one country and all others with which it has had any financial dealings. The balance-of-payments position of a country is determined by a combination of many factors, including, but not restricted to, its balance of trade. Other important items that go into the balance-of-payments picture are investments—both those made here by foreign companies and those made by U.S. companies abroad—and capital flows.* Indeed, capital flows, as we shall see, can be at times a far more significant factor than the balance of trade in the balance-of-payments ledger, for capital flows reflect the perception on the part of the international business community and central bankers of a country's economic well-being—its ability to maintain the value of its currency.

Ever since the election of President Ronald Reagan in November, 1980, as one example, international capital flows have moved strongly toward the United States. The result has been a strengthening of the U.S. dollar and a weakening of the West German mark. There was no particular economic action taken by the Reagan Administration to account for this new trend—indeed, it occurred in the three-month period between Reagan's election and his taking office. Nor can the likelihood of contin-

* Capital flows refer to the movement of money into or out of the United States.

ued high or even higher interest rates explain this new trend in international monetary flows because interest rates did not rise during this early period. On the contrary, President-elect Reagan's promises of substantial budget reductions made their decline more likely. International financiers simply decided that Reagan economic philosophy would favor a strong domestic currency.*

Thus the question of perception by those who control money, to which we will refer frequently during the course of this book, is all-important in understanding international monetary affairs. Indeed, the best lay definition of what is a strong currency as opposed to a weak one may be that a strong currency is one in which international investors have expressed confidence.

In nature, lack of motion is death; to establish that there is life, one must find movement. In the human body, there is the vascular system, as well as any number of recognizable patterns of electrical signals; in international economic terms, there is the monetary flow, reflecting capital-investment decisions as well as the payments made for goods and services bought and sold. Because these capital investments are often made or not made on the basis of informed risk-taking rather than as a consequence of any hard factual analysis offered by economists, they are difficult to anticipate. Nevertheless, anyone wishing to understand coming changes in exchange rates between key currencies ought to bear in mind the extent to which in the world of international finance the movement of money is affected by the perceptions, accurate or not, of those who either have wealth or control its movement.

As with nature's living organisms, the balance-of-payments system has its little mysteries; unilateral transfers, leads and lags, autonomous and accommodating transactions, transitory flows, errors and omissions. It will be the purpose of this first chapter to make this jargon clear, to reduce the U.S. balance-of-payments concept to its basic money-movement components—those generated by the trade of goods and services (for services are growing in importance), by foreign capital investment, and by the flow of exchange earnings homeward that such investments generate.

* Of course it can and will be argued by some that it is not confidence in Reagan's policies that has strengthened the dollar but rather a lack of confidence. According to this line of reasoning, Reagan's tax cuts will more than compensate for the anti-inflationary thrust of the budget cuts, forcing the Federal Reserve Board to continue to support high interest rates to check inflation, and that it is these anticipated high interest rates that are attracting investment in the U.S. dollar.

Put in simplest terms, the balance of payments can be said to be a balance between two ledgers—the current account and the capital account. Central to the first is trade, to the second, the movement of capital. The explanations that follow, detailing the component elements of the balance-of-payment ledger, are important principally for those whose job it is to analyze exchange markets. Other readers may study Figure 1 to understand the flow of relevant data and then move on directly to the heading captioned "The Current-Account Balance," page 18. The important point for the general reader to note is that money flows, the capital account, are often more important than the trade figures, the current account.

To find a country's current-account position (see Figure 1), we start by calculating the "merchandise trade balance"—the value of the goods (merchandise manufactures and agricultural products) sold against those purchased and determine the balance. To this figure is added or subtracted the net value of exports and imports of services—banking, accounting, insurance, transportation and other nonproduct items, the service balance. The export of services has become increasingly important for the United States and other industrialized nations. As developing nations begin to industrialize, they need increasingly to import the services as well as the machinery necessary to the modern industrialized economies they are trying to build. Next there is added the income from foreign direct investment* abroad by U.S. companies and the expenditures by foreign tourists within the United States less the sum of expenditures abroad for our military forces, expenditures abroad of American tourists, and foreign earnings from direct investments in the United States.

Having determined the balance of trade (in goods and services) we simply add in what are called unilateral transfers to arrive at the balance on current account. In these are included all one-way transfers of money or credit—private remittances abroad by foreigners working in the United States; pension payments made to Americans living abroad, such as U.S. citizens retired in Poland or Costa Rica; private aid abroad, such as that sent by U.S. religious institutions; government grants; and foreign aid other than military expenditures, which are placed under the category

*Foreign Direct Investment in the United States is defined by the U.S. Department of Commerce as foreign ownership or control of 10 percent or more of the voting securities of an incorporated U.S. business enterprise or an equivalent interest in an unincorporated U.S. business enterprise. Before 1974, foreign direct investment was based on a 25 percent ownership interest. Portfolio investments, on the other hand, are net purchases of U.S. equity and debt securities by private foreigners and international financial institutions.

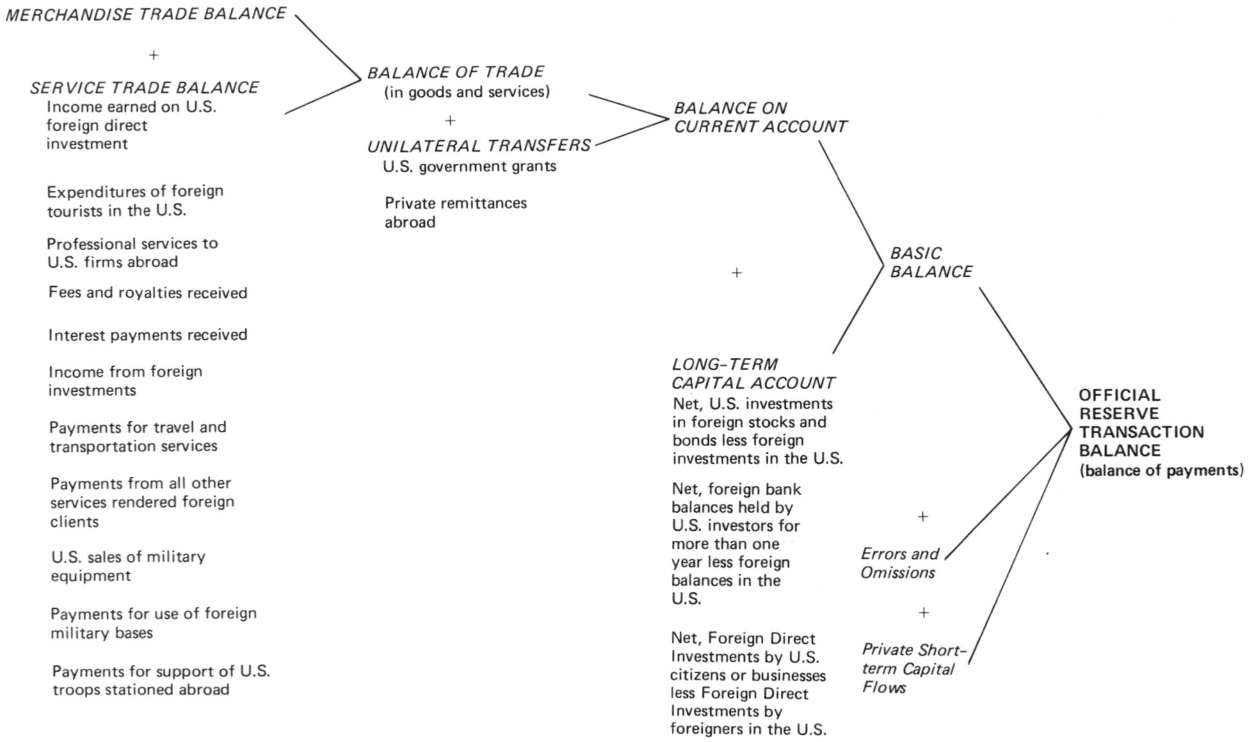

Figure 1. Official reserve transaction balance (*Balance of payments*)

of services so as not to attract undue attention. Into the current-account balance, then, are entered all international *nonfinancial* transactions, i.e., those transactions that do not involve the purchase or sale of financial assets (e.g., the purchase of currencies or gold).

The capital account, on the other hand, refers to the international ebb and flow of financial assets.* It is, in effect, the investment account in the balance of payments. It is important to remember that day-to-day transactions, whether merchandise trade, sale of services, or unilateral transfers, go into the current-account balance, while investments (short- or long-term) enter into the capital account.

Economists, in describing movements in the capital account, frequently separate long-term capital items from nonliquid, short-term capital flows, and again from short-term monetary capital flows. There is merit in making these distinctions. The so-called basic balance of payments adds to the current-account balance the net long-term movement of capital items, the capital accounts—the incoming foreign direct investments, U.S. bank balances held by foreigners for more than one year, and foreign-held investment in U.S. stocks and bonds, reduced by increases in the same investments by U.S. citizens abroad. The purpose of computing the basic balance is to indicate long-term trends in a country's external position. Is a current-balance deficit more than compensated for by growing investments from abroad, so that the outflow of dollars to make up the deficit on current account is balanced by foreign capital inflows seeking U.S. investments? This was the case in the United States through the end of 1980 and the beginning of 1981—which is one reason why the dollar regained strength at this point despite a continuing deficit in the country's current account. But there is a problem here: the dollar is said to be stronger than it was because our interest rates are higher than elsewhere. Long-term investments in the United States are being made by foreign businesses because with interest rates high, equity (investments that entail ownership rights or risk interests) tends to drop in price† and foreigners can purchase U.S. assets cheaply. This creates employment in the United

*Sometimes the term "capital account" refers only to international flows of nonmonetary financial assets, including international transfers of currencies, international reserves, or gold. In other instances it includes the totality of international financial transactions. To simplify the relationship between the current account and the capital account, the tables in this book, when speaking of the "capital account," will refer to the totality of international financial transactions.

†This phenomenon is most clearly illustrated on the stock exchanges of the world. Rising interest rates act to depress stock prices; falling interest rates to drive stock prices up.

States but causes Congress to wonder whether foreigners should be entitled to control American businesses.

In the period from the end of World War II to the late 1960s the reverse was true: the United States had a large current balance due mainly to its trade-export surplus. This, in turn, was adjusted by very substantial outflows of dollars in the form of foreign direct investments by U.S companies abroad, therefore adding to U.S. wealth, power, and international standing abroad.

The necessity for adjustment of the basic balance is evident. A persistent basic-balance deficit will indicate that major *structural* problems exist in a country's economic position. If the Congress, as it threatens from time to time to do, limited foreign direct investment in the United States during a period when the country had recurring current-account-balance deficits, the U.S. currency might well have to lose a substantial part of its foreign-exchange value. There is then an important relationship between the current-account balance, capital inflows and outflows, and exchange-rate adjustments.

From the basic balance, economists pass to the Official Reserve Transaction Balance (the balance of payments, or overall balance), which adds short-term capital flows plus errors and omissions, including "leads" and "lags"* found in international trade transactions as a result of short-term loans extended by international traders. These statistical discrepancies are cured over time by entry into other accounts, but their amount at any one time can be very substantial.

In our society a person faces bankruptcy if he cannot meet his debts as they mature. So it is with nations. The overall balance is used by central bankers to determine whether or not at any given point in time a country can meet demands for payment of monetary claims against the country. It indicates whether the exchange rate of that country's currency can, in fact, be defended. In 1971, for example, the U.S. overall balance was seriously eroded. When the French and others demanded conversion of a portion of their dollar claims into gold, as they had the right to do under the monetary system then in effect, President Nixon was obliged to abandon the system unilaterally, declaring that the United States would no longer allow conversion of official dollar claims into gold.[1] At the same time, he reduced the exchange-rate value of the dollar and placed a temporary embargo on additional imports. In effect, then, the United

* A lag results when the importer has received his goods but delays payment. A lead is caused by prepayment in advance of shipment of the goods.

States was refusing to pay its debts except by issuance of its own paper currency.

Final adjustments in arriving at the overall balance of a country are frequently very revealing, because they show what multinational companies and banks perceive to be the strengths or weaknesses of a given currency. Treasurers of multinational corporations and their money-center banks are expected to watch, and take advantage of, currency movements. They will move out of weaker currencies into those they believe will soon strengthen, so that as bills are due these bills can be paid by conversion at a more favorable rate. They will also anticipate payments owed in strong currencies by their Swiss or German subsidiaries and, by the same token, delay payments in Canada, or, until recently, the United States, because these were perceived to be declining currencies, and hence delaying payment would eventuate in payment being made in dollars of lower exchange value. As a result companies and banks may, by their own actions, and without acting in concert, bring about in a given currency the very strength or weakness they anticipate. This happened in Great Britain in 1967, in West Germany in 1970, and in the United States in 1971, 1978, and early 1981. It can, of course, happen much more easily now that currencies are free to float* in relation to each other.

Capital movements through the basic balance are sometimes referred to as "autonomous" transactions because they are not planned; adjustments that must be made to arrive at the Official Reserve Transaction Balance are referred to as "accommodating transactions" because they are transitory rather than permanent in nature. These latter include short-term capital flows seeking to take advantage of a temporary, perceived exchange-rate adjustment. They also include adjustments made by central banks among themselves to keep the Official Reserve Transaction Balance of each country in equilibrium and thereby avoid unwanted changes in exchange rates.

Table 1 and Figure 2 show the balance of payments of the United States for the period 1970 to 1980 in accordance with these definitions. As has been seen, there are, with each definition, reasons for including the items called for under each separate heading. Figure 1 shows in graphic form just how the flow of data is reported in order to arrive at the official reserve transaction balance. If one wants to understand what is likely to happen to a given currency as a result of changes in the

269 * In chapter 4, the free float of currencies will be examined in detail.

Table 1. U.S. balance of payments 1970–1980 (*In billions of dollars*)[a]

	1970	1975	1979	1980
Merchandise trade balance	$ 2,603	$ 9,047	$−29,386	$−27,354
Exports	42,469	107,088	182,068	221,781
Imports	−39,866	−98,041	−221,454	−249,135
Services balance, net	3,018	13,847	34,346	34,431
Investment income, net	7,877	16,043	37,996	32,535
Balance of trade (in goods and services)	5,621	22,894	4,960	7,077
Unilateral transfers	−3,294	−4,613	−5,066	−6,958
Balance on current account	2,327	18,281	−706	119
Long-term capital, net	−5,816	−18,866	−15,260	−10,551
Private capital flows, net	−4,227	−15,392	−11,477	−5,440
U.S. direct investment abroad	−7,589	−14,244	−24,319	−20,592
Foreign direct investment in U.S.	1,464	2,603	9,713	8,204
Short-term capital, Net	−6,551	−11,345	6,463	−35,921
Balance on capital account	−12,367	−30,211	−8,797	−46,472
Errors and ommissions	−216	5,753	23,765	37,177
Official reserve transaction balance (Balance of payments)	−9,389	−6,178	15,401	8,024

[a]*For a more detailed presentation of the balance of payments for each of the years 1970–80, see Appendix I.*

balance of payments, it is, therefore, important to be able to analyze the movements in the individual balances referred to, since each gives its own indications. To take just one example, the long-term capital-account items included in the basic balance can have an effect upon the balance on current account: the outflows of long-term capital will be registered as a debit in the basic balance. But, if this outflow from the United States represents foreign direct investment by U.S. firms, exports of goods and services to those overseas operations will generate a credit in the balance on current account. The deficit due to capital outflows has been affected by an increase in exports credited to current account as well as reflected in the trade balance. In order to understand how the balance-of-payments mechanism functions, bear in mind the individual balance accounts and the complex effects of each upon the others.

In judging a country's balance-of-payments position at any given time, one should focus first on the balance on current account. If this account is continually in deficit, something will have to be done to bring it into

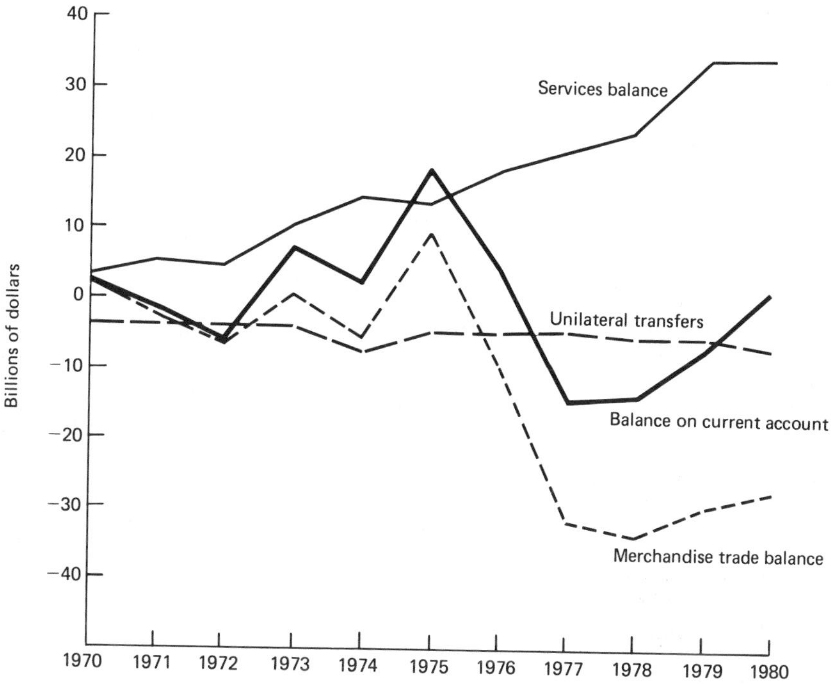

Figure 2. Balance on current account, 1970–1980 (*In billions of dollars*)
Source: From data released to author by Export-Import Bank of the United States staff.

balance: the exchange value of the currency may have to be adjusted downward; the country may have to borrow from others or from the International Monetary Fund* (as an increasing number of developing country members have had to do recently); imports may have to be curtailed (as Brazil had to do in 1980); exporters may have to be motivated through special tax advantages or through financial subsidies; foreign direct investments may have to be encouraged (as in Brazil from 1975 to 1980); foreign investments abroad may have to be discouraged (as the United States did in 1962 through the Interest Equalization Tax, followed by involuntary controls over foreign credit transactions by U.S. individuals or firms); tourist expenditures abroad may have to be discouraged (as President Kennedy attempted to do in 1961); foreigners may have to be encouraged to visit the United States (as President Nixon

* The role of the International Monetary Fund will be discussed in chapters 4 and 6.

attempted to do in 1969–71 through special programs directed at foreign tourists); U.S. aid programs to developing countries may have to be reduced, as several administrations have talked of doing (e.g., President Carter's threat to reduce the U.S. military presence in South Korea in 1977); or currency controls may have to be established to discourage U.S. citizens from holding foreign currency (the Nixon Administration forced U.S. citizens to report holdings in foreign banks or brokerage firms, and the U.S. Congress considered a bill in 1980 that would have given the executive branch the power to introduce exchange controls).

To understand more closely the relationship between current transactions (the current-account balance), capital transactions (the capital-account balance), i.e., net long-term foreign direct investments, portfolio investments (stocks and bonds), or bank deposits, and the adjustment mechanisms that *must* be employed to keep the accounts in balance (private, short-term capital movements and official central-bank transactions), the rest of the chapter will consider in a historical analysis: 1. the current-account balance; 2. the capital-account balance; 3. the adjustment process, including the role of multinational companies in the exchange markets (private, short-term capital flows) and official swap transactions.

We will also discuss how the U.S. government, to restore the necessary balance, has used both devaluations of its own currency and increases in interest rates to bring about future adjustments in the current-account or in the capital-account balances. A devaluation makes U.S. products more competitive in the international marketplace, thereby stimulating exports and improving the trade balance; an increase in interest rates makes it attractive for foreigners, private or government, to leave money on deposit in the United States, thereby helping to restore the capital account balance.

The Current-Account Balance

When World War II ended, the United States was the only industrialized country whose manufacturing plant had not been severely damaged. For this reason the United States was able to quickly convert its industries back to the production of capital equipment and consumer goods. The worldwide demand for such goods could be satisfied only if the United States agreed either to accept, in exchange for the goods, promises to pay in the future or to furnish such goods as a form of foreign aid. Agricultural grants under Public Law 480, the Marshall Plan, Agency for International Development loans to Europe and to Japan, all represent U.S. effort in the years immediately following the war to reconstruct the economies of the industrialized world.

But neither the Marshall Plan nor the loans were sufficient to establish the resources abroad through which the demand for U.S. products could be met. To help meet this demand, the U.S. government began encouraging American companies to establish plants outside the United States and to transfer U.S. equipment to such plants to satisfy foreign markets through localized production of U.S. goods. In the 1950s and 1960s, U.S. firms established manufacturing plants throughout the world. This was a clear instance of using foreign investment as a means of balancing the current-account surplus, which the United States had earned through its positive balance of trade.

It was not until the beginning of the 1960s, during the Kennedy years, that all of a sudden the balance of trade of the United States turned negative. This balance went into deficit during a period of substantial capital outflows as American companies continued to establish plants abroad, particularly in the industrialized countries of Europe. It was at this time that President Kennedy instituted the Interest Equalization Tax (IET) to force U.S. business firms and banks operating abroad to borrow U.S. dollars there rather than from U.S. deposits. This represented a turning point in the U.S. government's perception of the balance-of-payments problem.

Nevertheless, there was little fundamental understanding of anything but a need to have cash-outflow totals balanced by inflows.* Kennedy himself proposed exempting Canada† from the IET, not realizing that a government cannot put walls around money that has left its sovereignty. The result of the exemption was that U.S. dollars flowed to Canadian banks, attracting them through increased rates on deposits. From there the dollars flowed on to the London Eurodollar markets,‡ where U.S. corporations, to fund the capital requirements of their European affiliates, borrowed them at even higher rates.

*The Secretary of the Treasury during the Kennedy Administration at one point boasted of improvements in the balance of payments but, in fact, such improvements had been brought about by nothing more than the prepayment of old loans by Britain and France.

†This may have been due to the warmth with which the President was received in Canada—where the government made its appeal for continued U.S. investments in the Canadian economy—as compared to the stern lectures he received from General de Gaulle in Paris and the angry exchanges with Khrushchev in Vienna later on during the same trip abroad.

‡The Eurodollar markets will be discussed in chapter 5.

This one example merely suggests the myriad of reciprocally provocative relationships that exist among interest rates, capital movements, current-account balances, currency flows, and ultimately exchange-rate changes. In the end the IET served a purpose opposite to that which it had been intended to serve—it encouraged U.S. currency flows to Europe.

All through the 1960s the current-account balance tended to go into greater deficit. Worse, the balance of trade was necessarily bound to go into increased deficit, as the Europeans and Japanese adopted U.S. technologies, rebuilt their industries, and became increasingly competitive in trade. Finally in 1971, the merchandise-trade balance went into deficit. After twenty-five years of having merchandise-trade surpluses (because the United States was a net supplier of goods to the rest of the world), the U.S. merchandise-trade balance went into the negative, first in 1971, then in 1972, and then again in 1974. Since then, the merchandise-trade balance has gone from a surplus of $9 billion in 1975 to a deficit of $9.2 billion in 1977, a deficit of $33.76 billion in 1978, a deficit of $29.45 billion in 1979, and a deficit of $21.2 billion in the first three quarters of 1980.

Today, the United States is no longer conceded by anyone as having the technological lead it has had, until only recently, in most manufacturing sectors. For example, Japanese, French, and German autos are perceived by prospective buyers anywhere in the world to be at least the equivalent of ours. Furthermore, there is increased indication that manufacturing companies in other OECD* countries are no longer even willing to concede to the United States a special position of leadership in the development of new commercial products. Indeed, they are carefully monitoring U.S. technological innovations so as to rapidly obtain manufacturing licenses as new products of general interest are developed. This has happened recently in robots, in semiconductors, and in biogenics, three important industrial-development areas in which much of the pioneering work was done in the United States.

Nor is there reason to believe that the merchandise-trade balance will improve enough in the future to offset the increased dollar value of our imports, particularly oil, automobiles, and certain capital goods unless U.S. government policies change in A. removing disincentives to exports among U.S. companies, or B. by encouraging the commitment of U.S. commercial resources to the development of the newer technologies rather than to attempting to maintain an old dominance in the produc-

* Organization for Economic Cooperation and Development, which includes the principal industrialized nations.

tion of steel, or in the light manufactures, textiles, or shoes, in which there is increasing competition from the developing countries.

Similarly, although the demand for agricultural products can be expected to increase considerably in the future as a result of climatic changes in various parts of the world and the decline in agricultural production in the socialist countries and the Third World, it is unlikely that U.S. production can be greatly increased. It is already unusually efficient and highly developed. True, as chapter 3 will make clear, we are in a position to use surplus food production to reduce our dependence on imported oil, but this may take several years to accomplish and may in the end do little more than balance the expected decline in the export of manufactured products.

Fortunately, in recent years the U.S. services balance has progressed substantially. In 1975, services provided a positive balance of $13.9 billion to the current account; in 1976, $18.9 billion; in 1977, $21.4 billion; in 1978, $25.4 billion; in 1979, $34.8 billion; in 1980 the balance may approximate $45 billion. The growth in the positive U.S. service balance has been due in part to the massive investment abroad made by U.S. multinational businesses in the 1950s and 1960s. The Commerce Department, since 1975, reports all income earned by affiliates of U.S. corporations as income received from outside the United States and therefore as a positive addition to the current-account balance, even though a portion of such earnings has not been converted into dollars and transferred to the United States. These amounts of earnings retained abroad are then put into the capital account as outflows, as if they had been received at home and then reinvested abroad.

Recently service income has been artificially increased by the growing earnings from abroad of U.S. oil companies as a result of OPEC price increases. But, in fact, such earnings may not have been repatriated. The net expenditures of tourists have also turned favorable as U.S. tourists find it more expensive to travel to Europe and the Europeans and Japanese now find a trip to the United States relatively low in cost, both in terms of the actual cost of travel and in the price of merchandise available here. Americans may find that clothes, food, and household furnishings cost increasingly more, but to Europeans, Asians, and Latin Americans, U.S. goods are relatively inexpensive. These price differences can be expected to continue; distribution and selling costs in the United States are much lower than in other parts of the world and can be expected to remain so.

In terms of professional services the United States again can be expected to remain very competitive. As other countries have industrialized, the need for services to complement and accompany increased manufacturing capability has also grown. Earnings to the United States from foreign banking services, insurance, accounting, legal, medical, engineering, and computer services can be expected to continue to rise, particularly as developing countries modernize their economies. U.S. sales of military equipment can also be expected to increase in a Republican administration and should help to balance the increased costs to the United States of maintaining an enhanced military presence abroad.* In services, therefore, it is likely that the United States will continue to have a growing positive balance to offset merchandise-trade deficits in the current account.

Unilateral transfers, which constitute the third portion of the current-account balance, have remained relatively constant in deficit over the past few years at approximately $5 billion per year.

A detailed analysis of the U.S. balance on current account reveals how little government policy has had to do with the results. In 1975, the United States had a surplus in current account of $18.3 billion; in 1976 a surplus of $4.6 billion; in 1977 a deficit of $14.1 billion; in 1978 a deficit of $13.9 billion; in 1980, a surplus of perhaps as much as $2 billion. Why the movement from surplus to deficit and now back to surplus? The answers are interesting because they illustrate the relationship between differing economic conditions in various parts of the world on trade, as well as the effect of exchange-rate changes.

In 1977, the Carter Administration continued efforts to reduce unemployment by increased government expenditures. The consequential increase in the U.S. money supply resulted in the increased purchase of imported, as well as of domestic products, by Americans. The gross effect then was to create a higher trade deficit, a larger budget deficit, and a reduced value for the U.S. dollar. In November 1978, the U.S. government suddenly became alarmed by the decline in the value of the currency and reversed course, engaging in swap transactions† to prevent a further decline in the currency, and encouraging U.S. interest rates to rise

* Please recall that the sale of military equipment is treated as the sale of a service.

† Swap transactions take place when central bankers agree to lend one another their currencies so that the borrower whose currency is then weakest can sell that currency to buy his own, thus enabling him to maintain the stability of his currency's exchange rate. In November, 1978, for example, the swap of dollars for West German marks and Swiss francs enabled the Federal Reserve to sell those currencies for dollars, thus preventing a further decline in the exchange value of the dollar against those currencies. In 1979, as the dollar turned firm, the transactions were effectively reversed.

so as to motivate capital inflows from abroad. At the same time, the recession was ending in the rest of the world, and U.S. exports had begun to increase. The decline in the value of the dollar had also made imports more expensive while increasing the price competitiveness of U.S. products for export.

Perhaps more important was that during 1978 Alaskan oil at last started to flow. In 1978 and early 1979, OPEC increases in the price of oil did not match in percentage the rise in consumer prices in the United States. This also helped the U.S. current account. In 1979, as a result of the decline in the exchange rate of the dollar, the price of imports (other than oil, which is payable in dollars) increased. Consequently the inflation rate in the United States, affected by the rising price of imports, climbed the following year.

In 1980, the rise in interest rates encouraged by the U.S. government to maintain the value of the dollar caused the U.S. economy to turn downward. New pressures on the American consumer again reduced imports and again would have helped the trade balance if at the same time OPEC increases in the price of oil had not more than made up for the reduced merchandise imports. Since these OPEC increases were very much predicated on the failure of OPEC to keep pace with increases in the prices of OECD manufactured goods during 1977 and 1978, the whole sequence illustrates how complex international economic relationships can become and how counterproductive government "beggar thy neighbor" policies can be. An important lesson that must come out of all this is that it does little good for one country to seek unilateral advantage by reducing the value of its currency to increase its exports. Only increased productivity under conditions of world monetary stability can reduce the impact of increases in the cost of energy.

The Capital-Account Balance

International flows of capital and financial assets make up the capital-account balance. Whenever a country has a deficit in its trade account for goods and services combined with transfers (a current-account deficit) it can make up the difference through a net inflow of private capital, or if not, through a transfer of financial assets. It can do the latter by borrowing from abroad, or by transferring reserve currencies or other monetary assets such as gold. The important consideration is the necessity of maintaining the equilibrium between the country's current account and its capital account (including official financial transfers) during any given time period. Given this requirement, it seems useful to examine in the first instance the changes that have taken place since World War II within the U.S. balance-of-payments picture in the capital-account balance compared with the country's current-account balance. We should then examine to what extent the United States has had to make official transfers of reserves to balance increased account deficits. There will also be noted how currency adjustments have been required whenever recurrent trade deficits were not compensated for by inflows of private capital.

In the immediate postwar period businesses in the United States invested their capital in plant and equipment needed in the switch from wartime to peacetime production. There was no need to invest outside the United States; foreigners purchased all the American consumer goods they had the dollar exchange to buy. It was not until the mid-1950s that American business began to focus on supplying markets abroad through the establishment of plants there, particularly in Europe. Gradually, over a period of years, the merchandise-trade balance of the United States went into deficit as other industrialized countries rebuilt their own industrial bases. Faced with the possible loss of their overseas markets, U.S. firms began to transfer capital to Europe for the plant and equipment investment that might allow them to hold these markets. U.S. direct investment abroad increased from $31.9 billion at the end of 1960 to $94.3 billion by the end of 1972. Thus a deficit in the current account was accompanied by deficits in the capital account, necessitating official transfers of reserves.

What has happened to private capital flows in more recent years? Table 2 shows the changes in the U.S. capital account from 1975 to 1980. It will be noted immediately that there have been changes in net private capital flows during this period. While the change in U.S. private assets abroad from 1975 to 1979 represents a capital outflow of approximately $20 billion, the change in foreign private assets in the U.S. has grown from $8.6 billion in 1975 to 51.8 billion in 1979, resulting in a net decline in the outflow of private capital in that year. Why? The answer is at once meaningful and very instructive as it illustrates the influence of changing perceptions by corporate treasurers and their bankers on private capital flows.

As the U.S. current account moved from deficit to balance in late 1978, the need for large inflows of capital disappeared. As this occurred, accompanied as it was by President Carter's decision to reverse prior policy and to strengthen the dollar through swap transactions with foreign central banks and sharp increases in U.S. interest rates, U.S. and foreign

Table 2. U.S. capital account, 1975–1980 (*In billions of dollars, seasonally adjusted*)

	1975	1976	1977	1978	1979	1980[a]
Private flows						
Change in U.S. private assets abroad, net	$−35.4[b]	$−44.5	$−31.7	$−57.0	$−56.9	$−71.2
Change in foreign private assets in United States, net	8.6	18.8	14.2	30.0	51.8	31.4
Total private flows, net	−26.7	−25.7	−17.6	−27.1	−5.1	−39.8
Official flows						
Change in U.S. official reserve assets, net	−0.8	−2.6	−0.4	0.7	−1.1	−8.2
Change in foreign official assets in United States						
Industrial countries[c]	0.9	8.4	28.8	34.3	−14.3	+16.2
OPEC	7.1	9.6	6.4	−0.7	n.a.[d]	n.a.
Others	−1.2	−0.4	1.5	0.2	n.a.	n.a.
Total official flows, net	5.9	15.0	36.3	34.5	−15.4	8.0
Change in U.S. government assets other than official reserve assets, net	−3.5	−4.2	−3.7	−4.7	−3.8	−5.1
Statistical discrepancy	5.9	10.3	−0.9	11.1	23.8	37.2
Total flows, net	−18.3	−4.6	14.1	13.9	−0.5	0.3

Source: U.S. Department of Commerce, Bureau of Economic Analysis, "The U.S. Balance of International Payments and the U.S. Economy: Developments in 1978 and Early 1979," Background Paper, (November, 1979). Details may not add to totals because of rounding.

[a] Preliminary figures for 1980 subject to wide fluctuations.
[b] Negative entries indicate capital outflows.
[c] Australia, Canada, Japan, New Zealand, South Africa, and Western Europe.
[d] n.a. = data not available.

bankers and businessmen concluded that the dollar would indeed strengthen and they transferred foreign currency holdings into dollars. In the fourth quarter of 1978 alone the capital inflow into the United States came to $16 billion.

The mistake of the Carter Administration prior to November, 1978 was in believing that a weak dollar was essential to bringing about an increase in U.S. merchandise trade competitiveness and a consequent amelioration in the current-account balance. What such a policy did in fact cause was an outflow of private capital from the United States into bank deposits in foreign currencies, mainly the West German mark and the Swiss franc. Attempts, therefore, by the U.S. government to solve the trade-deficit problem by reducing the value of the currency simply made the larger problem worse. A nation that is a net importer of goods—and the United States seems condemned by the necessity to import continuously growing dollar amounts of oil to remain such a net-importing nation—should maintain the value of its currency and not seek its effective devaluation. Prior to the end of 1978, while private capital moved out of the United States, foreign central banks, to keep their currencies from strengthening further, purchased dollars in large quantities; they too feared the negative impact on their foreign trade of an appreciating currency.

Thus in order to keep exchange rates from fluctuating even more, *private* capital outflows were balanced in 1977 and 1978 by *official* capital inflows. In 1979 and 1980, the reverse occurred. As private capital moved back into dollars, foreign central banks were able to dispose of the dollars they had purchased in the swap transactions of November, 1978. There was one important difference, however, between the private capital flows of 1977–78 and those of 1979–1980. The U.S. outflows were temporary in nature, while the inflows from abroad in the more recent period represent, to a much greater degree, foreign direct investments in the U.S. business economy. If such foreign investments continue to increase, this might foretell a significant change for the future. (But this is not certain because when the U.S. economy turned sluggish in 1980, foreign private investment turned down.)

To a great extent the U.S. current account has in the past decade been kept in some sort of equilibrium by the flow back of foreign earnings of U.S. multinational companies. If foreign multinationals continue to invest heavily in the United States, these investments will result eventually in the transfer of U.S. earnings abroad, thus balancing out in due course the current large surplus to the United States in service transactions. The answer to this threat to the United States, of course, lies not in restrictive regulations or confiscatory taxes on investors but rather in programs that increase the technological know-how of American businesses, that end the subsidization of inefficient industries, and that encourage in every way possible the development of an industrial community profitable enough to attract an increased flow of domestic savings.

The Adjustment Process

As was noted earlier, whenever the current account is in deficit, changes in the capital account *must* make up the deficit, either through private capital inflows encouraged by high interest rates or through government borrowing or transfer of reserves. When the United States had sizeable current-account surpluses in the two decades following World War II, U.S. businessmen were encouraged to invest abroad. In 1977 and 1978, when the reverse occurred, foreign businesses were encouraged by the weakness of the dollar to invest in U.S. businesses. The United States became a net importer of capital. If the U.S. currency now remains strong there will be a tendency for foreign takeovers to subside.

Foreign Direct Investment

It is to be hoped that the Reagan Administration will recognize the beneficial consequence of maintaining the value of the currency as well as the more obvious advantage of reducing domestic inflation by reducing the cost of necessary imports. As will be demonstrated in more detail later, it is better to maintain the competitiveness of U.S. products even through finance subsidization of exports, as our industrial trading partners do, than to allow a weakened dollar to create this competitive edge, a policy that will later require as compensation that one raise interest rates, the very course upon which the Carter Administration found itself forced in November, 1978 and again in 1979. The biggest losers in a period of high interest rates are the small, high-technology growth companies, whose rapid growth tends to outstrip their own financial resources. Because they are new, generally undercapitalized, and growing in sales and receivables, they have particular difficulty competing for new funds in a tight money market.

The U.S. government has had difficulty in understanding that the very perception of a currency-value decline by private interests will cause the decline to occur. This is an important lesson to be learned from the chain of consequences set in motion by U.S. government action in 1977–78. The government-incited decline in the value of the dollar also substantially increased world inflation by causing the Germans and the Swiss to buy dollars and invest them in U.S. government securities, thereby adding to the international money supply. At the same time the OPEC nations sold dollars to invest in West German or Swiss currencies and in late 1978 even threatened to require that payments for oil be in currencies other than dollars. Has anyone in the U.S. government considered what it would mean to the United States if $75 billion of imported oil had to be paid for in currencies other than the dollar? Certainly the actions of the Carter Administration at the very least encouraged the maintenance of dollar holdings outside the United States, a pattern that needs to be reversed. We should not discourage the flow of funds into the United States regardless of whether these represent the repatriation of domestic funds or new investments from foreigners.

Foreign Direct Investment by United States companies has continued to grow in the period 1975–81. Nevertheless FDI flows into the United States are growing much faster. In 1979 alone, foreign investors spent $11.53 billion to acquire or establish some 792 businesses in the United States. This has now begun to concern the Congress. Based on a study by the Commerce, Consumer, and Monetary Affairs Subcommittee, the Committee on Government Operations of the House approved in August, 1980 a report entitled "The Adequacy of the Federal Response to Foreign Investment in the United States" (called the Rosenthal Report after its chairman, Benjamin S. Rosenthal), which is highly critical of U.S. policy on foreign investment.

The report would have the United States register and screen incoming foreign investments. It is only the latest of numerous proposals in the Congress to discourage foreign investment in the United States. If such a proposal were to become law, it would invite retaliation that might seriously affect the balance of payments of the United States. Such legislation might also reduce the value of the dollar. It would certainly reduce domestic investment and would increase U.S. unemployment. It would represent a complete reversal of U.S. policy since the end of World War II.

The question of foreign direct investment and its effects on the balance of payments in both directions is worth careful examination. For the reasons previously outlined, investment by United States companies abroad has generally been in the form of direct investment by U.S. business firms rather than portfolio investment by American individuals or firms purchasing shares in foreign equity markets. Foreign capital investments in the United States on the contrary have tended to be portfolio rather than direct investments, the purchase of shares quoted on the New York Stock Exchange, the American Stock Exchange, or the over-the-counter markets.

In the last few years, however, the pattern of investment has changed—in both directions. As companies in Europe and Japan have grown, developed their own international operations, and made their products almost as well known in the United States as in their domestic markets, American interest in foreign portfolio investment has grown commensurately. American Depository Receipts (ADRs) of foreign companies are traded in the United States; specialized funds with investments outside the United States have come into being. On the other hand, foreign business firms have recently made direct investments in the United States, either through the acquisition of U.S. companies or through the establishment of manufacturing entities here. There have been some twenty-two affiliates of Finnish companies alone established in the United States in the past three years.

What has brought about this desire on the part of foreign business to make direct investments in the United States? Several important factors can be cited: 1. the growth in size of foreign business firms and their own tendency to become multinational companies; 2. the attractiveness of the American market because of its size and purchasing power; 3. the devaluation of the dollar since 1971 on an almost continual basis, which has made investment in the United States increasingly inexpensive; 4. the fact that U.S. securities, particularly those quoted on the various securities exchanges, sell at a much lower price-earnings ratio than do those in Europe or Japan;* 5. much better relations between management and labor in the United States than in Western Europe, for example; 6. the growing protectionist climate in the United States, which causes foreign companies to seek to protect the marketing base they have built through exports by establishing manufacturing or assembly plants in the United States. (Volkswagen, SONY, Phillips, Matsushita are but a few examples of a growing trend); 7. the stability of the U.S. business environment, both in terms of business relations with government and with labor unions. Surprisingly, while American businessmen frequently complain of increased government interference in their affairs, Europeans find our economy relatively free of the burdens of social welfare states—price controls, rapidly rising labor costs, increased labor militancy; (8) the growth of a foreign bank network in the United States available to give financial support to foreign firms establishing operations in the United States for the first time.

Among foreign countries with direct investments in the United States, the Netherlands is the principal investor, followed by the United Kingdom, Canada, West Germany, Switzerland, Japan, and France. These seven countries account for 85 percent of all direct investment in the United States. The OPEC countries account for less than 1 percent of total direct foreign investment in the United States and that investment

*To cite but one instance, the most active stock on the Athens Stock Exchange is a cement company, which sells in good years for seventy times earnings, in bad years for forty times earnings. In the United States, cement companies generally sell for four to five times earnings.

appears to be mainly in real estate holdings. From time to time fears are expressed in the press or in Congress that the farmland of the United States is passing into foreign hands. This does not appear to be founded in fact.

How has foreign direct investment in the United States grown in recent years and how does it compare with direct investment by the United States abroad? The figures are interesting. According to the Commerce Department, FDI in the United States stood at $52.26 billion at the end of 1979, compared to U.S. direct investment abroad at the end of the same year of $192.65 billion. Thus, while foreign direct investment in the United States has grown much faster than U.S. direct investment abroad in the last few years, the total is still less than 30 percent of the U.S. foreign direct investment.

This percentage can, however, be expected to continue to increase in the future. This means that in the future the earnings of U.S. firms abroad when netted out against the earnings of foreign investment in the United States will decline as a factor in the U.S. balance of payments. At the end of 1979, for example, U.S. FDI produced $37.82 billion in earnings, compared to earnings in the U.S. by foreign direct investment of $6.03 billion. The change will thus come slowly.

Why haven't U.S. foreign direct investments continued to grow as rapidly as in the past? Several reasons can be given: 1. disincentives adopted by the U.S. government such as the antibribery statute and antiboycott legislation, and tax laws making it less attractive for Americans to work abroad; 2. a pattern of increased nationalization of foreign investment in the developing countries; 3. more rapidly rising wage rates in Western Europe than in the United States, which make direct investments in Europe less attractive than heretofore; 4. efforts in the United Nations to establish controls over the activities of foreign multinational companies in Third World countries; 5. pressure in the Congress to limit foreign direct investment by U.S. companies because it is said to "export" U.S. jobs; 6. unwillingness on the part of many U.S. corporations to engage in joint ventures abroad because U.S. firms have always preferred to exercise management control over their foreign plants.

It would indeed be a pity if the government of the United States adopted a more restrictive attitude either toward foreign direct investment by U.S. business abroad or by foreign business in the United States. Whether or not our policymakers choose to recognize it, consumers everywhere can only benefit from additional competition across borders.

The United States, in particular, has never had much to fear from business competition if the rules are fairly applied.

Conclusions

The relationship between trade, investment, and the value of the currency has been outlined in this chapter. A strong current-account balance adds to income and employment in the United States provided such strength in the current account is not due to a reduction in imports brought about by a lagging U.S. economy. A strong current-account balance encourages a strong currency, which discourages capital inflows for foreign direct investment in the United States while encouraging portfolio investment and the reinvestment in the United States of dollars held abroad. It also makes it unnecessary for the United States to raise interest rates as a means of protecting the value of the dollar by encouraging foreign investors to buy government securities.

In order to maintain a strong current balance, the United States needs to encourage exports as a matter of national policy. This means elimination of disincentives to exports, encouragement of high-technology industries, a program to subsidize exports by giving additional support to the Export-Import Bank so that the United States can compete successfully with export support programs adopted by other industrialized countries. It also means the encouragement of exports by stimulating the formation and growth of export-oriented industries through appropriate changes in tax legislation. The United States has a particular opportunity now to do something about improving the trade balance because so little has been done in the past. Until recently, it seemed that U.S. business was only minimally interested in exports because the size of the U.S. market made it unnecessary to place any reliance on overseas markets.

On the service side, where the United States has a strong position, additional focus might well be given to finding ways to encourage further growth through (a) Export-Import Bank financing for feasibility studies, insurance coverage, and other services, and (b) preventing attempts to limit restrictions abroad on imports of U.S. services. Because of the positive role played by dividend and interest payments from foreign direct investments in the current balance the United States should neither discourage U.S. FDIs nor seek to control foreign investment in the United States.

As the value of the dollar remains high, the necessity for government to encourage high-technology exports will increase; these sales are less vulnerable to currency fluctuations, commanding a market, as they do, not by their price but by their distinctive utility.

As the dollar remains strong, there will be an increased tendency for foreign capital, especially OPEC surplus funds, to be invested in U.S. securities. Such portfolio investments should not be discouraged; they are a means of reversing the outflow of dollars caused by past failures not only of U.S. energy planning but of U.S. monetary policy.* In 1980 alone, transfers to OPEC exceeded $120 billion, much of which was added to dollar funds in the Eurocurrency banks. These funds, representing short-term deposits, are then loaned to developing countries on a long-term basis. This borrowing short to lend long only increases the illiquidity of the international banking system. As we shall see in chapter 5, the consequences are not pleasant to contemplate.

As will be noted from a detailed examination of the trade balance in the two chapters that follow, the United States is the only industrialized country with the capacity to really do something about its trade deficit simply because so much of this deficit is due to oil imports and the United States, of all the industrialized countries, has by far the most realistic possibility of solving its energy-import problem.

* U.S. monetary policy since the end of World War II is discussed in detail in chapter 4.

2

The U.S. Balance of Trade

The trade balance is the most important component of the balance of payments. It is therefore useful to analyze trends in U.S. exports and imports over the course of the past twenty years. Such analysis will help us understand more clearly how the role of the United States in international trade has changed through this period, the role it plays today, and what might be expected of it in the future.

For our purposes it is not necessary to analyze detailed international trade statistics year by year. For those interested, an analysis by category of goods can be found in Appendix 2.

It is clear that since the end of World War II international trade has grown enormously, but as a consequence of very different factors from those that motivated prewar planners. Before the war, a number of powerful nations, short of particular raw materials and food stocks, had sought to create trade blocs. Their principle purpose was simply to assure themselves, as part of their preparations for war, adequate access to necessary food and raw materials. This was true of Germany, and perhaps even more so of Japan, whose prewar Asian Co-Prosperity Sphere constituted an attempt to create regional self-sufficiency and, consequently, Japanese self-sufficiency in raw materials and food. Only within the Comecon bloc* does this attempt at economic self-sufficiency continue today, and the attempt here has not been particularly successful.

Regional development is still sought today, but for different reasons. In the European Community (EC) and in Africa the thrust has been political. In Latin America, a perceived need to show potential investors greater market size has provided the impetus. Over the course of the past thirty years, trade has become for most economic planners a way of accelerating development rather than a means of insuring the economic-military self-sufficiency military strategists once thought so necessary.

* An acronym for Communist Economic bloc, a group of seven Eastern European countries under control of the Soviet Union exchanging goods with one another through a trade and monetary association. It represents an attempt to imitate the European Economic Community created by the Treaty of Rome in 1958.

If trade blocs consisting of neighboring countries do not better succeed in stimulating more rapid economic development, it is often because each country within the particular region is likely to be producing similar goods to satisfy similar market demands, depriving the region of the stimulus more diverse outside markets would produce. What such regional groupings generally succeed in accomplishing, however, are that they cause each country within the area to examine its own natural advantages for export trade with its neighbors; that they heighten competition *within* the region; and that they create a unified marketing and distribution area to attract investment from the outside. As a result, trade within the entity tends to grow, disrupting, at times, old and well established trade patterns often with countries geographically very distant.

Trade within the European Community, for instance, has grown substantially. As the EC expands to include Spain and Portugal, following Greece, these additional countries will see the opportunity, through membership, to develop protected markets for their agricultural products and light industries. Among Latin American countries, the pattern in the past was to ship raw materials and semifinished goods to the United States rather than to try to increase trade among themselves. More recently, they too have sought to increase trade within the region through such regional groupings as LAFTA and the Andean Common Market.

The economic policy of the U.S. government since World War II has contributed greatly to changing trade patterns throughout the world. Three factors have been of paramount importance in bringing about this policy. First has been the political concern in America that Europe might, if it did not become more unified, fall prey to Soviet expansion westward. Second, American planners seemed unable to understand the importance of developing closer ties, both political and economic, with other countries of the Western Hemisphere. The Europeans have sensed the importance of developing closer trade links with the natural wealth of Africa and the Middle East while Japan is attempting to rebuild its economic base in Asia. But periodic bursts of rhetoric aside, the United States has done relatively little to establish really significant developmental plans with either Central or South America. Third, the United States for policy reasons encouraged Great Britain to abandon its Commonwealth system, as a vestige of an earlier colonialist era, in favor of a new role as a leader of the European Economic Community "to stabilize the French and Germans."

In order to understand the U.S. role, it is necessary that we put ourselves in the world economic situation as it existed in 1945, at the end of World War II. The United States had come through the war with its industrial plant unscathed, as contrasted with the situation in most of industrialized Europe, including Britain, France, Italy, Belgium, the Netherlands, and the Eastern European nations, and, of course, the Soviet Union. The policy of the United States in the immediate postwar years focused upon the economic rehabilitation of Western Europe as a means of preventing the region, as a whole, from turning to Communism and falling under eventual Soviet domination. This was the economic purpose of the Marshall Plan and later of the Truman Doctrine.

As political strategy, the policy was, of course, highly successful. U.S. economic assistance made it possible for the European economies to resurge from the ashes of wartime destruction. But there were unforeseen consequences on the economic side. Because of the size of the rapidly revitalized European market, and the fact that for many years following the war labor rates in Europe were substantially lower than were those in the United States, American multinational companies saw a clear advantage in establishing manufacturing plants in one or several European countries to produce for the European market products designed and previously manufactured only in the United States.

After a period of time, U.S. companies gradually modified the pattern in two ways: first, they observed that the product cycle of manufactured goods made it advantageous for their products to be first launched in the United States, then later transferred overseas, thus extending the life cycle of individual products. This pattern of treating the domestic and European markets sequentially enabled businesses with large investments in equipment to transfer this equipment at a later stage in the business cycle to manufacturing plants located abroad, thus making room in the United States for new equipment that would produce replacement products at the first stage of a new product cycle. Still later, U.S. businessmen further observed that differing regulations among foreign countries might make it advantageous to manufacture products outside the United States for sale not only within the country in which they were manufactured but in other markets, including the United States itself. Indeed, one of the reasons why General de Gaulle, who understood very well and very early the full implications of the incipient Common Market, was reluctant to see it come about, was that he understood that France would no longer be able to protect its inefficient industrial production from the effects of U.S. competition. If de Gaulle refused to allow American businessmen to establish plants in France they would simply go to Belgium or West Germany, with the products necessarily allowed into France under the treaty rules of the European Economic Community.

The effect of the European Economic Community has thus been to force economic competition among nations that had managed ever since the start of the Industrial Revolution to protect themselves through tariff barriers against outside competition. Because of the political power of the agricultural sector of the population, it took much longer for de Gaulle to bring about competitive changes in French agriculture, which may have been even more backward than French industry. But after years during which the Common Agricultural Policy (CAP) of the Community, under pressure from de Gaulle, protected French farmers, this policy too has changed, while simultaneously the forced increased size of French farms, mandated by de Gaulle's policies, has begun to take effect.

Through painful adjustments within the economies of the countries of Western Europe, the system of open competition within the EC is having the desired effect of increasing productivity. Gradual elimination of government protection within this market has forced individual businesses either to modernize and hence, prosper, or to disappear because they are unable to compete.

Of course, such an end was not seen by all as inevitable, or even as desirable. De Gaulle, for one, could never understand why the British, who had created over a period of centuries an efficient industrial and agricultural system with other members of the Commonwealth that allowed British manufactured goods to be exported to distant members of the association in exchange for agricultural and semifinished industrial products, would allow their system to be destroyed through Britain's entry into the Common Market.

The role that British banks, British shipping, and British insurance companies played in the old system had made it highly profitable to Britain as well as self-perpetuating. As one example, it used to cost more to ship goods from Liverpool, England to Dublin, Ireland—a distance of a few hundred miles—than it did to ship those same goods from Liverpool to Sidney, Australia, a distance of several thousand miles. Ireland was not a member of the Commonwealth but Australia was. Now the system is gone and its demise has resulted in an enormous change in the direction of flow as well as in the cost of international trade.

Writings on trade have not sufficiently focused on the impact of Britain's withdrawal from its former control of trade financing, insurance of goods in transit, and particularly, control of the Shipping Conference rates, which had been established to assure that trade with fellow Commonwealth nations would give maximum competitive advantage to Great Britain. It may take years for Britain to adjust to its new role as a part of Europe, while the other Commonwealth nations have to develop trade patterns with the rest of the world on new and different bases. As for consequences to the United States, there may be irony but no lack of logic in the fact that its own postwar economic policy, which supported the creation of the European Economic Community to counter the threat of Communism from Eastern Europe, has succeeded so well that the United States is now facing increased *economic* competition from a grouping of nations it helped to create for sound *political* reasons.

The U.S. government policy of rebuilding the manufacturing capability of Western Europe was subsequently extended to newly developing countries, with a particular emphasis on Latin America, through a postwar tax policy that encouraged American business firms to invest outside the United States. Since income tax could be deferred until profits were brought home, there was an incentive to reinvest profits earned abroad in new ventures or in the expansion of current investments outside the United States. We tend to forget that during the Truman and Eisenhower Administrations, successive commissions of businessmen and government experts examined the question of how business investments in Europe and Latin America might best be fostered, and that President Kennedy's plan for an Alliance for Progress focused on the same objective through a modified approach.

The idea, unchallenged through all three administrations, was that government policy in favor of economic development abroad could best be made effective by stimulating foreign direct investment by American business, thereby encouraging the development around the world of democratic, business-oriented consumer societies similar to the United States itself. No one worried in those days about the export of American jobs or about competition from Europe or Japan, which such massive investment was making possible. Wasn't the U.S. economic system, with its highly developed industrial society and its work ethic, the envy of countries everywhere? It was not until the Revenue Act of 1962 that the U.S. tax system stopped encouraging foreign investment and even then it was done not out of consideration of the long-term consequences for the strength of the dollar but only at the instigation of labor unions representing motion picture employees, who wished to discourage the making of motion pictures outside the United States.

On the other side of the globe, in Japan, an industrialized society was recreated in a manner quite different from what General MacArthur's postwar military government had intended, and quite free of the type of American economic support characterized by the Marshall Plan in Europe. In Japan, of course, there was no fear of a Communist takeover if industrial jobs were not created for workers returning from the war. Japan was a highly structured society where individual aspirations were subordinated to the demands of the state. Further, postwar Japan interpreted the victory of the United States as that of a society capable of producing more and better goods, using its production more efficiently in the national interest when challenged. Because the United States won the war, U.S. productive efficiency became a Japanese goal. Japan, so the Japanese thought, would have to redefine its national goals in new terms—production efficiency rather than military superiority. To do so, little else in the Japanese social system needed to be changed.

In 1954, when the peace negotiations between the United States and Japan were finally concluded, the Japanese immediately set out on their own to transform a poor agricultural country with no wealth or national resources and a relatively barren land into an industrial giant, using their own special advantages to bring about the transformation: a government of the elite, a highly developed educational system, a well developed work ethic, and a disciplined population accustomed to deferring the purchase of consumer goods in order to save and invest for the future of the country.

Since the patents and the know-how of industrialization belonged to the Americans, the Japanese government encouraged the purchase of manufacturing licenses by Japanese firms on the basis of priorities carefully established by government experts so as to make maximum use of scarce foreign-exchange resources. Since raw materials and food had to be imported, the country would focus on promoting those industries capable of producing goods for export; exporters would be given government assistance in financing plant and equipment and motivated through the creation of tax advantages available only to exporters.

It is true that during this entire period of post-war reindustrialization the Japanese did not have to direct investment capital into military expenditures because the United States had taken on the burden of assuring the country's protection. Nevertheless, the Japanese economic miracle must be credited to the special manner in which the government, the business community, labor, and the Japanese people themselves have, with singular consistency and perseverance, managed their affairs on the basis of national goals established immediately following the signing of a peace treaty with the United States.*

In analyzing the position of the United States in international trade it will be helpful to examine the problem under three different headings: 1. problems arising from bilateral trade between the United States and certain other countries; 2. development of the service sector in U.S. trade; 3. analysis of our trade position by type of product exported or imported by the United States.

Bilateral Trade with Individual Countries

It is useful here to describe two recent phenomena that are beginning to affect the U.S. trade balance and are important for the future. The first relates to the change in the nature of the competitor the U.S. exporter faces—the state-owned or controlled business.

In the United States, business has always been privately owned. It is expected that business must, as a general rule, be able to compete without government aid or assistance. True, we have seen in the case of Lockheed a few years ago, and more recently in the case of Chrysler, government intervention to save private businesses in serious trouble, the justification for such intervention resting on the assumption that large numbers of employees would otherwise have lost their jobs. But such decisions have, even in these isolated cases, posed difficult philosophical questions, both for government and for private industry. Within the American political philosophy it is not the role of government to bail out management, bankers, or stockholders, or to shield them from the natural consequences of poor management decisions; business knows that if it supports the idea that there is a government obligation to bail out firms that get themselves into trouble, it will be difficult to argue against ongoing government oversight of all business decisions. For purposes of arguments being made here, however, it should be noted that in the case of Lockheed and Chrysler, the U.S. government was dealing with difficulties of U.S. companies arising out of their domestic operations. Except for its investment in Britain, Chrysler was profitable outside the United States and indeed was able to postpone its domestic crisis by selling profit-producing overseas assets.

* In chapter 10 there will be a detailed discussion of what the United States now needs to do to reacquire from the Japanese the business methods they so well learned from us over the past twenty-five years.

The question now faced by the U.S. government and U.S. business is far harder: to what extent, if any, should the U.S. government intervene to protect private U.S. businesses in international trade transactions in which they find themselves in competition with foreign states? Boeing's competition today comes from the Airbus, an aircraft assembled by Aerospatiale, which is, in turn, owned by the French government. Its planes are marketed by a company owned by a consortium of four governments—France, West Germany, the Netherlands, and Britain—each of whose nationally owned airlines make up an important part of Boeing's potential market. Will a private American company be able to compete successfully in sales to government-controlled airlines against manufacturers that are themselves owned or controlled by one or more of such foreign governments?

In the oil and petrochemical business we see the same phenomenon. How will privately owned U.S. oil companies be able to compete in the future with petroleum concerns owned by OPEC governments or even with Petrocan or Pemex in our neighbor countries of Canada and Mexico? In October, 1980, the Canadian government announced its intention of forcing the sale of privately owned or controlled oil and gas companies to state-owned entities by 1990. If the political standing of the United States continues to decline, and state-owned enterprises of the European Community or of the developing countries increase in political power and financial support, how will our multinational business enterprises based in America be able to compete successfully in these foreign markets?

Already in Brazil there are more than five hundred state-owned business corporations competing with private sector companies. All over the world governments, ostensibly to meet the very formidable competition from entrenched multinational companies, are creating new state enterprises. In state-controlled economies, such as exist in many parts of the developing world, the state creates purchasing entities that import goods from abroad. Since decisions made by government agencies will always be political as well as economic, free movement of goods in international trade, through free competition may become seriously compromised.

A second danger arises out of the growing inability of private industry in the developing countries, as well as of their governments, to continue to meet their foreign debt obligations as foreign exchange is increasingly absorbed by increased oil import costs. As a result, bankers are more apt to require government guarantees before issuing credit to private companies looking to import foreign products. Quite naturally, then, once the government is asked to give its guarantee to private business it may increasingly exact for its guarantee either a voice in management, control of the business, or even substantial government participation in the operation of the company. By increasingly demanding guarantees from national governments, U.S. business and banking interests run the risk of bringing about more government control of business worldwide. As a consequence, competition to private business in international trade by government-owned or -controlled companies will be encouraged.

But with or without this encouragement we should expect that trade with the developing countries will be increasingly with, and in competition against, state-owned entities financed directly by the government. In international trade this will mean more state-to-state barter transactions of the type currently in use within the Communist bloc. Industrialized countries must focus on this problem because if this trend continues, it may soon no longer be possible for privately owned business firms to compete effectively in international trade.

In the case of the United States, trade patterns with individual countries during the past few years have reflected clear trends. We have unfavorable trade balances with OPEC countries in particular with Nigeria and to a lesser degree with the Arab countries of the Middle East, because of the rising cost of our oil imports. We also have unfavorable balances with Japan because of growing demand in the United States for Japanese automobiles, radios, television sets, and peripheral equipment. We have unfavorable balances with Canada ever since the treaty in 1965 on automobile components.*[1] We have, on the other hand, a favorable balance of trade with the EC as a whole, which approximately balances the deficit with Japan. In terms of individual country balances, therefore, the U.S. trade problem would appear simple to solve: how can we increase exports to Japan, Canada, West Germany, and the oil-exporting countries? If oil imports constitute the problem why can we not emulate the policies of Japan and West Germany, two countries even more dependent upon imported oil that yet manage year after year to achieve trade surpluses?

We have discussed the case of Japan. Why is West Germany so much better able than the United States to achieve a positive balance of trade? The answers are interesting because they point up some clear structural differences between the two countries.

Despite a substantial depreciation of the value of the U.S. dollar compared to the West German mark since 1971, the balance of trade be-

* This treaty made it possible for automobile parts manufactured in Canada by American automotive companies to come into the United States at exceptionally favorable tariff rates.

tween West Germany and the United States continued during this period to be positive for West Germany. As we will see throughout this book, and is clear to anyone who has examined bilateral trade between France and West Germany since World War II, depreciation of the exchange value of one's currency does little to improve the balance of trade, contrary to what U.S. government officials in the last administration were saying in urging a continued devaluation in the value of the U.S. currency.*

Quite obviously, there are other and more important reasons why trade balances between the United States and West Germany have continued until 1980 in favor of the Germans, many related to structural and attitudinal differences between the two countries. But perhaps the most important factor has been the German reluctance in the past few years, when the German currency has been strong, to encourage additional economic growth.

Despite great pressure from the Carter Administration to expand the economy under the so-called "locomotive" theory that envisioned German economic expansion pulling the rest of Europe out of a recession, the German attitude has been to restrain growth out of a fear of accelerating inflation. Indeed, because of the calamitous effect on former German societies of runaway inflation, first in 1923 and again in 1948, any German leader advocating economic policies that might increase inflation would face an immediate adverse response from the electorate.

In addition, West Germany is, statistically, a nation of savers rather than spenders. The rate of savings is high (15 percent annually), and such savings tend to go promptly into investments in German industry, many of which contribute significantly to higher productivity, thereby neutralizing the disadvantages that accrue to the seller of German-made goods due to the strength of the West German mark. In the United States on the contrary, by the end of 1979 the savings rate had declined to zero and consumer debt exceeded $300 billion. Because inflation in the United States is now at a double-digit level, there is an even stronger disincentive to save than heretofore. On the other hand, in West Germany, where the return on savings is not cancelled out by inflation, there continues to be an incentive for the public to save, and hence to create funds for investment.

* The reader will remember that the depreciation of a country's currency tends to make that country's products more competitive abroad. There are those who believe this aspect of the problem makes it mandatory for such a country to have frequent currency devaluations as a matter of national policy.

Another difference relates to the absolute necessity for West Germany to import oil. Because of this, the Germans have developed capital equipment that utilizes less energy than counterpart equipment developed in the United States, where, until recently, energy was very cheap. As the cost of energy mounts all over the world, West German equipment has become more saleable abroad and U.S. equipment less so. It should be recognized that there is a fundamental structural problem here, that in a world that may never again see cheap energy, American industrial equipment, designed to be energy intensive, is now in need of a redesigning almost as radical as that which American automobiles have had to undergo.

There are also other factors that have played a role. Because Germany has, ever since its own industrial revolution in the 1860s, lacked the raw materials required by its industries, the population fully accepts the need to promote exports to generate foreign exchange. Two world wars were fought and lost by the Germans in unsuccessful attempts to gain political control over sources of raw materials for their industrial base. Once it was faced at the end of World War II that these materials could be obtained only through foreign exchange earned by exports, the highly efficient German banking system assumed the responsibility to act as the financial arm of the export effort, working in close cooperation with both industry and government.

In order to further the emphasis on producing industrial equipment in demand outside Germany, the government has devoted substantial financial assistance to promoting the German high-technology industries, particularly power plants, generating equipment, transportation equipment, and machine tools. While the U.S. government has tended to focus on protecting its domestic markets against imports—especially in heavily unionized industries such as steel and textiles, where the labor unions affected have had the political strength to demand protection from successive Congresses over the past twenty years, West Germany (and in particular its industrial sector labor unions) has concentrated on creating new employment through additional exports.

In developing this new export business the West Germans have exploited two additional advantages they have over the Americans. First, if a country purchases politically sensitive German capital equipment (nuclear plants, for example), the German government, unlike the U.S. government, will not later condition the granting of export licenses upon the purchaser's meeting political conditions established long after the order was accepted and/or paid for. In the United States, it will often happen that by the time an order is ready for delivery, our government will have introduced, for what are perceived as sound if not compelling reasons, impediments to the actual transfer of the goods, impediments most often related to human rights or environmental considerations, but which were not part of the negotiations at the time the order was placed. Further, if a government is observed to move too suddenly to the right or to the left it may be threatened with cancellation of the delivery of equipment it has purchased and is now awaiting, even if such change puts the government far short of extreme positions, in either direction, taken by other governments with which the United States still does business. Thus it is that West Germany presents itself as a more reliable supplier to the international trade than does the United States.

Second, the Germans seem not to be concerned with whether or not equipment ordered abroad may be used to manufacture goods that may then be exported back to Germany and thereby produce an adverse domestic labor impact. West Germans freely make deals to export steel plants, nuclear plants, or textile mills without any regard for the effect on future competition with West German products produced at home. All this makes West Germany a formidable competitor in international trade.

The Canadian balance-of-trade advantage with the United States rests upon the manufacture in Canada by the U.S. automobile companies of automobile parts that are then exported to the United States under the 1965 treaty. Recently, the export of gas from the fields of Alberta and British Columbia have added to the balance of trade in favor of Canada. Both these advantages will tend to disappear in the future. The American automobile industry will have to be modernized to regain its competitive edge, even in its own domestic markets. It is likely that the new equipment developed by the American auto companies will then be installed in the United States rather than Canada. Also, as increased reserves of deep gas are found in the United States, the United States is less likely to import gas from Canada.

Given Canadian Prime Minister Trudeau's apparent antipathy toward oil and gas producers in Canada, it is more likely that Canadian companies will invest in the United States than in Canada. Thus the Canadian government's effort to nationalize parts of the Canadian oil and gas industry will likely serve to reduce Canadian production and Canadian energy development, weaken the value of the currency, and reduce or eliminate the Canadian trade surplus. Will Canada furnish one more instance of a government impeding the economic development of its natural resources through nationalization of such assets? Many developing countries have restricted their own growth in the same manner.*

The Service Sector

There are those who have started to refer to the United States as a post-industrial society, one in which ever-increasing numbers of workers are engaged in the so-called service sector. Indeed, in 1979 approximately 67 percent of American workers were reported to be engaged in service industries. These include accounting, banking, advertising, auto/truck leasing, communications, computer services, construction/engineering, education services, employment services, equipment leasing, franchising, health services, hotel/motel operation, insurance, legal services, motion picture distribution and exhibition, and air and sea transportation.

For years a growing portion of U.S. international trade has been represented by this service sector. Yet it was only in the Trade Act of 1975 that "trade" came to be defined as including both "goods" and "services." Approximately 25 percent of current U.S. exports are described as in the service sector. Yet, here too, competition from other industrialized countries has been growing, particularly from Japan, West Germany, and France. The service industries in which competition is increasing most rapidly are banking, communications, construction and engineering, and transportation. In the future, we may expect additional competition from advanced and intermediate developing countries, such as from South Korea in construction projects, particularly in the Middle East and Latin America.

In addition, the United States faces numerous barriers to expansion of its service sector exports as other countries seek to develop their own service industries and to protect them against U.S. competition. Discrimination may take many forms: discriminatory licensing, forced deposits, nationality restrictions, employee restrictions, limitations on the number and type of activities that can be performed by foreign firms, discriminatory taxation, currency regulations, and limitations on advertising by nonnationals.

So far little attention has been given to trade restrictions in the service sector because the sector involves so many different activities exercised in so many different ways through so many people. The United States, however, should, in the future, be increasingly concerned with discrimination

*See chapter 8 for a detailed discussion of such nationalization policies in developing countries.

against its service sector. If trading-company legislation currently pending in the U.S. Congress should be adopted, the Congress may be required to focus more extensively on this problem as the trading-company concept takes hold abroad and barriers begin to be raised to discourage the growth of U.S. trade-representation offices in foreign countries. The United States cannot afford to lose any portion of the $45 billion surplus it earns in the service sector to balance out a substantial portion of its annual trade deficit in goods.

Analysis by Type of Product Traded

While the international trade of the United States has grown substantially in the ten-year period 1970 to 1980, from 12 percent of the Gross National Product to almost 25 percent, serious problems nevertheless remain. These can best be illustrated by analyzing this growth in trade by category of product.

First, we need to point out that while exports of manufactured products have indeed grown, exports of agricultural products have increased even faster. With the projected increase in the world's population in the next decade and recurrent bad harvests in such areas as the Soviet Union and certain parts of Africa, it is likely that the world will increasingly depend on U.S. agricultural exports. The same is certainly not true of manufactured goods.

Japanese and European Common Market high-technology products and new competition resulting from the industrialization of developing countries will tend to cause a deficit trend in manufactured goods to accelerate further. An analysis of the U.S. trade balance in manufactured products over the ten-year period 1970–1980 is revealing in that it shows the United States becoming a net importer of such items as automobiles, machinery, and others for which U.S. brand names were once known the world over. In 1980, for example, the United States was a net importer of $20 billion of autos, largely from Japan.

What happened to change the U.S. trade picture in manufactured goods over the ten-year period? Throughout the 1950s and 1960s the United States consistently maintained a merchandise trade surplus. The size of the surplus varied from $7.8 billion in 1957 down to $2.4 billion in 1964. The fluctuations can largely be ascribed to changing business conditions abroad—as foreign economies weakened, U.S. exports fell, and, as they regained strength, U.S. exports again increased. By contrast, during this entire period the U.S. economy was consistently expanding, and the demand for imported products was thus increasing steadily.

It was only toward the end of the 1960s that a real decline in the U.S. trade balance was detected. The U.S. percentage of world trade, for example, declined from 17.5 percent in 1964 to 14.2 percent in 1971 as Japanese and West German goods became increasingly competitive. A recession in the United States in 1970 caused a sharp decline in imports, but the economy revived in 1971 bringing a renewed surge in imports and a $2.8 billion trade deficit. During 1973 the beginnings of sharp deficits with Japan ($1.4 billion), West Germany ($1.6 billion), and Canada ($2.6 billion) appeared, setting a pattern that would be sustained throughout the 1970s.

In response to the trade deficit apparent in 1971, which spurred foreign holders of dollars to convert their U.S. currency into gold and stronger currencies, President Nixon in August, 1971, unilaterally halted the right to exchange dollars into U.S. gold, ending the monetary system established at the end of World War II in which dollars were automatically convertible into gold at a fixed rate of $35 an ounce, and bringing about a depreciation in the value of the U.S. currency of about 9 percent. In terms of trade it was hoped that this would make American goods more competitive in world markets, while imports, thus raised in price in terms of dollars, were expected to decline. At the same time the U.S. government put a 10 percent surcharge on all imports into the United States and adopted a ninety-day wage and price freeze to quell inflation and further contribute to making U.S. goods more price competitive.

Despite these measures, however, the U.S. trade deficit more than doubled in 1972 to $6.4 billion. After a small surplus of $900 million in 1973, the trade balance went over to a $5.4 billion deficit in 1974, very much because of the three-fold increase in petroleum imports to $24 billion. It thus becomes necessary to see U.S. trade deficits from 1973 onwards in terms of the import bill for oil, and of the inability of the United States to balance off this item through large increases in trade with the OPEC nations. In 1976, for example, the United States ran a $12.1 billion deficit in trade with OPEC nations; the total deficit for the year came to $9.4 billion. But in 1977 the United States had the worst trade deficit in its history—$31 billion—not all of it attributable to the rising cost of oil imports.

In 1977 the Carter Administration continued to "prime the pump" to reduce unemployment, thus generating additional imports. It also "talked down" the value of the U.S. currency, while unsuccessfully urging West Germany and Japan to "inflate" their economies so as to pull other industrialized countries out of a momentary recession and help U.S. exports increase. The results were not satisfactory. In 1978, the U.S. trade deficit increased again to $34 billion, with Japan's share alone amounting to $11.6 billion. It was evident that while the United States had no energy policy and therefore increased the value of its petroleum imports annually, other countries, particularly Japan, through better productivity, concentration on product quality, government policies to encourage exports, and effective barriers against imported goods, were successfully balancing their bill for imported oil by improving their balance of trade with the United States.

As the United States continued to neglect its balance of trade, its currency weakened further. This in turn set the stage for the actions taken by the U.S. government in 1978 to protect the currency through the swap arrangements described in Chapter 1 and, in 1979, through measures taken by the Federal Reserve to increase interest rates. Thus the failure of the U.S. government, year after year, to take necessary steps to protect its trade balance, has brought about drastic alternative policies that have resulted in new dislocations in the U.S. domestic economy. In March, 1980, the United States was forced to take measures to control credit in order to keep interest rates from climbing even higher.

In 1981 the United States faces new and perhaps more serious dislocations brought about (at least in part) by the continued enormous merchandise trade deficit: rising interest rates, reduced productivity, an economic recovery retarded or even aborted by the necessity of maintaining high interest rates to protect the value of the dollar, increased unemployment, and sharply increasing budget deficits brought about, among other things, by the reluctance of the Carter Administration to restrict the growth of social welfare programs, even during a period (1977–79) of relative prosperity.

The relationship of the United States to the OPEC nations at the present time is not dissimilar to the relationship that existed in the years immediately following World War II between Europe and Japan on the one hand and the United States on the other—except that now it is the United States that needs to forego consumer expenditures in favor of increasing exports. But unlike the Europeans and the Japanese of that other time, we are working toward no better day. For as long as we are not able to bring about a domestic solution to our energy problem we will face the need to make great sacrifices for little apparent gain. Increasing domestic energy supplies must be a priority goal under current conditions.

The lesson to be learned is that a continued failure to effect a balance in U.S. international trade will necessarily force the adoption of government policies that in themselves cause further dislocations in the domestic economy and undesirable adjustments in our standard of living.

Given these realities, what can we predict for the future?

It is true that in political and economic terms, the world is a constantly shifting stage. Evaluations of relative military power, political stability, economic development, within regions as well as globally, are constantly changing, although the awareness that such changes have occurred is sometimes very much delayed. But these changes do not come about in a haphazard fashion and as early as 1960, today's political, economic, and trade-development scenario might well have been predictable to careful observers. Should we not have been capable of anticipating the Japanese growth in trade given their unwavering policy of encouraging the manufacture of products capable of establishing a strong export base? Should we not have foreseen the military position of the USSR, given that its commitment to attaining such a position has not changed since Stalin's day? And now, looking into the future, should we not be able to evaluate what the economic entity called Western Europe will mean to the United States in economic terms over these next ten or twenty years? Can we not foresee that the creation of new industries in the developing countries will mean increased competition for a U.S. economy that attempts to maintain its primacy in those same product areas it dominated twenty and thirty years ago?

Of course, it is not the United States alone that faces a future of dramatic change. We already have many signs that the political system established in the Soviet Union will have to deal with continually increasing economic pressures. And as long as the emphasis on greater individual productivity fails to be introduced, such pressures will continue. The result is likely to be further bureaucratization, reduced industrial and agricultural output in relative terms, leading to additional pressures for relaxation of government controls, and finally new cracks in the monolithic infrastructure now controlled entirely by one small group of people from one small segment of the Soviet system itself. This may in due course bring about substantial alterations in the Communist system itself, and thus affect greatly the U.S. trade position.*

* Development of the Soviet Union's growing role in international trade (but not with the United States) is examined in detail in chapter 9.

As for the European Community, having established at last its economic base in mutual trade, it will likely pass on to growing monetary adjustment, and, in time, to a regional political unit having one military and foreign policy voice, while continuing to observe cultural and educational distinctions based on former political divisions. As economic pragmatism subverts old ethnic prejudices, Western Europe should become more cohesive in a political sense while Eastern Europe, whose economic and political relationships were imposed by Soviet force, should show signs of declining cohesiveness.

3

The Growing Role of Energy in Trade

> Where the willingness is great, the difficulties cannot be great.
>
> NICCOLO MACHIAVELLI, *The Prince*

> The whole of science is nothing more than a refinement of everyday thinking.
>
> ALBERT EINSTEIN

If both Einstein and Machiavelli—one a scientist and the other a political adviser—had been given the task of solving America's energy problem it is likely that each would have found fault with the solution of the other. The reason, of course, is that the problem is political as well as technical and must be treated as such.

The impact of oil imports on the U.S. trade balance has become staggering in recent years and may get even worse in the immediate future (Table 3). Finding a way to deal with the consequences of this dollar hemorrhage must become one of our most important concerns. It is appropriate to question why it has taken us so long to recognize the gravity of the problem. Other industrialized countries are already far ahead of the United States in their analyses of the problem and in their efforts to solve it. Yet, as of the end of 1980 there was still no consensus within the U.S. government as to what needed to be done. Or even whether the problem did, in fact, exist.

There are many who believe the government cannot solve the problem because it is not the kind of problem government ought to be made to cope with in the first place. They support their position with the following arguments:

1. The energy crisis did not come about through any suddenly created shortage of product. There is plenty of fossil fuel in the world. The problem is one of price. Oil—particularly gasoline and heating oil—was subsidized at so low a price for so long that the public has been led to buy

Table 3. U.S. imports of petroleum and petroleum products[a]

Year	Billions of dollars
1960	$ 1.55
1965	2.22
1970	3.08
1973	8.17
1974	25.45
1975	26.48
1976	34.00
1977	44.54
1978	42.11
1979	60.21
1980[b]	75.14

Source: U.S. Department of Commerce.

[a]Based on FAS (Freight Aboard Ship) transactions.
[b]For the first six months of 1980 oil imports amounted to $40.2 billion compared with $24.5 billion in 1979. While consumption was down, the United States was importing in dollar value almost twice as much oil in 1980 as it had the year before. In the second half of calendar 1980 the quantity of oil imported diminished appreciably, but the dollar value continued to increase. In 1981, unless OPEC increases further the price of oil, there should be a decrease in the dollar amount of oil imports.

inefficient automobiles, to waste electricity, to keep homes and offices too warm in winter and too cool in summer. As an example these critics point to regulations that continue to direct public utilities to charge their customers lower rates if they use more electricity, thereby encouraging greater use of a scarce commodity.

2. In terms of encouraging production, the argument made is that the regulations of the Department of Energy have often been confusing and inconsistent. Worse, these rules have tended to discourage domestic exploration and production because under them controls over prices were to be phased out only over a long period of time; hence good business practice dictated postponing exploration. In 1981, it should be noted, President Reagan accelerated oil-price decontrol. The hope, of course, is that such accelerated decontrol will bring about more immediate implementation of formerly postponed exploration projects.

3. For yet another reason an accusing finger is pointed at the Department of Energy by these critics. Not only does the department produce no energy, and indeed, its regulations discourage others from

producing it, but it is itself highly inflationary. Its $17 billion annual budget exceeds half the 1976 value of all imported oil; its work force of more than 19,000 employees represents a money and manpower drain on resources that, these critics argue, might better be applied to long-range programs for energy source development.

Two years ago, according to a commonly cited example, the President of the United States and the Prime Minister of Canada signed a treaty to enable Alaskan gas to flow to the Midwest; the Canadians have already finished their part of the planning, while the Department of Energy and other agencies of the U.S. government are still so hopelessly ensnarled in jurisdictional disputes that little progress has been made on the U.S. end. In the meantime, the cost of the pipeline has increased so appreciably that it will now probably never be built.

The whole notion of insuring product availability by government regulation seems to these critics an extraordinary distortion of the manner in which private initiative can best be motivated in a free enterprise economy such as that of the United States. But before attempting to pass judgment on these criticisms it might be well to examine briefly where we were just a few years ago and the manner in which we passed to this present state of affairs.

Clearly, our Western industrial society has had its base in energy since the days of the invention of the steam engine. At first coal was the principle energy component, but since the early 1830s we have passed from coal to oil to natural gas and on to nuclear energy—this last, especially, a resulting benefit of the unlimited expenditures for research and development made primarily in connection with defense or wartime needs.

There is an irony in this gradual development—from wood, the country's pre-industrial source of energy, to nuclear fuel, its most recent energy alternative—for there are now those among us who would reverse the process, giving up the technological lead we have developed in nuclear energy, rejecting the private competitive system by which U.S. companies first became clearly preponderant in the discovery, refining, and distribution of fossil fuels, and attempting a return to reliance upon windmills, the wood stove, and the bicycle. The promise of such regression is that it would reward us with a less dangerous community, cleaner air, and a more healthful standard of living. The trade-off, however, is not insignificant. Before we even consider seriously such a drastic alternative, we need to look at our energy problems more carefully. We would have to sacrifice much in the process, and man, capable of discov-

Table 4. U.S. production and consumption of petroleum (*In millions of barrels per year*)

Year	Production: Petroleum	Natural gas liquids	Total	Consumption[a]	Dependence gap
1970	3,517	606	4,123	5,364	1,241
1971	3,454	618	4,072	5,553	1,481
1972	3,455	638	4,093	5,990	1,879
1973	3,361	634	3,995	6,317	2,322
1974	3,203	616	3,818	6,078	2,259
1975	3,057	596	3,653	5,958	2,305
1976	2,976	587	3,563	6,391	2,828
1977	3,009	590	3,599	6,727	3,128
1978	3,178	572	3,750	6,879	3,129
1979	3,108	607	3,715	6,707	2,992

Source: Energy Information Administration, *Annual Report to Congress* (Washington, D.C., 1979), vol. II.

[a]Refined petroleum products, including gas liquids and crude oil burned as fuel.

ering and using nuclear energy, is equally capable of controlling its use. We have not abandoned the use of fire because violent men are capable of arson.

To understand fully the situation in which the United States finds itself today in its imports of foreign oil, it is worthwhile to look not only at prices (both domestic and foreign) but also at *demand* and *domestic supply.* Table 4 gives the data on domestic oil production and consumption for the period 1970–1979. At the beginning of the period, the United States was the world's major oil producer. Today it is third, behind only the Soviet Union and Saudi Arabia, hardly a calamitous situation.

In terms of price, however, the OPEC increases of 1973–74, compounded by the new increases of 1979 and 1980, have driven imported oil from $2.30 per barrel to well above $30 and, in some cases, up to $40 per barrel. In 1973–74 alone, the price increase was 366 percent, an increase that cost the nation "between $15 billion and $20 billion in gross national product and half a million jobs, and added five percentage points to the consumer price index."[1] In 1976 a study estimated that a new oil embargo might cause a loss of between $39 billion and $56 billion in GNP and well above 1 million jobs if it lasted as long as six months.[2] The effects of the substantial new price increases of 1979–80 are still being evaluated. The threat of embargo and of further price increases make clear the necessity of treating the energy situation as a

Table 5. The declining supply of U.S. crude oil (*In thousands of barrels*)

Year	Proved reserves at start of Year	Reserve revisions, extensions and discoveries, during year	Production during year[a]	Proved reserves at year-end	Net change in reserves during year	Indicated years supply of year-end proved reserves
1948	21,487,685	3,795,207	2,002,448	23,280,444	1,792,759	11.6
1950	24,649,439	2,562,685	1,943,776	25,268,398	618,909	13.0
1952	27,468,031	2,749,288	2,256,765	27,960,554	492,523	12.4
1954	28,944,828	2,873,037	2,257,119	29,560,746	615,918	13.1
1956	30,012,170	2,974,336	2,551,857	30,434,649	422,479	11.9
1958	30,300,405	2,608,242	2,372,730	30,535,917	235,512	12.9
1960	31,719,347	2,365,328	2,471,464	31,613,211	−106,136	12.8
1962	31,758,505	2,180,896	2,550,178	31,389,223	−369,282	12.3
1964	30,969,990	2,664,767	2,644,247	30,990,510	20,520	11.7
1956	31,352,391	2,963,978	2,864,242	31,452,127	99,736	11.0
1968	31,376,670	2,454,635	3,124,188	30,707,117	−669,553	9.8
1970	29,631,862	3,088,918	3,319,445	39,001,335[b]	−230,527	11.7[b]
1972	38,062,957[b]	1,557,848	3,281,397	36,339,408[b]	−1,723,549	11.1[b]
1974	35,299,839[b]	1,993,573	3,043,456	34,249,956[b]	−1,049,883	11.3[b]
1976	32,682,127[b]	1,085,291	2,825,252	30,942,166[b]	−1,739,961	11.0[b]
1978	29,486,402	1,347,616	3,029,898	27,803,760	−1,682,642	9.2

Source: American Petroleum Institute, Committee on Reserves, April, 1979.

[a] Production is the amount originally estimated and used by API in prior reserves reports.
[b] Figures include 9.6 billion barrels located in Prudhoe Bay, Alaska.

primary national concern. Yet various polls have indicated that more than 50 percent of Americans either don't believe that we have an energy shortage or blame it on oil company manipulation.

There are essentially three reasons for this. In the first place, successive administrations have, for one reason or another, been unable to create a public understanding of the root cause of the problem, even when in 1974 and again in 1979 long gas lines appeared in various parts of the country.

Second, the government has failed to discourage the continually rising consumption of oil (as is apparent from Table 5) by failing to impose additional taxes either at the pump or as import duties. To the contrary, until 1981 the government artificially kept the price of oil low, through price controls, with the entirely predictable result that public utilities, industry, and individual citizens alike were discouraged from switching to those other kinds of fuel whose price was not maintained below an artificial ceiling. It is as though the government had planned to motivate business and the public to import more, rather than less, oil.

Third, the government placed price controls on domestic oil that it could not impose on imported oil, with the result that domestic oil companies were encouraged to produce less at home and import more from abroad, and to sell domestic production wherever possible outside the United States in order to benefit from higher prices obtainable outside the government's jurisdiction. The government thereby used price manipulation to accomplish exactly what it should have been trying to avoid—lower domestic production, more imported oil sold within the United States at inflationary prices, while domestically produced oil, with unnecessary transportation costs tacked on, was shipped for sale abroad.

From the very beginning there appears to have been a failure of understanding. In allowing this dependency on imported oil to develop, the United States was simply tempting foreign nations to exploit the situation, which they did, by nationalizing private producing companies and creating a cartel of oil-producing countries. And yet despite the fact that OPEC was in existence for some time, and the United States had been given ample warning of the type of actions this cartel was capable of taking, the events of 1973–74 appeared to have taken the government by surprise. Indeed, in the early 1970s the government had even required that public utilities abandon coal-fired generators in favor of oil and gas turbines. Five years later the same government reversed its policy to require a switch back to coal, all at enormous cost.

Other recent domestic energy policies have done little to improve the government's reputation for consistency; in many instances the overall thrust of government policy has been impossible to fathom. President Carter, in calling for a "comprehensive national energy policy," stated: "We can have an effective and comprehensive energy policy only if the federal government takes responsibility for it,"[3] ignoring the advice of most economists who specialize in energy matters and seeming to contradict the anti–big-government message he had sent out on his road to the White House. Unfortunately, the advice he did follow substituted government edict for the market forces that normally determine product distribution patterns. As a result, regulations have tended to be more and more complicated as government officials have tried in vain to fine tune unworkable control mechanisms.

It would be a mistake to single out any administration for blame for America's failure to deal with the nation's energy problems. Through successive administrations, federal energy policies have been confusing and contradictory, often going to great lengths and great expense to offset incentives to corporate practices that had been created by former policies. For instance, in 1950 the National Security Council devised the program, designed to give the Saudi monarch more revenue, that allowed Aramco to pay income taxes to Saudi Arabia and credit such payments against the Aramco partners' U.S. tax. In effect this program was equivalent to a direct payment by the U.S. government to the government of Saudi Arabia.

Perhaps at the beginning there was a rational intent—such tax incentives would encourage the exploitation of foreign reserves, leaving domestic reserves relatively intact for the future. Yet once this foreign-produced oil came in and started to compete with the oil of American producers, the directly affected constituencies—management, labor, and the affected local communities—started lobbying the government to establish oil-import quotas; in 1959, during the Eisenhower Administration, such quotas were established. Predictably, domestic production was spurred to fill the newly created void in the domestic marketplace, thereby accelerating the depletion of U.S. reserves, an end diametrically opposite to that originally intended. Tax credits to U.S. oil companies today can best be justified for new foreign drilling in non-OPEC areas. Might the purpose of having the tax credit system in place after 1973 have been to encourage Arab countries to rearm in order to withstand a political Soviet threat to the Persian Gulf? We shall probably never know to what extent, if any, the Nixon Administration may have encouraged, in 1973, increases in the price of Saudi Arabian and Iranian oil with this in mind.

But even more bizarre was another consequence of this same sequence of governmental interpositions. And that was that some of this foreign oil production subsidized by U.S. tax concessions but now barred from the United States was diverted to European markets. In effect, tax dollars had been used to reduce prices to consumers outside the United States, including many industrial users who would be able to factor in such lowered energy costs in pricing products that were often in competition with American-produced goods.

The imposition of price controls on natural gas is another example of a mistaken policy leading to additional regulatory inconsistency. These controls go all the way back to 1938, but a Supreme Court decision in 1954 changed dramatically their effect on the American scene. When the Court ruled that the controls could apply only to gas that flowed in interstate commerce, great regional differences developed in the price of natural gas. Within states that produced their own gas, prices jumped but supplies became plentiful, while in areas that had to "import" their gas across state lines buyers enjoyed the apparent benefit of low price but had great difficulty in obtaining the product. It is interesting to note that businesses forced to make decisions regarding new locations during this period opted not for the areas in which utilities would have to supply gas at the lower, controlled rate, but in favor of states like Texas, California and Louisiana, where there would be an assurance of continued supply, even though at an uncontrolled price.

Again, when the Nixon Administration imposed price controls on crude oil and its products in 1971 the results should have been obvious– a decline in domestic production and increased imports. But now two new wrinkles were added. As part of its control over prices, the administration introduced multiple-tier pricing. The question then came up as to which companies would have access to which tiers of pricing, and in what proportions. In attempts to establish fairness, a complicated system of allocations was developed under which certain companies had to sell crude to others. This strange corporate income redistribution system imposed among competitors was productive principally in creating new government employment and boundless confusion, the additional cost of which inevitably worked its way onto the consumer's fuel bill.

At the same time, it was decided that the price-control system created inequities between producers and refiners. A complicated system of so-called "entitlements" was therefore imposed by the government, which required large amounts of money (more than $1 billion per year) to be paid by one refinery to another. Even the Executive Office of the President was obliged to admit that the entitlements program had become "an administrative nightmare."[4] To give but one example of the inequity created: Under the program, refineries using relatively cheap price-controlled domestic oil, sent monthly subsidization checks to refineries using more expensive foreign oil. You would have expected Sohio, the biggest producer of "inexpensive" Alaskan oil, to be sending checks to others. Not so. Sohio was the biggest receiver of entitlements checks. Under the program, Alaskan oil was considered "foreign" oil, because in 1977 the Department of Energy decided that Alaskan oil had to be subsidized to be competitive.

The historical record does not suggest that in 1981 the new administration and the new Congress will find it any easier to arrive at a workable "comprehensive energy policy," despite some real progress made in the 1977–81 period. President Carter and the 1978 Congress are certainly to be commended for adopting the Natural Gas Act of 1978. The recent decontrol of oil prices by President Reagan has also been a great step forward. As market mechanisms start to express themselves, production should increase, with prices adjusting moderately upward and demand declining. Above all, if market forces are allowed to function they will ultimately reduce oil imports as oil price increases gradually discourage demand for oil and encourage switching to alternative energy sources. In time we may even expect pressure on individual members of the OPEC cartel to increase sharply—leading to price stabilization or a breakup, as individual countries of OPEC begin to engage in bilateral barter transactions with consumers.

It is not surprising that oil and gas legislation and regulation have historically been so inconsistent, unproductive, and costly to the country.

Reducing Energy Demand

Credit is certainly due the Carter Administration for insisting on the need for an energy policy. The policy presented to Congress by the Administration, however, had many shortcomings. While the President stressed conservation, the Congress tended to focus on production. A brief discussion of conservation efforts is in order.

We can reduce our demand for imported oil in any one of three ways: 1. because we are constrained to do so by government action; 2. because we voluntarily see the need for conservation; 3. because if we do, we will be rewarded, or if we don't, we will incur a penalty, all through the operation of the price mechanism. If the government established another quota system on foreign oil, it would be employing option one. Option two, voluntary conservation, was urged by President Carter throughout his term with very little success. Nor is there any evidence that this method, which was also employed in Europe, functions any better there. Option three, which is based on economic motivation, is the yet untried alternative. How might it be approached?

In terms of penalty provisions, the simplest would be to place special duties on foreign oil (which would, however, invite retribution against U.S. exports to OPEC countries) or do what other industrialized countries do so effectively—levy a corresponding sales tax at the gas pump matching every successive OPEC price increase. This would reduce consumption by raising prices and putting OPEC on notice that the effect of any further price increases would be to reduce demand by doubling the price hike. Other means might be to offer tax credits for home insulation, excise taxes on cars based on their horsepower as in Europe, or special subsidies for mass transportation—subways, buses, railroads, and the like—to motivate more people to use public transport. All these methods are good and should be implemented.[5]

There are some who would have us raise the price of energy to make manpower a more attractive alternative. A recent study conducted by two Harvard faculty members suggests that employment will increase 5 percent for each doubling of the price of energy.[6] Interesting that it should be suggested that we might return to pre-industrial times in order to create additional employment. Surely, there are better ways of handling unemployment than by substituting manpower for mechanical or electrical horsepower.

It should also be reported that environmental groups have had a similar approach to conservation. They see a reduction in energy use as a positive development that would assure a return to nature in its prior state—clean water and clean air and healthier people who would benefit from a return to the way in which mankind lived in times long past.

History suggests that the most effective factor in increasing conservation is the price mechanism itself. As the price of oil-generated energy increases (particularly for electricity), human ingenuity will apply itself to product conversions, to distributing energy more efficiently, or to developing more competitive alternate domestic sources so as to reduce oil imports.

Let us now turn for an analysis of the production side of the equation. What can we do to increase the production of domestic supplies of energy so as to cut our bill for imported fuel? Because there are many options, this part of the chapter is divided into these subheadings: domestic oil, natural gas, coal, nuclear energy, and, finally, alternate energy sources, including solar energy, wind and tides, gasohol, etc.

The Situation Regarding Oil

So much has been written on the dependence of the industrialized countries on OPEC that it needs no further elaboration here. Our only interest is in examining whether or not such dependence is endemic, given the role played by oil imports in the U.S. trade balance (Table 6).

A few brief comments can be made. First, world oil production is clearly a political rather than an economic problem. We now know, or should know, that whenever consumption is reduced in the OECD countries through conservation or other means, production will be reduced by OPEC. In March, 1980, when oil reserves increased in the OECD countries and the U.S. press began to talk of an oil glut, Kuwait, Libya, and even Venezuela began to cut production. Even Saudi Arabia, despite the discovery of new oil deposits, has made no move to increase production to anywhere near capacity. However, at least through the first quarter of 1981, it has maintained the production from currently producing fields far in excess of need, and well in excess of production prior to the Iran-Iraq conflict. Nonetheless, the Saudis have already made the demand, as a condition for maintaining current production, that the United States make no further effort to stockpile crude. The pressure brought about by threats of production cutbacks can be expected to continue to be applied until the OECD countries have taken concerted action to reduce their oil imports from OPEC.

Second, the decline in economic power of the private oil companies in favor of the state-owned oil monopolies in the oil-producing countries has made price increases—rather than production increases—the key to maintenance of revenue flows. As the governments of the oil-producing countries have boosted their control over the production and sale of oil through these state-owned companies, production control has become increasingly political. In 1980, the movement of more than 42 percent of the world's crude supply (13 million barrels per day) was controlled by producer governments.[7] This was five times the amount controlled by these governments in 1973.

Third, as the new OPEC state-owned companies increasingly enter phases of the oil business other than the production of crude—i.e., oil refining, transportation, distribution, and eventually, petrochemical production—the role of the major oil companies in the OECD countries, those formerly known as the Seven Sisters,* will decline even further. As the Shah of Iran once said: "Oil is too precious a commodity to be sold as crude." As producer nations increasingly take to converting crude oil into more valuable products to be marketed by them, their share of oil-trade income will increase while that of the OECD countries decreases—a discouraging but realistic prospect for the future.

Given this scenario for the future, what can be done to increase the production of oil outside OPEC? There are, of course, some possibilities. Recent discoveries in Alaska, the Arctic islands of Canada, the Beaufort

* Exxon, Mobil, Texaco, Gulf and Standard Oil of California (U.S. companies), B-P (British), and Royal Dutch/Shell (60 percent Dutch, 40 percent British).

Sea, offshore Newfoundland and Labrador, additional parts of the North Sea, Mexico, Guatemala, Argentina, China, and west Africa all indicate that future exploration will yield some results. Nevertheless, as consumption continues to increase, and particularly, as the developing countries industrialize, we are unlikely to increase reserves fast enough to meet the increasing demand. It has been estimated that demand for oil outside the Soviet bloc will reach anywhere from 59 million to 68.4 million barrels per day in 1985, and 66.8 million to 78.2 million barrels per day by 1990,[8] with non-OPEC production ranging between 22 to 28 million barrels by 1985 and 23.7 million to 31.2 million barrels by 1990. If OPEC production levels remain constant at 30 million barrels per day, there will be a serious shortfall. It is irrational to expect these OPEC countries, many of whom cannot absorb additional funds into their own development programs, to increase or even to maintain current production simply to compensate for this shortfall.

On the contrary, we must expect OPEC increasingly to use its control of supplies to exact political or economic concessions from consumer countries. There have already been many instances to illustrate that the OPEC countries understand the power they have and are prepared to use it. The best remembered instance, of course, is the 1973 oil embargo, during which Americans suddenly found themselves waiting in long gasoline lines as punishment for their government's failure to extend political support to the allies of certain oil-producing nations. A few more recent examples of this type of political pressure can be cited:

1. Saudi Arabia halted oil sales to Italy's state-owned oil company, ENI, after the Italian press mentioned payments to members of the Saudi Royal family;

2. Saudi Arabia has warned the United States, as we have mentioned earlier, about possible production cutbacks if the United States added to its Strategic Petroleum Reserve;

3. Algeria recently cancelled its gas contract with El Paso gas company of Texas and with French buyers because the buyers would not agree to an arbitrary price increase in violation of formerly agreed-upon contract terms;

4. Kuwait arbitrarily notified its major customers that it would no longer make deliveries of oil as required by its contracts, preferring instead to sell its oil on the spot market (Libya, Nigeria, and Iran have also unilaterally modified their deliveries under binding sales contracts).

We can also expect other alterations in our relationships with oil-producing nations. From the more developed countries among the oil producers, we should expect new demands for trade concessions on other products. For instance, the Canadians are already exerting pressure for tariff reductions on petrochemical products in return for higher sales of natural gas to the United States, and the Mexicans are requesting changes in U.S. policies on immigration and on agricultural imports as conditions for their allowing increased exports of fossil fuels.

Second, additional investments in producing countries will continue to be curtailed. Saudi Arabia could easily increase its production but, in no rush to exhaust its source of wealth and power, will not permit Aramco to make the necessary investments. In other countries production will fail to increase, and may even decrease, because, in the shift of control from technical people to bureaucrats, appropriate maintenance procedures to protect the productive capacity of the oil fields have not been followed. In Iran, the fields are chaotically maintained and the Abadan refinery, even before its bombardment by the Iraqis, had been permitted to deteriorate to a point where serious breakdowns were inevitable.

Third, we should expect very little new investment, particularly in those developing countries that have created state-owned oil companies. For the often inadequately trained managers who all too frequently run these companies for their governments are reluctant to bring back into the oil-production cycle technicians capable of expressing informed advice on exploration or production. Thus, practical working agreements with private companies having appropriate expertise in exploration, development, or in the building and maintenance of refineries are unlikely as long as this type of management can prevent it. In fact, rather than increasing production in existing fields and developing new sources of production, the world outside the OECD is making little effort to add to its oil reserves. This is particularly discouraging when we look at the figures on oil drilling to date.

According to a December, 1979 article in *The Wall Street Journal,* "there are approximately 600 prospective petroleum basins in the world. Of these, 160 are commercially productive, 240 are partially or moderately explored, and the remaining 200 are essentially unexplored. Around the globe, 3,444,564 wells had been drilled up to 1978. Of this number, 2,513,000, or 73% had been drilled in the United States."[9]

But the United States is also the world's largest energy consumer, accounting for 40 percent of the world's oil consumption. As such, our consumption patterns and government policies are as important in influencing the future world oil market as is the reluctance of OPEC nations to increase production.

Oil and gas supply more than three-fourths of total U.S. energy consumed, with oil accounting for 47 percent of this amount. Exxon's most recent forecast is that U.S. imports of oil and gas will remain at about 9 million to 11 million barrels per day through the 1980s. This oil cost the U.S. approximately $60 billion in 1979; it could easily rise to $150 billion per year by 1985.[10] Can this be avoided? What can the United States do to increase its production and lessen its dependence on the world market?

A December, 1979 article in *The Oil and Gas Journal* estimated that the United States had "proved" reserves of 641 billion barrels.[11] Except for one jump in 1970 when Alaskan reserves were first reported, these reserves have been declining steadily since 1967. (See Table 7) Between 1970 and 1975, proved oil reserves declined by 23 percent, and production declined by 16 percent.[12]

The United States is currently producing about 3 billion barrels of oil yearly, making it the third largest oil producer in the world. This is as much oil as Saudi Arabia produces, but U.S. reserves are being exhausted six times faster. If this level of production is maintained throughout the next decade, assuming no additions to reserves, the United States will run out of oil before the end of the century. Estimates of the cumulative reserve requirements that would be needed to sustain U.S. oil production at 10 million barrels per day until the year 2000 range from the Department of Commerce's prediction of 97 billion barrels to the Department of Energy's 136 billion barrels.[13]

New enhanced oil-recovery methods may be developed to extract additional oil (about 50 percent more) remaining in the ground following application of initial recovery programs. One method, called secondary recovery, involves applying pressure to force up oil through gas or water injection; tertiary recovery consists of using chemical and thermal methods. As a result of price increases, it has become more advantageous to stimulate production from old fields. Undoubtedly, new methods will be developed, such as "dense drilling," to apply increased pressure to the reservoirs and, in that way, increase oil recovery.

In a recent government report, it is estimated that without the additions to U.S. oil production from Alaska, from the Outer Continental Shelf, and from enhanced oil-recovery methods, U.S. oil production in the 1990s will decline to approximately half the production of 1978.[14] If these new sources are included, the forecast is a little more optimistic (Tables 6 and 7), but still not bright.

Private industry in the United States drills more than four times as many wells as does the rest of the non-Communist world combined.[15]

Table 6. Estimated trend of U.S. petroleum production by sources (*In millions of barrels per day*)

	1978	1980	1985	1990	1995	2000
CRUDE OIL						
Lower 48 onshore	6.3	6.0	5.0	4.2	3.9	3.7
Alaska						
Existing	1.2	1.5	1.6	0.9	0.4	0.2
Frontier	—	—	0.1	0.4	0.9	1.3
Total	1.2	1.5	1.7	1.3	1.3	1.5
Lower 48 offshore						
Existing	0.7	0.6	0.5	0.4	0.3	0.2
Frontier	—	—	0.1	0.2	0.3	0.4
Total	0.7	0.6	0.6	0.6	0.6	0.6
EOR[a]	—	—	—	0.2	0.5	1.0
Natural gas liquids	1.9	1.8	1.6	1.7	1.7	1.7
Totals	10.1	9.9	8.9	8.0	8.0	8.5

Source: Government Accounting Office, *Analysis of Current Trends in U.S. Petroleum and Natural Gas Production,* Report to the Congress (Washington, D.C., Dec. 7, 1979), p. ii.

[a]EOR = Enhanced Oil Recovery.

Table 7. Estimated U.S. petroleum production from selected studies 1980 to 2000 (*In millions of barrels a day oil equivalent*)

Year	Shell[a]	Exxon[b]	Tenneco[c]	PIRF[d]	DOE[e]	CRS[f]	DOC[g]	WAES[h]	SHC[i]	AGA
1980	9.9	10.0	10.2	10.4	9.8–10.4	9.5–10.3		10.3	10.3	9.9
1985	8.5	8.5	11.1	10.8	10.9	9.5–12.9	10.0	10.0–12.7	11.2	8.9
1990	9.3	7.2	11.5	10.4	11.5	10.1–13.2	—	—	11.7	8.0
1995	—	—	10.8	—	11.8	—	—	—		8.0
2000	—	—	10.0	—	11.6	—	7.2	6.4–7.2	11.7	8.5

Source: U.S. General Accounting Office, *Analysis of Current Trends in U.S. Petroleum and Natural Gas Production,* Report to the Congress (Washington, D.C., Dec. 7, 1979), pp. 47, 48.

[a]Shell, *The National Energy Outlook 1980–1990,* February, 1979.

[b]Exxon, *U.S.A.'s Energy Outlook 1979–1980,* December, 1978.

[c]Tenneco, *Energy 1979–2000,* June, 1979.

[d]Petroleum Industry Research Foundation, Inc., *U.S. Oil Supply and Demand to 1990,* October, 1977.

[e]Department of Energy, *EIA Administrators Annual Report, 1978,* July, 1979.

[f]Congressional Research Service, Project Interdependence: U.S. and World Energy Outlook through 1990, November, 1977.

[g]Department of Commerce, *Forecast of Likely U.S. Energy Supply/Demand Balances for 1985 and 2000 and Implications for U.S. Energy Policy,* January, 1977.

[h]Workshop on Alternative Energy Strategies, 1977.

[i]Sherman H. Clark, Associates, *Evaluation of the World Energy Developments Their Economic Significance,* January, 1977.

[j]American Gas Association, *The Future for Gas Energy in the U.S.,* 1979.

Yet, in 1978, when 48,513 new wells were drilled, reserves dropped by 1.7 billion barrels. Unfortunately, because most of the promising areas have already been explored, almost 90 percent of this new drilling was for development of known reserves, and only about 10 percent for exploratory drilling adding to new reserves.[16]

Drilling is expected to increase by as much as 75 percent in the next six years, but will the requisite new reserves be found? Optimistic predictions place yearly reserve additions from the lower forty-eight states at 45 million barrels a year until the turn of the century.

There is much promising land, including the Overthrust Belt of the Rockies and the Alaskan North Slope, but most of this land is owned by the federal government. Future leasing and exploration of these areas will be pivotal in determining future U.S. oil-production levels.

Production from the Prudhoe Bay field in the North Slope of Alaska, which began in July, 1977, is expected to reach a level in 1985 of 1.6 million barrels per day, after that, it is expected that production there will begin to decline. It is these frontier areas of Alaska, both on the land and offshore, that are believed to hold the greatest hope for additions to U.S. oil production. Predictions for these areas are difficult to make. To date, exploratory activity has been disappointing, and restrictions established by the U.S. government under pressure from environmentalists will make exploration nearly impossible in the future, effectively closing these public lands to mineral exploration of any kind. To establish a proper frame of reference under which to examine the conflict between the nation's need for energy and the very admirable desire of many to preserve at least a part of this planet in its original natural state, it must be kept in mind that the North Slope field in Alaska covers only 400 square miles in a state of 566,000 square miles. With proper care, therefore, it should be possible to accommodate both points of view.

In this connection, it is interesting to recall how the Prudhoe Bay area happened to be developed. When Alaska became a state, the new governor requested of the federal government that a portion of the federal wilderness area be ceded to the state. The Department of the Interior then selected the Prudhoe Bay area because it had no population to speak of, no timber, and little scenic beauty. Within three weeks after Governor Walter J. Hickel, Sr. took office on December 5, 1966, the salient elements of Prudhoe Bay oil exploration had been assembled and by May 8, 1967, the first well drilled. The rest is history. The area to the east, all the way to the Canadian frontier, would probably be just as rewarding for oil exploration. The federal government, however, has taken no action to permit exploration in areas under its control.

Decreases in U.S. oil production from known reserves are thus very likely over the next few years. New large reservoirs must be found in order to counter this trend. Policies designed to stimulate drilling, particularly in frontier areas, are essential. The two long-standing major proposals have been: 1. to deregulate oil prices, and 2. to grant offshore licenses. The first has already come about.

Allowing oil prices to rise to world "market" levels, it was argued, would reduce U.S. domestic demand, encourage exploration, encourage attempts at novel or unconventional production, and stimulate the development of new enhanced recovery methods. Part of President Carter's energy program, a phased process of decontrol, was designed to lead to the total decontrol of prices by September 31, 1981. As part of the package, Congress was asked to adopt the misnamed "Windfall Profits Tax," which became law in 1980. The two measures were at cross purposes. Decontrol, which would have had more dramatic results had it taken effect at one moment, was designed to increase the production of oil. The "Windfall Profits Tax," not a tax on profits at all but an excise tax on gross sales, works to penalize efforts to increase production. Adopted under the Carter Administration more as a means of increasing government revenues, it will clearly reduce incentives to produce more oil in the United States.[17]

High prices will dampen demand for oil, although to what extent the demand for oil is price elastic* remains a hotly debated subject. Moreover, on the supply side, the General Accounting Office estimates that higher prices will have only a marginal effect on stimulating the discovery of new U.S. reserves and increasing production levels. The estimate is based on the agency's belief that higher prices will more likely increase investment in enhanced oil recovery methods of oil in place,[18] rather than in exploration and production in the difficult but promising frontier areas.

The U.S. oil industry is divided between those companies referred to as the majors and the independents. Approximately 10,000 independent oil and gas producers account for almost 90 percent of the exploratory drilling in the United States.[19] It is these independents, who lack the huge reserves of oil held by the majors, who will be particularly hard hit by the Windfall Profits Tax. Without reserves of oil to convert quickly to sales, these companies will benefit less from the decontrol of prices than

* Price elasticity describes the increase or decrease in demand for any product that is capable of being brought about by reductions or increases in the price of the product. When price changes in a product have little effect on demand, the product's demand is said to be price inelastic.

will the majors, while the Windfall Profits Tax will make exploration outside the United States, where the majors are more likely to control rights, more attractive than domestic exploration.

The Oil and Gas Journal predicts that this excise tax could result in the availability of 1.6 million barrels per day less crude than would otherwise have been the case.[20] This estimate, from an admittedly biased source, may be an exaggeration, but any disincentive to produce must be avoided if the United States is to cope with the inevitable supply stringencies of the next twenty years. This dishonestly named and poorly thought out excise tax does little to encourage greater U.S. self-sufficiency.

Turning to the second proposal, offshore licensing must be accelerated. Because of government regulations, most of the geologically promising Arctic Ocean area is presently not open for exploration. The General Accounting Office estimates that if these areas are not opened up, U.S. oil production could soon decline to pre–Prudhoe Bay levels,[21] a reduction the United States could not tolerate without greatly increasing its dependence on foreign suppliers.

In summary, then, decontrol and leasing of federal lands for exploration are essential ingredients in any plans to increase U.S. oil reserves. They will *not,* however, lead to U.S. energy self-sufficiency, and the United States must be prepared to deal with continued dependence on an extremely volatile region of the world—the Middle East. The creation of a strategic petroleum reserve (SPR) will, however, provide the United States with a cushion to soften the shock of short-term supply cutoffs or shortfalls similar to those that took place at various times over the past decade, the most recent in late 1979 after the revolution in Iran.

To date, the attempt to build this SPR, a commitment the United States made at the International Energy Agency with other oil-importing nations, has been an unmitigated failure. The original goal of the SPR, as presented by President Ford in 1975, was a stand-by reserve of 150 million barrels of oil by 1982. President Carter set 1 billion barrels as the new goal, an amount thought necessary to give the United States time to develop a planned response to any cutoff or shortfall. In March, 1981, the United States had a strategic stock of about 118 million barrels, equivalent to less than fifteen days worth of imports.

Saudi Arabia, arguing that it has been attempting to stabilize the world oil market by producing 1 million barrels per day over its OPEC production ceiling of 8.5 million barrels has warned the United States that attempts to fill the SPR out of this excess production would destabilize the world market, and has threatened to cut back its own production if the United States goes ahead.

Angering Saudi Arabia at this point in time would clearly be unwise. But neither can we concede OPEC a permanent trump card. The Saudis are not, however, our only source for acquiring SPR oil. Alaskan production or a certain portion of imports could be diverted for such usage. Whichever method is chosen, a strategic reserve must be created. We have had sufficient warning about the implications of an oil cutoff on the economic and political health of every oil-importing nation. Continued delay would not only prove risky; it could be disastrous.

U.S. domestic oil policy must encourage conservation and the development of alternatives to oil although neither would significantly reduce U.S. import dependence during the 1980s. The U.S. government must provide new and better incentives for domestic exploration in difficult and uneconomical areas. Finally, the United States must accept that oil in the foreseeable future will remain an essential commodity under the control of foreign nations. The creation of a SPR is one of the few ways to address the immediate dilemma. In addition, we must begin converting to alternative energy sources wherever such conversion is technologically feasible. In the rest of this chapter, we will discuss how this can be accomplished.

The oil picture could be immediately improved if the U.S. government were to concentrate its efforts on encouraging the technology that will allow greater recovery of a special class of petroleum raw material called "heavy oil."* The recoverable reserves of heavy oil in the United States now amount to about 15 billion barrels. The total heavy-oil reserves are probably 200 billion barrels, but extraction and conversion is difficult and costly. The Carter Administration, in finally decontrolling the price of heavy oils, encouraged the development of new recovery techniques, which will not only reduce the cost of production but also enable U.S. companies to export that technology to develop the vast heavy-oil reserves located in Canada and Venezuela.

Recoverable quantities in the Athabasca tar sands in Canada are estimated at about 300 billion barrels out of total reserves of about 900 billion. In Venezuela there may be about 3 trillion barrels in the Orinoco basin. In due course, these vast reserves must be available at a competitive price. Given that combined United States and Canadian consumption of oil is less than 8 billion barrels per year, surely these large reserves of heavy oil suggest one answer. Exxon, which planned to spend $6 billion

*Heavy oil is a dense, viscous form of petroleum, which must be heated, or otherwise coaxed to flow, before it can be pumped out of the ground. It may be found in homogeneous deposits as in the Orinoco Basin of Venezuela, but more commonly it is found mixed with other materials, such as tar sands.

just to convert the tar sands at Cold Lake, Alberta, certainly thinks so. This should encourage the United States to concentrate on Western Hemisphere development on a priority basis. The oil shales* in the United States, discussed in detail further on in this chapter, also offer definite possibilities. Through cooperation, rather than confrontation with the environmentalists, it should be feasible to develop this source of oil in the next few years.

Meanwhile, one can only wonder why the United States, faced with the increased instability in the Middle East, shuts off more and more domestic public lands to exploration, retains any controls at all over the price of domestic production, and now taxes domestic production at the wellhead in order to finance synfuel projects.[22] If our remaining oil reserves are to be developed effectively, it would be well for the U.S. government to revise its priorities.

The Natural Gas Option

Two points must be made in discussing the role of natural gas in the energy future of the United States. The first is that natural gas has always been associated with oil in the literature on the subject. Perhaps this comes from the fact that there is always a certain amount of gas with the oil. Normally, such gas is either flared or reinjected into the reservoir in order to add to the pressure and enable the reservoir to yield more of its oil. Water, gas, synthetic gas—all are used in secondary or tertiary recovery. (The Chinese, wiser than we, have used bamboo gas pipe lines for thousands of years. In the modern industrial world it is only very recently that we have begun to think of gas independently of oil.)

The second point to make is that we have always had a tendency to associate gas with oil in geological terms. Gas was thought to have been created just as oil and coal obviously were, through the decomposition of plant matter that, under intense pressure and heat, was turned first into peat, then coal, then ultimately into oil *and* gas. Thus, our geologists had become convinced that gas would *necessarily* be found only in sedimentary basins, where oil is found.

We have now discovered that this need not be so. Geologists began a very few years ago to find gas in odd corners of the globe, in areas far from sedimentary basins, where deep faults existed. Perhaps the most

* In the geologist's lexicon, oil shale is not a shale but a rock called marlstone. Some samples are so rich in hydrocarbons that they can be lighted with a match.

famous find was the discovery of large quantities of natural gas at the bottom of Kivu Lake in Zaire. At first, such phenomena were put aside as freak occurrences in nature. Only when the U.S. space probe in 1979 discovered that two moons of Jupiter were made of solid methane did our scientists begin to realize that perhaps the core of our earth also consisted of methane gas and that geographical efforts ought to be directed at locating trap rocks in the earth's surface where deep faults were located.

The results are beginning to show. In the United States, nonassociated gas has been found in the Williston Basin of Montana and North Dakota, the Overthrust Belt of eastern Utah and southwestern Wyoming, the Anadarko Basin in western Oklahoma, and now the Tuscaloosa Trend in northern Louisiana. The eastern Overthrust Belt, in the Appalachian region and the Northeast, should also yield many additional pockets of gas. As one scientist has stated: "The astronomers have shown us that what we suspected we now realize is true. As a result, we must do our geophysical work all over again."[23] Fortunately, the Natural Gas Act of 1978 removed price controls from so-called deep gas found below 15,000 feet.

There are six additional comments that ought to be made about natural gas in the broader context of current geophysical knowledge. The first is that there is nothing unique about the geology of the United States. It was only a few years ago that the chairman of Shell in England declared that gas might be found in the English North Sea but never oil, an assessment that has been proved in error by the enormous North Sea oil finds of the late 1970s. The heavy development of fossil fuels in the United States and the USSR, compared with the rest of the world, is less likely due to geophysical coincidence than to the fact that there has been in these two countries over the past fifty years a special marriage of adequate technology and strong incentive to explore and develop sedimentary basins. Of all the oil drilling done in the world, more than 75 percent has taken place in the United States.

The technology and incentive to go after gas already exist. All that remains to be established is that prospects for finding gas in locations formerly thought of as unpromising have improved. We will probably be found to have been as mistaken about the location of oil and gas reserves in the rest of the world as was the Shell chairman about finding oil under the North Sea. Indeed, with oil as well as with gas, recent finds off the coast of Labrador are but the latest proof of how rudimentary our understanding remains of where the earth's crust has stored its energy.

A second comment to be made is that the computer has revolutionized geophysics within the last five years; we can now test more thoroughly and much deeper than ever before. Oil is generally found in shallow basins, gas often in much deeper basins, except where volcanic activity or earth movements have raised deposits nearer the surface. Our drilling equipment has also developed very noticeably during the past few years. What this means is that we are now at the threshold of our capacity to find new gas reservoirs located in deeper areas offshore or below 15,000 feet onshore, and when such reservoirs are found to drill them. Today, for example, we have developed the technology to drill to more than 40,000 feet, a feat deemed impossible two or three years ago. Since such exploration and drilling is necessarily far more costly than that required to develop the shallow Texas basins discovered a few decades ago, the penalty for price controls on gas is all the greater.

The third point to remember is that gas is the cleanest form of energy now used by man and the least dangerous. At a time when environmentalists have effectively stalled the building of nuclear plants and reduced the cost-effectiveness of coal, there seems to be no rational environmental objection to gas.

Fourth, we need to consider that while natural gas can supply our needs for the next twenty or thirty years, if not longer, we will, ultimately, have to turn to other source materials. By the time we do, we should be at such a stage in the perfection of new technologies in the gasification of coal to make possible the use of our present gas-fired utility plants. Our million-mile gas pipeline system could then receive the product of gasification plants right at the coal beds and distribute it efficiently throughout the country.

Finally, we need to remember that on both sides of our borders, in Western Canada and in Mexico, gas has been found to supplement our own domestic gas discoveries in abundant quantities. In 1977 we lost an opportunity to get Mexican supplies by foolishly refusing to pay the negotiated price; those empowered to make the decision had not yet appreciated the fact that price controls over gas in our own country could not be made to apply to imports from abroad. We made the same mistake in Canada. It is to be hoped that these mistakes will not be repeated in the future. The initial price of the product is of little long-range importance. It serves to amortize the cost of the pipeline to the United States but once built, it will only be available to service U.S. customers and the price will tend to adjust downward to approach that which is paid in the U.S. domestic market.

Available statistical forecasts regarding U.S. reserves of gas have not yet been adjusted, either to the effect of eliminating price controls on new offshore or deep onshore gas or to the probable results of the new geophysical approach just suggested. It is very likely that reserves of natural gas will increase substantially in North America in the next few years. If we doubt this, we have only to compare the extent of current drilling and new discoveries with that of five years ago. We are in the middle of a technological revolution that is not generally recognized.

Recent authoritative estimates of remaining recoverable conventional gas reserves in the United States are in the range of 700 to 1,200 trillion cubic feet. Since the current U.S. consumption rate is about 20 trillion cubic feet per year, there are, based just on current estimates, between thirty-five and sixty years of conventional U.S. gas supplies still to be produced. These estimates, as we have indicated, are probably low. In addition, these numbers do not include the vast additional reserves recently found in Mexico and Canada, a portion of which will certainly be available for sale in the United States. It is sad to reflect on, but major suppliers of Canadian and Mexican gas would already have been available for sale in the United States had it not been for American failings, largely diplomatic in the Mexican case and bureaucratic in the Canadian case.

Looking at world reserves, one finds figures that are even more startling. Present estimates show about 2,400 trillion cubic feet and remaining recoverable resources at about 10,000 trillion cubic feet or two hundred times the current annual production.[24] Among these, of course, are the very significant proved reserves and potential resources of Mexico and Canada, whose gas can be conveniently delivered to the United States by pipeline. Again, it should be pointed out that recent finds can increase these reserves very substantially. Off Qatar, in the Persian Gulf, for example, discovery of what is probably the largest gas field in the world was announced in 1980 by a group headed by the German company Wintershall. This field, where the first well was drilled in 1974, very likely links up with a huge, previously known offshore gas field off southern Iran. If so, the Persian Gulf from north to south would contain one massive gas field in the Khuff formation at depths of about 13,000 feet, a source of supply that might itself meet the needs of Europe for many decades. Similarly, in Egypt, near the Mediterranean Coast, there are indications of vast new reserves, which will provide power for the electrification and industrialization of this area so vital to U.S. strategic policy in the Middle East.

Even the OPEC countries are beginning to modify formerly wasteful procedures in the extraction of natural gas. Because of the constantly increasing value of exported oil, these countries are now trying to avoid flaring gas or reinjecting it into the oil reserves so that these gas supplies can satisfy domestic energy needs. In time, probably, these countries will find it more productive to build liquid natural gas plants, but the cost of packaging and delivering gas in this form—involving, as it does better cryogenic technology and special liquid natural gas ships—currently makes this alternative still some years off.

Under these circumstances, how can we justify a policy that causes the Department of Energy to spend only a paltry 8 percent of its total research and development budget on new methods of utilizing gas, including coal gasification? Such a distorted sense of proportion in the allocation of the department's huge budget tends to support the argument of those who would abolish the department altogether.

Even using reserve figures from out-dated geophysical approaches, from currently unsatisfactory technological appraisal methods, and from very limited exploration efforts, world resources of natural gas in place at year end 1978 were estimated at 90.3 percent of the original recoverable resource. Less than 10 percent has been produced, with more than half of this production taking place in the United States. Given these statistics, even with current state-of-the-art techniques, it does seem disingenuous of our leaders to generate support for their special programs of alternate energy development by constant pessimistic references to a calamitous, unending decline of the world's primary energy resources.

One of the problems in correctly determining reserves is the time lag in adding new discoveries to the statistics. Even today, the major discoveries in Melville Island and the Beaufort Sea in Canada have not been added to that country's reserves because, supposedly, the delivery system is not in place. Today we are satisfied that the Williston Basin in North Dakota and Montana, the Overthrust Belt in eastern Utah and southwestern Wyoming, the Anadarko Basin in western Oklahoma, and undoubtedly also the Tuscaloosa Trend in northern Louisiana will yield very substantial amounts of gas. In the Overthrust Belt alone, it is likely that two recent finds in Wyoming will eventually link up, forming a giant gas field fifteen miles in length and four miles wide, with recoverable gas reserves of from 5 to 10 trillion cubic feet.[25]

Both north and south of this area, there are probably two other super giants that will add up to 230 trillion cubic feet to known U.S. reserves.[26] Drilling to date has been insufficient to add more than the yields of a few wells to swell the reserve figures. In the meantime, the majors who report on the old gas fields in Texas are reporting substantial declines in reserves due to drawdowns. Thus, new fields tend to be added only gradually to reservoirs, while declines in old reservoirs are immediately reflected.

It is interesting to note that if we apply the source-reserve criteria to world oil reserves and production we find that here again the figures give no cause for panic. World statistics for 1978 show 79.9 percent of world oil reserves still in place. This means that only 20 percent of the world's oil reserves had been consumed by year-end 1978. When we consider that most OPEC governments (Iraq, Iran, and Saudi Arabia being the classic cases) are making little effort to find additional reserves, because they prefer to raise prices rather than production, then we must conclude that while more effort has been made by private companies to find oil than gas, there is no prospect of a global failure of supply in either category of product. The energy crisis of the industrialized world is, in reality, a political, rather than an economic crisis; the problem is that energy availability dictates industrialization, and that energy sources are no longer under the political control of the major industrialized countries that discovered and developed these resources for their industrial plants.

We have shown that reserves of natural gas are sufficient for many years to come, both in the United States and in the world at large. Nevertheless, as demand increases over time, our domestic reserves must necessarily decline to the point where alternative sources will have to come on stream. We must be ready at that point to turn to synthetic gas.

What are the chances for such a scenario twenty to thirty years from now? Given what we have just spoken of with respect to man's capability to develop new technology when needed, we must try to project our thinking for the future not in terms of where we are today but rather in terms of probable technological breakthroughs that can be expected in the years to come: better geophysical capabilities, better drilling methods, the capacity to drill deeper, newer recovery methods. We can, with some assurance, list the areas of research most likely to yield results. With equal assurance, we can even project cost and time estimates within the defined limits of our demand/production/reserve ratios. We must also, if we are sensible, make the switch to these substitute products gradually, while we can still effectively utilize previously developed energy systems.

When we speak of oil or gas as an energy system, we are describing the steps involved in the exploration, production, refining or cleaning, delivery, conversion into heat or power, and utilization of these products. The less we have to change parts of the total system other than product, the better off we are. It makes sense, therefore, to address our immediate technological efforts not to finding ways to satisfy our industrial and consumer needs through conversion to coal, or solar energy, or exotic fuels, or even nuclear energy, but on finding a way to substitute for gas without discarding more of our plant than we have to. The path ahead seems clear. We must be ready twenty or thirty years from now, if we are lucky, to feed synthetic gas into the distribution, conversion, and user system we have already developed. The way to do so is to find better means of transforming our vast reserves of coal into gas or liquids to take, in due course, the place of oil and natural gas.

There is little new in today's technology on coal liquefaction. It was used extensively in Hitler's Germany. In the USSR, coal liquefaction has been used for a long time. The SASOL project in South Africa essentially uses the same European technology but on a much bigger scale. Reductions in cost tend to come through increases in plant size; the only way to reduce cost seems to be to build a full-sized plant and then tinker with it. We shall certainly obtain valuable information from the South African experience. We shall also obtain valuable design information from the pilot plants in shale oil extraction, tar sands conversion, and eventually from plants designed to convert the heavy oils of eastern Venezuela.

But coal is still of primary importance to the United States because, if for no other reason, we have enough reserves to last us several hundred years. Furthermore, overcoming environmental concerns about land restoration—as compared to the environmental problems arising out of the direct burning of coal—represents no insurmountable cost problem. Western coal seams, in particular, are thick enough and near enough to the surface that the cost of subsequent landscaping would pose no barrier.

We discussed coal liquefaction earlier when we analyzed the prospects for synthetic oil. Here we focus on direct synthetic gas production from coal as a byproduct of synthetic oil.

It seems likely that by 1985 coal-based synthetic natural gas will already represent a partial supply source of gas. Several projects are in various stages of government clearing procedures. The most important is the Great Plains Coal Gasification Project in North Dakota. When completed, this plant is designed to produce about 125 mmcf per day, equivalent to 20,000 barrels of oil. The Department of Energy has agreed to guarantee the debt on the project to the extent of $1.5 billion, but at the moment, between regulatory agency rulings and court rulings,* the proj-

* An appelate court has recently ruled that the Federal Energy Regulatory Commission cannot issue a tariff under which synthetic gas can be sold.

ect has been stalled, perhaps permanently. As reserves of natural gas are found to be increasing it is not unlikely that projects for synthetic natural gas will be deferred in favor of oil shale development. One of the processes under consideration is the Lurgi gasifier with methanation, which was first invented in Germany in 1930 and improved through various stages, including modifications at the SASOL project in South Africa. It is particularly useful in areas where the coal has a high ash, low energy content or where geographic isolation makes it impractical to use coal as a direct product without conversion.

While the Reagan Administration is faced with difficult decisions in determining which programs of the Department of Energy and/or the Synfuels Corporation are to be retained in a period of budgetary constraints, it is to be hoped that projects dealing with coal liquefication or gasification will be favored over others.

Of particular interest is the concept of the U.S. Synthetic Fuels Corporation, as created by the Congress in June, 1980.* The purpose of this corporation is to fund synthetic fuel projects out of an Energy Security Reserve created by Congress for synthetic fuel projects, biomass energy projects funded by the Department of Energy, and alternate fuel projects funded by the Department of Energy under the Nonnuclear Act of 1974. The Reagan Administration and the new Congress will presumably decide to what extent the $19 billion appropriated to the Energy Security Reserve will be allocable by the Department of Energy and by the Synthetic Fuels Corporation.

One policy change will be likely in view of budget constraints: on every project the industry participants will be required to increase their equity. The number of projects will also probably be reduced. It would certainly be preferable to have only one energy financing agency within the government, and this agency should preferably not be the Department of Energy. The U.S. Synthetic Fuels Corporation can do a better job with a leaner budget, concentrating on guarantees rather than direct loans, and on only those few projects ready for commercial development. Were it not for the fact that the Windfall Profits Tax was to be used for the purpose of financing the development of alternate energy programs, there would appear to be little justification for the creation of a special agency of government to finance energy development. The energy companies in the United States have enormous capital resources available for

* Title I of Energy Security Act, which became law on June 30, 1980, created the U.S. Synthetic Fuels Corporation and authorized it to provide various forms of financial assistance for the development of commercial synthetic fuel projects.

this purpose. Government should mainly seek to encourage development by avoiding overregulation, price controls, or special taxes aimed at production.

There are a number of other new technologies to be looked at in the coming years to help bring forth new supplies of gas from previously overlooked sources. A few examples can be cited. It has been said, for example, that *in situ* coal gasification could triple useful coal reserves in the United States by gasifying coal seams too deep or too difficult to mine. Other sources just beginning to be explored include peat gasification using the 740 quads of peat located just in Alaska, as well as supplies in eastern North Carolina; geopressured gas resources in Texas and Louisiana; gasification of Devonian shale in the eastern United States; tight sands; gas produced from marine biomass; and, of course, gas from organic wastes.

Some of these sources currently appear to show promise. As prices for gas increase, Devonian shale and tight sands are likely to be increasingly exploited and may add to reserves significantly. But then, as we have indicated, the nature of the problem is such that any product must be capable of being produced cost-effectively to play a role, given the relatively advanced state of the art that already exists in coal gasification.

As we indicated, the position of the United States in concentrating on natural gas as the preferred energy option is heightened by the fact that both to the north and to the south there have been increasing finds of natural gas, and the opportunity to tie into the U.S. gas pipeline network at a reduced and stable cost makes it very worthwhile to consider natural gas reserves and subsequently coal gasification as a North American, not simply a U.S., solution to the energy crisis. Talk of a North American economic common market has been perceived by our neighbors as an attempt to increase economic domination of the area; joint planning in natural gas development, pipeline construction, and finance, and, ultimately, the technology of coal gasification on a regional cooperative basis would seem to hold much more promise without affronting national sensibilities. Why have we done so little to develop economic ties with Canada and Mexico, when all three countries stand to benefit so much? A brief analysis of recent relationships will be helpful.

First, Canada. As we discuss elsewhere in this study, Canada has certain regional political, economic, and cultural problems quite different from those of the United States. While the center of economic activity has been, until recently, in the east, energy supplies come from the western part of the country, particularly Alberta and British Columbia. Producers in the west preferred to sell their gas to the United States at high prices, but that gas sold at subsidized low prices domestically, was needed by the factories, homes, and refineries in the east. Fortunately, recent new gas finds off Sable Island and oil off Newfoundland, both in eastern Canada, make it likely that eastern Canada will eventually become self-sufficient in oil and gas, and western gas could then go south in larger quantities, freeing the more easily transportable western coal for shipment to Japan.

The opportunity to run the Alaskan gas pipeline through Canada, hooking up with a line coming from the Beaufort Sea, has made the first cooperative venture between Canada and the United States a very practical project for both countries. In fact, the Canadians have immediately taken steps to implement their part of the bargain. Regulatory agencies in the United States, however, have done very little. As a result, the cost of the proposed pipeline keeps mounting from month to month, and the completion date keeps getting postponed from year to year. In their supposed aim to protect the consumer, the executive agencies and Congress have created delays that can only cause the consumer to pay enormous additional costs if the project is not scuttled altogether. The visit to Canada in March, 1981 by President Reagan, accompanied by his principal foreign economic advisors, indicates the importance the new administration attaches to developing a closer trade relationship with our northern neighbor.

To the immediate south, the deterioration of relations with Mexico has come about differently but with similar consequences. Here the problem has not been bureaucratic procrastination but diplomatic misunderstandings at the highest level, accompanied by a failure in Congress to anticipate and respect Mexican sensibilities. In 1976, Mexico discovered large quantities of natural gas in the Reforma fields near Cardenas on the Gulf Coast's Bay of Campeche. Since the initial discovery, reserves have been continually increasing. As of January, 1980 they amounted to at least 67 trillion cubic feet proven reserves and an additional 340 trillion cubic feet potentially available.[28]

In August, 1977, Mexico entered into an agreement with a consortium of six U.S. gas companies to deliver a maximum of 2 billion cubic feet per day by 1979 via a forty-three-inch pipeline to McAllen, Texas, at a price equivalent to that of No. 2 fuel oil landed in New York harbor, or about $2.60 per 1,000 cubic feet as of that time. The price was set after long and difficult negotiations that took into account political relations on both sides of the border. Nevertheless, the U.S. Senate effectively put an end to the project by preventing the Export-Import Bank of the U.S. from financing the $1.5 billion cost of the pipeline. The Senate's position was that the loan should not be made until the Department of Energy could state that the price was fair to U.S. consumers.

Because the Canadian delivery price was then $2.16, the Energy Department failed to approve the Mexican transaction, even though the Mexicans would have to take into account paying the enormous cost of the pipeline. Thus, once again, through the Energy Department's failure and the shortsighted attitude of Congress, the United States lost an opportunity to purchase gas supplies at what would today be a very reasonable price. In addition, of course, the United States lost the opportunity to export $400 million of pipe that was subsequently purchased from the Japanese.

There are certainly better ways of approaching this kind of problem. The consequences of past failures should alert us to the possibility that real opportunities can be missed through the failure to properly order priorities.

What does this analysis of gas potential mean today and in the future to the U.S. trade balance? From January to November, 1979, increased natural gas sales in the United States displaced oil in energy markets at the rate of 435,000 barrels per day, saving $10.4 million per day in the trade balance.[29] Through June, 1980 this figure could be increased by an additional 116,000 barrels per day, reducing by $3.1 million per day the cost to the United States of imported oil. We have only to blame ourselves and our pricing policies if this figure is not substantially increased for the period 1981–85.

We have seen how important a factor pricing has been in deciding whether or not we will add to our reserves of natural gas. Drilling activity over the past few years has not taken place in regions containing the majority of potential gas resources but rather in the more mature areas, where costs of drilling or of product delivery, or both, have been significantly lower. Now that we have begun the process of freeing the price of natural gas (to be completed by 1985 as to wells drilled since 1977), the offshore and deep onshore sites that are high-potential areas have become attractive drilling sites.*

The most significant event brought about by enactment of the Natural

*A conventional gas well of less than 6500 feet will cost less than $500,000, but the drilling of a deep well from 15,000 feet to 30,000 feet may require an investment of from $4.5 million to $12 million. One well currently drilling (in May, 1981) to 33,000 feet in the Anadarko Basin will cost approximately $20 million.

Gas Act of 1978, as we have indicated, has been the elimination of price controls on deep gas (over 15,000 feet). As a result, we can expect the reserve figures on domestic natural gas to rise appreciably. Already in 1979, additions to proved domestic natural gas reserves totaled 14.3 billion cubic feet, up 35 percent from 1978. Just as in 1979, Department of Energy estimates for 1980 will prove to have been conservative. Natural gas production need not be expected to decline at all through the rest of this century. Indeed, the opposite is likely.[30] Already the U.S. Geological Survey (USGS) has recently increased reserve estimates of natural gas by 15 percent. Reserves in old fields continue to decline, but new discoveries are only just now—in 1981—beginning to add substantially to reserve figures.[31] By administrative action within the Department of Energy, the government can also hasten the price adjustment process, and hence encourage increased production of domestic gas, without having to ask Congress to amend the National Gas Act. The Congress may well be reluctant to revise the act in view of its phase-out provisions.

Coal as an Answer

It is evident that the United States has enough coal reserves to last three hundred years. Whether the coal will ever be fully exploited, however, is another matter. Opinion is divided. Many energy companies, including Exxon, Arco, and Standard Oil of California, believe that coal may have an important future as a substitute for oil in the production of electricity. Thanks to an acquisition policy that began more than a decade ago, eleven large oil companies now own 25 percent of all the coal in the United States. (The U.S. government is still the largest owner of coal in the country, holding 34 percent of recoverable reserves, of which only a small portion is under lease.)

The oil companies have plans to increase their coal production rapidly so that by 1985 they will be producing 50 percent of the total U.S. output. Production is rapidly moving to the western part of the United States, where coal seams can be found on the surface and are thus much cheaper to mine than the underground deposits of the Appalachian region. The oil companies are counting on new legislation that would force the public utilities to convert to coal even though the Energy Department's five-year conversion effort has been a failure to date.

The new, increased effort will clearly be in the West, where the miners are not unionized, the cost of mining is far lower, and the problem is mainly one of transportation cost, since the mines are located far from the public utilities. It is in the West, therefore, that synthetic fuel plants from coal liquefication may be expected to be established, thereby avoiding the transportation problem but raising water conservation and air quality issues, as well as questions about the socioeconomic impact caused by new town construction in areas unprepared for rapid population growth.

Other observers, including many Europeans, believe that coal as a fuel can play only a limited role in replacing imported oil. While we should not discount the ultimate feasibility of using synfuel plants to convert coal into liquids or gas, for use as a direct boiler fuel for public utilities, coal does raise the following difficulties: (1) conversion costs from oil-fired plants, (2) air pollution problems, (3) transportation difficulties, (4) labor problems, and (5) high regulation costs capable of being imposed at every level of government.

First, there is the enormous cost in converting from oil back to coal as a boiler fuel for the production of electricity. Only a few years ago the U.S. government encouraged public utilities to convert from coal to oil at very great expense. To convert back now would mean reversing the process, at an even higher cost today than that of the first conversion. On the other hand, as we have seen, it is simple and relatively inexpensive to convert from oil to gas.

Second, because of the high level of pollutants introduced into the air, environmental protection legislation has made coal burning by public utilities and industrial plants a costly undertaking. In addition, the need to make application for federal, state, and municipal permits,* which applications can be subject to litigation by any public group at each stage, makes coal conversion an even more costly and time-consuming process.†

The problem of acid rain will probably make environmental controls on coal burning even harder to satisfy. This acid rain comes about when emissions of sulphurs and nitrogen-oxides from power plants or industrial activities, borne in the upper atmosphere over long distances, finally come down to earth with rain or snow and are changed into acids that seep into lakes and destroy aquatic life. The best-known case originated at the Inco smelter at Sudbury, Ontario; the acid rain killed fish in ponds

* The new Secretary of Interior, James Watt, plans to relax federal controls on strip mining by transferring these to local officials.

† Nevertheless, coal-fired power plants that comply fully with clean-air rules under the Clean Air Act of 1970 (which comes up for renewal in 1981), are coming on line. Twenty-five were put into operation in 1979, and 33 in 1980.

in New Hampshire, despite the fact that the smelter has a 1,200-foot stack constructed on orders from the Canadian Government.

As a result of new coal-fired plants constructed in the Middle West, the Canadians have been having the same problem on their side. They complained to President Reagan, during his trip to Canada in March, 1981, that acid rain is polluting lakes and streams in Ontario and Quebec. Thus, acid rain threatens to become increasingly a political problem across national boundaries. In addition, if countries across the earth switch to coal on a large scale in the next few years, the excessive heat introduced to the atmosphere by such massive coal burning could bring about climatic changes. Better technology may make a difference here in time. Already, a Swedish company, Stal-Laval Turbin AB, has developed a system that uses fluidized beds to increase combustion efficiency while reducing pollution.

Third, coal is a very difficult product to transport. The railroads, particularly in the West and Midwest, have, through lobbying efforts, managed to maintain their hold over the transportation of coal, despite the enormous cost of moving it—even in unit trains—by rail. Boeing engineers and others have designed coal slurry pipeline systems that hold considerable promise, but to date the railroads have successfully prevented their use. It is important to note that the low-sulfur western coals are far from most of the centers of population that particularly need relatively nonpolluting fuels. Hence the cost of transportation becomes an especially important factor with coal.

And the transportation problems are indeed enormous: a 1,000-megawatt coal-fired electrical generating plant, for example, devours more than 100 rail cars of coal each day. A similar nuclear plant need be refueled only once a year. (As a rule of thumb, 600,000 rail cars of coal are the energy equivalent of 100 truckloads of nuclear fuel.) The Carter Administration, rather than ask Congress for additional subsidies for passenger rail transportation, found it preferable to let the railroads increase their freight charges. Because grain and coal are money-earners, particularly in the export market, they have been allowed to provide the subsidy, creating a situation in which coal buyers, including foreign buyers, are subsidizing U.S. passenger transportation. It is now more expensive to transport coal the few hundred miles from Wyoming to Houston,—$20 per ton—than from Australia to Houston—$13 per ton. Under bills pending in Congress, railroads would be able to increase freight charges on coal by 10 percent, in addition to an automatic annual increase based on the inflation rate for the year (estimated at 15 percent for 1981). Under such a law, rail freight rates on coal transport might go up by over 25 percent more.

Fourth, coal unions have always been an independent group that have not easily acknowledged the decisions of their leaders. Because coal mining became a major industry in the United States at a time of substantial labor abuse, there has developed an ingrown distrust between management and labor that is unfortunately as evident today as it was fifty years ago. Leadership biases on both sides tend to be self-perpetuating. The public is largely uninterested. It regards coal mining as a "dirty" business, unattractive to modern man and obviously worth high wages. It is true that western coal mining is largely nonunionized and that since 1977 there have been no wildcat strikes in the Appalachian region. But union leadership is still not fully in control of the membership, and the old distrusts persist.

Fifth, there are numerous government laws and regulations adopted in recent years that have increased the cost of using coal as a fuel: the Clean Air Act of 1970; the EPA regulations affecting standards of atmospheric conditions; and various general environmental regulations. In addition, coal mining is necessarily a hazardous occupation—in the case of underground mining, very hazardous—and new OSHA regulations have increased the cost of coal even further by increasing mining costs.

To produce enough energy to replace even 1 barrel of oil a day would take 76 tons of coal on an equivalent basis. Since such bulk is quite logically difficult and expensive to transport, it would be more economic to convert coal to liquids or gas right where it is mined, and then transport the resulting product to the public utilities located near the population centers.

The first problem is the cost of a conversion plant. The larger the plant the more reasonable the cost per barrel of oil produced. A commercial-scale coal liquefaction plant could cost as much as $25 billion to $40 billion today. This means that the cost per barrel of oil produced would still be substantially higher than that paid by the consumer of conventional oil; although if the price of oil continues to rise—and the price of a coal conversion plant does not increase proportionately—there will come a time when the cost of synthetic fuel will approximate the cost of natural oil.

Only SASOL in South Africa has attempted, on a commercial scale, to convert coal into gasoline. It currently produces about twenty American gallons of gas for every ten tons of coal using the Fischer-Tropch process developed by the Germans prior to World War II. The United States is currently experimenting with some new processes for coal conversion, but it may be many years before these are competitive.

The chemical industry can undoubtedly help us develop new technologies to avoid using oil to produce base chemicals, substituting coal instead. The first step would be to convert the coal or synthetic gas into methanol. Then, using zeolite catalysts, the base chemicals would be diffused out of the methanol, thus producing the main building blocks of petrochemistry, including ethylene, propylene, butylene, benzene, toluene, and xylene. Mobil Corporation is the leader in this technology. Gasoline can also be produced by converting methanol. This is what New Zealand proposes to do with its Maui offshore gas finds. Recently the Japanese have also been pushing chemical research in the same direction, using a government-financed consortium approach.

Although coal will continue to be a useful product, converting oil-fired public utility plants to coal use does not appear to be a viable energy alternative. The Carter Administration's plans to subsidize public utility conversion back to coal would thus seem to have been a mistake. It would appear preferable, as has been indicated, to continue to foster research expenditures on coal gasification and liquefaction.

Perhaps what will turn out to be the most interesting aspect of our renewed interest in coal will come in the area of the chemistry of coal itself. Historically, the development of chemicals from hydrocarbons was tied to the introduction of oil and gas to replace coal as a fuel. Hence chemicals and petrochemicals are practically all oil and gas derivatives rather than coal derivatives. Now that we are turning to the liquefication and gasification of coal on a large scale, we will necessarily develop from the chemistry of coal, not only feedstock substitutes for those previously derived from oil and gas but also interesting by-products that may in turn serve as base chemicals for new industries in the future.

While it may be doubtful that U.S. coal reserves will ever again be used as boiler fuel in public utility plants on a large scale, nevertheless, the country is likely to find a growing market for its coal as a fuel in Japan, Denmark, France, Sweden, Italy, Spain, Portugal, West Germany, and most of the non-energy-producing developing countries. At the moment our further exports of coal are limited by the inadequacy of our port facilities. However, the bottleneck of port capacity may be on its way to a solution. If we can solve this problem, U.S. exporters, according to an interim report released by the Federal Interagency Coal Export Task Force, may be in a position to capture 18 percent of the world steam-coal market by 1985, and 38 percent by the year 2000. Several foreign countries (France, Sweden, Denmark, and Japan) have even said that they are willing to use their own funds to develop an East Coast port to ship this needed coal.

Despite the port facility problem, the export figures are impressive. In 1979, the United States exported 14 million tons of steam coal. An MIT study in 1979 estimated that by the year 2000 this figure could reach 65 million tons. In the meantime, all this has caused great congestion in the major export terminals of Hampton Roads and Baltimore.

What is truly surprising is our government's apparent unwillingness to fund even a portion of the cost of a new port to facilitate coal exports. A terminal capable of handling 50 million tons annually would probably cost between $700 million and $1 billion. Since the United States exports approximately 10 percent of the total coal mined, it would seem well worth our while to support this export effort.

The Nuclear Challenge

Can the United States solve its energy problem by developing a nuclear energy base? Had the question been asked thirty years ago, the answer would have been clear: nuclear energy will certainly supply an increasing share of the nation's total energy needs in the United States in the years to come. Today the prognosis is uncertain. Why? Is it due to a fear of technological challenge, or to a lack of confidence in our own capability to control atomic devices?

Regardless of the reason, the results are apparent. Because of a change in national attitude, we have grievously damaged the U.S. nuclear trade position. We not only have increased our dependence on foreign oil imports but also have decreased our ability to export nuclear plants and enriched fuel. In an ironic twist, our failure to maintain our lead in nuclear technology has also diminished substantially our ability to insist on nuclear nonproliferation standards from the rest of the world, thereby very much increasing, rather than decreasing, the possibility of a serious nuclear accident.

As shown in Table 8, it is clear that our use of nuclear plants to furnish energy is a program of the past. In 1973 U.S. utilities ordered 38 reactors; in 1979 there were no new orders and 11 cancellations of earlier ones. The growth of electrical power generated by nuclear reactors has also slowed. In 1975, 55 licensed units were capable of supplying up to 8.4 percent of the country's electricity needs, according to the Nuclear Regulatory Commission (NRC). By March, 1979, when the Three Mile

Table 8. The changed market for nuclear power

Years	Number of operating units	New plant[a] orders	Order cancellations
1972–74	53	100	14
1975–77	67	11	22
1978–80	75	2	35

Source: Computed from data released by Atomic Industrial Forum, *The New York Times,* March 8, 1980.

[a] A plant consists of one to four units.

Island accident took place, 70 reactors were capable of supplying 12.9 percent of our electricity.

Total electric-power generation measured in trillions of kilowatt hours has risen steadily in the last ten years from just over 1.4 trillion in 1970 to over 2.25 trillion in 1979. The nuclear percentage share of this power generation grew sharply from 1.4 percent to over 12 percent by 1978, but is now declining and may be expected to decline even further unless the policies and perceptions of the Carter Administration are reversed dramatically by President Reagan. Eight new reactors were denied licenses in 1979, and some utilities are considering converting nuclear reactors currently under construction to coal. The Nuclear Regulatory Commission has now proposed some 100 separate modifications for existing nuclear plants as a result of the Three Mile Island accident. This will cost some $30 million per plant and these new costs come at a time when utilities, because of a recent trend toward using debt financing rather than equity for their capital requirements, are less able than they have been in the past to absorb such suddenly imposed new costs. At the start of 1981, there were eleven nuclear plants nearing completion, but these plants, once completed, cannot begin operations until the award of a license by the Nuclear Regulatory Commission. While idle, a plant costs $1 million a day, an additional expense that will be passed on to the utility's customers.

What is the situation in other countries? Antinuclear groups in Western Europe and Japan reacted very similarly to the way their counterparts did in the United States, but aside from Austria, where a referendum decided against activating the one nuclear plant in the country, results have been quite different. In a recent referendum Sweden's vote was in favor of adding six new nuclear plants to the six already built or

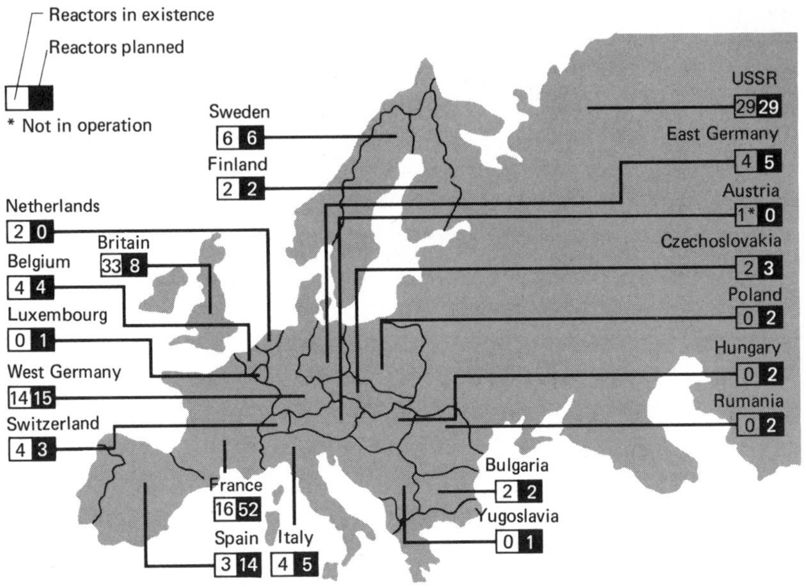

Figure 3. Europe's nuclear progress

Source: The New York Times, March 16, 1980.

currently under construction. In West Germany, the government, taking heart from the Swedish vote, has revived its construction program. Figure 3 shows nuclear building programs in Europe as of the second quarter of 1980.

In Sweden, interestingly enough, support for nuclear construction reflected concerns that employment levels would decline if energy needs were not met from domestic sources; in Germany the government chose to go ahead with construction in part because of overseas demand for German nuclear technology. Unfortunately, neither argument appears to have had much impact in the United States.

In France, meanwhile, following the Three Mile Island furor, the government took a very strong stand in favor of maintaining the nuclear plant construction program, and opposition seems to have evaporated. It will now be interesting to see if government policy will change as a result of the election to the French presidency of François Mitterand. In Spain, where some 14 plants are under construction by the private sector—the only country in Europe not to have government control of nuclear installations—building programs, if anything, have accelerated. In Japan, on the other hand, where one would expect the population to be particularly sensitive about nuclear disasters, there has been a tendency to halt nuclear construction and examine alternatives, particularly coal.

The negative U.S. policy toward nuclear plant construction has had a substantial effect on our foreign trade. Through 1974, the United States had received about 70 percent of all nuclear plant construction awards in the world. Since 1975, U.S. suppliers have seen their proportionate share of such orders shrink dramatically as French and German manufacturers have become increasingly competitive in world markets. This has four unfortunate effects: 1. the failure to get just one export order means the loss of approximately 60,000 man-years of employment; 2. it also means an erosion of technical leadership because foreign engineers are adapting their technical knowledge through on-the-job learning while U.S. engineers are not getting sufficient practical experience in nuclear construction and technology; 3. the U.S. balance of trade is seriously affected. (Two nuclear plants financed by the U.S. Export-Import Bank in fiscal 1980 will result in more than $1 billion in exports. From inception, through March 31, 1980, the Export-Import Bank has financed $8.4 billion in export value of nuclear plants, of which $6.7 billion represents equipment and $1.7 billion represents fuel); and 4. with every new plant built abroad without the assistance of the United States, the United States loses that much more of its practical ability to influence nonproliferation policies in other countries.

Table 9 shows the potential market for nuclear plants, with the market each creates for nuclear fuel in various countries: 106 to 172 plants for Europe, and 64 to 76 plants in other parts of the world. In terms of plants, the increased competition is coming from West Germany, France, the USSR, Sweden, Japan, Canada, and Italy; in terms of fuel it is coming largely from France and the USSR.

Why have U.S. orders declined in the past few years? In part this decline is due to delays in U.S. export licensing brought about by the government's ambiguous nonproliferation policy, the uncertainty of the U.S. enrichment services, increased interest by other nations in competing in this market and their increased ability to do so, and the belief by purchasing nations that the United States may condition continued supplies of parts or fuel to future political behavior. At the time of the inauguration of President Reagan, this last was perceived abroad as a quite serious threat; the Carter Administration had already held other exports hostage to foreign compliance with certain U.S. human rights standards. Probably the greatest source of this dissatisfaction with the United States as a nu-

Table 9. The nuclear export market

Country	Imported energy dependence (%Fossil fuels imported)[a]	New nuclear orders for operation by 1995 (Megawatts)	
		Low	High
European:			
Belgium[b]	88	2,600	6,500
Denmark	99	0	5,200
Finland	80	1,300	3,000
France[b]	84	30,800	41,800
Germany[b]	56	20,300	32,800
Greece	62	2,200	2,200
Ireland	85	1,000	1,000
Italy[b]	87	26,600	46,600
Netherlands	(Net exporter)	0	3,000
Portugal	96	3,600	3,600
Spain[b]	83	13,900	18,900
Sweden	97	0	900
Turkey	43	600	600
United Kingdom	36	6,300	6,300
Total European		109,200	172,400
Non-European:			
Argentina	15	1,900	3,500
Brazil	43	21,900	24,900
Egypt	0	600	600
India	10	1,500	4,500
Israel	100	900	900
Mexico	0	10,500	10,500
South Korea	54	21,100	23,200
Taiwan	70	5,400	7,800
Thailand	63	600	600
Total Non-European:		64,400	76,500

Source: The International Nuclear Fuel Cycle Evaluation Survey, 1978.

[a] 1976 Data—International Atomic Energy Authority

[b] Countries with little or no export potential for the United States.

clear plant and fuel supplier, however, comes from the Nuclear Non-Proliferation Act (NNPA) of 1978. This act, the latest U.S. attempt to control the spread of nuclear technology throughout the world by controlling supplies, calls for an embargo of U.S. enrichment services to any foreign government using U.S.-supplied fuel that does not, after a two-year discussion period, accept U.S. authority over the future reprocessing of fuel. The policy has been counterproductive.[32] As a consequence of its implementation, the Soviet Union now supplies one-third of Europe's needs of enriched uranium. Other countries are also preparing to enter the enrichment business. Needless to say, the United States exerts no influence whatsoever on how this fuel will be reprocessed.

Another result of the U.S. nuclear policy has been that the Europeans, including France, West Germany, the Netherlands, Italy, and Belgium, have now formed a jointly owned concern to promote the rapid development and sale of nuclear reactors abroad. The Commission of the European Communities has officially declared its support.

The U.S. nuclear policy is particularly shortsighted when one considers that both Japan and Europe are increasingly at the mercy of oil price increases from the OPEC countries. The recent action by Algeria in refusing to ship any more liquefied natural gas to Europe despite a contract running to 1990 indicates the extent to which energy-dependent countries are vulnerable and how pressing is their need to find reliable substitutes for imported fuels. As one author has noted:

> If the United States ignores the energy security needs of others, or worse, heightens their feelings of vulnerability, the historical record shows that these countries will take steps to ensure themselves against external disruptions. Such a reaction may produce, and probably is already producing, the very evolution [that] U.S. policy aims to prevent.[33]

There are two very obvious and important difficulties with using nuclear plants as a source of energy to create electricity. How do you protect the plant against an accident that could cause death or destruction? How do you dispose of radioactive waste materials that may remain dangerous for thousands of years? The dangers in either case are so great and our knowledge of the substances dealt with so limited that almost any risk seems too much.

Are there any solutions to the problem? When the Three Mile Island accident occurred, France's President Giscard d'Estaing immediately addressed the nation on television. He said there were some proper questions that had to be answered. Was it necessary to rely on nuclear plants for energy, and was the system of controls established in France more reliable than that which had been shown to be deficient in the United States? As to the first, he stated that by 1985 about 50 percent of France's electrical energy would be produced in nuclear plants because the nation could not afford to be at the mercy of OPEC, and that no alternative was available. "If you demonstrate, you will be arrested," he said, "because the nation depends upon nuclear plants for its very survival." As to the second, he said that in France, unlike in the United States, nuclear plants were built by the state and operated by the state, and furthermore, that the safety inspectors were recruited directly from the finest technical schools and had all graduated near the top of their class. In the United States, he claimed, the jobs are often treated as political favors, dispensed by those in charge of federal or state regulatory agencies. French plants, Giscard stated, could therefore be considered safe.

The Kemeny report (Dr. John George Kemeny, president of Dartmouth College, was appointed by President Carter in 1979 to head a panel of experts to investigate the Three Mile Island nuclear incident and make recommendations) indeed indicated that President Giscard had raised two very delicate issues. Ownership and operation of nuclear plants by private utilities first raises the question whether all plants will be equally carefully managed. An inherently dangerous facility will be run under properly administered safeguards by a private firm only when that firm's management insists on the application of the best safeguards. In the United States the military has for years managed inherently dangerous nuclear installations: the Air Force in the case of missiles, and the Navy in the case of nuclear-powered warships or missile-carrying submarines. A tradition of care and competence has been established within those services in the same manner as in the EDF in France.

Would it be sensible for nuclear fuel plants in the United States to be constructed by the military and operated either by the Air Force or by the Navy with production sold to local public utilities? The public has come to rely on the military to operate nuclear facilities safely. It would probably be ready to accept the assurance that the military would follow proper safeguards and would always give the very top priority to reducing the possibility of human error.

In Argentina the entire nuclear program is under the direct command of its top naval officer; operation is by naval personnel. Should we consider adopting this formula in the United States? After all, the United States has the original "nuclear admiral" in Hyman Rickover, and his training system is known to be exacting and rigorous. If this were done, Giscard's other question—of expensive safety procedures as implemented by employees of profit-making utilities and monitored by political appointees—would be answered. The Nuclear Regulatory Commission (NRC) would continue, of course, to assure civilian supervisory control over the management of nuclear plants. Nevertheless, regardless of the accepted competence of the military on nuclear matters, and the assured maintenance of close civilian supervision, a serious question remains. Would the public be ready to accept operation of nuclear public utility plants by the military and under what conditions? *

The question of waste, while quite serious, is not as acute a problem as it is often depicted to be. For years now, a nuclear waste inventory, created by various defense programs, has been successfully managed. In terms of volume, annual spent-fuel discharge from a large reactor could involve about 45 cubic feet of waste held in a "form" of borosilicate glass. The "form" is then emplaced into what is considered by the Atomic Energy Commission to be a nonleachable, inert, and radiation-resistant solidified geologic formation such as a salt-dome deposit.

Under the Reagan Administration, it is expected that the role of nuclear energy in the production of electricity in the United States will be examined much more carefully than it has been in the past few years. There has to be a place for nuclear energy in the United States if it is ever to become totally independent of oil imports. We cannot forget that one 7-pound pellet of enriched uranium has the same energy power as 3 barrels of oil or one ton of coal.

Perhaps the most serious problem ahead in consideration of the use of nuclear plants for energy is the question of the breeder reactor. France and the USSR now have perhaps as much as a ten-year lead over the United States in this advanced reactor technology.

In France, the revolutionary Super-Phoenix fast-breeder reactor is expected to go into service at the end of 1983. Fueled by 5,000 tons of plutonium, it cost $2.5 billion to build. But it will produce more plutonium as a by-product than it will consume in creating energy. The project involves the electricity industries of France, Italy, and West Germany, which own 51 percent, 33 percent, and 16 percent, respectively, of the plant. The French now plan to build one breeder reactor every three years until the end of the century. The USSR already has a fast-breeder reactor in the Urals, and is planning a number of additional plants, despite its wealth in oil and gas.

President Reagan has now declared his support for the Clinch River breeder reactor project in Tennessee, which was halted by the Carter Administration. This is an important step forward toward the realization that if the United States is not ahead of other countries in this particular

* A thesis of this book has been that government should not participate in business operations. The justification here must be the unavoidable inherent danger to the community, which makes government involvement mandatory.

technology, it risks its safety and that of its allies in an increasingly dangerous world.

Improved Electricity Generation

It is conceded by all that in the years to come the United States will have to produce electricity in increasing amounts from coal or nuclear energy instead of from oil. But what of energy savings within the system of electrical generation? There is much that can be done here also.[34] When energy was cheap, motor manufacturers created no sales problems for themselves when they gradually reduced the efficiency of windings—the heart of the motor—to save on the cost of copper. Today, given the price of energy, educated buyers—public or private—should start demanding more efficient motors. Similarly, we need to capitalize on advances in motor drives, particularly for motors with industrial applications. Electronic versions will be arriving on the market; they can be expected to cut power consumption by half. There are many savings possible in the generation of electrical power, savings that will surface as soon as cost of purchase versus cost of operation ratios are better understood. Human ingenuity will respond to the ensuing demand.

The idea of "co-generation,"* about which so much has been written,[35] could enable us to save as much as 2 million to 3 million barrels of oil per day, or replace some 50 large reactors.[36] In West Germany, co-generation supplies more than 20 percent of that nation's electricity needs; in the United States it is only 4 percent. Why have we not done more? Because the price of energy continues to be subsidized, and 3,000 conflicting and obsolete building codes remain in force in the absence of the "price crises" that would motivate us to revise them. A showcase $20 million pilot project is now under construction at the Hoffman-LaRoche Plant in Belvedere, New Jersey, financed in part by the U.S. government (to the extent of $7 million). Excess power will be sold to the local public utility. Results should encourage similar plants elsewhere.

Other Sources of New Technologies

The Carter Administration, influenced by the position of Amory Lovins[37] that we should turn to conservation and to what he calls the "soft" technologies of solar, wood, biomass, wind, and tide for a long-term solution

* "Co-generation" generally refers to the combined production of electricity and steam at industrial sites, with electricity as a by-product of steam generation, mainly for heating purposes.

to our energy problems, managed to complicate an already difficult problem in two ways. While the Carter Administration properly sought to convince Congress and the public that the development of new domestic energy sources was of the highest priority, it nevertheless did little to motivate the public to conserve energy, through price increases or tax allowances, for example. It taxed the production of domestic oil to fund searches for new energy sources using technologies in which businessmen who were familiar with energy problems had little confidence. Because of the influence of environmental thinking at the White House, the programs of the Department of Energy tended to focus on solar and biomass, energy sources that can produce no more than marginal benefits in the immediate future, rather than on finding new sources and new exploration methods for the conventional fuels. We now examine briefly the possibilities of oil shale, geopressured methane, solar, and biomass as new sources of energy.

Most of these technologies, including solar energy and biomass, appear—at least at the present time—to have only limited application. Solar energy does lend itself to limited use in some home heating situations, and biomass, as an adjunct material to the creation of electrical energy. Geopressured methane may, in the course of time, prove useful if we can develop the technology to extract the gas from very deep geopressured areas off the Texas and Louisiana Gulf Coast, and solve the special accompanying problems of corrosion and salt-water disposal. Estimates of this gas in-place range up to 30,000 trillion cubic feet, but estimates of what is recoverable are more in the range of 2,000 trillion cubic feet maximum, already a very substantial amount.

Of these additional sources of energy, it seems clear that oil shale offers the most interesting prospect. Here, the figures themselves are startling. There are said to be an estimated 28 billion barrels of oil locked up in shale deposits in at least thirteen states. In a 17,000 square-mile area at the intersection of Colorado, Utah, and Wyoming lies the world's largest known deposit of shale with 20 to 25 gallons of oil per ton of rock. These deposits are said to contain some 600 billion barrels of oil, of which it is estimated that 200 billion can be extracted. When we consider that the United States uses only 7 billion barrels of oil per year and has proven reserves of only 28 billion barrels of crude oil, it is obvious that we should make every effort to develop the technology and to encourage the production of these additional reserves. Unfortunately, quite the opposite has happened until very recently.

Shale oil is not a crude oil as we know it but a solid waxy material called "kerogen." In order to extract it, the rock must first be broken into small pieces and then heated to some 900°F. Unfortunately, after extraction, the remaining material is four times the dimensions of the original rock mass, creating a problem about what to do with the residue. This problem is solved if the oil can be extracted from deposits below the surface through an *in situ* process.

Several different processes of this kind have been effectively developed by Tosco, Occidental Petroleum, Union Oil Co., and Superior Oil. These companies have also developed surface retorts* to produce oil from shale. Some, like Occidental, have spent almost $100 million in the last few years to prove out their processes. All are now ready to pass to commercial development if they can obtain the necessary permits from the federal, state, and municipal authorities claiming jurisdiction.

In the last months of the Carter Administration, senior White House officials spoke of a new city in western Colorado that would be larger than Houston in 5 to 10 years, once oil shale was fully developed. No one knows what the cost will be when the *in situ* extraction process is developed on a commercial scale, but as the price of OPEC oil continues to rise there will come a time when oil extracted from shale will be competitive with imported oil. We may even have passed that point already. Union Oil speaks of $15 per barrel crude shale oil at the production site and $24 after transportation and upgrading into refinery feedstock.

From an economic standpoint, we thus appear able, through shale oil, to place a ceiling on the ultimate price of OPEC oil—at least as far as U.S. purchases are concerned. The engineering and environmental problems remain. To produce a million barrels of oil per day using surface retorts, the industry would have to mine almost 2 million tons of rock per day. Water is needed in the process but total needs for an industry of this size would be less than 300,000 acre-feet of water per year. *In situ* mining would present no water problems whatever. There are, therefore, no reasons other than self-imposed limitations why the extraction of oil shale on a gradually increased basis cannot play a significant role in meeting our oil needs in the future, particularly if, at the same time, we develop fully our natural gas reserves, convert coal into gas, adopt more prudent energy-use habits, increase the efficiency of our electrical generation and distribution systems, and utilize solar and biomass energy where these sources are capable of being used efficiently.

* These are huge ovens in which the shale is heated to extract the oil.

If this is so, why have many hundreds of millions of dollars, if not billions, been spent in pursuing will-o'-the-wisp dreams that promise to make solar, wood, tides, or wind a primary energy source? Why was such an effort made to encourage the rapid development of gasohol plants, each capable of producing 50 million gallons of alcohol per year from corn or barley, when the world is increasingly short of food? People may indeed wonder in future years at the wealth of the U.S. government and at its citizens' willingness to be taxed without question for the purpose of pursuing new energy-producing schemes that appear much less capable of being brought to fruition than older plans to fully utilize the wealth the country has in oil, gas, and coal.

Conclusions

While hardly justifying the vast amounts of money that have been spent, or excusing the creation of additional burdensome regulatory systems, the Department of Energy will have served some purpose if it turns out to have created incentives for the development of new technologies for new industries and stimulated creative minds to think in new directions.

It might be possible to rationalize the idea of an incentive-destroying tax on oil production (such as the misnamed "Windfall Profits Tax") if the money were truly to be set aside to stimulate the development of new technologies. However, if the tax is used only to create revenue for a perpetually out-of-balance federal budget, then the tax will be no more than another effort on the part of government to alleviate its chronic cash flow problem by punitive taxation of a sector of the economy that is successful but out of favor with the general public.

The Reagan Administration is capable of bringing a fresh approach to our energy problem. It has an opportunity to point out to the Congress that the principal purpose of this tax was supposed to be to stimulate, through transfer payments for research and development, the creation of additional new sources of domestic energy. It would indeed be discouraging if the tax were now retained but the development programs of the Department of Energy and the Synthetic Fuels Corporation dropped. As we have said so many times, the role of government is to direct the nation's energies in areas clearly perceived to be consonant with national goals. Government is most effective in a democratic society when it motivates the private sector through appropriate incentives, encourages innovation and problem solving, but avoids engaging directly in business operations. It should not be government's responsibility to drill for oil, or mine coal, or even carry on research directly.*

Problem solving in our current energy crisis will require the finest innovative and creative talents we possess as a nation. We need to encourage in every way possible both individuals and businesses capable of making a contribution. In particular, the government needs to 1. avoid diverting funds from the production of energy; 2. encourage oil and gas production and coal conversion technology through research grants and tax advantages; 3. adopt import duties on imported oil to encourage domestic alternatives; and 4. finance pilot plants, where appropriate, in such new technologies as coal conversion, the development of more fuel-efficient automobiles, or new transportation methods. Above all, government needs to modify ruthlessly its own permit procedures and land-use powers. The country as a whole must address the special problems created when, as has happened, the judicial system is used to block interminably the implementation of plans approved by appropriate agencies and supported by a majority of the public at large. Finally, we need to develop a better balance between energy needs for a growing economy and the protection of our environment.

Surely, we have the technological capabilities to restore our trade balance by substituting domestic sources of energy for imported oil. Given our wealth in natural resources—particularly coal, oil, and natural gas—our only problem appears to be our reluctance to date to act effectively and promptly.

* Obviously there have to be exceptions where safety or national security are involved—air-traffic controllers, for example, or possibly operation of nuclear plants or military installations of any kind.

4

Breakdown of the World Monetary System

> In the past five hundred years there have been only two periods of about fifty years each (the Elizabethan and Victorian Ages) when the use of money for the conduct of international trade can be said to have 'worked.'
>
> JOHN MAYNARD KEYNES

> They wonder much to hear that gold, which in itself is so useless a thing, should be everywhere so much esteemed, that even men for whom it was made, and by whom it has its value, should yet be thought of less value than *it* is.
>
> SIR THOMAS MORE

John Maynard Keynes has dominated economic theory since 1923, when his first great work on the nature of money appeared. His was the genius that guided the establishment of the monetary system enacted at Bretton Woods in 1944. As we shall see, had his recommendations been more closely followed, the Bretton Woods system might still be functioning today.

For all his innovative genius, however, Keynes was also a product of his age. He had seen at first hand what had happened in Britain during the terrible depression years after 1931 and was resolved to make sure that this would not happen again. In times of recession, he urged, governments ought to go into deficit to "prime the pump" until the economy could generate its own momentum. He conceded, however, that despite the implementation of his theories to combat the Great Depression, unemployment in Britain seemed to be greater than ever by the end of the decade, when World War II came along to cure it. But even within the dynamics of his own theory, Keynes saw the necessity of creating budgetary surpluses in good times, so as to be prepared to increase government spending when the economy faltered.

Keynes's intellectual heirs, who have played so great a role both in the formulation of domestic economic policies and in the establishment of international monetary relationships since the adoption of the Bretton Woods system, developed their ideas on economic theory during this very period of worldwide unemployment and severe depression. Unfortunately, having caught hold of the revolutionary idea that economic depression was best treated by massive government expenditures, they failed to understand the importance Keynes had given to restoring surpluses during periods of economic expansion. Keynes's wise words of caution were ignored and soon his narrowly focused theories on combatting depressions with deficit spending were used to support the argument that governments could assure permanent prosperity by ever-growing government expenditures, regardless of deficits. Since there are always desirable social programs to be funded, too many American presidents have been disposed to follow such advice. The result, in the United States at least, has been the greatest government debt in history, and continual inflationary spurts in cycles ever more frequent and steeper. Because pumping unearned money into the economy without surcease must necessarily reduce the money's value, we have seen the value of gold go from \$35 an ounce to more than \$700, a twenty-fold increase. We have seen the value of crude oil go from \$2.35 a barrel on the international market in 1973 to well over \$30 a barrel in 1980, a twenty-fold increase. We have seen the price of wheat in export markets go from 45 cents a bushel to \$4.50 a bushel, a ten-fold increase.

Although there is hope now that this generation of economists is about to be replaced in government by a new generation of more cautious men who will be more careful to advise the governments they counsel that budget deficits, even through normal times, can only result in the continuous creation of additional supplies of money, and hence continued inflation, here we are principally concerned with what the neo-Keynesian influence on successive governments in the United States has done to the value of the dollar outside the United States and to international monetary relationships, which must be kept stable if international trade is to grow. It is indeed an ironic twist of history that the very disciples of the great Keynes were the ones who would bring to an end the international monetary system that he was so instrumental in creating in 1944.

Without going back five hundred years, as Keynes suggested, let us analyze the relatively recent evolution in the use of money in international trade—from the gold standard, to the gold-exchange currency, to the "cosmetic" gold-exchange standard of President Johnson, and then to the unadorned dollar standard created when President Nixon announced in August, 1971 that the United States would no longer honor requests for gold to satisfy its international obligations. We will examine world monetary "progress" from the "fixed" exchange-rate standard to the "flexible" or "floating" exchange-rate standard of today and will consider the possibility of going back at some future date to a fixed exchange-rate standard.

There is a basic confrontation here: businessmen have trouble living in a world of exchange-rate unpredictability while politicians, most of whom have never had any experience or training in international business, can pursue domestic economic goals free from international accountability under the floating exchange-rate system. Since theirs is not the pragmatic world of day-to-day business decisions, which need to be made on the basis of some exchange-rate stability, policymakers in the United States have tended to rely for advice on these matters upon economists from academic institutions rather than men with business experience.

We will also see how, waiting in the wings, may be the ideas of two men who are both policymakers by training and experience, heads of state, with deep experience in international finance. Given both time and the smile of fortune, the calling of these two men may be to lead the world full cycle back to an environment in which international trade once again takes place in a climate of monetary certainty. Finally, we shall try to do all this without losing the reader along the way in the thickets of economic jargon.

It often seems that economists are not held accountable for their recommendations. When a remedy does not work it is never because it was the wrong remedy, but instead because it was applied too early or too late or with insufficient vigor. No matter what comes, the philosophy is not subject to refutation simply on the basis of its record of success or failure.

The power of the economist lies in the mystery of his calling, a mystery that survives because of lay ignorance of the general principles at work. In this chapter we will try to dissipate this aura of the arcane so that a rather simple succession of events can be understood and realistic conclusions drawn from them.

Any international monetary system must perform three functions: 1. determine exchange rates, 2. adjust disturbances in the balance of payments, and 3. provide international liquidity.[1] In this century the world has experienced a gold standard, two gold-exchange standards, and periods of "benignly neglected," "managed," and downright "dirty" floating exchange rates. None of these systems (some really ought not to be called systems but improvisations) can be said to have "worked," if by that we mean that they provided an adequate adjustment mechanism for deficit and surplus countries, or generated sufficient international liquidity without creating currency crises or transmitting inflation worldwide. Yet, even more important, each of these systems failed in the sense that not one of them freed the international economy from the effects of domestic monetary mismanagement.

As countries become more economically interdependent in the future, domestic monetary responsibility will become even more important. It is the thesis of this chapter that no international monetary system will long survive if the country with the key currency is allowed to pursue its own domestic aims without regard to the economic effect on other countries. Thus it is no wonder that the Bretton Woods system collapsed in 1971 and vanished in 1973 after the United States—which had created the system—stopped playing by the rules in the late 1960s and early 1970s. But also important to the collapse of the Bretton Woods system, and to the abandonment of the gold exchange standard in early 1973, is what we shall call the key, or reserve-currency, dilemma that was characteristic of this gold exchange standard.

The gold standard was, in one form or another, the essential monetary system for trade among the Western European countries since the start of the Lombard banks in Italy during the Renaissance. It was based on the simple premise that sellers of goods wished to be paid in specie that they could then use to purchase other goods. The reason for using gold coins issued by a government or a governmental banking institution was equally simple: Everyone could be sure that the coin actually contained a certain, warranted amount and quality of gold.*

While the gold standard is thus a simple, workable system, it contains elements that are anathema to today's government economists. For instance, in dealing with each other under a gold standard, governments must periodically settle their accounts either in goods or in gold. If a nation were to engage in broad domestic social programs that resulted in increased prices, its goods would no longer be competitive and the country would be obliged to pay much of its debt in gold until the gold has

* It is an interesting commentary on the credibility of modern institutions that the current British government is manufacturing gold coins for sale with the year "1913" engraved on them, while the French government today manufactures and sells gold coins embossed with the head of Louis Napoleon.

run out. In order to avoid national bankruptcy, a country in such a situation must increase its exports by cutting prices—which means cutting wages. This has been called the price-specie flow mechanism. As wages and prices are cut, exports increase, and the country's balance of trade is reestablished.

The easiest way to explain how the mechanism operates is in terms of a two-country relationship. Let us assume that country A has a deficit in its balance of payments with country B. Country B necessarily has a surplus. Since the countries are on a gold standard, the deficit country must send gold or specie to the surplus country. Because of the quantity theory of money, the money shortage in the deficit country causes what we today call deflation; the surplus country, with a new inflow of money, goes into an inflationary situation. The deficit country's exports thus become cheaper, and imports from the surplus country become more expensive because of the inflation there. As a result, an adjustment takes place. The deficit country tends to export more and import less; the surplus country does the reverse. The result is a sort of self-adjusting equilibrium in the balance of payments between country A and country B.

All this appeared simple in the nineteenth century, but the adjustments were often painful because they resulted in unemployment and a decline in the standard of living in the deficit country.*

In the twentieth century two new factors have made it difficult for our government to accept the discipline of a gold standard. First, the demand for imports and exports is relatively inelastic, it does not vary greatly from year to year; second, strong resistance to any downward movement of wages and prices (caused in great part by the growth in political strength of labor unions) makes the price-specie flow mechanism ineffective.

The gold-exchange standard adopted at the Genoa Conference of 1922, which was attended by the principal trading powers led by Great Britain, was described as only a step towards full restoration of the pre-World War I gold standard. The conference participants agreed on the following resolutions:

> *Resolution 5:* Gold is the only common standard which all European countries could at present agree to adopt.
>
> *Resolution 6:* It is in the general interest that European Governments

* American readers may recall from their study of history William Jennings Bryan's cry of anguish in the presidential campaign of 1896 about the population's crucixion on a "Cross of Gold."

> should declare now that the establishment of a gold standard is their ultimate object, and should agree on the program by way of which they intend to achieve it.[2]

The pre-World War I gold standard was to be reestablished by "economizing the use of gold by maintaining reserves in the form of foreign balances, such, for example, as the gold standard or an international clearing system."[3]

The rationale behind the adoption of the gold-exchange standard in 1922 was therefore similar to the rationale that led to the adoption of an essentially similar standard at Bretton Woods in 1944. In 1922, shortly after World War I, there was a liquidity problem that could not be solved by an immediate return to the gold standard. After four years of war, the victorious countries, headed by Britain, France, and Italy, desperately needed liquidity to rebuild cities, plants, and housing, to say nothing of providing the consumer goods that people had done without during the war. The gold stock was insufficient and was physically in the United States, which had finished the war with its manufacturing plant intact and most of the world's liquid assets. Sterling was thus substituted for gold until a normal redistribution of the metal through trade could take place. The United States, in the interest of re-establishing international monetary stability, supported the program.

At Bretton Woods, two decades later, the victorious but bankrupt European Allies turned to the U.S. dollar as the key currency, particularly since the British were confident that the United States would again help generously in the rebuilding of Europe. In each of the postwar periods, therefore, *liquidity* was considered more important than *stability*. Unfortunately, even though our policymakers started with a program of sound aims, they failed over time to adapt it to changed circumstances. As the need for further liquidity ceased, they nonetheless continued to add to the supply of dollars, thereby creating the massive inflation that continues unabated to the present day.

Why was there such a strong desire to return to the gold standard in 1922? The answer lies in part in the contribution that the gold standard had made to the expansion of world trade and investment.

During the late nineteenth century, England was the financial center of the world, with the Bank of England acting as the world's central bank. Most world trade—the percentage has been estimated at more than 90 percent—was financed in London.[4] Thus, before World War I the lynchpin of the monetary system was the confidence that trading nations had in the integrity of the Bank of England, which served as guarantor of an international trading system that relied ultimately on British banks and insurance companies, and hence on sterling for financing. Since the sterling bank notes were fully convertible into gold, there was no flaw in the system.[5]

The nineteenth-century gold standard had also overcome two of the major difficulties characteristic of such a standard: It had solved the problem of providing for a rate of growth of the supply of gold approximately equal or closely related to the growth of demand for international reserves at stable prices; and it had dealt with the problem of maintaining confidence in the ultimate convertibility of the gold substitute (sterling notes) into gold.[6]

The new monetary gold-exchange standard established at Genoa in 1922 did not fare nearly as well because the position of Britain in the twentieth century was no longer what it had been in the nineteenth. The main reason for the failure of this new system (as well as the inherent flaw in any gold-exchange standard) was the lack of confidence nations had in the convertibility of the key currency into proportionally smaller supplies of gold. In the gold-exchange standard of 1922, sterling was to be the key international currency, and it was to be pegged to and convertible into gold.

It is not that gold supplies shrink or that gold loses its value; it is simply that the country with the key currency ultimately adds to the money supply faster than the normal increase in the supply of gold. Thus, as international trade increased in the 1920s, bringing an increased demand for sterling and gold, the weakness of the gold-exchange standard was manifested in the extremely small supply of gold available relative to Britain's ever-growing sterling drafts. With the international financial crisis of 1931, Britain abandoned its peg to gold, terminating the gold-exchange standard.

The gold-exchange standard based on sterling failed for reasons not much different from those that would subsequently cause the failure of the standard based on the dollar established at Bretton Woods in 1944. The earlier system failed because the British increased their currency supply until it could no longer be converted into gold; for the same reason, President Nixon was forced to admit in 1971 that the dollar had become too watered down in value to be convertible into gold.

In all fairness, the breakdown of the gold-exchange standard in 1931 was noted by the founders of the Bretton Woods system. Consequently, the two most significant shortcomings of the gold-exchange standard would be addressed in the new Bretton Woods agreement. First, the national full-employment policies of the major allies—which had been thwarted by what was believed to be an inherent deflationary bias of the gold standard—would be protected by leaving countries free to devalue when their currency was in "fundamental disequilibrium." Second, the inadequacy of stable sources of international liquidity in the gold-exchange standard would be remedied by providing international credit substitutes for gold. The new system was thus designed to be better than the old, because it would provide both *flexibility* and *additional liquidity* when required.

The truly sad aspect of Bretton Woods was that Keynes, representing Britain, suggested the creation of an international bank of issue, but the Americans, with the same insularity that the British had demonstrated in 1922, insisted that the dollar be designated as the key currency. Unfortunately, the world missed an extraordinary opportunity to establish a monetary system based neither on a key currency nor entirely on gold.

The Bretton Woods System

Central to the formation of the Bretton Woods system was the belief that exchange rates should be "fixed and adjustable." This would allow each government the freedom to pursue domestic priorities and macroeconomic policies without the significant balance-of-payments constraints that were so typical of the gold standard.

Since the Bretton Woods conferees were not prepared to accept deflation—and the consequent large-scale unemployment and/or a decline in wage rates—as a way of eliminating a balance-of-payments deficit, they needed a source of international liquidity in addition to the limited amount of gold reserves that any nation could tap. They also wanted to establish fixed relationships for the various currencies, both in relation to the dollar and to gold, with provisions for adjustments under proper supervision. The International Monetary Fund (IMF) was thus established to provide for the adjustment, liquidity, and exchange rates necessary to a properly functioning international monetary system.

The international monetary concept reflected in the IMF was one of the truly creative economic ideas of recent times because it recognized the difficulty inherent in a fixed exchange-rate system. Furthermore, it recognized the difficulty of imposing periodic austerity on countries—especially the democracies—for the purpose of balancing payments. It presumed that countries might, for political or social reasons, take certain steps from time to time that would cause a disequilibrium in their balance-of-payments position. The purpose of the IMF was to step in, if called upon by the country in difficulty, and advance sufficient funds to tide that country over until it could reestablish its balance-of-payments equilibrium. The IMF directors have, to their credit, treated rich and poor in the same manner whenever either has experienced balance-of-payments difficulties.* The IMF rules have therefore been imposed as strictly against Great Britain and Italy as they were against Peru, Turkey, Zaire, and Jamaica. Only the United States has been able to ignore the IMF because it has held the key currency.

The avowed purpose of the IMF is "to promote international monetary cooperation through a permanent institution which provides the machinery for consultation and collaboration on international monetary problems."[7] To do this, the Fund uses a detailed code of international monetary conduct based on four fundamental principles.[8]

First, all member countries must establish par values for their currencies, expressed in terms of gold or U.S. dollars of specified gold content, and they may not change these values without consulting the IMF.

Second, exchange controls on current international payments are prohibited.

Third, national gold and currency reserves are to be increased so that countries are not forced to meet short-run balance-of-payments deficits by suffering domestic deflation and unemployment. This increase in liquidity is to be in the form of a prescribed "drawing right" on a member country's "quota," or the amount of its subscription to the fund. At the outset the initial total of quotas in the fund was approximately $8.8 billion, one-third the size that Keynes recommended as adequate to finance postwar international economic expansion. Here again Keynes's vision proved correct over the timid consensus of lesser men. Had the IMF at the outset been given a larger quota against which drawing rights could be applied, it might not have been necessary to create dollar liquidity in later years, and the Eurodollar market might not have taken on the role it has in meeting countries' balance-of-payments needs.

Fourth, the IMF adopted the principle that a balance-of-payments disequilibrium is necessarily two-sided, and therefore adjustment obligations should be the joint responsibility of both the surplus and deficit countries involved. Unfortunately, as a practical matter, the IMF was given no real means to enforce this principle against a surplus country.

* New problems facing the IMF in the future are discussed in more detail in Chapter 6.

The U.S. commitment to Bretton Woods has been summarized as follows: "At Brettton Woods, the United States alone chose to maintain the international value of the dollar by making it interconvertible with gold through transactions with official monetary authorities; other countries maintained the value of their currencies by using the dollar as the intervention currency, entering the foreign exchange markets to buy or sell dollars as needed to maintain their currencies with 1% on either side of the par value."[9]

Because the United States owned practically all the liquid capital wealth of the world after World War II, it seemed natural to use the dollar as the key currency and to make dollar deposits at the IMF the equivalent of gold. Like a small boy who has all the marbles but wishes to have his friends join in the game, the United States was prepared to lend its currency to others in order to let them participate in the game of international trade. If a nation did not have gold to pay for U.S. goods, the United States would advance it the dollars, on the understanding that in due course that nation would earn enough dollars through its exports to repay the loan.

The Operation of the Bretton Woods System

So needy was the rest of the world for products, plants, and machinery, which only the United States was in a position to supply, that not even the $100 billion advanced by the United States in Marshall Plan funds could keep the other players in the game.

In the years immediately after World War II, the United States amassed some $61.5 billion in balance-of-payments surpluses, thus encouraging devaluations by the major industrial nations. In 1949 Britain devalued by 30.5 percent, as did Sweden. Holland devalued by 30.1 percent, Belgium by 12.3 percent, and Canada by 9.1 percent. West Germany reconstituted its currency by issuing new Deutschemarks (now called West German marks) for Reichsmarks, and then additionally devalued 20.7 percent against the dollar. From the end of World War II through 1949, the total depreciation of the Italian lira was 63.9 percent. The prewar Japanese yen had been worth some 23.4 U.S. cents, or a bit more than 4 yen to the dollar. The postwar rate was set at 371 yen to the dollar, a 98.4 percent devaluation. France, even though it was a victorious nation, had devalued by 66 percent from the end of the war through 1949.

In the early 1950s, the United States began accumulating balance-of-payments deficits. These deficits were happily accepted by our trading partners, since a definite overseas dollar shortage was perceived to exist. Perhaps this psychology affected the U.S. policymakers, causing them to view the payments deficits as a friendly and helpful gesture by the industrialized free world so that others could increase their trade.* Indeed, U.S. deficits did provide much of the growth in international liquidity during the postwar years. The problem, however, was that each additional dollar sent abroad through payments deficits constituted an additional, potential claim on the fixed and slowly diminishing U.S. gold stock. With the help of hindsight we can see the dollar slowly putting itself into the classic key-currency dilemma. As the supply of dollars held by foreigners increased far beyond the total U.S. supply of gold at the official $35-a-ounce price it became only a matter of time before the faith in the ultimate convertibility of dollars into gold would be questioned.

The day of reckoning was made inevitable near the end of 1958, when convertibility was restored among the European currencies and exchange controls were lifted. Almost immediately, many European countries found themselves holding what they felt were too many dollars. They started cashing these dollars in for gold, and between 1958 and 1960, U.S. gold reserves were depleted by $5.1 billion.

Another factor leading to problems for the dollar and the U.S. balance of payments was the establishment of the Common Market in 1958, which increased incentives for American multinational corporations to invest in production facilities in the Common Market nations, and led, thereby, to a significant capital outflow from the United States. The Kennedy Administration later developed the Interest Equalization Tax (IET) in an attempt to curb U.S. direct investment abroad and thus reverse the dollar outflow brought about by payments deficits.

Criticism of the U.S. balance-of-payments policy first surfaced in the early 1960s. The French, for instance, began criticizing the United States for financing its deficits by issuing more dollars. Indeed, this was the beginning of an increasingly severe period of monetary mismanagement in the United States characterized by continual budgetary deficits. The United States continued to ignore the effect that its money creation was having outside the country, given the dollar's status as the reserve currency of the post-World War II gold-exchange standard.

It may be argued that the United States needed to run deficits for a period of time after World War II in order to ensure sufficient liquidity for the postwar expansion of the industrialized world. The Europeans

* Treasury Secretary Blumenthal would use the same arguments in speeches abroad in 1977.

were understandably glad to have an overvalued dollar because it made their exports to the United States more competitive. And U.S. investments in Europe were welcomed as a way of increasing the dollar reserves that were needed to rebuild the capital equipment for heavy industry and public utilities. But starting around 1958 it was evident that additional U.S. deficits were beginning to jeopardize the international monetary system that the United States had been so instrumental in creating at Bretton Woods.

In October, 1960 the first gold crisis of the Bretton Woods system occurred, with an upsurge in the private demand for gold. This reflected both diminished confidence in the dollar and the possibility of a U.S. devaluation. Quotations for gold went as high as $40 per ounce.

This break in the official $35 price resulted in the creation of a gold pool by the major industrialized nations, with the United States contributing 50 percent. The pool functioned much as domestic price-support programs for grain do and worked reasonably well until the gold crisis of 1968. At the same time that the gold pool was being created, international monetary experts began to discuss what might be done to replace the dollar flows that had been so useful in the past in creating additional liquidity.

It was gradually accepted by the late 1960s that, to meet the need for a new form of international liquidity, dollar outflows should be replaced by the creation of a new credit-reserve asset, or Special Drawing Right (SDR),* that would be issued by the IMF in proportion to members' reserve deposits at the fund. Unfortunately, by the time policymakers made the decision to add to international liquidity, there were already too many dollars in the system.[10]

Thus, there was no longer any need for more liquidity, but there was a need for an asset other than the dollar.

As it was, the inauguration of the SDR system, because it simply added new liquidity without taking away any dollars, further fueled the inflationary fire.† Politically, it was a useful decision; it enabled the "rich"

* The SDR (Special Drawing Right) is an international reserve asset created by the International Monetary Fund (IMF) to supplement existing reserve assets. As of January 1, 1981, a basket of five currencies—the U.S. dollar, the West German mark, the French franc, the Japanese yen, and the British pound sterling—serves as the basis for determining both the valuation and the *interest rate* of the SDR. In accordance with the rules established by the IMF, SDRs can be used in a wide variety of transactions and operations among *holders*.

† Central bankers, now aware of the problem, are talking of a "substitution account" to substitute SDRs for U.S. dollars as official reserves when requested.

countries to add reserves to the "poor" countries so that they would be able to buy more from the rich. But economically, it was a disaster.

Already as far back as the Kennedy Administration, the government had introduced controls to reduce long-term capital outflows from the United States, and thus reverse the balance-of-payments deficit. The administration had levied a special tax on investments and loans abroad, the IET,* and the Joint Economic Committee of Congress had made this interesting observation:

> It is one of the ironies and inconsistencies of modern life that to protect fixed exchange rates—the means—we have compromised freedom of capital movements and, to some extent, trade—the ends—which the fixed exchange rates are intended to serve.[11]

With the Johnson Administration came an escalation of the Vietnam War and the introduction of the Great Society, but with no increase in taxes. During his presidency, Johnson ensured the passage of more social legislation than had any other president in the history of the United States. As a result, by fiscal 1979, the budget of just the Department of Health, Education and Welfare had reached $113 billion, or more than the entire budget of the first year of the Johnson Administration. The aim of this legislation is not questioned here. Nevertheless it must be pointed out that the Johnson Administration took these steps in the middle of a war that was already creating large budget deficits.

The war was unpopular. Tax increases would have made it more so. By not increasing taxes, however, the Johnson Administration added to the nation's budget deficit and hence to the money supply. In turn, these excess dollars flowed out of the country into the Eurocurrency banks and into such stronger currencies as the West German mark and the Swiss franc—in essence exporting inflation from the United States to Europe and throughout the world.

It is interesting to note that about this same time one of our most respected Keynesian economists, Dr. Walter Heller, was addressing a Harvard Commencement audience in the following terms.

> Economics has come of age in the 1960s. Two Presidents have recognized and drawn on modern economics as a source of national strength and Presidential power. Their willingness to use, for the first time, the full range of modern economic tools underlies the unbroken

* The IET was aimed at curbing the large volume of foreign capital issues in the United States that occurred after mid-1962 by placing a tax on the purchase of foreign securities by Americans.

> U.S. expansion since 1961. The economist "arrived" on the New Frontier and is firmly entrenched in the Great Society.[12]

By the time the agreement to create SDRs was finally reached in September, 1967, there had already been a massive transfer of U.S. inflation to the world. One writer, Richard J. Whalen, has stated this point of view in the following terms:

> The dollar crisis grows out of the intellectual bankruptcy of orthodox, neo-Keynesian economic theory, which rationalizes mounting deficits as the sure-fire stimulus to achieve "full employment." Instead, the deficits now yield higher levels of inflation, a rapidly expanding Federal borrowing requirement, and disappointingly slow growth.[13]

Back in 1965 the Interest Equalization Tax had been extended to cover lending by banks and by such nonbank financial corporations as insurance companies. Government officials, in fact, had been so pleased with the effects of this IET extension that they applied it to U.S. business as well. This policy allowed for continued government spending deficits at the expense of foreign lending and direct investment by U.S. multinational corporations. The degree of criticism by business of this governmental action was somewhat muted by the fact that U.S. businesses could now borrow from the Eurodollar market.

What is important to note here is that at approximately the same time three events occurred that added vastly to the creation of liquid assets in the world economy: the Johnson Administration budgetary deficits, which created sharp increases in the money supply; the creation of the new SDRs; and the increase in dollars generated by the Eurocurrency markets.

On March 15, 1968, pressures against the dollar and the French franc and in favor of revaluation of the West German mark caused gold purchases to reach frantic proportions in Europe. The United States lost $2 billion to the gold pool, which attempted in vain to offset the purchases. The gold pool thus proved forever ineffective, and with its disintegration came a two-tier system for gold pricing: a free-market price was to coexist with the then-official price of $35 an ounce, with the central banks agreeing not to buy or sell gold at other than the official rate.

By the late 1960s a U.S. devaluation had become inevitable. The Bretton Woods system was facing crucial challenges to its ability to hold the economies of the industrialized world together through exchange rates. A joint report by the Treasury and the Federal Reserve on foreign-exchange operations, reviewing the period from September, 1968 to March, 1969, indicates the multitude of unstable factors permeating the Bretton Woods system.

> The major development in the exchange markets during the period under review was the surging *wave of speculation* last fall on a simultaneous revaluation of the German mark and devaluation of the French franc and possible other currencies. Between late August and the Bonn Conference in November 1968, the German Federal Bank was swamped by record gross market purchases of more than $4 billion. Over the same period The Bank of France and the Bank of England suffered reserve losses, largely attributable to speculation of over $2 billion. *The flood of money across the exchanges, probably the largest in international financial history, was rooted in national currency problems rather than basic flaws in the international financial system.* The extraordinary competitive strength of German exports, the struggle of France to restabilize the franc after the "events of May," the lagging recovery of sterling after the devaluation of November 1967, and more generally, concern over the erosion by inflation of the value of the dollar—these and other fears had kept the exchange markets in a state of continuous anxiety and vulnerability to any persuasive rumor.[14] (*emphasis mine*)

Emphasis has been added to certain significant lines in the above quote because they affirm the thesis that no international monetary system using relatively fixed-exchange rates could have survived the domestic economic and political irresponsibility that characterized the late 1960s and most of the 1970s.

Further, one might note that whenever U.S. government officials find it advisable to take unpleasant monetary steps made necessary through policy shortcomings, they inevitably blame such action on a need to outwit unidentified speculators, generally foreign. Might not the same paragraph have been written about events exactly ten years later in October, 1978?

What brought the situation to an immediate head in 1968 was the decision by French President de Gaulle to stop the apparent takeover of European business by American companies using the same overvalued dollar that had once been so useful to the rebuilding of industrial Europe. DeGaulle was concerned that the United States under the Johnson Administration was spending—in government-sponsored social programs and particularly on the disastrous war in Vietnam—vast sums of money generated via the printing press rather than taxation. To stop the U.S. government from exporting its inflation through the American banks operating in the London based Eurodollar market, the French were determined to force the United States either to devalue or to pay its foreign creditors with the U.S. gold stock. Toward this end, the French started to demand that their dollars be redeemed in U.S. gold.

When Congress balked at transferring gold, a compromise was reached that took the United States off the gold standard for private debts. In exchange, the European central banks agreed to forego demanding gold unless special circumstances made it necessary. In effect, the United States was buying time to put its financial house in order, time that it was soon to squander.

When President Nixon was elected in 1968, he promised to return to "sound money" and asked Dr. Arthur Burns, the new chairman of the Federal Reserve to tighten credit. During the first few months of 1969, U.S. interest rates increased sharply. Starved for credit, the country's productive capacity slowed as factories began to lay off workers and the country entered a recession. The big U.S. money center banks were forced to repatriate $13 billion from their London branches in order to continue to extend credit to their biggest corporate customers. As a result, the London interbank rate (LIBOR) increased from 6 percent to more than 12 percent. After the president of the New York Stock Exchange visited the White House in the Spring of 1969 and told President Nixon that in the ensuing weeks such key corporations as Penn Central, Lockheed, and Chrysler would go bankrupt for lack of credit facilities, Nixon reversed the tight money policy and the Federal Reserve again made funds available to the banks. A little later President Nixon publicly announced that "I, too, have become a Keynesian."

In the meantime, with the continuing war in Vietnam, the U.S. international financial position continued to aggravate until the President was forced in August, 1971 to take the country completely off the gold standard by refusing to sell gold at the established rate. By that time, for the United States to be in a position to pay its foreign creditors by exchanging its gold for dollars, the official gold price would have had to be very sharply increased over the official price of $35 an ounce. Probably, at $100 per ounce the foreign debt could have been paid. But then the United States, as the French suggested, would have had to keep its expenditures under control in the future or it would have found itself in trouble again, and with no further gold supply to pay off its new debt. It appeared preferable to the U.S. government simply to destroy the monetary system. The world's central banks—loaded as they were with surplus dollar claims against the United States—had either to accept President

Nixon's decision to abandon the gold standard or admit that their dollar reserves had to be sharply devalued.

By this failure to take action, the world's most powerful central banks accepted an arrangement to go on a paper-dollar monetary standard with no way of controlling the creation by the United States of new money. Thus was assured the continuation of inflation worldwide.

As far back as 1969 it had been clear that the life of the Bretton Woods gold-exchange standard was coming to a violent end. It seemed that there was no way for the United States to unilaterally devalue the dollar, as it argued it had to do, because several other leading countries threatened to immediately devalue their currencies by the same amount. During Republican pre-election meetings, an idea of Gottfried Haverler's began to circulate: Adopt a policy of "benign neglect" of the dollar problem in order to force other countries to permit a U.S. unilateral devaluation. All that was needed was to let foreign governments keep accumulating inconvertible dollar balances until a U.S. devaluation would be a necessity. As a result of this policy (or nonpolicy), short-term capital outflows from the United States increased dramatically, and in 1970 the U.S. balance-of-payments deficit reached a record $9.3 billion—of which $5.1 billion was in the form of short-term capital outflows.

Early in 1971 the international financial markets began to sense an impending dollar crisis. Reports on the U.S. foreign-trade balance continued to show bigger and bigger volume deficits as the year progressed. According to Department of Commerce figures, the trade deficit for the second quarter of 1971 was $1 billion, while the overall U.S. balance-of-payments deficit for the first half of the year soared to $11.6 billion on an official settlements basis.

On Friday, August 6, a report by the House Subcommittee on International Banking indicated that the dollar was overvalued and that a general realignment of exchange rates was needed. Over the following week, the flight from the dollar accelerated sharply as $3.7 billion moved through the exchange markets into the central banks. Finally, on the evening of August 15, President Nixon suddenly and without warning announced the end of the Bretton Woods era. The President introduced a 10 percent temporary surcharge on dutiable imports into the United States and announced a suspension of the convertibility of the dollar into gold and other reserve assets. As Nixon explained his action to the nation at the time:

> Prosperity without war requires action on three fronts: we must create more and better jobs; we must stop the rise in the cost of living,

> we must protect the dollar from *the attacks of international money speculators.*
>
> In the past seven years, there has been an average of one international monetary crisis every year. Who gains from these crises? Not the workingman, not the investor, not the real producers of wealth. *The gainers are the international money speculators.* Because they thrive on crisis, they help create them.
>
> In recent weeks, *the speculators* have been waging an all-out war on the American dollar. The strength of a nation's currency is based on the strength of that nation's economy—and the American economy is by far the strongest in the world. Accordingly, I have directed the Secretary of the Treasury to take the action necessary to *defend the dollar against the speculators.*[15] (*emphasis mine*)

By October 8, the rates of the major trading currencies of the world had already moved to percentage premiums of anywhere from 1 to 9 percent over their former official ceilings.

It is important to note that this change in the exchange-rate structure was for the most part the product of controlled rather than free floating.

Four months after the declaration that no further transfers of gold would be made to settle official claims against the dollar, the so-called Group of Ten countries (the world's leading industrialized countries) held a meeting in Washington. The result was the Smithsonian Agreement, which was promptly hailed by President Nixon as "the most important monetary event of our time." It lasted only a few months.

The devaluation of the dollar might have taken the classic form of a depreciation in terms of the other principal currencies. Since the French in particular did not want their currency to be seen as appreciating against the dollar, it was agreed that the dollar devaluation would be announced in terms of the dollar's new relationship to gold.

The agreement specified an exchange-rate realignment based on an 8.5 percent increase in the official gold price from $35 per ounce to $38 (in essence an 8.5 percent devaluation of the dollar). This devaluation of the dollar was accompanied by relatively smaller devaluations of the Swiss franc, the Italian lira, and the Swedish krona against gold, thus slightly reducing their effective appreciation against the dollar. It was also agreed that the trading bands surrounding the new central rates would be widened to 4.5 percent from 1 percent. Table 10 shows the appreciation of the Group of Ten countries against the dollar after the Smithsonian Agreement was concluded.

Table 10. Appreciation of major currencies after the Smithsonian Agreement

Currency	Percent appreciation of parity against U.S. dollar
Belgian franc	11.57%
Pound sterling	8.57
French franc	8.57
West German mark	13.58
Italian lira	7.48
Japanese yen	16.88
Dutch guilder	11.57
Swedish krona	7.49
Swiss franc	6.36

Source: Federal Reserve Board, March, 1972.

After the Smithsonian Agreement, the dollar showed some signs of recovery. This lasted until June, 1972, when the actions of the British government forced the pound to float.

As we saw in Chapter 2, however, the balance of trade of the United States in the first six months of 1972 was particularly poor. On July 19, 1972, the United States resumed operations in the foreign-exchange markets in the form of West German mark offerings on the New York market.

This intervention was carried on briefly the next day. It was subsequently defended by the U.S. Treasury Department as a necessary response to speculative forces.

> The action reflects the willingness of the U.S. to intervene in the exchange markets on occasion when it feels it is desirable *to help deal with speculative forces.* The action indicates absolutely no change in our basic policy approach toward monetary reform and the necessary efforts on all fronts to achieve a sustainable equilibrium in our balance of payments.[16] (*emphasis mine*)

When data was released on January 24, 1973, showing a further increase in the U.S. trade deficit for December, 1972, the foreign-exchange markets began to react. On the following Monday, German trade data was released showing the substantial growth in the German trade surplus during 1972. The mark began to move up strongly on heavy demand. By the close of business on Friday, February 9, the reserve gain of the German federal bank for the seven trading days of the month had amounted to nearly $6 billion while sales of marks in the New York market by the Federal Reserve Bank of New York came to a total of $318.6 million. On the evening of February 12, 1973, Treasury Secretary John Connally announced that the dollar would be devalued by 10 percent, thereby conclusively terminating the Bretton Woods system. One month later, five European Economic Community countries—Germany, France, Belgium, the Netherlands, and Denmark—organized the joint float. The yen, Swiss franc, sterling, and the lira each floated independently.

The policy issue of whether the ensuing float would be "clean" or "managed" was addressed at the Paris meeting of the Group of Ten ministers in March, 1973. The ministers agreed in principle that "official intervention in the exchange markets might be useful at appropriate times to facilitate the maintenance of orderly conditions."[17] In the language of the money markets, the float would be "managed" or "dirty." The fixed exchange-rate system inaugurated at Bretton Woods was in that manner replaced by a managed, floating exchange-rate system that has persisted to the present day. So ends the sad story of the Bretton Woods system that had served the world so well for so long—throughout the entire difficult postwar readjustment period. What has happened since?

When the foreign-exchange markets were officially reopened on March 19, 1973, the dollar saw approximately six weeks of modest improvements. By June and July, however, the currency was driven down in what one expert described as "recurrent bursts of heavy selling unjustified and undesirable on any reasonable assessment of the outlook for the U.S. payments position."[18] What this and other authorities had overlooked was the effect of domestic conditions, and future expectations about the behavior of the dollar, on its exchange rate. The dollar continued to depreciate against the mark, and by slightly lesser amounts against the French franc and other currencies in the European Economic Community (EEC) bloc. This depreciation of the dollar exacerbated inflationary pressures in the United States and also contributed to disorderly "speculation" in the international commodity markets.[19]

Consequently, the Federal Open Market Committee approved a resumption of exchange operations, and the swap network was increased from $11.7 billion to nearly $18 billion. As a consequence of investor's expectations of massive Federal Reserve intervention, the dollar then inched back up against the mark and other major currencies. When this intervention did not occur, the dollar again began to depreciate against the mark. In late July, 1973, the market stabilized, reinforced by an improvement in the June trade figures for the United States. In early September, dollar rates against the mark and French franc were respectively some 20 percent and 11.5 percent above their July 6 lows.

The March, 1974 *Federal Reserve Bulletin* reported that, between August, 1973 and January, 1974, the dollar "recovered strongly" from the "speculative attack" of the first week of July, 1973. This recovery was abetted by the eruption of the oil crisis in late 1973 and early 1974, as the foreign-exchange markets acted on the belief that the United States was less dependent on imported oil than were Europe and Japan. It was then also believed that a major share of the oil producers' higher revenues would be attracted to dollar-denominated assets and investments, and this positive assessment of the U.S. position initiated a strong movement of short-term funds out of the major European currencies and the Japanese yen into dollars.[20] (At times of OPEC price increases, the dollar will generally be stronger than the currencies of the industrial countries that are more dependent on imported oil, as indicated by the action of the dollar in 1979 and 1980). Consequently, by mid-January, 1974, the German mark and Swiss franc had fallen by approximately 23 percent against the dollar from their peak levels of early July, 1973, and the other major European currencies followed suit in the depreciation against the stronger dollar.

The random-walk nature of foreign-exchange rates prevailed, however, as the dollar again weakened in 1974 between late January and mid-May. According to the *Federal Reserve Bulletin* of September, 1974, "the adverse shift of market sentiment against the dollar coincided with the complete elimination of U.S. capital controls on January 29, 1974, and also the easing of European barriers against capital inflows."[21] Adding fuel to the fire, U.S. interest rates dipped while rates abroad remained steady, thereby encouraging outflows of U.S. funds to foreign markets. By mid-May, the dollar had fallen 21 percent below its January rate against the mark.

One of the most significant impacts of floating rates on trade was witnessed by the failure in June, 1974 of the Herstatt Bank of Germany. This awakened the banking and business communities to the inherent risk of playing the foreign-exchange markets under floating rates. As a result, traders began to limit new transactions to customers of "only the highest quality," and the New York Clearing House banks "sought to make payments for their correspondents only after assurance that covering receipts were in hand."[22] These measures did not work, however, and the Clearing House subsequently modified its procedures, facilitating a recovery in trading volume. According to the *Federal Reserve Bulletin,* "a more lasting consequence of the Herstatt affair was to compound the trading difficulties faced by small- and medium-sized banks, not only in the foreign exchange but also in the 'Eurodollar' market, as a worldwide review of bank credit lines resulted in a tightening of credit limits for all but the very best names."[23]

Franklin National Bank also failed in 1974, adding to the cautious behavior of banks and others in the foreign-exchange markets. The result was "to make exchange markets thin and volatile as participants hesitated to engage in 'stabilizing speculation' (buying or selling a currency when its value was judged to have fallen too low or risen too high)."[24]

From October, 1974 to January, 1975, the dollar again weakened against the German mark and the other currencies in the European monetary bloc. Fears of a U.S. recession, together with fears that the OPEC nations might diversify their assets and hold fewer dollars, contributed to the decline in the value of the dollar. Toward June and July of 1975 the dollar began to recover in the foreign-exchange markets, fueled by a more optimistic expectation of a U.S. economic recovery. The dollar regained strength until October, 1975, when U.S. interest rates declined relative to those abroad, and New York City's fiscal problems came to light. These factors contributed negatively to the dollar's international position.

From the advent of the Carter Administration until November, 1978, the dollar experienced severe instability in the foreign-exchange markets. While the dollar remained fairly steady in 1976, because of an upswing in the U.S. economy after the preceding recessionary year, the dollar began to decline relative to other major currencies in early 1977. From July, 1976 until the beginning of 1977, the dollar depreciated by a total of 10 percent against the German mark and the other currencies linked to it. By the end of January, 1977, the dollar had depreciated by a net 21 percent against the Swiss franc and by 10 percent against the Japanese yen. Reinforcing the dollar's decline were the trade figures for 1977. The U.S. trade deficit increased from $9 billion in 1976 to $31 billion in 1977.

The current-account deficit also increased from $1 billion in 1976 to $19 billion in 1977. In part, these figures reflected an increasing dollar outflow from the United States to pay for foreign imported oil; but they also reflected the more rapid growth in demand for imports in the United

States, relative to its major trading partners, due to the end of recession in the United States. Meanwhile, Japan and Germany were accumulating substantial trade and current-account surpluses. This fueled speculative pressures against the dollar. While this statistical information regarding trade account figures was analyzed in much greater depth in Chapter 2, it is nevertheless interesting to note that, contrary to what we were led to believe by the Carter Administration's economists, the trade figures worsened appreciably as the value of the dollar declined.

From the early days of the Carter Administration in 1977, the view was taken that "the mounting U.S. payments deficit was not an embarrassment but an exemplary American contribution to international financial stability and the collective adjustments to OPEC's steep levy on oil consumers."[25] While the increase in the dollar supply did in fact help ease the crunch of the OPEC price rise, its effect on the international financial system had to be to exacerbate the existing downward pressures on the dollar's value relative to the currencies of the other major industrialized countries.

The U.S. exchange-rate policy under the Carter Administration, as articulated by Secretary Blumenthal, has been described by political analyst Richard Whalen in the following terms:

> Noting the sharp swing in the U.S. payments position from an $11 billion surplus in 1975 to a larger and still growing deficit in 1977, the Secretary presumed to advise our allies on how to run their economies. He insisted that the other major trading nations, especially Japan and West Germany, should quickly reduce their surpluses, stimulate their sluggish domestic economies to absorb more imports, and allow the value of their currencies to rise against the dollar. Even at this point, after semi-public hectoring of Bonn and Tokyo, Blumenthal could have halted without too much damage to his own or the dollar's credibility. Instead, presenting a spectacle that shocked and dismayed foreigners, he rushed headlong to throw his weight against the dollar in foreign exchange markets.[26]

Blumenthal continued to make similar assertions in talks outside the United States: At a June, 1977 meeting of Western finance ministers in Paris, Blumenthal declared: "We need significant shifts—into deficit—in the balance of payments positions of such surplus countries as Japan, Germany, Switzerland, and the Netherlands."[27] Because of the Treasury Secretary's speeches on the dollar's overvaluation, foreigners shifted into the stronger currencies of West Germany and Switzerland. The result was that after mid-June the dollar started falling and continued to do so for the rest of 1977. By the end of 1977, it had declined by approximately 20 percent against the German mark and 30 percent against the yen.

Unfortunately, as Whalen noted, "long before producing any promised trade advantages, the cheaper dollar boosted the cost of imports and encouraged domestic producers (in import-competing industries) to hike their prices, thus worsening the overall inflationary threat to American consumers. . . ."[28]

On January 4, 1978, the Treasury and the Federal Reserve Board issued a joint statement announcing they would begin to intervene "actively" in foreign-exchange markets with borrowed German marks and other strong currencies. Exchange-market traders were unimpressed, however, and in a short while the dollar resumed its decline. The Administration's policy toward the dollar unfortunately did not take into account that exchange rate movements have very little effect on fundamental factors influencing the balance of payments and that in the short and intermediate run, exchange-rate fluctuations will only exacerbate inflationary pressures in a deficit country. This is precisely what happened to the U.S. economy from the beginning of the Carter Administration until November 1, 1978.

It is interesting to compare what happened over the two-week period prior to November 1: 1. the dollar depreciated against all major currencies, including 6.3 percent against the mark; 2. the Standard and Poor stock index dropped 11 percent; 3. short-term and long-term interest rates increased; 4. the price of gold increased by $18; and 5. the spot-commodity price index increased 3.6 percent.

On that same day, the White House and the Federal Reserve Board announced a series of strong measures to halt the sharp decline of the dollar in foreign-exchange markets. These measures included "an unprecedented pledge of massive U.S. intervention—backed by a huge $23.2 billion money pool—to bolster the dollar."[29] The money pool would be created by Treasury issuing $10 billion worth of foreign-denominated U.S. securities, a quadrupling of previously announced gold sales by the Treasury, a $7.6 billion expansion in swap agreements; and sales of Special Drawing Rights and other U.S. assets in the International Monetary Fund. Also announced was an increase in the discount rate by a full percentage point, to 9.5 percent, and an increase in the Federal Funds rate.

President Carter remarked that the continued decline of the dollar "is clearly not warranted" by basic economic conditions and "threatens the economic progress at home and abroad and the success of our anti-inflation programs."[30] A continued depreciation of the dollar, however modest, would have added significantly to the difficulty of reducing the rate of inflation. As a result of the announcement, the following events occurred: the dollar rebounded sharply on those exchange markets that were open on November 1, All Saints' Day, climbing against every major currency, including 8 percent against the Swiss franc and the German mark; the price of gold dropped $27 as investors switched from gold into American securities; short-term interest rates steadied while long-term interest rates fell 10 basis points; spot prices for commodities declined 0.6 percent, and the stock market rose a record 35.34 points. (It is interesting to note that the previous record was 32.93 points, on August 16, 1971, the day after Nixon announced the abandonment of the Bretton Woods monetary system.) This illustrates how quickly a reversal of a bad monetary policy can affect commodity prices, interest rates, stock prices, and the price of gold. Of course the question remains: why was the unfortunate policy of attacking the dollar proposed and adopted in the first place?

Perhaps the most important aspect of the steps taken by President Carter in November, 1978 was that these steps changed the perception of foreign observers. Many now believed that President Carter had made a fundamental decision to reverse the decline in the value of the dollar and was prepared to take steps to control the inflationary cycle in the United States.

What has happened since then? In 1979 the dollar decline was itself sharply reversed. By the end of May the dollar had increased 9 percent in value against the West German mark, 15 percent against the Swiss franc, and 20 percent against the yen. More important, from a dollar outflow of $16 billion in the fourth quarter of 1978, the United States achieved a $16 billion inflow in first quarter of 1979. Furthermore, as a result of the heavy buying of U.S. dollars in 1978, particularly by the German and the Swiss governments, inflation increased sharply in these countries in the first quarter of 1979. In February alone, consumer prices in Germany increased by 2.1 percent. As a result of the increased strength in the dollar, the United States was able to halt gold sales temporarily and to repay the swap transactions it had made earlier.

Floating Exchange Rates as Monetary Policy

While it is undoubtedly true that the courageous action taken by the Carter Administration in November, 1978 to reestablish confidence in the dollar resulted in a sharp revaluation upward, the reasons for its continued strength must be sought elsewhere. In 1979, the OPEC cartel was repeatedly leapfrogging increases in the price of oil; since oil was paid for in dollars, oil purchasers had continually to acquire those dollars, keeping upward pressure on the value of the U.S. currency.

By the autumn of 1979, however, the dollar began to weaken again and increased talk of utilizing a currency or group of currencies other than the dollar to pay for oil began to be heard. As a result of urgings on the United States at the World Bank meeting in Belgrade in September, 1979, Chairman Paul Volcker of the Federal Reserve returned to the United States and began to increase interest rates to hold the dollar firm. Then in March, 1980 came a new program of controls over bank reserves and over credit. Interest rates briefly touched 20 percent, then declined as credit restrictions took hold. The Federal Reserve then reversed itself—credit controls were abandoned, and the money supply through September, 1980 was sharply increased. The Carter Administration at the same time focused on increased social welfare expenditures, reinforcing doubts among Europeans about the U.S. commitment to making the dollar strong.

In November, Ronald Reagan was elected president.

We come now to a discussion of flexible exchange rates, the nature of the flexible-rate system we have had since 1973, and the impact of such a system on trade.

To the Keynesian economists who flocked to the Carter Administration from academia, "floating" exchange rates represented an answer to their prayers. Under such a system, the domestic economy could be stimulated to enhance employment without fear that the ensuing inflation would cause exports to drop off because in a floating exchange-rate system the value of the dollar would be bid down as new dollars were being printed, this natural devaluation working to make exports more competitive. (If money traders were not quick enough to react, the exchange value of the dollar could be "talked down.") We have noted how governmental confidence in this flawed economic thinking was abandoned by President Carter in November, 1978.

The U.S. experience with flexible rates since 1973 has not conformed in any way to the expectations of the theory of flexible rates. The foreign-exchange value of the dollar has fluctuated greatly against many of the currencies of the major industrial countries. For example, from 1973 to 1975, there were six periods in which the dollar rates of exchange for the currencies in the European joint float rose or fell by 10 percent or more in the course of four months.[31]

Flexible exchange rates have also not shielded the United States from incurring massive deficits in its current account, nor have they ameliorated the U.S. balance of trade or the country's payments problems.

One chief reason why flexible rates have not helped the U.S. trade or current-account positions is that too much emphasis has been placed on using exchange rates as a way of adjusting the balance of payments without taking the appropriate domestic fiscal and monetary measures. And if a country fails to take the corrective action to restrain excessive domestic demand (which leads to a greater import ratio), flexible rates will simply add inflation to a deficit country without improving the trade account or the balance-of-payments position. Money flows resulting from the perception of a currency's real value will inexorably adjust the exchange rate. Floating exchange rates can thus be said to enhance speculation against a currency.

We have never had a system of purely floating exchange rates. Rather, we have had "managed" or "dirty" floating exchange rates. Justifications for "managing" the exchange rate, or for intervening in the market to support an existing or a desired rate, have been given in detail by numerous economists. The idea seems to have great appeal. The temptation to tinker with a system so as to make it work better may simply be too great to resist. Here are the two arguments most often given for rate management: A. The free play of market forces leads, in the short run, to an inappropriate rate, i.e., a rate unduly influenced by temporary factors of a cyclical or speculative nature and therefore diverging from some longer-run equilibrium value better correlated to underlying economic conditions (purchasing-power parity); B. Exchange-rate flexibility is not a very effective means of reducing or eliminating payments disequilibriums and may have harmful consequences for domestic economic objectives, in particular the objective of price stability.[32]

Exchange rate movements, in these arguments, lead only to an offsetting of local currency price changes and result in a vicious circle of depreciation/inflation or appreciation/deflation. The U.S. experience with floating rates proves this point, namely that a floating exchange rate will tend to increase inflation at home without in any way reducing a chronic balance-of-payments deficit. Nevertheless, manipulation of world exchange rates continues. In 1978 alone the principal central banks spent $30 billion in "managing" exchange rates through purchases and sales.

Contrary to the predictions of many economists, the breakdown of the Bretton Woods international monetary system "was not accompanied by any significant consequential recession, let alone collapse, in world trade, production, and employment.[33] In fact, the 1973–74 oil price increase had a much greater impact on world trade and investment than did the shift from fixed to flexible exchange rates. It may even be argued persuasively that flexible rates have helped to ease the adjustment to this international exogenous shock for many economies, something a fixed exchange rate might not then have withstood.

As has been noted, three of America's principal competitors in international trade are the Japanese, the Germans, and the Swiss. These countries, all almost wholly dependent on imported energy, should have suffered in competiveness with the United States as oil prices jumped. Yet their competitive position was temporarily aided by the U.S. policy of reducing the value of the dollar. To Switzerland, for instance, the five-fold increase, in dollars, in the price of oil meant a 40 percent *decrease* in the price, in Swiss francs, of imported oil. Even with the newest price increases, Switzerland still paid less for oil in 1979 than it did prior to the organization of OPEC. Such reduced energy costs are factored into manufacturing costs, giving the strong-currency nations an edge in international trade.

Recycling of OPEC Funds

We come now to a very recent phenomenon in monetary history: the so-called recycling process, which has been going on since OPEC's five-fold increase in oil prices created a vast amount of unusable excess currency in the cartel countries. These funds, generally called petrodollars or oil dollars, are channeled from Kuwait, Saudi Arabia, and Libya into the Eurocurrency banks in dollars, and through these banks into development projects in the various developing countries. What is this new flow of money doing to international trade and development? How big is the flow? Where is it coming from, and where is it going? Are we creating a new international currency? Who controls it? What is its meaning? Is it still growing? What is its role in the trend of monetary development? Does it represent a new reserve currency?

There are many important questions to be raised about the role this "new money" will play in the growth of international trade, development, and banking. We need not dwell long on the "banking" factor, since it is covered in Chapter 5, which talks about the Eurocurrency banks and their role in trade. Suffice it to say here that the amounts flowing into the banking system in London alone are large—indeed, very large—and growing steadily; billions are being generated every day on oil purchases throughout the world in ever-increasing amounts that cannot immediately be invested in the OPEC countries, which are already surfeit with development projects.

Looking at the positive aspects first, we noted earlier that both Saudi Arabia and Kuwait had participated in the Witteveen facility to increase the funds available to the IMF for balance-of-payments loans. Thus, two of the countries that have created a severe new balance-of-payments problem for the non oil-producing developing countries are contributing a portion of their additional income to tiding over such countries until they have a means of exporting enough products to pay for imported oil. But what of the flow elsewhere? It is estimated that the OPEC countries, even though they increased the price of oil only modestly in 1980, generated an additional $120 billion in dollar transfers in 1980. Approximately two-thirds of this amount could not be effectively used in domestic infrastructure projects, therefore a large portion of the $80 billion excess was added to the Eurocurrency funds available for lending outside of OPEC. A portion of these funds have gone into government securities in such "rich" countries as the United States, Germany, Great Britain, Switzerland, France, and Japan.

The principal borrowers are, however, the developing countries, who would rather borrow from private commercial banks than from the IMF because in Eurocurrency banking few questions are asked and loans are not made conditional on the lender-country's committing itself to unpopular domestic actions in order to avoid balance-of-payments problems. Deposits are generally made for six months, and bank rolled-over loans may be for five years or more and carry high interest rates (currently 13 percent or more). The threat to international monetary stability is that new money has been created—in dollars—and the dollar supply outside the United States has thereby been substantially increased. The money has been loaned to countries that may not be able to repay the principal even if they can service the high interest rates charged. The OPEC deposits that have served as collateral for these medium-term loans are short-term deposits. Will they continue to be made available? Under what conditions?

The size alone of the deposits brings dramatically increased instability to the world monetary system. Are there any beneficiaries of all this chaos? The major oil companies have certainly not been hurt by the OPEC price increases. Instead of entrepreneurs acting for themselves in a high risk business, they have become distributors of a product with a market at virtually any price. With oil at $37 to $40 a barrel instead of $2.30, the oil companies can obviously make more gross profit simply as distributors with a smaller percentage as markup than they ever did as producer and distributor when oil was one-tenth that price.

The Eurocurrency banks have not been hurting either. They have become intermediaries on a vast scale, taking deposits and making loans that, on paper at least, carry substantial interest-rate differentials between deposit rates and loan rates. However, these banks seem prepared to continue to carry an almost unlimited number of these loans, ignoring the capital-to-outstanding loan ratios that were, until recently, considered prudent. As a further source of disquietude the banks are applying historical loss ratios to types of loans for which they have no history.

What of the Arab depositors? They, too, have little involvement. The loans are not their loans. They have only made deposits under tax-free certificates of deposit that in February, 1981 were bringing 20 percent or more. The Saudi Arabian Monetary Agency (SAMA) has become a special kind of international financing institution in this, a short-term depositor of first instance from whom all the Eurodollar banks draw to build their taller and taller debt pyramids among the less stable developing nations. It should be noted, however, that the SAMA is not a lender of last resort. Behind their deposits, they know, is the Federal Reserve of the United States as lender of last resort. In this game the principal players all appear to be winning; the Arabs, the banks in London, the major oil companies, the borrowing developing countries. How long can such a game continue?

Future Prospects for Monetary Policy

Since this chapter deals with monetary policy and its effect on relations between countries, it is important to consider carefully the cross-border relationships between money supply, interest rates, exchange rates, inflation, current-account positions, and unemployment. Making a difficult problem far worse has been the unfortunate tendency on the part of our political leaders to neglect the effect that any increase in the money supply will have, not only on the domestic inflation rate, but on the export of inflation to other countries, the consequent increase in the *global* supply of money adding to international liquidity and hence stimulating inflation *everywhere*.

When Treasury Secretary Blumenthal tried to persuade the Germans and the Japanese to reflate in 1977 and 1978 he was, in effect, urging that the rest of the industrialized world increase its inflation to match the inflation occurring in the United States. Fortunately, neither the Germans nor the Japanese followed his advice. On the contrary, the Americans were urged to stop the decline in the value of the dollar for fear that OPEC would match declines in the value of the dollar with increases in the price of oil. In November, 1978, when President Carter took the bold and correct step to revalue the dollar, with the good effects previously discussed, he unfortunately neglected to take the one additional step needed to help solve the problem of inflation. He did not insist that the growth in the money supply in the United States be curbed. It will be interesting to see whether President Reagan will have the courage in 1981 to take this all-important step.

Because of the role played by the United States in world Gross National Product what happens to the U.S. domestic money supply has repercussions all over the world. Just as a wave moving onto a beach encounters the return of the previous wave and raises the water level, so does the impact of U.S. monetary policy increase the money supply in other countries and result in increasing the worldwide effect of domestic inflation.

Let us make here a number of assumptions: 1. the Federal Reserve can and does control the money supply of the United States; 2. despite protestations of independence, the chairman of the Federal Reserve generally accedes to the policies on money supply requested of him by the president; 3. if the money supply in the United States is increased to any extent, whether by interest rate adjustments, by credit regulation changes, or by deficit spending, an increase in inflation will necessarily follow in due course; 4. because of the role played by the dollar in international trade, dollars so created will be added in great part to world liquidity, resulting in the export of domestic inflation; 5. as a result of the increase in the money supply on a worldwide scale, the price of goods will rise everywhere; 6. this rise in the price of goods affects the price of raw materials such as oil and also accelerates wage increases, thus causing the inflationary process to regenerate itself.

We saw in Chapter 1, and again in the historical review made in this chapter, how perception affects the direction of international capital flows. Investors and financiers continually shift out of assets denominated in weak currencies and into assets considered strong. Thus, if inflation in country A is persistently higher or lower than that of its trading partners, currency A will depreciate or appreciate accordingly, at a rate approximately reflecting the relevant inflation differentials. That is why the West German mark was strong from 1971 to 1979 and the dollar weak. Of course, a currency may also increase in value because of some technological advantage particular to that country. In the United Kingdom, for example, North Sea oil has strengthened the value of sterling unduly because it has given Britain a new source of exports; in Japan the yen has had a tendency to increase in value because of technological advances and improvements in industrial productivity.

If these are the consequences of domestic inflation, what then are its causes? It is generally agreed that a country's inflation rate mirrors the rate at which it produces money relative to the rate at which it produces goods and services. If money is produced faster than real output, prices for the same quality of goods rise, and inflation is said to have resulted. In simpler terms, it has often been said that too many dollars chasing too few goods causes prices to rise. Recently in the United States inflation has been stimulated by a war—the war in Vietnam, the cost of which was met by a huge increase in the money supply rather than by tax increases—and by social programs paid for by ever-increasing budget deficits. As Peter Korteweg has said:

> Whether the monetary authorities produce money too fast in order to finance a war or the welfare state, to keep interest rates low or exchange rates fixed, or to prevent wage claims in excess of productivity from being translated into unemployment, the unavoidable consequence of monetary growth persistently in excess of output growth is inflation.[34]

The dollars resulting from this creation of new money, as we have seen, have tended in large part to go overseas rather than remain in the United States. Oil payments payable in dollars and borrowings by the developing countries at high rates of interest account for much of this outward flow. In addition, as investors observe the dollar weakening they have sold dollars and invested in other currencies, largely the West German mark or the Swiss franc. Unfortunately, since the quantity of Swiss francs and German marks in circulation is only a fraction of that of U.S. dollars, these movements out of U.S. currency are often made difficult, further threatening to bid up the foreign currencies. In the case of those two countries, as a consequence, inflow has been purposefully discouraged by such steps as negative interest charges or rules forbidding foreigners to invest.

In order to understand better the interplay of foreign currency movements, it will be helpful to look more closely at the German experience from the last quarter of 1978 through the first quarter of 1981, a period of just two and a half years, when inflation, interest rates, and exchange rates were all highly volatile.

To the Germans, at the base of the problem is the necessity of importing energy: gas must come from the Soviet Union, and oil must be paid for in dollars. This ties the German monetary policy (just as it does that of other European countries and Japan) inexorably to the monetary policy of the United States. Normally, if the dollar rises, the West German mark falls, and vice versa, because of the flows of money so often noted in this book. But the German government is constantly faced with a dilemma: if the German mark rises in value its oil-import bill goes down but German goods become less competitive in the international market place, the balance of trade worsens,* and unemployment eventually rises. For a country that exports over 40 percent of the manufactured goods it produces, this is a serious matter.

On the other hand, if the mark loses its value relative to the dollar, as has been happening in 1980 and 1981, then the cost of imported oil rises. At that point, defense of the mark by the German government will necessitate using reserves, increasing interest rates to attract inflows of currency from outside the country, or selling German mark bonds on a large scale to OPEC-dollar-surplus countries as has been tried in 1980–81. This, in turn, implies that the foreign policy of West Germany, which has been since World War II carefully in tune with that of the United States, may be induced to tilt, for reasons of monetary policy, toward the Arab cause in the Middle East. All these difficulties facing German policymakers cause one to question the advantages of the floating-rate monetary system under which the world is currently operating.

We have seen how costly it is to central bankers to keep this floating exchange-rate system in balance. In 1980 the German Bundesbank lost 25 billion marks out of total reserves of 90 billion in trying to maintain the exchange rate with the dollar. Did it succeed? No. In one year's time, from February, 1980 to February, 1981, the German mark went down in value relative to the dollar by 19.1 percent. On the other hand, other continental European currencies have also fared badly. Relative to the dollar, the Swiss franc in the same period declined by 17.3 percent, the French franc by 18.2 percent, and the lira by 19.2 percent. Since Euro-

* The West German balance-of-payment deficit in 1980 did worsen. It reached 28 billion marks. In early 1981, the mark continued to weaken and the Bundesbank in February, 1981 raised interest notes to protect the currency.

pean central bankers are inclined to blame the strength of the dollar on the rise in interest rates in the United States, the German Bundesbank has been allowing interest rates in West Germany to rise in order to attract foreign investment.

Unfortunately this policy will increase the cost of business investment, slow down the economy, and ultimately increase unemployment. It may also have serious side effects. The decline in liquidity and asset value of the German commercial banking system was affected in early 1981 by four noteworthy occurrences. First, the decline in the value of the mark caused deposits to move into other currencies, outside of Germany; second, the increases in interest rates caused a substantial decline in the value of the bond portfolio of the banks; third, losses in Iran were followed by losses on Turkish loans, and the banking system still faces the possibility of extraordinary losses on Polish loans, only part of which have been guaranteed by the German government; fourth, German banks' investments in gold were affected by the decline in the price of gold. A fifth factor, one not yet brought into play, is that German banks have been active in the Eurodollar market where there is no Federal Reserve safety net to protect these banks in the event dollar loans to developing countries cannot be repaid.

It is probably here that the EMS* will play a helpful role in maintaining some stability among exchange rates within the European Community until a more stable rate can be established between the Community and the dollar. The differential is tight, however, since it may not exceed 2.5 percent. Inflation rates within the Community may vary so much that it may prove impossible under expected changes to come to maintain the EMS as it is. But one hopes the European nations will see the increasing need to coordinate monetary policy and synchronize better interest rates, inflation rates, and exchange rates.

What has been said of West Germany and the German banking system might also be said of the rest of continental Europe at a time when the dollar is gaining strength. Will the dollar continue to increase in value? It was pointed out that the dollar's recent strength has been the result more of a perception of strength than high interest rates. It is likely, however, as the Reagan anti-inflation economic program develops, that this perception will continue and that the exchange-rate value of the dollar will continue to rise. Of course, it goes without saying that if Presi-

* EMS refers to the European Monetary System developed in the late 1970s by Giscard d'Estaing of France and Helmut Schmidt of West Germany. It presently includes all the members of the European Community except the United Kingdom.

dent Reagan does not get his program through Congress, or if he does and it proves ineffective in reducing inflation, the world will quickly abandon its newly discovered confidence in the dollar.

Still, the Reagan Administration has a remarkable opportunity not only to reverse the economic policies of the past twenty years, which have resulted in a staggering increase in world money supply, high inflation, and declining productivity, but also to set a new path for economic and monetary cooperation for the future among the industrialized nations.

Before discussing what such a program might entail in the United States, it will be helpful to turn briefly to an analysis of the Thatcher government experience in Great Britain, since its policies have now been in effect for some eighteen months. What lessons for the Reagan Administration can be found in recent Tory policies? There are, of course, many differences between Great Britain and the United States: the class structure, long-existent labor antagonisms, failure of capital investment, nationalization of industry, a much more extensive social service system, including very broadly applied publicly funded health care programs, etc. Nevertheless, in both countries the government is seeking to reverse a long-standing governmental commitment to high spending, deficit budgets, increased regulation of industry, high inflation, increases in the money supply to meet the costs of social programs, high taxation, low capital investment, and declining productivity of the work force. Can it be said that the Thatcher policies have "worked" so that Reagan planners can adapt them to the needs of the U.S. economy? Obviously, if a commonality of policy can be found, the effect on other industrialized countries may at last find that common policy thread that is so essential to controlling the global inflation that affects them all.

It is, of course, very unfair to discuss the impact of Mrs. Thatcher's policies on the British economy in the middle of a turn-around situation. Nevertheless, it should be noted that each of those economic factors discussed in this chapter, both the positive and the negative, is in an upswing: money supply, interest rates, the exchange-rate value of the currency, inflation, current-account position, budget deficit, and unemployment. This highly unusual situation is the result of a number of factors, some of which are interrelated, others not. What is probably the key factor, the money supply, is up sharply.

In 1980–81 the government is having to borrow 27.6 billion pounds. In part this is due to the recession in the United Kingdom, which has caused the revenues to be overestimated and expenses, including unemployment insurance payments, to be underestimated.* Interest rates to the consumer have reached as much as 22 percent. The exchange rate has remained very high, largely because of exports of North Sea oil. One wonders why the Thatcher government has not sought to bring down the interest rate and the exchange rate so as to motivate equity investment and spur exports. For a government trying to improve the lot of private industry the policy on interest rates and the exchange appears quite counterproductive. High interest rates, as we have seen, increase foreign investment inflows and keep the exchange rate higher than it should be. Earnings from oil exports need to be directed by the government towards investment in other domestic industries, either by lowering the tax rate on industry through investment credits or through government-sponsored research grants aimed at high technology industries, such as electronics.

The inflation rate, which increased to 22 percent in July, 1980 appears to be coming down but is expected to be at 15 percent for the first six months of 1981. It is expected, hopefully, that the inflation rate will decline in 1982 to single-digit levels. It will, if industrial production begins to rise again. Wage settlements are the real problem here along with the increase in the money supply. The recent capitulation of the government on wage increases for the coal miners indicates how difficult it is for the government to maintain control over wage hikes. The rate savings in Britain, however, is high—17 percent. With a greater effort to encourage savings to flow into investment there could be hope that Britain will at last be on the way to rebuilding its industrial base.

Will the United States have to pass through the same difficult and painful period of shrinkage before rebuilding its economy on a new premise? It is difficult to foretell. All we know is that the government debt will pass one trillion dollars in the next few months. We have the hard, very painful, and unpleasant choice of liquidating that debt through default and bankruptcy or passing on to our children an even greater debt, which they will be even less able to repay. Some day the piper will be paid, or the debt forgiven, and a fresh start made. Either alternative is singularly unpleasant.

But the insolvency in the world monetary system continues to perpetuate itself, both individuals and businesses continue to borrow because without new loans they cannot repay loans previously made. The pyramid of debt continues to grow not solely through shortsightedness but also because failure to assure its growth will result in massive forced liquida-

* This is what Reagan budget planners have most to fear. As the economy slows, unemployment will rise, and the budget deficit will increase.

tion. There have been instances in world history when individual countries found themselves unable to pay: Germany in 1928, Britain in 1967, Italy in 1974, and more of the developing countries each passing year. But there has never been an instance when the global capital base and its entire economic structure depended upon the creation of constant additional debt in one single currency.

Yet this is the situation today. This global debt structure is maintained and nourished through the expansion of the dollar supply made possible by the actions of the Federal Reserve of the United States. It can at any time halt the process. The events of March, 1980 proved this, when credit was tightened and interest rates came down.* In France, in 1959, Jacques Rueff, who was President de Gaulle's principal economic advisor, by successfully stopping the Bank of France from buying French government securities, showed that it could be done, although in one country alone and under very different conditions from those prevailing in the United States today.

Today hundreds of millions of savers—the old, the poor, the young, all those to whom promises to pay or to repay have been made—are wondering whether there is any validity to those promises. On the other side are the borrowers—governments in debt, individuals with mortgage and installment debt, businessmen whose growing debt payments to meet increases in wages and the cost of raw materials are dependent upon new bank loans made possible only through increases in lending capacity dependent in turn on new Federal debt instruments created by the Federal Reserve. It must be evident that in this situation only the most careful collaboration between heads of state, central bankers of the major countries, and ministers of finance can bring about the necessary adjustment without causing the entire collapse of the world's credit structure. No one can predict just where the first crack in the wall will come. It may be a country, it may be another bank, like Herstatt (as happened in 1931 with Credit Anstalt), or it may be an overextended multinational business. In 1964, President Johnson saw what would happen if the war in Vietnam continued without an increase in taxes, and yet failed to ask for such a tax increase. In March, 1969, President Nixon saw what would happen to Penn Central, Chrysler, Lockheed, and other companies if

* Restricting the expansion of credit has also been tried successfully in Europe. The French call it "Encadrement du Credit." One solution would be to restrict credit throughout the OECD countries by putting a ceiling of say 5 percent on permitted increases in assets of central banks. This step might be taken in lieu of a return to a fixed exchange-rate standard such as gold, and might work well.

credit were not made available again to the banks, and he therefore asked the Federal Reserve to relax the restrictions; in 1978, 1979, and 1980, President Carter saw the necessity to restore the value of the dollar in the foreign-exchange markets, but from June to September, 1980, the Federal Reserve increased the money supply at a pace unheard of until then.

Today, the situation is certainly far more difficult to solve than it was in 1964 or 1969, or even 1980. It will take enormous courage to face the problem now. For the first time, however, since 1945, there appears to be an agreement on the part of government leaders all over the industrialized world that something needs to be done to halt this constant increase in money supply and the continuous growth in the world pyramid of credit. Emory Land, founder of the Polaroid Corporation, and, until recently, its chief executive, once said: "What takes the time of the inventor is determining just what it is that the product is expected to do. Once determined, the rest is only a question of mechanics."

We have learned that it is no longer possible for any country to act independently of others in this highly interdependent economic structure we have created in the years since World War II. The recent conversion and flow of currencies to the dollar indicates an awareness that perhaps there is a team in place in the United States that will be willing at last to face the problems of the U.S. economy on a priority and almost single-issue basis.

Restrictions on the growth of the money supply in the United States would have grave repercussions in the United States, but would also affect the economies of European countries, their interest rates, their exchange rates vis-a-vis the dollar, their growth rates and degree of unemployment. Such restrictions will similarly affect the economies of the intermediate developing countries, their trade with the industrialized countries, and, of course, the extent to which they may have to reschedule their own vast indebtedness. Since we are beginning to understand the extent of our international financial problem, there is hope that through collaboration we will be able to face the solutions ahead, difficult as they may turn out to be. Since there has long been no adequate alternative, the decision to shrink world monetary expansion starting with the U.S. dollar has, sooner or later, to be made. It should be hoped by all that the decision has in fact been made and that it is still soon enough.

5

The Changing Role of Banking in International Trade

We have shown in the preceding chapter the extent to which goods and services exchanged in international trade are currently paid for in U.S. dollars. Because of the sheer size of U.S. production compared with that of the rest of the world, there has been good reason in the past to use the dollar as the accepted medium of exchange. But this is somewhat less true today now that Japan, Germany, France, and now the European Community (considered as one trading entity) play a much greater role in trade. While in the future international trade may require a new form of monetary exchange unit not linked to or controlled by any one nation, we have not yet reached that stage of monetary development. Indeed, in 1981, the dollar appears to be regaining its former position as the preferred monetary unit of exchange.

This chapter discusses how goods are paid for in international trade, how the unit of exchange is determined, and how the private commercial banking system plays its role in financing these trade transactions.

There is, of course, trade financing through the domestic national banking system. If a U.S. manufacturer sells tractors to a Brazilian distributor of farm equipment, for example, the transaction may be financed in whatever currency the buyer and seller agree upon. If, as would most surely be the case here, the medium of exchange chosen were U.S. dollars, these dollars could be furnished either through the seller's or the buyer's domestic bank. Similarly, if credit is involved, the financing might be arranged through the seller's bank, by a supplier credit, or through the buyer's bank via an import credit. If the seller wants dollars and the buyer's bank in Brazil handles the credit, it would be apt to obtain these dollars from the London branch of Banco do Brasil, or from another bank operating in the Eurodollar market. Such a transaction would result in a flow of dollars from outside the United States returning to this country.

If the transaction were the reverse (e.g., a shipment of coffee from

Brazil to the United States), the transaction would normally be financed through a U.S. bank; in this case U.S. dollars would ultimately flow from the United States to Brazil, thus creating a foreign claim against a U.S. bank and, hence, additional Eurodollars.

In the early 1960s, when the term "Eurodollars" first came into widespread use, some people mistakenly believed that the term described some special issue of foreign currency, one perhaps backed by the full faith and credit of the U.S. government, but not U.S. dollars themselves.* Today, we all know that a Eurodollar is nothing more nor less than a claim held by a foreigner against an American bank. The rate of growth of this market for dollar claims outside the United States has been phenomenal. Lately, Eurodollars have been estimated to be growing at rates as high as 25 percent per year, and to have reached a total of over $1 trillion if interbank deposits are not netted out. Table 11 shows the growth in the size of the Eurocurrency market in recent years.

How did such growth occur? What are its implications in the context of international trade? Is this money market fueling global inflation? Is it making the role of the Federal Reserve Bank more difficult? Are there special risks to monetary stability in this system? Should there be controls? The purpose of this chapter is to examine these questions.

Historically, the development of the Eurodollar is simple to explain. The first Eurodollars were likely created during the Korean War when the USSR, which had kept a good deal of its foreign currency in U.S. dollars in New York banks, decided in 1953 that its dollar funds should be located elsewhere and transferred them to a Soviet-owned bank in London, the Norodny Bank. From London, these dollars were loaned out for short terms (three to six months) at interest rates comparable to what the dollars would have earned in New York.

The Eurodollar market received its first real boost when President Kennedy in an attempt to protect the value of the dollar, developed the Interest Equalization Tax (IET). Since the IET penalized American companies that borrowed in the United States for the purpose of investing or lending those funds outside the country, foreign subsidiaries of American multinational companies looked to borrow the funds in the London Eurodollar market.

* A few years ago the treasurer of an American company came to the investment banking office of the author and said that his company proposed to make a Eurodollar loan. Have you ever seen a Eurodollar? he was asked. He was then shown a dollar bill kept in the office on which the head of George Washington has been replaced with the unmistakable profile of General de Gaulle.

Table 11. Eurocurrency market size[a] (*In billions of dollars [rounded to nearest $5 billion], at end of period*)

	1971	1972	1973	1974	1975	1976	1977	1978	1979	1980 June	1980 Sept.
Estimated size											
Gross	150	205	310	390	480	590	725	925	1,185	1,310	1,370
Liabilities to nonbanks	30	35	55	75	80	100	125	170	230	265	n.a.[b]
Liabilities to central banks	15	25	40	60	70	85	110	120	155	160	n.a.
Liabilities to other banks[c]	105	145	215	255	330	405	490	635	800	885	n.a.
Net	85	110	160	215	250	310	380	485	600	670	700
Claims on nonbanks	35	45	65	100	115	150	195	245	295	340	n.a.
Claims on central banks and on banks outside market area[d]	35	45	75	95	115	135	155	195	245	260	n.a.
Conversions of Eurofunds into domestic currencies by banks in market area[e]	15	20	20	20	20	25	30	45	60	70	n.a.
Eurodollars as % of gross liabilities in all Eurocurrencies	76	78	73	77	78	79	76	74	72	72	*n.a.*

Source: Morgan Guaranty Trust Company of New York, *World Financial Markets,* February, 1981.

[a] Based on foreign-currency liabilities and claims of banks in major European countries, the Bahamas, Bahraim, Carjman Islands, Panama, Canada, Japan, Hong Kong, and Singapore.

[b] n.a. = not available.

[c] Includes unallocated liabilities.

[d] Includes unallocated claims.

[e] In European market area only.

And these funds were easily available. As pointed out earlier, there was a gaping hole in the IET system: money loaned to Canada was exempted from the tax. As a result, American banks loaned U.S. dollars to Canadian banks, which then transferred these funds to affiliated banks in London, where they were in turn loaned to the banks that engaged in dollar lending there. In this way, the law was neatly bypassed and the Eurodollar system was given new impetus, particularly since banks dealing in a foreign currency in London were not subject to the usual bank regulators' controls. The loans made were large ones—the larger the better—and the borrowers were generally subsidiaries of well-known multinational companies whose parents guaranteed the loans.

Banks making the Eurodollar loans borrowed freely from each other, thus creating what is now known as the interbank market. The cost of money in the interbank market in turn became known as the London interbank offer rate (LIBOR). It is this interbank lending—at rates fixed each day—that is the basis for the growth of the Eurocurrency market, since at all times and on short notice any bank operating in the market can obtain the funds its customers request. Generally the smaller banks supply their deposits through the interbank market to the larger banks, which, in turn, make the syndicated loans to the big borrowers at a higher rate of return.

In the early days of the Eurocurrency market, loans were made in dollars; the term of the loan was relatively short; the rate was generally a fraction more than the rate that would have been paid in New York. To a known corporate buyer, the paperwork required was simple; approval for the loan might even be given over the telephone. There were no government controls and no examination of balance sheets and financial statements was requested. Nor were there compensating balances required, as would be the case when a company borrowed from a U.S. bank in the United States, and there were no fees, as would be the case when borrowing from European banks in their domestic markets. Rates were and still are related to the interbank rate—the margin over LIBOR may vary, but it has always been less than the margin over the costs of funds charged by banks in domestic markets.

A brief historical analysis will be helpful in showing how the market has developed in the twenty to twenty-five years since its first effective use in international trade and investment.

The first important date in this development is 1958 when currency convertibility became generalized in Europe. It had taken Europe some thirteen years from the end of World War II to reestablish its domestic currencies so that these currencies could be freely convertible into dollars. In Eurocurrency terms, this meant that dollars borrowed in the market could be used in other than dollar transactions for the first time.

With the adoption of the IET in 1963 and with subsequent Johnson Administration controls limiting borrowing by foreigners or foreign subsidiaries of U.S. multinationals,* the Eurodollar market in London was given even more impetus. In 1967, foreign branches of U.S. banks were exempted from the provisions of the IET if the loans made were for longer than one year. This made it attractive for U.S. banks to transfer funds to their London branches. At the same time, treasurers of U.S. multinationals were increasingly using the opportunity to deposit short-term funds in what had become known as the Eurodollar market because the Federal Reserve's limitations on interest payable on deposits were not applicable abroad.† The market thus satisfied at once the needs of the banks, the depositors, and the borrowers.

In 1969 the banks that had been lending short term, for three or six months, and generally at fixed rates, developed a new scheme to permit them to make medium-term loans, five years and more, without taking the risk that interest rates might change during the term of the loan and leave them with outstanding loans at rates below the market. This was important to the banks, since their customers only made short-term deposits at fixed rates. To solve this problem and enable the Eurocurrency banks to make loans without interest risk for up to five or even ten years a "roll-over" loan was devised.‡ By agreement between the bank and the borrower, the interest rate on a medium- or long-term loan would be adjusted every six months (or in rare cases, every three months) to reflect changes in the interbank rate. As it moved up or down, the borrower's rate would be similarly adjusted.

Since the borrower's term was much longer than the depositor's, weren't the banks taking an undue risk themselves by borrowing short to lend long? Yes, the banks were, but they were also confident that the Eurodollar market would continue to expand. Table 11 shows how constant this growth has, in fact, been. The roll-over loan has thus become the feature of Eurodollar lending in today's volatile Eurocurrency markets.

* The Voluntary Credit Restraint Program of 1965 and the Mandatory Credit Restraint Program of 1968.

† Regulation Q limits the amount of interest that can be paid by commercial banks on short-term deposits.

‡ At times, this roll-over loan is called a "floating-rate" loan.

Additionally, in 1969, as a result of President Nixon's attempt to cut down on the extension of domestic credit, America had its first real post-war credit crunch. This ended in some $13 billion being returned from London branches of U.S. banks, along with sharp consequent increases in the cost of money in the London interbank market. The rate went from approximately 6 percent to 12 percent within just a few months. And while the big U.S. money center banks were repatriating their dollars to meet the loan requirements of their domestic clients, and to get around the credit-tightening efforts of the Federal Reserve, the major European banks started making dollar loans in London to the subsidiaries of the big American multinationals. As we shall see, this gave the Europeans and the Japanese—who had learned the ropes from their more innovative American competitors—a foothold in the Eurocurrency market that they have been expanding ever since.

That the tightening of domestic credit by President Nixon in 1969 brought about action by the money center banks in the United States withdrawing Eurodollar deposits from their branches in London so that they might be in a position to continue to lend to their large corporate borrowers in the United States, demonstrates quite clearly the close relationship between the Eurodollar market in London and the domestic money market.

It is sometimes said that Eurodollars come from transfers of dollars to OPEC to pay for oil or from deficits in the U.S. balance of trade. This is, of course, true. But it must also be realized that the dollar funds abroad at the present time move back and forth dependent upon whether a more profitable return is available in the Eurodollar market or through deposits in the domestic banks. Movements depend upon relative interest rates. In other words, when interest rates abroad rise relative to U.S. rates, money flows there. When they rise here relative to rates abroad, the flow reverses back to the United States. Because interest rates in the Eurodollar market are generally a bit higher than for deposits in the United States, the Eurodollar market tends to grow faster than does money in the domestic banking system.

At the same time the Eurocurrency market can also charge generally less to the borrower. This is because, as we have seen, there are no reserve requirements, no FDIC insurance, and no control mechanism or fees, as in the case of normal European bank transactions. This last is also one reason for the growing influx of other currencies in the Eurocurrency market, although it is generally considered that the dollar still accounts for approximately 75 percent of the Eurocurrency market, with the West German mark and the Swiss franc accounting for most of the balance.

The case of the West German mark is interesting. The Euromark market has grown even though the rate of inflation in Germany is low and Germany has, until recently, had no substantial balance-of-trade deficit. It is the interest-rate advantage and the lack of controls and costs that account primarily for the growth in the market.

Does this mean that the growth of international trade and the interdependence of the international banking system have made domestic controls over banks superflous or ineffective? Will the growth of the Eurocurrency market mean that governments will in time accept the necessity of doing away with national controls over banks in favor of an international system of controls operated by some central banking authority made up of central bankers* and perhaps, in time, a true international central bank? Trade growth and financial needs would seem to require that the flexibility of the Eurocurrency system be retained and expanded.

The next event of importance in the growth of the Eurocurrency market occurred in 1973–77 when OPEC raised the price of oil to the industrialized world from $2.50 to $12 a barrel. This brought about two important developments, the first a flow of deposits from certain OPEC countries with sudden access to dollar payments for oil that they could not immediately use domestically and had to place elsewhere in order to avoid massive inflation at home. Among these nations were Saudi Arabia, Kuwait, the Arab Emirates, and Libya.

For understandable reasons, OPEC governments were reluctant to invest in the United States; their funds might be seized on any number of political or economic pretexts. Nor did they want to make loans to the oil-short developing countries because such loans might not be repaid. The ideal answer turned out to be short-term, roll-over deposits in the principal Eurocurrency banks. The depositors did not care to whom the funds were eventually loaned; the banks of deposit remained liable, and the depositors were protected from government political pressure by the anonymity of their deposits. As it turned out, the early principal borrowers of these Eurocurrency deposits were those OECD countries that now needed large amounts of dollars to continue paying for imported oil.

* Presumably this would include the central banks of ten key countries: Belgium, Canada, France, Germany, Italy, Japan, Netherlands, Sweden, United Kingdom, and the United States. These countries and Switzerland are in the reporting network of the bank for International Settlements (BIS), which monitors the Eurocurrency market. Austria, Denmark, Ireland, and Luxembourg are also in the network.

Once again, the new banking system had responded by addressing each participant's need: the depositor had a safe and profitable investment; the new government borrowers were able to raise billions of dollars for medium-term loans at a spread as low as 0.625 percent over LIBOR; and the banks found both new borrowers and, more important, massive new deposits.

Even with this new wealth at their disposal, by 1975 the Eurocurrency banks faced the future with some trepidation. The monetary difficulties created by the bankruptcies of the Herstatt Bank and the Franklin National Bank, viewed as isolated instances of poor bank management and foreign-exchange speculative practices that more serious international banks could avoid, were still troubling. Indeed, the Herstatt failure, which caused momentary tie-ups of interbank transactions on both sides of the Atlantic, convinced OECD central bankers that they should do more to police speculation in the foreign-exchange markets. Since that time, any untoward transactions in foreign exchange are immediately reported and supervision of bank exchange traders has been severe. This is one more instance where central bankers have shown an ability to collaborate quickly and effectively.

There was only one catch in all this: the early borrowers in the market were the subsidiaries of well-known American multinational corporations whose paper was guaranteed by their parents. Later, European multinationals also became borrowers, since their credit standing was equally good. When Americans started to borrow again in the United States in 1974–75 (the IET penalties were removed in 1974), these American multinationals were replaced as borrowers by the major European and the Japanese governments, which needed large amounts of dollars to pay their higher oil bills. Gradually, however, as these countries began to increase their exports to the OPEC countries, they earned through trade more of the dollars needed to pay for their oil, and thus lessened their need to borrow.

Where would the Eurocurrency banks now lend the ever-increasing deposits coming from the OPEC countries? The answer was one calculated to cause bank regulators a great deal of concern. While the OECD countries gradually increased their exports to OPEC and thus solved their oil-payment problems, the non–oil-producing countries of the Third World lacked such flexibility: generally all they could market were raw materials or semifinished goods rather than the finished products of an industrialized society. So now they too sought Eurocurrency loans to tide them over until their own industrialization would enable them to pay for

OPEC oil with final products. For example, Brazil, Mexico, the National Republic of China, South Korea, and India,* along with other less creditworthy developing nations, began borrowing heavily from the Eurocurrency banks. Loans to the developing countries indeed expanded very rapidly during this period and have continued to do so to the present day.

Where do we stand today in the Eurocurrency market? Are the banks involved facing additional risks because of the decline in the standing of their borrowers? Will deposits continue to grow sufficiently to cushion the reschedulings that will result from delinquent loans to certain developing countries? What will be the effect of U.S. efforts to balance its domestic budget and reduce its balance-of-payments deficit? Will this shrink dollar holdings abroad and force the Eurocurrency banks to pay more for their dollar deposits? These are questions we need to address because the Eurocurrency banks have played such a useful role in the past, particularly in the recycling of the OPEC surpluses in 1974–75. But 1981 is not 1975. And the market is facing new and different challenges.

In understanding where we are today, we must take into account two developments in the money market: 1. the increased competition, and 2. the changes in composition of the participants. As we have pointed out, the market is highly competitive. The smaller banks provide the additional deposits or transfers that enter the interbank lending pool, while the larger banks serve as syndicate managers or even make the loans themselves. These larger banks may get an agent's commission or a fee as manager. As the lead banks they may also get deposits from the borrower or establish a key banking relationship with either the depositor or the borrower that will generate further business in the future. Because competition for deposits has grown enormously in the past twenty years, and because the difference between the cost of acquiring new money (the amount paid the depositor) and the interbank rate have narrowed, those banks engaged in the wholesale interbank market have had their profit-margins reduced.

For years individuals or corporations eager to get their funds out of South America, Africa, or Asia—where governments were unstable and assets subject to seizure—deposited their funds in dollars with American or with other banks in London, even though the return was less than might be earned at home. Today depositors are much more sophisticated and demand a better return for their funds. The result of the increased

* In chapter 8 there is a detailed discussion of how the so-called intermediate developing countries such as these hastened industrialization through Eurocurrency borrowings.

competition for both depositors and borrowers has been to make the Eurocurrency mechanism a highly efficient one, giving the depositor an increased return while at the same time taking a lower rate of interest from the borrower.

In recent years traditional relationships between borrowers and their bank lenders have turned into competitive auctions, where rates are the sole determinant of which bank gets the business. Unfortunately, just as bank profit margins started to decline steadily these banks started to make loans to riskier borrowers; the LDC borrowers today are nowhere near as good credit risks as were the well-established major multinational corporate borrowers of the 1960s and the early 1970s.

More important, there has been a major change in the composition of those banks engaged in Eurocurrency lending. We pointed out that American banks initially played a preponderant role. This changed in 1969 when the U.S. banks repatriated their funds and the European and Japanese banks established a position in the market. Recently, for a number of reasons, this trend has greatly accelerated.

In part, this is the result of the declining posture of American multinationals in international trade. As U.S. government regulations have created added "disincentives" to trade, (e.g., antitrust, antiboycott, and antibribery statues), American companies have found themselves playing by a set of rules different from those their competitors must deal with. As a consequence, European and Japanese multinationals have tended to secure the big trade projects worldwide in place of American firms.

At first, foreign banks were reluctant to participate in the Eurocurrency market, and their governments did not encourage them to do so. In Germany the change came in 1971, when the government made it attractive, through swap transactions, for German banks to lend dollars outside the country. In Switzerland the change came even later.

There were other reasons why the perception of foreign banks changed. 1. They saw how successful the American banks had been in "following their companies abroad;" 2. as the European governments accumulated additional dollars in their central banks, their domestic banks saw less of a risk in making dollar transactions, even though they had no "lender of last resort" as the American banks did in the U.S. Federal Reserve; 3. they adopted the American techniques of credit analysis, which were far more concerned with operating results than with the cumbersome balance-sheet appraisals and book-value calculations normally relied upon in Europe; 4. they saw how the interbank market worked to supply dollars needed for roll-over loans; 5. they increasingly opened branches in the United States to tap the U.S. money market; 6. they saw how budgetary deficits in the United States resulted in constant accretions of dollars outside the United States.

It was for these reasons then that foreign banks finally decided to par ticipate in the Eurocurrency market. But what is less clear is why, once they entered, their share of the market continued to increase. The answer to this question lies elsewhere. For one thing, the European and Japanese banks have capital structures different from those of banks in the United States. In France, for example, a capital ratio* of 1 percent is not uncommon. In Japan ratios are not much higher. The reason for this is that the central banks in these countries fully expect to support their domestic banks if they need additional discount facilities. The domestic banking system becomes an extension of the government in its economic planning, whether at home or abroad. Second, there may be government participation via deposits, long-term loans, or special discount facilities. Japan, for instance, offers this kind of government participation in support of private commercial banks. Third, because the capital ratios are smaller in foreign banks, the same return on assets will produce a much higher return on capital. Put another way, foreign banks can charge less for loans and still produce the same return on capital American banks do. Fourth, in most foreign countries a domestic bank with branches abroad need not pay domestic taxes on its foreign earnings.

Finally, as we explained earlier, foreign banks have had a tendency, much as American banks did before them, to follow their business enterprises abroad. As Japanese corporations have spread their investments to other nations through their trading companies and otherwise, the banks have followed, financing both overseas trade and investment. At the same time, American companies have retreated abroad, in part because of the increased competition from foreign multinationals, in part because of government-created disincentives to foreign trade and investment.

The effect of these changed perceptions by foreign and domestic banks has been clear. Sine 1978, American banks have reduced their participation in the Eurocurrency market while the Europeans and Japanese have increased theirs substantially. While American banks have thereby reduced their share in the riskier loans often made today in the Eurocurrency market, they have also sharply reduced their role in financing both foreign investment and world trade. Given the influence of banks on in-

*The "capital ratio" describes the relationship between the capital structure of the bank and the bank's loan portfolio.

ternational trade, this does not augur well for American participation in the growth of trade.

We now return to the questions posed at the beginning of this chapter: What role does the Eurocurrency market play in international trade and investment? What are the risks involved for monetary stability? Should controls be imposed?

In the summer of 1979, the House of Representatives held a series of hearings[2] to consider a bill, H.R. 3962, to amend the Federal Reserve Act to establish reserve requirements on Eurodollar liabilities of American banks abroad, provided foreign banks' deposits in dollars were subjected to the same requirements by their own countries. The gist of the testimony was that any such legislation was premature, particularly since there was little evidence that other countries would go along, and that in the absence of such concurrence, American banks would be severely handicapped. The intense interest rate competition in the market would make it simply too difficult to absorb the increased cost of reserve requirements.

There are essentially three questions to be asked in determining whether controls are advisable. 1. Has the Eurocurrency market added to world inflation? 2. Has it created exchange-rate instability? 3. Are the banks engaged in the market taking undue risks that may affect the stability of the international banking system? It is useful to look at each of these questions individually.

Has the Eurocurrency market added to inflation? The answer has to be that it probably has, in several ways. First, the system itself undoubtedly creates money, in part just because of the absence of reserve requirements. Money can be borrowed from one bank, deposited in a second bank, loaned again by that second bank, and the process repeated again and again. It is, of course, not possible to predict precisely the multiplier effect, but it has been estimated at anywhere from 2:1 to 7:1. In the 1960s and early 1970s a number of learned articles were written that tried to calculate just how much money was created by the system but in 1981 no one seems to have much interest in such calculations: money creation appears to have become an art form subject to constant innovation, internationally as well as domestically.

It is clear that the Eurocurrency market does contribute to inflationary pressures by increasing credit availability to deficit countries, particularly when such borrowings are made to solve balance-of-payments problems that would otherwise have to be alleviated by going to the International Monetary Fund and meeting its strict conditions for borrowers. The ready availability of funds through the Eurocurrency market may also encourage such LDCs as Brazil to continue borrowing for capital projects even through periods when repayment may become increasingly difficult. Any move to establish reserve requirements would, by increasing the cost to borrowers, certainly cause deferral of some capital projects in the developing countries. Such a move would also make it more difficult for developing countries to meet the rising cost of imported oil, which is, after all, the primary cause of inflation in the Third World: financing by the Eurocurrency system of these increased costs is a secondary cause. As Governor Henry Wallich of the Federal Reserve has said: "The Euromarket is an efficient conduit of stabilizing or destabilizing forces and is an amplifier of these forces but not an originator."[3]

Does the system add to exchange-rate instability? There seems to be no proof that it encourages speculative practices. It has certainly expanded international dollar liquidity and accelerated the international movement of capital. It is a thesis of this book that this movement is necessary and healthy and that any step taken to manage currency flows should be regarded as just one more attempt by governments (individually or in concert) to compensate for the unintended deleterious consequences of prior policy misjudgments. Preventing the normal functioning of monetary movements will, in the view of this author, create new dislocations in the monetary system.

Are banks taking undue risks under current conditions in the market? This is a more difficult question to answer. There are a number of disquieting trends to be watched if the international economy continues to slow down. The first is the mismatching of maturities, i.e., borrowing short to lend long. Bank of England figures indicate that about 40 percent of Eurobank liabilities in London are of one-month maturity or shorter. The weighted average of total liabilities is probably no more than three to four months. Such mismatching of maturities will cause grave difficulties if the Eurocurrency markets begin to shrink. Even then, as rates of interest are increased to maintain the level of deposits needed to offset long-term loans already outstanding, new funds will tend to be drawn from the United States outward, unless, of course, the U.S. government should establish exchange controls, a highly unlikely and undesirable possibility. Furthermore, such interest rate increases in short-term deposits would create losses for the banks since the interest rates on most syndicated loans are adjusted only every six months. Here again, outside flow adjustments would be needed to solve the problem.

Another potential risk is tied up with the credit-worthiness of the developing countries. The increase in OPEC deposits in 1980 to perhaps $80 billion and the increasing needs of developing countries to make balance-of-payments loans in the commercial markets have created a situation in which more and more loans, at higher risk, are made to the least stable in the pool of borrowers. However, because loans to countries are most often syndicated, the risk is very widely distributed among the Eurocurrency banks. It is difficult to evaluate how serious country-loan risk is at the present time: Zaire, Turkey, Poland, and, until recently, Peru, are the areas of concern to international bankers.

Two steps might be taken here to minimize the risk: The first, which ministers of finance in the industrialized countries have been advocating, is to substitute for commercial bank loans insofar as possible direct LDC borrowings from the OPEC countries. The second would be to increase IMF funds available to countries in balance-of-payments difficulties.*

A third type of risk involves the adequacy of Eurocurrency bank earnings and capital, given the competitiveness of the market at the present time, a risk linked in turn to the final risk—the possibility that the central banks will have to come in as lender of last resort should a substantial loss have to be taken at any time by one or more of the banks active in the market. In the Eurodollar market the Federal Reserve acts as lender of last resort to the branches of American banks. But what of the European or Japanese banks?

The Banque de France has warned French banks that it will not intervene, even in case of serious trouble, if its banks are engaged in dollar transactions in the Eurocurrency market. As has been noted, American banks are now playing a less active role; it is likely, therefore, that if a Eurocurrency bank gets into trouble, it will not be an American bank. Because of the interbank lending system, however, if any one major bank should not be able to meet its claims, all banks will be affected.

What is needed is an agreement among the central bankers of the principal OECD countries where the Eurocurrency banks have their domestic headquarters to establish a sort of safety net to be available in case of difficulty. Swap transactions between central banks to assure availability of dollars would assure depositors that they will be paid and avoid panic. The Bank for International Settlements (BIS)† should play a significant role in such an arrangement. Countries that are members or observers at the BIS have an important stake in the continued effectiveness of the

* As was done by the so-called Witteveen facility, named after the last Chairman of the Fund.

† The role of the BIS is discussed in detail in Chapter 6.

Eurocurrency system, because they remain very important borrowers in that market.

It is evident, given its present size, that the Eurocurrency market plays a preponderant role in the financing of international trade. It also perpetuates the use of the dollar as the medium of exchange. Other more stable currencies like the West German mark or the yen might be preferred by lenders, but the very stability of these currencies comes from the fact that both the German and the Japanese governments exercise great care to keep the amount of their own currency in circulation within bounds. Neither successive U.S. administrations nor the Federal Reserve have made any concerted effort to do so with the U.S. dollar. It is thus the weakness, not the strength, of the dollar that has preserved its role as the key currency in recent years. This weakness is also the reason, of course, that the world continues to suffer from growing inflation.

As we have observed, U.S. budgetary deficits cause the Federal Reserve to create more currency to finance an ever-growing national debt. This excess currency is then exported through ever-increasing trade deficits centered around the importation of oil from the OPEC countries. The excess dollars that are paid out for the oil, as we saw, are next funneled into the Eurocurrency market and then loaned to the developing countries.

This flow is not in itself bad; on the contrary, it has permitted a rate of industrial development in Latin America, Africa, and Asia that would not have been possible without the creation of this new liquidity. In effect, the process has created a vast redistribution of the world's wealth, with United States profligacy creating an ever-increasing debt structure that has financed the asset growth of the rest of the world. Since much of this debt will probably not be able to be repaid when due, either by the developing countries to the Eurocurrency banks, or by the United States, there will come a time when a massive rescheduling of international debt will have to take place.

We saw in chapter 4 the process by which the U.S. debt has grown since the end of World War II. In this chapter we have examined how the flow of dollars outward from the United States has permitted international trade to grow. We also have seen how this outflow has allowed the OECD countries to pay the many-fold increases in the price of oil, and how it has enabled the developing countries to build up their infrastructures and create the beginnings of an industrial base. Should the Eurocurrency market now be subject to controls? In the author's view, it should not. Controls have always perpetrated, rather than cured, a problem that can better be handled in other ways. At the heart of the problem is not the Eurocurrency system but rather the use of the U.S. dollar in international trade at the same time that the U.S. government refuses to control the amount of its currency in circulation by controlling its own expenditures. If any other nation were involved, the IMF would long ago have been called in to force those budgetary controls necessary to reestablish the balance of trade. If we do not ultimately find the will and the means to control the growth of international liquidity based on the growth of our dollar debt, our capitalistic society, as we have known it since the beginning of the industrial revolution, will be threatened with total collapse.

In this eventuality, the OPEC countries—by increasing the cost of the one product without which an industrial society cannot survive—will also be in a position of having played a key negative role. If a merchant demands for his product a price quite beyond reason, his customer will be tempted to give him in exchange something that has been correspondingly inflated beyond any pretension of real value. Such is the game being played today and the role of the dollar in it. One answer may surely lie in the dollar's replacement in international trade by a new form of currency that is not subject to the control of any one nation. Maximum cooperation in international money matters, as in nearly all international affairs, comes from mutual dependence, with shared responsibility, shared risk-taking, and shared benefits.

6

The Role of International Agencies in Trade

The need to increase the competitiveness of U.S. exports in the world market is clearly crucial to reestablishing the American trade balance. However, no steps taken by government, business, or labor to increase national productivity can succeed in increasing U.S. exports if the world is unable to buy them. No matter how attractive, seductive, or competitively priced U.S. exports are, they cannot be purchased except with cash or on credit. Given the shortage of hard currency or reserves in the developing countries, international institutions of finance play a particularly vital role in financing the growth of these countries' trade.

Many of these developing nations must obtain capital from outside sources in order to finance even the most basic infrastructure projects. Until these projects are completed, they cannot begin to participate in the international trade system, organized as it is around the increasingly competitive exchange of goods, services, and raw materials. This needed capital is available from a variety of sources: commercial banks and other private financial sources; government export-financing institutions of the industrialized countries; bilateral aid programs of the developed and OPEC nations; the International Monetary Fund (IMF); and the credits furnished by the various international financial institutions.

Because developing countries now purchase more U.S. capital goods than do Europe, Japan, and the Eastern Bloc combined, and constitute the United States' fastest growing export market, U.S. goals of export promotion are inextricably tied to the ability of these countries to finance these purchases.[1]

It would, therefore, be inappropriate in a book on international trade to forego reporting on the role of the Multinational Development Banks (MDBs),* which have done so much since the end of World War II to

* This chapter will use the term MDBs to refer to those international organizations that provide multilateral development assistance to promote economic growth in developing countries. It should also be noted that they are often referred to as IFIs (International Financial Institutions).

help the developing countries enter into the mainstream of modern commerce. In many ways the role of these institutions has not been an easy one. In the industrialized world they are considered by too many (including some in the U.S. Congress) to be engaged in redistributing wealth from the "rich" countries to the "poor" countries, to the detriment of working men and women in the former. To the poorer nations, on the other hand, the requirements of the MDBs for financial statistics and the establishment of controls over government expenditures seem far too stringent. As viewed by these countries, the MDBs' money "costs too much," their interference is "too great," and they ought not to "ask so many questions."

As it has turned out, the activities of the MDBs have proved beneficial to both the poorer and richer nations. They are criticized, it sometimes seems, only because they have not found a way to help those who are not willing to help themselves. All in all, the creation of the MDBs must surely be considered one of the successful steps taken by the community of nations since the end of World War II to ensure that gradual economic development and an accompanying growth in trade could indeed be accomplished. The MDBs have performed their roles admirably, with few exceptions, ignoring politics in favor of economics and substituting active loan programs in place of empty rhetoric.

It is indeed the thesis of this chapter that MDBs are essential to the continued development of newly industrialized nations and to the continued expansion of world trade. Although they do not account for the major portion of capital flows to the developing countries, they do represent a significant and, it can be hoped, expanding channel for capital flows between the developed and developing nations. Further, they serve as channels through which the United States and the other industrialized and wealthy nations can effectively promote economic goals on a world scale.

Multilateral credits channeled through the MDBs serve the economic interests of the United States as well as those of other contributing nations. Such credits are particularly helpful to the recipients because they are extended without political strings attached and solely in the interests of economic development. Most often they finance necessary infrastructure projects—ports, transportation facilities, public utilities, etc. Without such infrastructure, trade is almost impossible because the cost of manufacturing and moving goods becomes prohibitive.

Furthermore, as nationalism continues to intensify in many developing nations, multilateral channels tend to serve as more acceptable funnels for development credits than do aid programs from individual donor countries. One can bristle at, yet still accept harsh conditions requiring national discipline from an international organization, whereas such conditions would have to be rejected as an attack on sovereignty if demanded by one particular nation, such as the United States or the USSR.

The World Bank Group

The best known MDB is the World Bank, which actually consists of three related but separate organizations: the International Bank for Reconstruction and Development (IBRD); the International Development Association (IDA); and the International Finance Corporation (IFC). During fiscal 1980, the IBRD, IDA, and IFC combined committed more than $12 billion to the world's developing nations.[2] This represents a twelve-fold increase in lending through the period since Robert McNamara became president of the World Bank in 1968. Table 12 gives a list of the principal borrowers in fiscal year 1979.

The International Bank for Reconstruction and Development (IBRD) is the central institution of all Multinational Development Banks. Founded in 1945, it has a current membership totaling 135 nations. Upon its establishment, the IBRD focused its lending on the reconstruction of Europe and Japan and not, as it is commonly assumed, on development assistance to the less economically developed nations of the world. For instance, the development of the Japanese steel industry after World War II was largely financed by the IBRD. Even as late as 1964, more than one-third of IBRD's loans went to the industrially advanced nations.[3] This emphasis has slowly shifted, however. Throughout the 1960s and early 1970s, the IBRD has aimed primarily at serving as an intermediary between the developed nations and the so-called middle-income nations that were already on the road to development.

These intermediate nations, some forty countries often referred to as the Third World, generally have abundant natural resources, growing though still infant industries, and a rising standard of living. The capital needs of these nations are met very much through private market channels and only supplemented by loans from the MDBs. Past and present large IBRD borrowers include Mexico, Brazil, Indonesia, Spain, and Yugoslavia. (Yugoslavia, Romania, and now the People's Republic of China are the only Communist, nonmarket-economy nations that are members of the World Bank group.)

The loans negotiated between the IBRD and these relatively credit-

Table 12. The twenty largest MDB borrowers in fiscal year 1979 (*In millions of dollars*)

1. India	$1,492	6. Korea	$557	11. Argentina	$371	16. Pakistan	$277
2. Indonesia	1,065	7. Thailand	450	12. Morocco	349	17. Kenya	268
3. Brazil	949	8. Colombia	439	13. Egypt	343	18. Peru	246
4. Mexico	803	9. Bangladesh	386	14. Turkey	313	19. Malaysia	211
5. Philippines	618	10. Yugoslavia	385	15. Romania	295	20. Dominican Republic	197

Source: U.S. Treasury Department, as reported to the U.S. Congress, Senate, Committee on Appropriations, Subcommittee on Foreign Operations, testimony of G. William Miller, Treasury Secretary, 96th Cong., 2nd sess., February 26, 1980.

worthy nations are generally for specific infrastructure projects and are referred to as hard loans, a designation indicating that they carry interest at about the ongoing commercial rate. The funds lent by the IBRD are borrowed in international capital markets,* until recently, primarily in the United States, and are then relent at slightly higher interest rates to the governments of developing countries only for those very specific projects that have been meticulously analyzed by IBRD economists and found to be economically feasible.

The contributions of member nations to the IBRD are relied upon by lenders to support the IBRD's own borrowings in the capital markets. The direct contributions by donor-country governments to the total capital structure of the Bank are small. Only 10 percent of the subscriptions of member nations are actually required to be "paid-in" capital; there is a remaining 90 percent committed as "callable capital," which the donor nation stands ready to supply, should the need arise. To date, no MDB has had to request this callable capital. The charters of all MDBs allow them to issue only those bonds that are fully covered by callable capital. An additional general capital increase has now been proposed to permit an expansion of the World Bank's lending programs.†

Congress has frequently questioned the need for such institutions,‡ since nearly all the funds actually loaned out are supplied by existing

* At the beginning of 1980, the World Bank had $28 billion of debt outstanding, of which less than $7 billion was held in the United States. $8 billion was held by governments, with the largest holders being Saudi Arabia, Venezuela, West Germany, Japan, Yugoslavia, Nigeria, and Iran.

† This would increase the capital of the Bank from $40 billion to $80 billion. The U.S. share of the increase would be $8.4 billion. But, of course, most of this increase will only be callable.

‡ The Congress too often stands reluctant to accept the importance of participating in international undertakings where the United States does not control policy or investment. The International Labor Organization (ILO), to which both Poland and the Soviet Union

international capital markets. Although it might seem a less complicated arrangement to have the client countries arrange loans directly from those supplying the capital, such a system would not work in practice. By lending through the MDB, institutional lenders in the principal capital markets are willing to supply funds for development that they otherwise would refuse to lend if it meant lending directly to a developing country. Besides opening up such channels for capital, MDBs also help both lenders and developing countries by making sure that the funds are used for the most credit-worthy and beneficial projects.

Another type of loan, the concessional or soft loan, is offered by another member of the World Bank Group—the International Development Association. The IDA was created in 1960 to aid the poorest developing countries by offering special loans (officially referred to as credits in order to differentiate them from the loans offered by the IBRD) on very favorable terms. These soft loans are available to nations that have a per capita gross national product below $520 in 1975 dollars.[4] These countries, which account for more than 1 billion of the world's population, are commonly referred to as the Fourth World. Their economies are generally stagnant, there is massive illiteracy and endemic hunger, and their needs obviously differ from those of the Third World countries.

As of January, 1981, there were 120 member nations in the IDA. Unlike the IBRD, the resources of the IDA are totally dependent on donor-country contributions, since the lenient terms of the IDA's credit make it impossible to raise the necessary funds in the international capital markets.* IDA credits, made only to government or government-guaranteed projects, generally have ten-year grace periods with fifty-year maturities and no interest, although there is an annual service charge of 0.75 percent on the disbursed portion of each credit.[5]

In the last few years, both the IBRD and the IDA have changed the focus of their lending to apply greater emphasis on human needs. This

belong, is an interesting case in point. Shortly after World War II, an American director general of the organization, David Morse, was instrumental in obtaining passage of a regulation to which all members subscribed, establishing the right of workers freely to associate in labor unions. When Poland's Solidarity was organized in 1980, the Supreme Court of Poland was able to point to this agreement as justifying the attempt by Polish workers to organize a union of their choice. This ILO agreement may in time be recognized as one of the landmarks in the recognition of human rights and underlines the importance of active participation by the U.S. government in international organizations dedicated to human or economic development, even where the United States can exercise no veto power over policy.

* There is, unfortunately, great reluctance in Congress to continue to provide funds for the IDA. The United States has been in default on its contribution and is trying to stretch out payment of its past-due contributions over a period of years.

has meant increased lending for projects that deal with agriculture, health, education, and population control. For example, total lending in 1973 by the World Bank Group for agriculture amounted to $1 billion. In 1978, this rose to $3 billion. Basic needs thus continue to have priority in determining which projects are funded.[6]

The third and final member of the World Bank Group is the International Finance Corporation (IFC), with membership, as of January, 1981, of 108 countries. Established in 1956 to promote the growth of the private sector in developing counries, this effort is directed primarily toward the mobilization of domestic and foreign investment capital from others, but often also includes modest loans and direct equity investment of its own.

It is useful to recap briefly how the World Bank Group functions and what new policy trends can be discerned. It has been noted that for the first twenty-odd years the IBRD, the hard-loan member of the group and the one lending only to credit-worthy borrowers, made infrastructure and basic-industry loans to developed nations that had to rebuild industrial bases that had been destroyed in World War II. Client countries in this period included Britain, West Germany, Austria, Italy, and Japan. In the past fifteen years, the IBRD has gradually shifted its focus to the so-called intermediate developing countries: Brazil, Mexico, Taiwan, India, Yugoslavia, Malaysia, and Indonesia. In each of these countries, important factors—the size of the country, its natural resources, the educational level of the population, the existence of some advanced level of infrastructure already in place, and a government receptive to large-scale public projects—were found to create a climate appropriate for IBRD project financing. For those countries not yet ready to participate in such large-scale project financings—the so-called Fourth World countries—the IDA grants soft loans on extremely concessionary terms in the hope that by gradually raising the standard of living of these countries, a point will be reached at which IDA credits can be phased out and the countries brought into the IBRD development phase, with credits repayable at market rates and on more normal terms.

The logic of the program is indisputable. But has the program worked out as well as expected? Only in part. Rapid industrialization has been found to bring on other major problems, not the least of which is the rapid flow of people out of the agricultural areas and toward the cities in search of jobs in newly established factories.* As a result, the World

*This problem is discussed in detail in chapter 8.

Bank Group has now begun to focus more attention on agricultural development.

Complementing the work of the World Bank Group are the various Regional Development Banks (RDBs). Although many of their functions overlap those of the IBRD, IDA, and IFC, they have developed more narrowly focused geographic expertise that enhances the value of their work. There are three RDBs to which the United States contributes: InterAmerican Development Bank (IDB), the Asian Development Bank (ADB), and the African Development Fund (AFDF).*

InterAmerican Development Bank (IDB)

The InterAmerican Development Bank was established in 1959 to aid the Latin American nations in their development goals. Initially, the IDB focused on social projects, which up to then had not been funded by the IBRD. The original members were the United States and the Latin American nations, with the capital of the bank supplied largely by the U.S. government. American influence over the bank has always been strong. The Latin American countries were to state what projects they wanted funded and submit appropriate studies where their nominees on the bank staff would review these projects. As is to be expected under such circumstances, there was a good deal of behind-the-scenes trading among the various governments, which ensured that each country got its "share of the pie" based on its power within the Latin American community and its political standing at the moment with the U.S. government.

In a reverse of what is happening with the World Bank Group, the IDB is now beginning to direct more of its resources toward industrial and infrastructure projects.[7] Unlike the World Bank, the IDB relies much more on the suggestions of its Latin American nation-borrowers in selecting the development projects to be financed. Like the the World Bank's IDA, the IDB has a soft-loan window, established in 1965, which is known as the Fund for Special Operations (FSO). Until 1976, only those Western Hemisphere nations that were also members of the Orga-

* There are other regional development banks of which the United States is not a member. Several of the larger MDBs in this category include the East African Development Bank, the Caribbean Development Bank, the Central American Bank for Economic Integration, and the Andean Development Corporation. Also, the various groups set up by the OPEC nations fall into this category. These include the OPEC Special Fund and the Arab Bank for Economic Development in Africa.

nization of American States (OAS) were permitted to join the IDB; in 1976, however, twelve nonregional members were allowed to join.[8]

An analysis of the IDB and its operations shows just what makes the World Bank Group function so effectively and why the IDB is relatively ineffective as an institution. The World Bank does not rely on its constituency for analyses; it has an extremely capable staff of loan officers and economists from all over the world who not only have many years of experience in the analysis of development projects in various countries but also have years of experience observing why one type project has worked out well in the past and another has not. In this way the World Bank works not only as an institution that produces good results at an international level; it also provides an extraordinary learning experience and serves as a training ground for highly educated nationals who may then return to their own countries to direct economic planning ministries, central banks, or ministries of finance. The IDB, on the other hand, relies on its client countries to produce the studies on the projects they want, and it has only a very limited staff of its own to determine independently whether a project is indeed feasible.

The reason for this difference is that the *raison d' etre* of the IDB, in contrast with that of the World Bank, was *political* accommodation rather than strict economic development, and the two thrusts, as has been repeatedly noted in this study, do not mix well.* One wonders, without in any way denigrating the dedicated service of the IDB board or staff, whether it might not be better to have this organization merged into the World Bank. Such a move, of course, is highly improbable, since any international organization, successful or not, develops its own political constituency.†

* The extent of American participation in the IDB, particularly its dominant management role, has had the perhaps unfortunate effect of fostering development in Latin America patterned after the United States, resulting in undue emphasis on costly capital projects that have created levels of indebtedness too high for the debtor country to absorb. IDB financing has tended to focus on projects involving massive imports of capital goods (mostly from the United States) rather than on the implementation of national export development projects. As a result, the countries of Latin America have become increasingly indebted. These debts in time must be repaid by exports of agricultural products or raw materials, leaving no proceeds of exports to develop indigenous cottage industries or small-scale farming. For an interesting discussion of this "dependency theory," with particular reference to Costa Rica, *see,* R. Peter De Witt, Jr., *The Inter-American Development Bank and Political Influences,* (New York, Praeger, 1977).

† Ironically, because of the greater U.S. role in the IDB, the Congress is more inclined to fund the IDB than the World Bank.

Regional Development Banks

In 1966, the United States played a key role in the establishment of the Asian Development Bank (ADB). Its membership numbers forty-one and includes nations from Asia, Europe, and North America. It was created to aid Asian nations stabilize their domestic economies so that they might better resist external pressures and bring stability to the area. Like the IBRD, the greater part of ADB work is done through conventional or hard loans designed to develop infrastructure. The ADB also has the Asian Development Fund, established in 1974 as a soft-loan window, like the IDA and the FSO, for the poorer nations. Perhaps because of Japanese influence within this Bank, the ADB is viewed as the most conservative of the regional development banks, and it continues to place heavy emphasis on the least risky projects in the more credit-worthy Asian nations.

A final regional institution which the United States contributes is the African Development Fund (AFDF). As with the other MDBs, the AFDF is a concessional lending affiliate of the African Development Bank (AFDB). The African Development Bank allows only African nations to be members; however, in 1973 the AFDF was established and non-African nations were urged to join.

One wonders here again whether there is a real need today for MDBs organized on a regional basis. Instead of concentrating on a limited geographical area, would it not be preferable to focus our thinking on global rather than regional interdependence? We have only to look at the difficulties experienced by the Andean Pact countries of Latin America in trying to work out trade relationships where the economies are similar rather than complementary. With communication and transportation facilities what they are today, there should be no difficulty in handling development planning on a global rather than a regional basis.

MDBs Versus Other Sources of Capital

As noted, in every MDB that makes conventional or hard loans, the donor nations do not supply all the funds to be made available but make only an original capital contribution against which the MDB itself borrows in the capital markets. This is not true of the MDBs that make concessional or soft loans.* These are funded directly through contributions

* The difference is made clear by reference to Table 13, which gives the fiscal year 1981 appropriations requests to Congress for the MDBs.

Table 13. Fiscal year 1981 appropriations request for the multilateral development banks (*In millions of dollars*)

International Bank for Reconstruction and Development	$ 20.0
International Development Association	1,080.0
InterAmerican Development Bank	
Capital	51.5
Fund for Special Operations	318.0
Asian Development Bank	
Capital	25.2
Asian Development Fund	111.3
African Development Bank	18.0
African Development Fund	41.7
Total MDB	$1,665.7

Source: U.S. Treasury Department, as reported to the U.S. Congress, Senate, Committee on Appropriations, Subcommittee on Foreign Operations, testimony of G. William Miller, Treasury Secretary, 96th Cong., 2nd sess., February, 26, 1980.

made by the donor nations, and frequent replenishments are required. This, in turn, stimulates periodic debate in the U.S. Congress on the virtues of multilateral over bilateral aid. To answer the question of which best serves the U.S. national interest one must first determine the overall benefits of MDB loans versus other sources of credits available to the Third and Fourth World nations.

MDBs do not represent the only source of capital for developing countries; nor do they represent the largest. In 1974 MDB assistance represented only about 12 percent of the total net capital flows to developing nations, private financial markets about 34 percent.[9] Could these other sources, i.e., commercial banks for hard loans and bilateral aid for soft loans, replace MDB lending? The interest-rate differential between commercial lending and conventional MDB lending is relatively insignificant; except where the size of a project dictates a long payback period, commercial lending remains an attractive alternative to MDB loans for the higher-income developing countries. Following the 1974 OPEC oil price increase, the high-income developing nations generally chose to finance the increased cost of oil imports by borrowing in the commercial markets. The poorer nations had to go to alternatives (i.e., IMF loans and bilateral grants, etc.)[10] largely because they needed the longer repayment term.

Unlike the relatively minor differences between conventional MDB loans and commercial loans, the differences between bilateral aid and

MDB soft loans are substantial. Both bilateral aid and replenishments to MDBs for soft loans are controlled by Congress, which must decide which channel best serves U.S. national interests.

While the economic difference between bilateral aid and conventional multilateral lending through the MDB is negligible, the political differences are clear. When appropriating money for further MDB soft-loan funding, Congress is clearly concerned that it has no control over the ultimate use of these funds. Quite expectedly, the developing countries find multilateral aid generally more predictable than bilateral aid and not subject to the political strings frequently attached by the donor country in the case of bilateral aid.

However, attempts by the U.S. government to impose conditions on MDB lending through its executive directors or to refuse to provide future contributions have been counterproductive. Recent attempts, for example, by the United States to impose human rights criteria on MDB loans have not been tolerated by these institutions. As a result, such restrictions have actually limited the influence of the United States in determining which projects are finally approved, thereby reducing U.S. participation in the important process of economic development. Although clearly the United States would better serve its own national *economic* goals, as well as those of the recipient nations, by abandoning its effort to exercise *political* pressure on the various MDBs, the congressional debate over the relative merits of bilateral aid and MDB assistance is sure to continue, with Congress likely to reduce its MDB commitment in the future in favor of mixed credits for exports.*

MDB "Subsidies" to U.S. Competitors

Some members of the U.S. Congress have been critical of the MDBs for several reasons. One focus of their attack has been MDB financing of projects designed to expand production of certain agricultural commodities in the LDCs. Legislation passed by Congress in October, 1977 has required that the U.S. executive director to the MDBs vote against loans for projects that would expand the export-oriented production of palm oil, sugar, or citrus fruits if U.S. producers of those commodities would be hurt by such expanded production.[11] The argument has been made that MDB loans booked at better than commercial bank terms amount

* A mixed credit, frequently used by the French government as a means of financing large French export transactions, involves a government export-financing transaction combined with a very low interest, very long-term aid loan.

to a subsidy to foreign producers that puts U.S. producers at an unfair disadvantage.[12]

In compliance with this legislation, the Department of Treasury and the Department of Agriculture conducted special analyses of fifteen proposed MDB loans during fiscal year 1978, six involving palm oil, five involving sugar, and four involving citrus fruits. Opposition to the proposed loan was recommended in only two cases. In most of the other cases it was found that the project would increase production primarily for domestic consumption in the country involved, not export.

The two loans the Unites States opposed, for a sugar project in Swaziland and a palm oil project in Malaysia, were approved nonetheless by the board of executive directors, thus needlessly subjecting the United States to criticism by both donor countries and developing countries. The Malaysian palm oil project was opposed because it was thought that it would exert a downward pressure on oil prices and thus have an adverse effect on U.S. soybean-oil producers. The sugar project loan was opposed not because of any feared threat to U.S. producers but because the project was not deemed viable due to the depressed state of the world sugar market.[13]

Despite the fact that the United States has opposed only one loan on the grounds that it would constitute a subsidy for those in competition with U.S. producers—a loan that was approved anyway—the attitude motivating the U.S. legislation has generated much criticism. The tying of the U.S. executive director's vote to U.S. commercial interests has been seen as an inappropriate politicization of a multilateral institution.[14] Similar sentiments have been voiced at the annual meetings of the World Bank's board of governors.[15] It would appear that the congressional mandate to oppose loans for certain MDB commodity projects gives Americans producers little protection at a high price to U.S. credibility.

A second factor to be considered in the matter of MDB loans for sugar, palm oil, and citrus fruit projects is that by reducing the price of specific food products certain U.S. producers may be harmed, but the U.S. consumer benefits. That the Congress is more concerned when it comes to palm oil than to crude oil merely confirms that agricultural producers are a much more important political constituency than domestic oil producers.

In the end, assuming that these MDB-financed projects are successful in raising incomes in the developing countries, U.S. food exporters in general will stand to gain much more than they can possibly lose. Information supplied to Congress by the U.S. executive director at the World

Bank explains the direct correlation between higher LDC incomes and increased food exports by the United States.

> Higher economic growth in the developing countries brought about an increase in food consumption, production, and imports. As the world's largest agricultural exporter, the United States has been in a unique position to capitalize on this situation. That is why U.S. agricultural exports to these countries grew from $2 billion to $10 billion in the past decade, and it explains why the developing countries are likely to be one of the fastest growing agricultural markets throughout the rest of the century.[16]

An additional factor diminishing the effectiveness of U.S. efforts to curtail world commodity production by opposing certain MDB loans is the significant time delay between the approval of an MDB loan for a sugar, palm oil, or citrus fruit project and the sale of commodities from these projects to the world market. For instance, palm oil supplies would not reach the market for some ten years after a project loan is approved.[17]

Because the legislation designed to protect certain U.S. commodity producers against what are considered MDB "subsidies" is of dubious effect, because it may work to the disadvantage of both U.S. food exporters and U.S. consumers, because it opens the country to the charge of attempting to use the MDBs for its own protectionist interests, and because U.S. opposition on these narrow grounds is overruled anyway by the other MDB executive directors, it would be wise for the U.S. Congress to reconsider the position it has taken.

This reconsideration, however, seems not to be in the cards. On the contrary, some members of Congress have expressed a desire to extend the legislation in order to bar MDB loans that would finance steel production and textile manufacturing,[18] contending that the MDB loans, in effect, subsidize competition to U.S. steel and textile producers.

It may be useful at this juncture to note the significant influence of the United States at the Multinational Development Banks and that to be overriden it must take a position that attracts the support of virtually none of the other members. The United States currently holds 22 percent of the shares of the World Bank and therefore controls that percentage of voting power. While this does not provide a veto over individual projects, it does give the U.S. executive director power to veto major changes in World Bank policy and changes in its charter. Similarly, at the IDB, the U.S. executive director controls 42.05 percent of the vote, which, while not giving it a veto over ordinary loans, does mean veto power over the IDB's soft-loan window, the FSO.

However, the preponderant influence of the United States at these MDBs does not appear likely to last over the long term. The recovery of Western Europe since World War II, the more recent emergence of higher-income LDCs, and the growing political voice of the Third World generally has resulted in some relative decline in U.S. influence. The leaders of the Third World have been pushing for a greater "universality" of World Bank membership and a revised voting schedule that would give more power to OPEC and other non-Western members. Also, there have been discussions about expanding the funding of the MDBs by such means as a global tax on multinational corporations or a tax on sea-bed mining. These mechanisms would remove the power of the purse over MDB operations from such national legislatures as the U.S. Congress.[19]

MDBs and U.S. Exports

The United States has enjoyed certain direct economic benefits from its participation in the MDBs. According to a study commissioned by the Treasury Department:

> Accumulated receipts by all segments of the U.S. economy have exceeded outflows by $2.4 billion from the time of the inception of the MDBs to the middle of 1978. This figure constitutes the net cumulative balance-of-payments effect encompassing merchandise and service exports by the U.S. as a consequence of MDB lending to LDCs, U.S. Government contributions and subscriptions to MDBs, and the latter's portfolio capital flows (investment less borrowing) into the U.S. capital markets.[20]

Participation in the MDBs has created 50,000 to 100,000 jobs in the United States, directly through the supplying of MDB-financed procurements and indirectly as an effect of increased exports to LDCs made possible through financing by the MDBs.[21] In real terms, the U.S. Gross National Product has increased annually by $2.40 to $3.40 for each U.S. dollar contributed to the MDBs.[22] Measured in purely economic terms then, the United States is receiving more from the MDBs than it is putting in. This must be understood in the context that, cumulatively through 1979, the United States—which supplies almost 23 percent of the capital—drew approximately 18 percent of the total export business from member countries that had been made possible by World Bank financing.

Table 14. Cumulative U.S. procurement through June 30, 1978

MDB-financed projects	Total of procurements contracts (*In millions of dollars*) United States	All other nations	U.S. share (*As percentage of total*)
InterAmerican Development Bank/Fund for Special Operations	$1,701.9	$3,467.9	46
International Bank for Reconstruction and Development/International Development Association	6,503.0	33,586.7	16
Asian Development Bank/ Asian Development Fund[a]	178.6	2,304.9	7

Source: Computed from figures released by the National Advisory Council, *1978 Annual Report,* for first two MDBs; for third MDB, Asian Development Bank.

[a] Figures include consulting services.

Table 14 indicates how successful U.S. exporters have been in winning procurement contracts in MDB-financed projects.*

Claims have been made that executive directors from countries other than the United States have been instructed to give a hand to developing nations that are considering large projects, with an eye to recommending their own nations as suppliers. Also, some directors have been active in recommending to their home capitals that their own nationals do feasibility studies for the bank on the premise that knowledge of technical details and the writing of specifications will give their home suppliers an important advantage. It has been suggested that the U.S. executive directors, in a like manner, play a more active role in aiding U.S. firms to get contracts for MDB-financed projects.

However, rather than asking U.S. executive directors to adopt such a practice, it would be more desirable that such activities on the part of others be curtailed and the guidelines for international competitive bidding be more strictly enforced. The interests of the U.S. government in its dealing with the MDBs do not necessarily always coincide with the interests of U.S. business. The U.S. executive director's responsibility to his country's "investment" in the MDBs ought to focus on seeing that these funds are used wisely and in the best interests of the bank's clients. In

* Information on projects being considered for MDB loans is available from a number of sources: U.S. Treasury and Commerce Departments reports; World Bank, IDB, and ADB monthly operating summaries; the United Nations.[23]

addition, he ought to take account of the fact that the U.S. role in the MDBs reflects the nation's posture toward the Third World. Given these economic, political, and diplomatic concerns, any attempt by the U.S. executive director to act as a commercial attaché as well as the representative of the U.S. government is simply not feasible. It would appear that other means should be found to involve more U.S. firms in MDB-financed projects than using the U.S. executive directors in sales-promotion activities.*

MDBs and Energy

Since the sharp rise in OPEC oil prices, most of the non-OPEC LDCs have been hard pressed to pay for their petroleum imports. The effects on these LDCs have been grave. In the poorer nations, imported oil is vital to the operation of agricultural machinery; trucks, tractors, and gasoline-powered irrigation wells are necessary for crop production and the transport of produce to markets. In the wealthier, more advanced LDCs, rapid industrialization creates a need for increased energy both in terms of electricity and power, driving up energy consumption in these LDCs at a much faster rate than it is rising in the developed countries.[24] The increase in oil prices thus results in diverting scarce foreign exchange from other development projects.

The need to find reserves of oil and gas in the developing countries is clear. The question is how to accomplish this. In many LDCs, governments have been reluctant to deal with the international oil companies—particularly the majors. The fear, based in part upon past practices of these companies, is that the oil or gas will indeed be discovered but that the reserves will then be exported from the country instead of sold within the country, leaving the local government with neither product nor with adequate compensation for its export. As a result, many countries have created state-owned oil companies. These, however, generally do not have entrepreneurial managements or access to the technical expertise needed in oil exploration.†

Under these circumstances there is only a limited role which the World

*The Treasury and Commerce Department, the National Association of Manufacturers, and the U.S. Chamber of Commerce can do the job more effectively and without compromising the multinational character of the executive directors' role.

†Some authors do claim that governments in the LDCs are better equipped to solve their nation's energy problems than are private businesses.[25] The views expressed are similar to those expressed by the Carter Administration with respect to solving the energy problem in the United States.

Bank can play but it can certainly be of great assistance in two areas. Expertise developed by the World Bank staff in assisting one country through proper resource planning can frequently be useful in developing the resources in a neighboring country that may not yet have given thought to more rapid development of its energy potential. The World Bank can also give financial support for projects related to the infrastructure needed for the proper development of energy resources: pipelines, refineries, hydroelectric projects such as that at Itaipu in Brazil*—all generally very expensive and requiring very long term financing at fixed rates. With such assured financing, the technology can be purchased from various sources through international bidding procedures customarily used in capital equipment procurement.

The use of World Bank funds for geophysical studies or for exploration, or even for development projects in oil or gas, unless granted only to highly sophisticated, relatively independent state oil companies in the LDCs, appears much more questionable. Inherent risk-taking involved in exploration would better be left in the hands of private sector entrepreneurs willing to assume such risks. However, as has been indicated, the World Bank staff can be of help to local governments in making sure that negotiations for exploration or development contracts are fair to both parties and will result in 1. adequate compensation to the local government in taxes and royalties, 2. protection of the environment, 3. proper development of any resources developed, 4. adequate distribution of oil and gas within the country.

The plans of the Bank for energy assistance to the LDCs have been very ambitious. They encompass some $4 billion in loans over a four-year period ending in 1983, 40 percent for exploration and 60 percent toward production facilities.[26]

The Reagan Administration has indicated that it has some reservations about the World Bank's energy assistance program and this program may be restructured after the Bank's new president takes over in July, 1981. It cannot be said, however, that the Bank's program was not carefully developed after a good deal of effort and very careful study.†

* This hydroelectric project on the Parana River between Brazil and Paraguay will, when completed, provide enough electrical energy to fill 78 percent of what were Brazil's needs in 1980.

† In August, 1980 the World Bank published a study entitled *Energy in the Developing Countries* with interesting material on the possibilities in Latin America for oil and gas exploration: tar sands (Peru), heavy oils (Peru, Venezuela, Colombia), oil shale (Brazil), enhanced-recovery projects (Ecuador, Colombia, Peru), exploration (Argentina, Brazil and Chile).

Role of the International Monetary Fund (IMF)

International financing organizations other than the World Bank that play an important role in the financing of international trade are the International Monetary Fund (IMF) and the Bank for International Settlements (BIS). (Relatively little is known about the BIS outside the world's central banks, which it is designed to serve.)

The IMF, founded at Bretton Woods in 1945, has played a key role in maintaining the world's monetary balance and has been an absolutely necessary part of the international trade mechanism. The stated purpose of the IMF is to furnish funds to countries that find themselves in "temporary disequilibrium" for balance-of-payments reasons (a euphemism for the lack of foreign exchange or other reserves with which to pay for essential imports). If a country cannot pay with its foreign exchange, or if its currency is not convertible and it has no reserves (gold or SDRs), it must rely on credit (i.e., borrowings in foreign exchange, generally dollars, because the dollar is still the key currency in international trade).

Suppose, however, that the commercial banks refuse to advance any more credit. The country cannot apply to the World Bank because the loan would not be for projects but for straight import credits for such items as food, spare parts, day-to-day capital equipment, etc. It is in this instance that the country must apply to the IMF for help. The only other choice would be to go the route of bilateral loans, as Italy did several years ago with West Germany. Bilateral loans, however, often have political strings attached.

The IMF has the great advantage that it is apolitical. When necessary, it does apply rigorous conditions on its loans but the conditions are formulated to satisfy economic rather than political criteria; in setting these conditions the IMF treats rich and poor nations alike. The rules that might be applied to Britain, Italy, or any other "developed" country in difficulty would be no less stringent than those faced by Peru, Turkey, or Zaire. Furthermore, since the IMF is often called in to help when social programs that are highly popular with the electorate but have been disastrous for a country's budget, inflation rate, or balance of payments, it is most convenient for the local government to be able to blame the unpopular imposition of disciplines that reverse or restrict these programs on a financing institution, and a foreign one at that.

The IMF rules are relatively simple. Funds are made available after experts have examined the situation and insisted upon import restrictions, inflation controls, wage stabilization, and an end to further foreign-bank borrowings until the nation's balance-of-payments equilibrium has been restored. This may take anywhere from one to five years but the fund monitors its client's health carefully in the meantime, and even more important, makes its credits available in successive transactions carefully matched with economic reforms promised by the borrower. In certain cases, as for example in Zaire, the fund insists that someone acceptable to it (generally a technician from some outside central bank) is brought in to supervise the activities of the country's central bank and, indirectly, its ministry of finance. Under these circumstances, the country is generally cooperative in reversing its balance-of-payments difficulties and in repaying its IMF credits because it wants to recapture its financial sovereignty.

In the 1973–74 period, following the big OPEC oil price increases, the developing countries with limited oil production but growing petroleum needs faced very difficult balance-of-payments problems. In 1979, many of these nations, which in many cases had only just adjusted to the prior fuel increase, faced the same troubles again. Fortunately, funds available to the IMF had been substantially increased in 1978, and several countries, including the United States, Saudi Arabia, and Kuwait, were contributing substantial amounts to the IMF's "Witteveen facility," named after the chairman at the time, who had successfully urged that the fund be given additional financial support.

The IMF is thus performing a very necessary function today in adjusting individual countries' economies to balance-of-payments difficulties caused by too many imports or too few exports. Congress is to be commended for funding the U.S.'s increased participation in the IMF.[28]

The OPEC oil price increases of 1979–80—the second oil shock—has now caused the World Bank and the IMF to rethink carefully what changes should be made in their programs to address the special problems of those developing countries that are importers of oil. In the case of the IMF the question has been to what extent it should relax its conditions for loans now that the balance-of-payments problems of the oil-importing LDCs have so worsened and the problem of foreign exchange shortages has become endemic instead of temporary. Through the Supplementary Financing Facility—which provides for a 50 percent increase in total quotas*—the IMF has had sufficient funds available to meet its

* Member nations agreed to this quota increase in December, 1978. This increase raised the U.S. quota by SDR 4,202 million (about $5.5 billion) to SDR 12,607.5 million. The value of SDR varies, but is based on the value of a basket of currencies of five countries: United States, West Germany, Japan, France, United Kingdom.

commitments. But its conditions have remained strict and, as a result, some countries in difficulties have preferred to borrow from the commercial banks rather than meet the conditions of the Fund.*

Pressure from the developing countries for additional help has caused the IBRD to consider whether it should not provide loans for balance-of-payments purposes. Thus, one member of the World Bank group is now proposed as a substitute for another, even though that was not its intended purpose. President McNamara of the IBRD has suggested that this be done through a program of so-called "Lending for Structural Adjustment,"[29] to assist countries in severe balance-of-payments difficulties. Despite the very real need it is designed to meet, the proposal raises many problems. If the IBRD supplements the IMF's activities, countries will be even more reluctant to borrow from the IMF for balance-of-payments assistance because its conditions are more strict. In effect the IBRD will have diverted its own efforts and funds from project development to current general-purpose loans totally unrelated to country development. It is to be hoped that the World Bank's new president, A. W. Clausen, will see the importance of maintaining the functional distinction between goals of the Bank and those of the Fund, and that he will be able to obtain the support of the U.S. government toward this end. It would be a grave error to meld the functions of two organizations that have performed their disparate roles with such rare distinction.

Some academics have recommended the creation of new institutions to fill the gap in financing by MDBs.† The United Nations would also like to play a role. UNIDO is working on just such a proposal for a new international institution borrowing short term to lend long term for international investment in developing countries. This would result in the creation of one more international bureaucracy to supplement an activity already very adequately performed by the World Bank Group.

The Bank for International Settlements (BIS)

What of this other, more mysterious, financial institution—the Bank for International Settlements?

The beginning of the BIS dates back to 1928, when a group of central bankers and finance ministers, along with American commercial and in-

* Perhaps the clearest example was the Jamaican government's decision in 1980 under Prime Minister Manley to abandon efforts to borrow from the IMF and face election instead. His successor, Edward Seaga, is now negotiating again with the IMF.

† See, for example, Stephen Fromens, "Why the IMS is Increasing Its Roles in Recycling," *Euromoney,* January, 1981, p. 123.

vestment bankers, decided that an international financial organization should be formed to monitor the payment of war debts imposed on the Central Powers following their defeat in World War I.* We need concern ourselves here only with its current role in international trade and how that role, if deemed helpful in today's international trade climate, might be usefully expanded.

As presently constituted, the BIS has a small working staff headquartered in Basel, Switzerland that reports each month to its executive board, made up of central bankers from Western Europe together with observers from several other countries, including the United States. In 1980, its chairman was a well known Dutch banker, its vice-chairman—effectively chairman of the working committees of the Bank and its staff director—a former chairman of the Bank of England. Constituting almost a club of central bankers, including representatives from Eastern Europe and such nonaligned countries as Yugoslavia, these men are in a unique position to monitor what loans are made by the commercial banks that they help regulate and control and to give help to other central bankers who may have problems to resolve, either in the operations of individual regulatory systems or in areas with broader global implications.

Let us give some examples of the role that this very professional group plays. The Herstatt bank failure in Germany in 1975 could have been prevented had a mechanism then existed to monitor and report commercial transactions in the foreign exchange markets. Such a situation could not occur again because the BIS has set up a monitoring system that will pick up and report any unusual positions in the foreign exchange markets. Where commercial banks, acting individually in a number of different countries, extend lines of credit to banks or government industries in a developing country, these, too, will be monitored by the BIS and questions will be asked within the group to determine whether or not such activity represents an undue risk to the banking system. The reason the system functions so effectively is that, in a world with too little exchange of official information among central bankers, the BIS serves as a working forum of communication for the professionals who make the most important financial and monetary decisions in the key money-center countries.

Would it not be desirable, given the good job done by these international banking professionals, to extend their jurisdiction so that they

* The history of the BIS, as recorded by its former chairman, is a fascinating story. *See, BIS Annual Report,* 1937.

might offer assistance in the same quiet, apolitical way to their counterparts in the developing nations who may not yet have the equivalent knowledge, training, or experience? In view of the caliber of the BIS staff, it should be relatively easy to make appropriate recommendations without in any way involving issues of national sovereignty or political interference. Let us carry this idea one step further and indicate that it might not be amiss for the BIS to provide, through its central bank members, information that would guide the private commercial banking sector in making credit decisions involving developing nations. This organization is well equipped to prescribe the precise preventive medicine needed to make international credit mechanisms work more smoothly in the future without in any way raising the spectre of political interference or attempts to dictate trade, fiscal, or financial policy to individual countries.

This completes our analysis of the Multinational Development Banks and similar institutions. These organizations are performing a vital function by helping to boost international trade, and should be given increased support within the United States and an expanded role in the ways noted. As government officials in both developed and developing countries come to understand more fully that increased international trade is the only solution for the evils of poverty and armed conflict, the role of these institutions should continue to expand, to the benefit of rich and poor countries alike. After all, no matter how fine the product or how efficiently it was produced, one cannot sell to those who are not in a position to buy because they have nothing to offer in exchange.

7

Development of International Rules on Trade

> Free trade, one of the greatest blessings which a government can confer on a people, is in almost every country unpopular.
>
> THOMAS BABINGTON (Baron Macauley)

> There is no more deadly device against the price mechanism than the quota system, and its general use would blow up the capitalist system as a whole.
>
> JACQUES RUEFF, *The Age of Inflation.*

In this chapter, we will analyze the attempts by the nations principally engaged in international trade to set up agreed-upon rules under which products from one country may enter another country even though the entering goods may be in competition with quality, price, or service in products manufactured in that second country. Devising such a universally acceptable set of rules is not as easy to accomplish as it may sound to be. Nations have always sought to protect their domestic manufacturers. Most often, historically, governments have tried to favor new domestic industries that might not get started if they had to compete with long-established foreign producers abroad; also, more recently, governments have acted to protect domestic employment or to maintain or restore favorable balances of trade.

At the end of World War II, certain European nations resolved with the United States to establish an international code of conduct that would govern international trade among themselves and, by virtue of their key positions in international trade, among all nations. The first compact, "The General Agreement on Tariffs and Trade" (GATT), was signed in Geneva, Switzerland in 1947. It called for international cooperation, reciprocity, and nondiscrimination in international trade, and it established agreed-upon codes of conduct as well as ground rules for such trade.

GATT also established a framework for further trade and tariff liberalizations, which led to seven successive rounds of multilateral trade negotiations. By the end of the Kennedy Round in 1967, the weighted average tariff for the major trading nations had been reduced to 7.7 percent on all industrial products, 9.8 percent on finished manufactured products, 8 percent on semifinished products, and 2 percent on raw materials.[1]

At the time GATT was established, right after World War II, the United States had most of the wealth and the industrial capacity in the world. It was necessary and logical then that the United States agree to keep its own tariffs low so that European producers could supply goods to the United States in exchange for the U.S. dollars without which they would be unable to participate in trade. Since wage rates were substantially lower in Europe, and the United States, as a matter of policy, was eager to participate in the industrial reconstruction of Europe, the initial rules were essentially those that the Europeans wanted, with little concern paid to protecting United States industries from European competition. The basic premise was that the Europeans might keep their tariffs generally higher to protect the industrial base they now had to recreate, while the United States, having a productive capacity untouched by war, could well accept the entry of foreign products into its vast and rapidly growing domestic market. In any event, imports amounted to only a small portion of U.S. trade.

Unfortunately for the United States, the world did not stand still; other nations joined the GATT—Japan and those from other parts of the European basin—and they too demanded the same relationship with the United States and obtained it. Simultaneously, with newly built plants and the latest equipment, the countries of OECD started to make substantial headway in rebuilding their industrial bases. By the early 1960s they had become formidable competitors.

But as often happens, conditions change faster than the rules that govern them and few of the countries doing so well by these rules showed any inclination to modify them after the world situation had changed in their favor.* A first indication of how difficult it would be to change the rules so as to make them more equitable for the United States was given during the Kennedy Round in the 1960s. By the time the next round, the Tokyo Round, began in 1973, the Americans realized that substantial changes would have to be made to avoid increased political pressure at

* Indeed, as we shall stress elsewhere in this book, the United States now finds itself, in 1981, under intense pressure to reverse its free-trade policy of the last thirty-five years and succumb to protectionism to protect its industry from Japanese competition.

home for protection of those U.S. industries that were no longer competitive. The Vance Hartke Bill of 1974 reflected this growing pressure on the part of labor unions and their friends in Congress to protect America from those imports thought to represent the toughest competition—those coming from low-wage areas of the world. After six years of tedious and, at times, discouraging negotiations, the Tokyo Round was finally concluded in 1979 to take effect January 1, 1980.

We shall examine in this chapter what exactly was achieved in these negotiations and what the results may portend for the future. In doing this we shall have to bear in mind two changes in the scenario that the participants could not have foreseen when negotiations began. The first is that the United States is no longer a high-wage country; hourly wages for time worked here are fully in line with those of our principal competitors in the industrialized countries. But American productivity has been steadily declining in comparison with that of other industrialized countries, so that although American hourly rates are no longer high, labor costs to produce like products are rising.*

A second point to bear in mind is that there are new players in the game, the so-called intermediate developing countries—e.g. Brazil, Mexico, Taiwan, Hong Kong, Singapore, and South Korea—that have themselves become formidable competitors and should now be required to play by the same rules as do the industrialized states.†

The world has changed in other ways. Tariffs, as a means of discouraging imports of manufactured goods, have since World War II gradually been replaced by the creation of nontariff barriers to imports. In addition, new methods have been developed in the industrialized countries to favor their own exporters. Before World War II taxes on business were relatively minor. Today tax rates on business are very high and many countries have Value Added Taxes (VAT), which are waived in the case of exports but applied to imported goods. A French product, for example, subject to 23 percent VAT if sold in France, may be sold in the United States without the tax, whereas the same product manufactured in the United States would pay the 23 percent tax if sold in France. In certain countries income taxes are waived or diminished for income generated from products exported.

Finally, it should be noted that two events have occurred that make the adoption of generally agreed-upon rules governing international trade

* The question of U.S. productivity and export competitiveness is examined in detail in chapter 10.

† Mexico and Taiwan are not GATT members.

all the more important. The first of these is, of course, the advent of the OPEC cartel. The necessity of earning large amounts of foreign exchange to pay for imported oil has made export competitiveness critical in the non–oil-producing countries. Other imports must be reduced, or exports generally increased, to reduce the proportionate impact of imported oil on the trade balance of these countries. As the cost of imported oil continues to rise, this pressure grows.

The second event is the rapid industrialization that has taken place in developing countries. Previously, these countries had never been a significant factor in international trade except as exporters of coffee or cocoa, minerals, or other raw materials or agricultural products. Their development is, of course, gratifying, but it means that these countries will increasingly become competitors in the trade of manufactured goods.

As we have observed, the first rules of GATT dealt essentially with tariffs because tariffs had always been the principal means by which nations controlled imports. After 1947, however, a variety of nontariff barriers were enacted by protectionist-minded legislatures, both in the developed and the developing world. In the case of the developing countries, these new barriers were erected to accelerate the growth of domestic industry pursuant to an import-substitution strategy favoring domestic products over imports, even where the domestic product was of poor quality and higher in cost than the imported goods.* Nontariff barriers established in the developed world, on the other hand, have resulted either as a consequence of pressure by politically powerful agricultural or industrial sectors, by labor unions to protect employment in domestic industry, or by governments to maintain a reasonable balance of trade during a difficult economic period.†

The Tokyo Round, for the first time in the history of GATT, attempted to focus on the harm to trade done by these nontariff trade barriers and to control them. What were these barriers to trade and how and why did they come about? Further, why are nontarriff barriers so difficult to remove? Essentially, most nontariff trade barriers were enacted to fulfill domestic economic and social goals. Proponents argue that nontariff barriers enable governments to stabilize and promote employment in high unemployment areas, to develop priority industries, to maintain control over certain products, to safeguard a minimum production base in "nec-

* Import-substitution policies and their effect in developing countries are examined in more detail in the next chapter, which deals specifically with the industrialization of developing countries.

† The most recent instance is the pressure to reduce Japanese automobile imports in the United States.

essary" industries for national security reasons, to obtain a favorable balance of trade, or merely to protect consumers. It is evident that nontariff trade barriers are also often the by-product of laws enacted for reasons unrelated to trade.

Since our study of these matters is meant to discuss and illustrate rather than serve as a compendium of all the trade barriers enacted in different parts of the world, we will give a brief analysis of the different kinds in use, with a few country examples to illustrate or explain the mechanics. Any businessman planning to concentrate on exports to a particular country may use these elements as a check list for the questions he must have answered for that country.

A nontariff trade barrier has been defined as "any governmental or private regulation, practice, or policy, other than an ordinary customs duty, that interferes with a normal conduct of trade and tends to distort the volume, composition, or direction of trade flows."[2] For ease of analysis, nontariff trade barriers may be divided into six major categories: 1. quantitative restrictions and similar specific restrictions on trade; 2. nontariff charges on imports; 3. government participation in or interference with trade; 4. establishment of standards that serve as technical barriers to imports; 5. customs procedures and administrative practices designed to discourage imports; 6. discriminatory ocean freight rates.

Quantitative Restrictions and Similar Specific Restrictions on Trade

As has been noted earlier, a basic tenet of the GATT has been to urge nations pursuing protectionist policies to implement these policies through the use of tariffs and not through quantitative restrictions.[3] Under certain narrowly defined circumstances, quantitative restrictions are permitted: first, to stop a serious decline in monetary reserves;[4] second, to meet the balance-of-payments problem of a developing country;[5] and third, to support domestic agricultural programs.[6] Nonetheless, all countries have some forms of quantitative or other restrictions of a nontariff nature.

There are many different forms of quantitative and other specific restrictions on trade. They include licensing requirements, quotas, embargoes, export restraints (voluntary), exchange and other monetary or financial controls, minimum or maximum price controls, local content and mixing requirements, restrictive business practices, discriminatory bilateral agreements, and discriminatory sourcing.[7] It is as though human ingenuity had outdone itself in finding ways to keep out foreign imports and reduce trade despite the GATT. However, of these methods, licensing requirements, quotas, and embargoes are the ones most often used and will be the focus of our analysis.

Licensing arrangements can be used to administer announced quotas, where exporters or importers of certain products are required to have the appropriate documentation to enable customs officials to administer quotas; to impose discretionary controls on trade, i.e., where the permitted level of trade is not publicly announced and thus the control is effected through the requirement of obtaining a license; or to enforce regulations, such as sanitary requirements not related to quantitative controls.[8] Each of these forms of licensing serves to create barriers to trade, in that they create uncertainty, the possibility of delays in the shipment of goods, discrimination in the processing of applications, and costs of documentation. A veritable quagmire exists for the uninitiated exporter and a golden opportunity presents itself for the badly paid official who chooses to cause delays or lose applications if he or she is not compensated.

There are four main categories of quotas: absolute, open-ended, global, and tariff-quotas.[9] In an absolute quota, the maximum amount of trade permitted in a given product or commodity is officially announced by the government of the importing country. With the open-ended quota, the product is declared to be under quantitative restriction, but the amount of trade permitted in that product is not stated. This type of quota is similar to the second category of licensing arrangements discussed above, where the ceiling on the level of trade in a certain product is not publicly declared. The purpose is to create great uncertainty for foreign exporters or domestic importers of products falling under this type quota or licensing arrangement and thus discourage the import. A global quota specifies the quota amount on a given product for the whole world, and not for individual countries. Finally, tariff-quotas permit an unlimited amount of imports into a country, with the exception that only a specified quantity is permitted to enter at a set rate of duty during a designated time period. Imports in excess of the specified quantity are then subject to a higher tariff. This type quota is less restrictive than are other kinds to the degree that the product under quota can still be brought in if the importer is willing to pay the higher tariff. The choice is up to the consumer to choose between the higher-priced import or domestic substitutes. Depending on elasticities of demand for the imported product and its domestic substitute, there is a chance to maintain a market for such a product under tariff-quota by assuring deliveries. In practice, however, the tariff applied under the tariff-quota system is generally so high that it is in practice restrictive.

The open-ended quotas and the tariff-quotas cause the most problems, because they introduce great uncertainty into any decision to trade in the product covered by the quota. For example, under a tariff-quota how can you determine which of two rates of duty—the normal rate or the higher penalty rate—will be applicable to your product?

Embargoes are resorted to mainly by the developing countries, although some advanced countries maintain them on certain imports or exports of rare or sensitive goods. Since this type nontariff barrier is self-explanatory, we will forego an analysis of its impact until later in this chapter.

"Voluntary" export restraints have increased in importance and number in recent years as nontariff barriers to trade. For example, significant voluntary restraints on textiles and steel have been negotiated during this decade. One thing must be made clear: there is nothing voluntary about this restrictive trade practice. Japan has been forced to implement voluntary export controls on such products as textiles and steel shipped to the United States, rather than face the threat of harsh, formal protectionist action. The United States has used voluntary export restraints and orderly marketing agreements with several of our major trading partners, most notably Japan and to a lesser extent the European Community, to curtail a variety of imported manufactured goods and textiles. The United States has also induced many textile-exporting countries to "voluntarily" restrain their exports to the United States. On the other hand, the Japanese, sensing the protectionist mood of the U.S. Congress several years ago, exported many of their textile plants to S. Korea and Taiwan, on the assumption that the Congress would be less likely to halt imports from those countries, whose economies we are pledged to support for political reasons.

Another type of quantitative or specific restriction on imports is a system of interference with the payments and/or financial cycle of a trade transaction, including multiple exchange rates (i.e., one exchange rate for financial transactions, one for capital goods, one for noncapital goods or raw materials), allocation of foreign exchange only to holders of import licenses, and other types of restrictions aimed at conserving foreign exchange.[10]

Discriminatory sourcing is a type of bilateral agreement favoring certain countries as sources of specified imports. The most prevalent example of this is "tied" aid, where an advanced or developed country obliges a developing country to buy the former's exports of certain products in return for financial or other aid. This type of nontariff barrier is closely tied to government-sponsored mixed credits, where the government mixes official export subsidies with foreign aid to arrive at concessional financing terms for its exports. It is also found in the "countertrade" requirements used by Eastern European countries in their foreign trade.*

Analysis by Country of Quantitative or Specific Restrictions

For analysis, the following countries have been chosen, providing an interesting and diverse example of the various nontariff barriers to trade: Canada, France, West Germany, the United Kingdom, Japan, Switzerland, Mexico, South Korea, and Brazil. Some of these countries tend to employ one type of barrier over another. Others (as anyone who has tried exporting to Japan knows) use a variety of legislative, bureaucratic, and customs regulations to discourage imports of foreign products. This discussion will illustrate to the reader the various methods and barriers used. Suffice it to say that international trade would be very different if these governmental barriers to imports did not exist.

Canada

Canada currently limits imports of most textiles and apparel under an action taken to protect domestic producers from injurious import competition. Canada also imposes quantitative restrictions on imports of footwear and has a near total embargo on the importation of used cars and trucks.

France

France maintains an extensive licensing and quota system. While the French system is so broad in nature as to include a wide range of products, the problem appears to be most severe in the agricultural product sector. Other goods adversely affected by quotas and/or licensing include wine, rum, wool yarns and fabrics, cotton and other textiles, watches, radio electrical apparatus, and semiconductors.

* The question of countertrade is discussed in chapter 9.

Recently, many of the licenses and quotas have been liberalized to provide the French with increased access to products exported from the United States and other sources. Nonetheless, the licensing procedure continues to result in significant uncertainty and delay in international trade.

Since France has become a signatory to the Multilateral Trade Negotiations Licensing Code adopted at the Tokyo Round by the GATT, this should serve to alleviate many of the licensing and quota problems for traders with France in the future.

West Germany

West Germany currently maintains thirty-five licensing requirements—thirteen of which are discretionary in nature. The commodities affected are mostly agricultural products, with other products affected being bituminous coal, briquettes, solid fuels made from coal, crude petroleum, and certain heavy oils.

The West German government also maintains quantitative restrictions in 145 areas in the form of global quotas, bilateral quotas, export restraints, seasonal quotas and prohibitions. Commodities affected are mostly agricultural products but include tableware, certain fabrics and apparel, ceramic products, wines, casein, refractory bricks, statuettes, electrical goods, insulators, petroleum products, certain chemicals, wood products, leather footwear, artificial jewelry, pipes and tubes, cycles, furniture, toys, and buttons.

United Kingdom

In the United Kingdom, quantitative restrictions and import licensing requirements are applied in a discriminatory fashion to coal, coke, solid fuels made from coal, cigars, rum, jute, and fabrics of a specified makeup. In addition, both global and country quotas are applied to imports of cotton textiles and butter.

From the U.S. standpoint, the most serious U.K. quantitative restrictions are screen-time quotas applied to foreign television films and movies. When applied to television films, the restrictions set a low quota (about 20 percent) for the number of foreign-produced films that can be shown on British TV stations. Prior to showing such films, stations must secure the approval of the postmaster general. Separate, and more restrictive provisions apply to prime-time programming. Movie houses are required to show "British-Quota" films for specified percentages of screen times, and penalties are assessed on those movie houses that fail to comply with the restrictions.

Japan

Under the Japanese Import Quota System, government permission must be obtained prior to the importation of a wide range of items. In addition, these items may only be imported under a Ministry of International Trade and Investment (MITI)-authorized import-quota certificate. Included in the quota items are the following: leather, leather shoes, cigarettes, aircraft, aircraft engines and parts, drugs, coal, petroleum, citrus fruit and juices, meat, tobacco, wheat, barley, rice. Japan also, as might be expected, has considerable quotas on fish imports to protect its own fishing industry.

As a result of the multinational trade negotiations at the Tokyo Round and recent bilateral efforts undertaken by the United States, quantitative restrictions on many of the items listed above (leather, aircraft and engines, citrus, and beef) have either been eliminated or will now be significantly liberalized, according to U.S. officials.

Switzerland

Imports of wine into Switzerland are covered under two quotas: under the first, country quotas are applied to certain specified sources; under the second, other countries' wines must enter under a global quota. Protection of the wine industry in the French-speaking part of Switzerland from French and Italian imports by the German-speaking majority in the Swiss Parliament is a classic example of 1. the strength of the agricultural sector in every legislature, and 2. the effectiveness of the Swiss system of government where the majority is careful to maintain minority support.

Textiles are also covered under quantitative restrictions in Switzerland. Import licenses are not issued on various textiles unless imports can be certified at not less than a certain percentage of the normal price of a comparable article produced and sold in Switzerland.

On the other hand, Switzerland maintains a liberal licensing system on a limited range of goods, including trucks, jute textiles, clothing, cotton fabrics, and various minerals and chemicals. Licenses are granted automatically on these products after the payment of a modest fee.

India

As one of the poorest countries in the world on a per capita basis, with a rapidly increasing population and high unemployment, India tries to keep out imports whenever possible in order to expand domestic manufacturing and increase domestic employment. On the other hand, India is a very large exporter of textiles.

All imports not on government account require licenses issued by the chief controller of imports and exports in the Ministry of Commerce. Licenses are normally granted only after it has been determined that the goods in question are not available from domestic suppliers. This system also excludes most consumer and luxury goods. In order to obtain a license, importers must list their preferred country of supply; indicate alternative sources of supply; and demonstrate that they have enough rupees to take advantage of the license.

Mexico

The mainstay of Mexico's foreign-trade system is the imposition of a prior import-licensing requirement. Under the system, the importation of most products except basic, noncompetitive raw materials and capital goods can be denied if 1. the identical product would compete with domestic production that is acceptable in terms of price, quality, quantity, and delivery time; 2. there is a reasonable domestic substitute; or 3. such import is judged as not suitable for the Mexican economy.

Until recently some 65 percent of the 15,000 items in the Mexican Tariff Schedule were also subject to restrictive licensing. The primary products hit by the licensing system are mass-consumption goods such as processed foods, beverages, apparel, consumer durables, and automobiles.

As a result of massive finds of oil and gas, Mexico has very recently become an exporting nation. Mexico has begun to replace its licensing system with tariffs, but has decided not to join the GATT at present.

South Korea

Under South Korea's "Negative List" of categories subject to import controls, all import items not listed as restricted or prohibited are automatically importable into Korea by qualified traders. The Negative List is revised every six months and published as the Semi-Annual Trade Plan.

Foreign exporters seem to have difficulty determining if their products are affected by the controls, since listed items change frequently and the plan is generally not available in languages other than Korean. As expected, this acts as a significant nontariff barrier to trade with Korea.

Brazil

Nearly all imports into Brazil require a license issued by CACEX (Foreign Trade Department, Bank of Brazil). The license must be issued to an importer prior to shipment, and each request for a license must include the manufacturers' price list and catalogue. If these are not available, a certificate from the exporter must be obtained certifying that the prices are those current in the exporting country and that no catalogue or price list exist. CACEX tightens the administration of these requirements when, as in 1980–81, the balance of payments is in deficit. In 1980 the slowdown of license approvals (Operation Tortoise) was particularly onerous.

In addition to general licensing requirements, import licenses for civil aircraft require special approvals. Special import permits are also required for imports of fishery products. The purpose in each instance is to develop a domestic industry with particularly favorable *potential* for development: aircraft because of Brazil's transportation needs; fisheries because of the length of Brazil's coastline.

Nontariff Charges on Imports

As mentioned earlier, the second most common nontariff trade barrier is nontariff charges on imports. In general, a variety of charges and taxes beyond a customs duty are often levied against imports. These charges are collected at various points of the product's distribution channel, in such forms as border taxes, charges assessed later in the distribution channel, and taxes on the final sale of the product to a consumer in a foreign country. It has been said that some of the most significant barriers to world trade lie in these charges.

The basic nontariff charges on imports include the following: 1. "border" taxes; 2. port and statistical taxes (i.e., fees on vessels and/or cargo using the port); 3. nondiscriminatory use and excise taxes and registration fees; 4. discriminatory excise taxes, government-controlled insurance, film taxes, use taxes and commodity taxes; 5. nondiscriminatory sales taxes; 6. discriminatory sales taxes; 7. prior-import deposit systems (requiring importers to deposit a percentage of the value of an import); 8. variable levies; 9. consular fees (i.e., charges usually made in relation to the issuance of a consular invoice or other documentation); 10. stamp taxes (excise taxes paid through the purchase of stamps that must be affixed to articles or documents before they can be lawfully sold); and 11. import surcharges (taxes or levies in addition to the normal duty, and sometimes collected as a percentage of the normal duty.[11]

These nontariff charges sometimes serve as protective devices, that is, they curtail or impede imports, such as the "variable levy" applied to agricultural imports into most of Europe; or they may be collected to equalize the tax value added on to domestic products, such as the United States' excise taxes and the Value Added Tax (VAT) in Europe. The most prevalent nontariff charges affecting imports are the border tax adjustments and other entry taxes, imposed for either of the two above reasons. These nontariff charges will be the focus of our analysis in this section.

Border tax adjustments have been defined as "any fiscal measure which enables imported products to be charged with some or all of a tax charged in the importing country on similar domestic products and which enables exported products to be relieved of some or all of the tax charged in the exporting country on domestic products."[12] Border tax adjustments include the imposition of taxes on imports not only at the time of importation, but also at any subsequent point in the distribution channel, and the exemption from tax, including the return of any monies already collected as taxes, on products that are exported.[13] The effect of the use of border tax adjustments by the major trading partners of the United States has been stated as follows:

> . . . The use of indirect taxes by our major trading partners disadvantages the United States which relies primarily on direct taxes as the major source of national receipts. The disadvantage to the U.S. manufacturer is very substantial. A European or Japanese manufacturer absorbs in his costs the domestic taxes imposed in his country on products sold for domestic consumption, but his costs are reduced on products exported because a substantial portion of these taxes is rebated when he sells the product for export. When these exports enter the U.S., the foreign manufacturer does not have to pick up any part of the U.S. tax bill, since the U.S. does not have a border tax. Therefore, the foreign manufacturer's costs are favorably affected by the remission of part of his domestic tax burden, while his costs reflect no part of the U.S. tax burden.
>
> The U.S. manufacturer faces an opposite situation. His U.S. tax costs are not reduced when he exports since we have no border tax rebates. In addition, his export costs are increased by the obligation

> to pay at the border of the foreign country a portion of a foreign country's tax burden in the amount of the border tax imposed. The unfairness to the United States of such a situation is obvious and serious, and, in my judgement, is a major reason why the U.S. trade balance will not improve.[14]

It is indeed ironic that this statement was made as far back as July, 1971.*

There are many other nontariff charges on imports aside from those specified above. Many countries impose taxes or other charges on transport equipment, especially automobiles. These charges are exorbitant in many developing countries. There are film taxes in many countries, which consist of discriminatory fees or taxes charged on motion pictures. There are a variety of taxes and non tariff charges levied on alcoholic beverages, ranging from border tax adjustments to stamp taxes, prior-import deposits, and consular fees.

Some countries collect excessive port charges, which may be as high as 10–15 percent of the value of the imported goods, freight and insurance included. Also, frequently used is the prior-import deposit, where the importer is required to deposit with the government, usually in a non–interest-bearing account and for a fixed term, a percentage of the value of the import.[15] The commitment of capital for this purpose has the effect of increasing the cost of the imports by an amount equal to the rate of return obtainable from alternative uses of this money.[16] Thus, prior-import deposits may effectively work to curtail imports.

Different countries employ the prior-import deposit for varying purposes. Japan, until 1970, for statistical purposes required a 1 percent deposit on the value of imported goods, which was held from the time an import license was issued until the goods were imported. The United Kingdom, on the other hand, imposed an import deposit of 50 percent in 1968 when it experienced grave problems in its balance of payments. Many developing countries, especially those in Latin America, use the prior-import deposit to help solve balance-of-payments problems. Since these problems are currently worsening in most developing countries, we may expect in the future to find additional prior-import deposits established or the amount of the deposit required increasing.

* In chapter 10 there is a discussion of efforts made by other governments to aid their exporters through favorable domestic tax legislation. The trouble in the United States is that there is relatively little focus on tax planning as an instrument to accomplish national goals. With federal tax receipts exceeding $600 billion, it would seem to be imperative that both the executive and the legislative branches of government develop tax-planning strategies for national objectives.

The overall impact of nontariff charges on imports can be illustrated by a quick look at specifics in just two countries, France and Brazil. In France, a special Customs Stamp tax is imposed on all imports. The tax is levied at a rate equal to 2 percent of all import charges borne by a product and is intended to pay for the costs associated with the French customs administration. Imported products, of course, also pay the French Value Added Tax (TVA) which can be as high as 30 percent of the value of the imported goods.

In Brazil charges on imports (other than import duties) include a 2 percent (c.i.f.)* port-improvement charge; a 20 percent (of freight charges) Merchant Marine Improvement Tax; and a warehousing tax on a goods' dutiable value that starts at 1 percent and doubles every fifteen days until a maximum 8 percent level is reached.

Government Participation in Trade

The last nontariff trade barrier we will discuss in detail is that created by direct government participation or interference in trade. Government action can have a significant impact on imports. It tends to express itself in five broad ways: 1. subsidies and other aids to domestic business; 2. state trading, government monopolies, and exclusive franchises; 3. laws and practices that discourage imports; 4. a policy of government intervention; and 5. government procurement. A brief analysis of several of these measures appears worthwhile.

Throughout this book, references have been made to the various ways in which governments subsidize exports. In the reverse, as a means of curtailing imports, governments can also provide subsidies to domestic producers to produce goods that would otherwise have to be obtained through imports. This is called "import substitution," and is a highly inefficient means of alleviating shortages of foreign exchange or reducing balance-of-payments disequilibriums. It is a system very frequently used in developing countries although the more successful developing nations have abandoned this practice as costly and inefficient.†

Governments also tend to be the largest single purchasers of goods and services in many countries of the world. As such, in their procurement policies, they will favor domestic suppliers. Many nations complain that the bidding time for other government's contracts is too short, thus effectively eliminating foreign bidding on government procurement. The re-

* Cost, insurance and freight.

† Chapter 8 gives a detailed analysis of this practise in some developing countries.

cent Multilateral Trade Negotiations have specifically addressed this question of government procurement. The effects of these changes in the GATT are discussed in greater detail later in this chapter.

But one phenomenon in trade that should be brought up under this heading of import restriction is the constantly increasing tendency of governments to participate directly in the manufacturing process through state-owned or state-controlled enterprises. One such enterprise is the European consortium which sells the Airbus aircraft in competition with the planes manufactured by Boeing, McDonnell-Douglas, or Lockheed. The manufacturer of the airframe used in the Airbus aircraft is a French concern, Aerospatiale, owned by the French government and hence freely subsidized.

Other areas of manufacture have also come under government control or ownership. Concerns in Great Britain such as British Steel, British Leyland, and Rolls Royce, which were not established as chosen government instruments but came under government control because they could not compete in the private market, are other examples of state-owned or controlled enterprises. Will Chrysler eventually have to change from a private business to be a similarly subsidized government-controlled consortium? Will the U.S. government, as a result, then take steps to reduce imports of Japanese, French, and German automobiles into the United States, which would then be in competition not just with a U.S. business but with the U.S. government itself? Or will we, instead, do what some of our competitors do, and insist that our government buy only those products made by its own government-owned manufacturing entities? We recognize a new and growing problem here that needs to be addressed.

Yet manufacturing is but one instance. Distribution is perhaps an even more difficult facet of the same problem. In Algeria, for example, distribution of capital equipment needed for factories and farms is handled by government-owned agencies that buy in large quantities. Because of this quantity order, they are quoted a much more favorable price and the financing terms are much more desirable than would be the case if the importer were a private-sector company. The economic advantages of large-scale purchasing by specialized government agencies in such countries as Algeria may lead other countries to do the same. If this happens, the role of the private sector in international trade transactions will be reduced further.

Standards as Technical Nontariff Barriers to Trade

Standards are laws, regulations, specifications, or other requirements with respect to the properties of products or the manner, conditions, or circumstances under which products are produced or marketed.[17] Standards usually concern quality, purity, component materials, dimensions, level of performance, and the like; or the health, sanitary, safety, technical, or other conditions under which a product is produced or marketed; or a product's packaging or labeling.[18]

Governments may effectively curtail imports in certain countries through the establishment of national standards that differ from those of the exporting country. The types of standards most frequently cited as nontariff barriers to trade are: 1. health and safety standards; 2. pharmaceutical standards; 3. product-content requirements; 4. processing standards; 5. industrial standards; 6. requirements on weights and measures; 7. labeling and container requirements; 8. marking requirements; 9. packaging requirements; and 10. trademark problems.[19]

Nearly every country has laws to protect the health of its own population, its cattle, or its agricultural products, by seeking to prevent the introduction and spread of disease, insuring sanitary conditions and minimum health standards in processing food for human or animal consumption, and by prohibiting the sale of unwholesome or contaminated food.[20] The curtailment of trade arises when these health and sanitation standards vary significantly among countries.

Industrial and product standards relate to weights, measures, container sizes, nomenclature, quality, product content, production processes, safety, ecology, and environment.[21] The sectors most closely regulated by these standards are electrical and electronic equipment, and automotive products.

Examples of such standards include the following: the Multipartite Accord for Assessment and Certification of Electronic Components in the European Community, which establishes standards, quality-control inspection, and harmonization of specifications and inspection procedures for electronic components in member countries; and the Underwriters Laboratory guarantee of inspection on electrical appliances and products, medical, gas and oil-burning equipment.[22] Problems obviously arise when these standards differ in specification tests or in inspection procedures.

Nontariff barriers to trade through the application of standards in pharmaceutical products usually involve requirements for testing, plant inspection, special documentation, and the use of a specific pharmacopoeia.[23] The greatest problems lie again in variance of the standards among countries. For example some countries do not accept the validity of U.S. Food and Drug Administration (FDA) tests. Other countries have strict and costly testing requirements, which may effectively impede or curtail imports. The U.S. Food and Drug Administration has its own tests, which are notably more strict than those of other countries. The Europeans (and some U.S. doctors) claim to be able to cite numerous instances when the FDA has used its powers to keep out a European pharmaceutical product on the grounds that it has not been proved that such product is superior to an American product or simply because there are already similar products marketed in the United States.

The growth of consumer protection movements in many of the major industrialized countries has resulted in an increased number of products being brought under various requirements and standards. For example, labeling and marking requirements, and specifically "marks of origin,"* have been roundly criticized by exporters as unnecessary and merely imposed for the purpose of hindering imports. Labeling requirements for certain products, such as alcoholic beverages and pharmaceutical products, may be especially costly to comply with, because they can vary country by country making it impossible to standardize the label.

A few examples of the imposition of standards as a technical barrier to trade may be helpful in showing what individual countries do to control imports: most relate to the importation of electrical products, wood products, or textiles. In the United States boilers and pressure vessels, whether foreign or domestic, must be inspected by an inspector licensed by the American Society of Mechanical Engineers (ASME). Until 1973, ASME would not certify boilers and pressure vessels outside the United States or Canada. This, of course, effectively kept out products from other countries. Threat of a civil antitrust suit against ASME from the Department of Justice brought about a change and foreign goods are now inspected.

The French counterpart to ASME is the Union Technique de l'Electricité (UTE); in West Germany it is the Trade Inspection Office. Neither accept ASME certifications on U.S. products and require satisfactory testing by local inspectors, often after disassembly.

On wood products, Canada and West Germany maintain restrictive standards that have the effect of restricting imports from the United

* Often products themselves contain ingredients imported from third countries. It is obviously burdensome to specify the origin of all constituent ingredients.

States. The use of CDX plywood (most commonly used in the United States) is not permitted in a wide range of applications in Canada. In West Germany, standards on the use of preservatives in plywood restrict the types of plywood that can be imported from the United States.

In Japan, approval from the Ministry of International Trade and Investment (MITI) is required as a condition to the sale of electrical equipment. The approval can be secured following the procedures outlined below. Importers must submit an application for material/product testing together with the products to be tested and be prepared to pay a fee of up to 200,000 yen to the Japan Electrical Testing Laboratory (JETL) in Tokyo. If the equipment conforms to the applicable standard, JETL issues a Quality Approval Certificate. The importer submits an application for type approval to the Technology Section, MITI, together with JETL's certification. If MITI approves, a notice of type approval is published in the official register.

In Switzerland, a material testing station examines and approves all forms of electrical appliances. Testing authorities are empowered to levy fines on producers of electrical equipment that does not meet the standards set by Swiss Elektrotechnisher Verein (SEV). The cost of undergoing the testing procedures can often be high and, depending on the product, can result in long delays. Complaints have been received that the SEV facility will easily and quickly approve highly sophisticated items for which there is no competitive Swiss product, but when products compete with less sophisticated, domestically produced equipment, the procedures are so tedious and time consuming as to discourage the importation of foreign goods.

Since all the countries briefly reviewed in this section are signatories to the Code on Technical Barriers to Trade, the so-called Standards Code which has been one of the results of the recent Multinational Trade Negotiations (The Tokyo Round), it is expected that the problem of standards will be less onerous to international trade in the future than it has been in the past.

Customs Procedures and Administrative Practices

Customs procedures, regulations, and administrative practices may constitute significant barriers to trade when these procedures and practices are overly complex or strict, or when officials in a country have broad discretion with respect to customs classification and valuation for tax and duty purposes. The result of this situation is uncertainty for the trader, which effectively impedes trade in his products. Barriers to trade may be found in these areas: 1. antidumping practices; 2. customs valuation; 3. consular formalities; 4. documentation requirements; 5. administrative difficulties; 6. classification of merchandise; 7. regulations on samples, returned goods, and reexports; 8. countervailing duties; and 9. emergency action.[24] Of these, customs valuation practices and documentation requirements are among the most prevalent barriers.

When *ad valorem* tariff rates are used, the value assigned to imported merchandise is as important as the tariff rate itself in determining the amount of duty to be collected, and the valuation may be of greater concern to the importer than the tariff rate.[25] For this reason, the Brussels Definition of Value* was adopted formally by twenty-six countries and is applied by at least fifty-eight other countries. One problem, however, is that the United States, Canada, Australia, New Zealand, and South Africa do not use the Brussels definition. In fact, the European Community, Japan, the Nordic countries, and the United States are now signatories to the Customs Valuation Agreement, which renounces the Brussels definition of value. The agreement limits the situations in which additions can be made to invoice valuations.

A problem in virtually all valuation systems is establishing a correct customs value for imports not shipped as arms-length transactions between independent unrelated parties.[26] Most countries tend to adjust upward the invoice values of such imports to establish the customs value, which is commonly referred to as an "uplift." Many countries have complained about these uplift procedures.

Another problem faced especially by U.S. exporters is that c.i.f. (cost, insurance, and freight) values are used widely for customs valuation purposes in many countries. This contrasts with the prevalent use of lower f.o.b. (freight on board) values by United States customs valuation authorities. Since the American system does not include insurance and shipping expense, customs duties are lower on U.S. imported goods.

Documentation requirements and consular formalities tend to act as barriers to trade when they are excessive in terms of quantity, formality, complexity, and other procedures or requirements. Some nations require special customs invoices shipped to them. The United States has been criticized for its alleged expensive and excessive documentation requirements. The United States had also been criticized for the American Selling Price (ASP)—an arbitrary domestic price used for evaluation purposes—

* This represents an attempt by certain countries to standardize customs nomenclature.

on four of its imports, benzenoid chemicals, rubber footwear, low-priced wool-knit gloves, and canned clams.

American business executives frequently criticize other nations for using unfair practices to exclude American products. Nevertheless U.S. authorities have been just as arbitrary, particularly when they have found themselves either under pressure from the very industry they are supposed to regulate (the FDA, for example, under pressure from the Pharmaceutical Manufacturers Association) or when, for political reasons, the government wants to exclude the products of a particular country. A well-known instance of this occurred in 1962 when a shipment of several million French hypodermic needles was kept in customs for well over a year on the pretense of improper sterilization. In fact, the difficulty was that the needles were made of stainless steel in which the nickel content may have come from Cuba and Cuban products were not allowed to come into the United States.

The United States and Canada have also been criticized for their application of countervailing duties* and antidumping statutes. Many countries have claimed that the procedures used by these two countries are arbitrary and thus trade-impeding. The U.S. tire industry, for example, sought a countervailing duty on Michelin tires manufactured in Canada on the grounds that Michelin had obtained government financing for its plant and that this constituted a subsidy.

Discriminatory Ocean Freight Rates

Some U.S. exporters maintain that ocean freight rates on many commodities shipped from the United States to Japan and other countries are higher than comparable rates from Japan and other countries to the U.S. To the degree this complaint is true, it represents a serious disadvantage faced by exporters and importers of American products. Shipping lines are predominantly organized in conferences, which set one-way freight rates for various commodities. Conferences tend to employ many different rates, which creates the possibility of variations in freight rates even between two ports. As a result, trade can easily be distorted.

* A countervailing duty is a special duty imposed when a foreign product is sold in the United States for less than its selling price in the country of origin or when its cost is subsidized in violation of GATT rules. Countervailing duties in the United States, found after lengthy investigation to be payable, have nevertheless not been collected by the Treasury Department. This function has now been transferred to the Commerce Department which promises to follow through on collections in the future.

For many years the conferences were controlled by the British. The rates established consequently favored shipments between various parts of the Empire and subsequently the Commonwealth. As an example, it cost more to ship from Liverpool to Dublin, a distance of two hundred miles than from Liverpool to Sidney, Australia, some eight thousand miles. Similarly, freight rates from Liverpool to Rio de Janeiro were only a few years ago far less than the rates from Rio to Caracas, Venezuela. The British controlled the conferences and the conferences fixed the rates with a view to accommodating British trade.

Impact of Tokyo Multinational Trade Negotiations on Nontariff Barriers to Trade

As noted, the Tokyo Round of the Multilateral Trade Negotiations (MTN) began in 1973. Six years later, on April 12, 1979, agreements were signed by representatives of forty-one trading nations, establishing tariff cuts averaging 30 percent, and six major codes of conduct in international trade.

What exactly did the Tokyo Round accomplish? This round of negotiations has established codes of international conduct in the following areas of nontariff barriers: subsidies and countervailing measures; government procurement; standards as technical barriers to trade; customs valuation; and import licensing. An analysis of the negotiated codes, keeping in mind the nontariff barriers discussed earlier in this chapter, should provide us with an accurate picture of the nontariff barriers that will be eliminated or reduced by the Tokyo Round of GATT.

Subsidies and Countervailing Measures

A major goal of this code was to control the effects subsidies have on trade, in part by providing new international rules on the use of countervailing duties and other countermeasures to offset the negative effects of subsidies on trade. The code expands existing GATT rules by expressly prohibiting countries from using export subsidies for nonprimary (industrial) products and primary mineral products. Regarding export subsidies on primary (agricultural and other raw material) products, new GATT rules prohibit the use of export subsidies for those products destined for a particular market, where such subsidies would result in prices substantially lower than those of other suppliers to the same market.

The code requires signatory countries to structure their internal subsidy programs to avoid: A. causing undue injury to domestic industries of other signatories; B. nullifying the benefits of their own tariff concessions through subsidies to domestic producers; and C. prejudicing the interests of other suppliers to a third-country market.[27] To assist in identifying harmful subsidies to be eliminated under the code, an "Illustrative List of Export Subsidies" was prepared.

The Subsidies and Countervailing Measures Code also reaffirm the GATT principle that countervailing duties be imposed only when subsidies have been found that threaten injury to domestic industries. This provision is aimed primarily at the United States, the only major industrial country that formerly imposed countervailing duties without requiring a determination of injury. This code also mandates guidelines for the size and duration of countervailing duties to be imposed.

Under this code, the developing countries are specifically exempted from the prohibition against export subsidies. In return, these countries are asked to pledge the elimination of subsidies as rapidly as their economic development permits.

Government Procurement

Since the inception of GATT, government procurement has been specifically exempt from the general provisions of reciprocity and nondiscrimination contained in that agreement, leaving governments free to discriminate against foreign products in their procurement decisions. Under this new code, all signatory governments are required to treat products originating in any other signatory country no less favorably than they would domestic products or the products of any other country.

Under this code, governments are therefore required to open up the process by which specifications are set, bids accepted, and contracts awarded. Signatory countries to this code are now required to publish winning bids for procurement contracts and to review complaints of unfair treatment from foreign producers. Procurement by governments and by national entities under the "substantial control" of the government are also covered under this code. Although the definition of what constitutes a national entity under "substantial control" has caused intense negotiation.

Each party to the agreement has submitted a list of national entities to which the code will apply, but several other enterprises not listed by the member party as national entities have had to be individually negotiated. The most significant of these was Nippon Telephone and Telegraph

(NTT), a large purchaser of sophisticated electronic equipment. The United States was determined to open this market to U.S. producers, who are generally recognized as highly competitive in both quality and price. The Japanese representatives finally agreed that the new code would apply to this company also.*

The code does not apply to service contracts, except those incidental to the purchase of goods. This is unfortunate. There should be a GATT covering services as they are growing in importance in international trade. It also does not cover construction contracts, national security items, purchases by state and local governments, or purchases by any noncovered entity. To ensure compliance with the code, there are enforcement provisions for dealing with both individual contract violations and larger, more systemic violations.[28] There are also dispute settlement procedures to adjudicate violations of the code. It has been estimated that this specific code will open a $25 billion market in international trade to U.S. suppliers.

Standards as Technical Barriers to Trade

The purpose of this code is to discourage discriminatory manipulation of product standards, product testing, and product certification systems. The standards code will also encourage the use of open procedures in the adoption of standards and will encourage international standardization of procedures. A major tenet of this code, like those of the others, is that imported products are to be treated no less favorably than domestic products. This is consistent with the GATT theme of reciprocity and nondiscrimination with respect to another country's exports.

The code establishes international procedures by which signatories may complain of code violations by other signatories, may secure reviews of their complaints, and, if a valid complaint rests unsettled, may ultimately take some sort of retaliatory action.

While the standards code covers both industrial and agricultural standards, it is not applicable to standards involving services, technical specifications included in government procurement contracts, or standards established by individual companies for their own use.

* NTT will open its procurement to international competitive bidding on those items covered by the code (approximately $1.5 billion of NTT's purchases). The remainder ($1.8 billion) is covered by a bilateral agreement between Japan and the United States.

Customs Valuation

This code establishes the "transaction value" of a product to be "the price actually paid or payable for the goods when sold for export," plus certain other costs and expenses associated with the transaction, as the primary method to calculate the value of imports for duty purposes. As a result of this code, a more equitable and uniform valuation of goods for duty purposes will, one hopes, be achieved.

One instance where the transaction value does not have to be used is in a sale between related parties, where the relationship may have affected the price charged (i.e., non-arms-length pricing strategies). In this case, other formulas of value may be used, in the following order: 1. the price of identical goods; 2. the price of similar goods; 3. the resale price of the goods with allowances for factors such as profits and costs associated with resale of the goods; and 4. the cost of producing the goods. The first valuation method to be ascertained shall be the one used.

Also contained within this code are provisions ensuring the right of importers to an impartial appeals procedure and to the establishment of a strong dispute settlement mechanism to protect its provisions.

Import Licensing

The purpose of this code is to reduce the administrative impediments to trade that were discussed earlier in this chapter. Among the requirements set forth in this code are the following: A. publication of the rules governing procedures for submission of applications for import licenses, as well as publication of other useful information about licensing systems; B. simplification of application and renewal procedures for obtaining a license; C. provision that import licenses are not to be refused for minor variations in value, quantity, or weight of the product under license; and D. specification that foreign exchange necessary to pay for imports is to be made available for imports subject to licensing on the same basis as it is for goods not subject to licensing.[29]

This code requires import licensing procedures to be as simple and open as possible, applied in a nondiscriminatory manner to products from all signatory countries. This code also prohibits the rejection of applications for import licenses because of minor errors in documentation; it also prohibits the refusal of imports because of minor variations in quantity or weight from amounts designated in the license.[30]

It is thus clear that the Tokyo Round has had some significant successes following very arduous negotiations. As a result, the GATT is now facing an expanded role in regulating international trade. How it will work out in practice nobody knows. The Europeans have always been in favor of moving slowly in the GATT, negotiation to them meaning progress in a series of little steps, to which everyone can agree. The Americans always take the position that where they see a problem there is a call for an immediate solution even though agreement is sometimes forced. The Tokyo Round just ended clearly breaks new ground towards freer trade.

Whether the new codes will apply in such a way that the carefully developed nontariff barriers to trade will be eliminated remains to be seen. The Americans have been some of the worst offenders in this respect in the past by insisting, through bilateral negotiations, on agreements to limit exports to the United States to a certain quota. Indeed, Ambassador Robert Strauss with great understanding of the legislative process negotiated the "accord" with the Japanese to "voluntarily" restrain Japanese textile exports to the United States in time to make it much easier for Congress to approve the Tokyo Round agreement.* These bilateral agreements establishing quotas constitute an effective nontariff trade barrier and quite obviously represent a step towards protectionism and away from further progress toward free trade.

Perhaps the greatest accomplishment of the Tokyo Round negotiations is what cannot be quantified: the close working relationship developed between trade officials in the executive branch, members of the trade oversight committees (Ways and Means in the House of Representatives and Finance in the Senate), and private-sector representatives from industry, agriculture, and labor. As always, the representatives from agricultural associations were particularly persuasive, knowing just what they wished to accomplish, and sending their own delegations to determine the factual situation in different countries. By comparison, certain industry groups were active, others far less so. On the whole, private-sector participation, mandated by the 1974 Trade Act, made possible the accomplishments of the Tokyo Round negotiations because it gave unusually

* In the first months of the Reagan Administration, the United States government faced pressure from Congress once again for protectionist legislation—this time on automobile imports from Japan. Having pushed continuously for free trade since the end of World War II, despite the reluctance of other industrialized countries, the U.S. government in April, 1981 forced a reduction in the importation of Japanese automobiles through "voluntary" quotas, in order to save its own automobile industry. This decision will probably affect the course of international trade for years to come.

capable U.S. government negotiators the technical and informational support without which no progress could have taken place.

If we assume that the Tokyo Round agreements do represent a great step forward in freeing international trade from burdensome barriers, what did the negotiations fail to accomplish, and what should be the goals of future negotiators in making trade easier?

There are probably three areas where much still remains to be done:

The first is the question of safeguards, which, as we have seen, threaten to get more difficult rather than easier to solve. Will the United States and the European Community be willing to risk temporary increases in unemployment in order to force increases in domestic productivity in those industries most susceptible to Japanese competition—automobiles, electronic equipment, semiconductors, in effect the technologies of the future?

Second, will the United States be able to withstand the pressure to limit its exports of vital supplies, such as agricultural products, as a means of forcing other countries to increase their exports of other products, such as oil, which the OPEC cartel limits in order to ensure continuing price increases?

Third, will the United States be able and willing to make a greater effort to insist that services be included in future trade agreements, particularly since services (banking, insurance, transportation) are playing an ever-increasing role in trade?

The temptations to further protectionism are great in a period when the industrialized countries are being forced to export more to pay for imports of energy. The pressures to link exports of agricultural products to greater exports of oil by other countries are very great. It will be a measure of American tenacity and long-range self-interest if we are capable of maintaining our determination to build upon the accomplishments of the Tokyo Round.

8

A New Force in International Trade: The Developing Countries

> The boundaries of democracy have to be widened now so as to include economic quality also. This is the great revolution through which we are all passing.
>
> JAWAHARLAL NEHRU

> The open society, the unrestricted access to knowledge, the unplanned and uninhibited association of men for its furtherance—these are what may make a vast, complex, ever-growing, ever changing, ever more socialized and expert technological world, nevertheless a world of human community.
>
> J. ROBERT OPPENHEIMER

Nowhere is change occurring more rapidly than in the developing nations. Nowhere are contrasts greater; nowhere are those tensions created by the side-by-side existence of starvation, on the one hand, and incredible wealth and ease, on the other, more evident. Yet adjustment to the changes brought about by the transfer of technology and assets to others less fortunate will work out only if the creation of new wealth in the developing world does not at the same time reduce the standard of living in the more advanced countries. It is a thesis of this chapter that technology can be transferred to the developing nations and new wealth created without reducing the quality of life in the developed portion of the globe. We do have the capacity to create new and better economic conditions in other parts of the world without reducing our own standard of living.

To a certain degree we have done this over the past thirty years, but it has been through the greatest creation of paper money the world has ever known. How to absorb and liquidate this "unrepayable debt" out of the new "real" assets that have been created is the economic challenge of this and coming generations. As has been noted throughout this book, there are, unfortunately, no economic miracles. This debt, in all likelihood, must ultimately be forgiven, or its payment made possible through accelerated inflation, which causes such payment to be ultimately effected by charging a certain amount to each person who has any monetary assets to be drawn upon. History has provided at least one puzzling exception, however, to what appears to be a rigid rule that unrestrained printing of money must result in wide-scale inflation. This happened in the United States, in the period from 1865 to 1914, when a massive national debt was liquidated out of earnings from newly-created assets.

In 1865 the War Between the States ended. Because in the last fiscal year of that war the federal government collected in taxes only 25 percent of what it spent, it was forced to resort to the printing presses for paper money on a scale unheard of up to then. The result should have been enormous inflation in succeeding years. Yet this did not happen. The vast expansion of money representing claims against the government in the banks of Boston, Philadelphia, and New York was, in turn, loaned outside the Northeast, invested in the development of the new western lands on which the young men from the farms and the cities of the East settled. It was as if the war had first displaced these people and then had stimulated them to go into undeveloped spaces where they might homestead and prosper.

It is not surprising that the intermediaries in this temporary transfer of wealth from the Eastern banks to the Western borrowers for development were such entrepreneurial traders as Lehman (cotton brokers from Memphis), or Lazard (cloth merchants from San Francisco). They became, by supplying necessities to the West, the regional, if not international, merchant bankers of the period. Instead of self-fueling inflation, the result was economic development of a formerly backward region of the country on a vast scale.

From 1865 to the start of World War I, prices did not increase; on the contrary, they gradually came down. The combined dynamics of thrift, hard work in the creation of new assets, and a stream of new production earning enough to repay the debt created a special economic climate. All this took place at a time when government hardly intervened at all, or at least did not attempt to use its taxing power to redistribute wealth. The word from Washington was work, produce, and prosper—or perish. There was little help for those unwilling to struggle for themselves: no

PL 480s to bring food, no soft-loan windows, no AID programs for schools or fertilizers.*

The results were truly astounding. Might not this historical economic experience in the development of one country hold promise for what the world faces today in the development not of one half of one country but of a vast section of our world? Might not the development process be best accelerated through myriad private loans for specific limited projects, directed at the creation of new sources of wealth in the developing nations? These loans could be repaid out of the new wealth created by new productivity. They would be made in lieu of massive transfers of money or other assets usually made by government to government or by international organizations to governments for *public investments,* which seldom if ever create earnings significantly capable of repaying the loans. The essential point of this chapter, as indeed of this book, is that we must constantly look to create new real assets, rather than focus on the redistribution of assets already created. Throwing money at economic problems does not solve them. Doing so may temporarily satisfy the donor's conscience and give the recipient new time to figure out how to motivate the donor to give again. But new debt not used to create new wealth will somewhere down the line either have to be forgiven or renewed.

Country development as a scientific endeavor is new to economics. Before World War II there were government-to-government loans, many on a large scale, but they were as nothing compared to what has happened recently. It can be said that colonial empires grew out of unpaid debts. This method of debt collection, used by wealthy European nations in China (from 1840 to 1937), in India, and in Africa, as well as elsewhere, resulted in a colonial system in which the maritime powers—Great Britain, France, Holland, and later the United States—obtained the natural resources they needed for their industrialized economies. Jute from India, coffee from Colombia or Brazil, rubber from Indonesia, silk from China, copper from Africa, and tin from Malaysia were taken by the colonial powers in exchange for finished products from Europe and the United States.

There have been, of course, many instances of specialized development of certain specific sectors of the industrial capability of certain countries.

* This does not imply that governments should not care for the needy. At issue here are means not ends. PL 480, for example, has tended to discourage domestic food production in many parts of the world where it is thought that domestic needs will continue to be met by American surpluses. This can only lead to increased food shortages.

Most of the technology of oil retrieval, for example, was designed and put in place in the OPEC countries by European or American private companies. But until recently these programs were narrowly focused and not directed at uplifting entire economies. The idea that a systemic modernization of a country could be effected by another for the benefit of the first was born out of post-World War II American idealism, and was, at the time, totally new to classical international economic ideology.

By now, however, almost four decades after the end of World War II, the development mechanism has been nationalized, bureaucratized, and internationalized. It has become top-heavy and inefficient. Concurrently, the system still demands technology transfers from the developed countries to the developing countries on a country-to-country basis, generally in an international forum, where the demander is often not the technologically proficient ultimate employer of the technology, but a government official trained in politics or economics rather than in engineering or production.

The issue of technology transfer is perhaps the most emotional problem between the so-called developed and developing countries. To proponents of the "New International Economic Order" in the United Nations, this issue has become a rallying cry, as though the industrialized countries had seized upon some source of wealth that belonged to all nations and were now insisting on deciding with whom they would share it. On the other hand, there has often been a fear, expressed particularly among union leaders in the United States, that the transfer of technology would bring about increased unemployment in the United States as the developing countries produced goods more cheaply and undersold U.S. products in the international market place. These critics cite the recent tendency on the part of U.S. semiconductor companies to establish plants in Taiwan or Hong Kong rather than in the United States.

A kind of mythology has been created on the subject that has tended to obscure realities. We have long since passed the time when the populations of the former European colonies could be considered to be, in the Biblical phrase, "drawers of water and hewers of wood." When Congress does not permit the U.S. Export-Import Bank to finance plant projects in the developing countries out of a fear that steel, textile, or agricultural products produced in these plants may be imported into the United States, the result, all too frequently, is that U.S. firms lose the order to foreign competitors, who are not bound by the same restrictions, with the products of the plants exported to the United States anyway.

The United States is currently the only industrialized country to require that an impact analysis of the effect on domestic employment be made by its export finance institution before an export transaction can be financed. The effect of such restrictions is that firms in the United States that depend upon exports for their survival are disappearing. Unfortunately among these are the engineering companies responsible for our machine tool industry, textile machinery industry, steel-making machinery, and similar concerns that depend upon foreign orders to maintain their engineering staffs and, more important, their research and development capabilities.

This is just another illustration of American preoccupation with outdated axioms. Rather than trying to hoard today's industrial know-how, we should be freely transferring it, as our industrialized competitors do, and concentrating on tomorrow's technology. In the United States we have become captive to a Frankenstein psychology, increasingly fearful of developing the technologies of the future, either because we distrust our ability to control the technology—as in the case of nuclear plants or advanced biological experiments affecting human life itself—or else because we fear that workers in old industries made uncompetitive by the new technology may lose their jobs and suffer dislocation in trying to retrain themselves.

As a result, we are now importing capital goods in such fields as autos, farm machinery, machine tools, etc., where in the past the United States exported these products throughout the world. To cite here but one instance: in the Chrysler plant where the new U.S. army tank is being produced the tank-building machines are made entirely by Mitsubishi of Japan. There are other examples in chapter 10, in which will be found a detailed discussion of the problem of U.S. productivity in the U.S. market itself.

The developing countries should have the opportunity to import whatever products they want and can pay for. The problem of technology transfer, however, is far more complicated than the endless UNCTAD discussions would indicate. In general, technological advances belong not to governments but to business firms, which are naturally reluctant to make such transfers without adequate compensation or an assurance that if technological capability is brought into the country as an investment, the investment will not be seized or the company threatened with forced and poorly compensated nationalization in the future. Today this is the case with investments in the Andean Common Market and, more recently, in the oil and gas industry in western Canada.

Increasingly, in recent years, industrialization in the developing countries is taking place through the acquisition by state-owned enterprises of advanced technologies from the industrial countries, often financed at subsidized rates of interest from state export finance agencies in the exporter's country. Most often these transactions are approved for financing without adequate provision having been made for personnel to operate or maintain the equipment purchased. The exporter doesn't care; he has made his sale. But the importing firm has been badly served. It expected to purchase a system to do a task. But seeking to acquire performance, it received instead, machinery.

A developing country more often than not is not buying road-building equipment, or a drilling rig, but the system by which the equipment will be operated, maintained, and serviced; it is the production capability that is needed, not the production tool. Too often American exporters are unaware of this need abroad; they assume that selling complicated machinery to a developing country is no different from selling the same machinery to a sophisticated buyer in the United States who understands how to operate and maintain complicated machinery. For this reason a firm such as Caterpillar is much more successful than its competitors abroad. The equipment is very expensive but the dealers are well financed, and the buyer gets training in use of the equipment, excellent service, and a stock of parts that insures the original price of the equipment will not turn out to have been wasted.

It would appear to be high time to abandon the empty rhetoric of the "New International Economic Order" in favor of a new atmosphere of cooperation between developed and developing countries. A new North–South dialogue is needed in which practical businessmen with international experience can participate. The aim of both must be the same because a successful transfer process benefits all.

In the United States, there has been too often since the end of World War II a tendency to confuse economic assistance to the developing countries with political or military considerations. It is indeed a perplexing problem. If economic development does not benefit a majority of the population, the government may in due course be changed as a result of revolutionary activity. Any such revolution from the left immediately raises spectres on the political right in the United States of domino theories and the presence of Soviet nuclear weaponry nearer our shores. Some of us who experienced at first hand as far away as in Southeast Asia the effects of this type of thinking are particularly sensitive to it. The United States certainly needs to continue to fear and respect Soviet military might and take all steps necessary to build a defense posture against it.

We certainly need not fear, however, the economic effectiveness or moral values of the Marxist system. Nor must we confound the one with the other. The governments of developing countries can see for themselves what has happened to economic development in such countries as Ghana, Guinea, Ethiopia, Cuba, Burma, Vietnam, and Cambodia, which applied Marxist economic programs, compared to Singapore, South Korea, Colombia, Brazil, and the Ivory Coast which relied on the private sector to develop the economy and create new jobs. The United States government under the Reagan Administration now threatens to limit the activities of American companies in Libya, Angola, Nicaragua and elsewhere where politically unpopular regimes are in power. By so doing, we may bring about exactly what we seek most to avoid, the establishment of even more repressive governments.

Recent political events in France may help to bring about a change in thinking by the Western democracies. It is likely that the election of François Mitterand in France may bring about new policies regarding the development process in the Third and Fourth World countries, much closer to the ideas of Brandt in Germany and Kreisky in Austria; men who are fully aware of the need to strengthen the Western alliance *militarily* under American leadership, but who are not ready to accept what appears to be the Reagan Administration's notion that socialist governments in developing countries will necessarily and eventually become Soviet-controlled. The election of Mitterand will also bring spirited discussion within OECD countries on the development process. Perhaps a consensus can be developed to recognize that prevention of military action by others does not require military intervention by the United States, that education, free expression, redistribution of land holdings into peasant cooperatives, and development of a middle class actively participating in the process of government are aims acceptable to both socialists and conservatives in the OECD countries. Recent events in France may hasten this consensus.

Yet despite the environment in which international development is taking place, it is an indisputable fact that since World War II the development process has accelerated rapidly in many parts of the world. Tables 15 and 16 show, respectively, the comparative growth of production and international merchandise trade in developed and developing countries in recent years. The tables show that growth among developing countries has not been uniform and that certain countries, not necessarily the most richly endowed with resources, have progressed much faster than others. It is one of the purposes of this chapter to examine what contributes to

Table 15. Comparative growth of production[a] 1970–78 (*Average annual percentage growth rate*)

	GDP[b]	Agriculture	Industry	Manufacturing	Services[c]
Low-income countries	3.6%	2.0%	4.5%	4.2%	4.3%
Middle-income countries (Includes newly industrialized countries)	5.7	3.1	7.1	6.8	5.8
Industrialized countries	3.2	1.0	3.4	3.3	3.7

Source: World Bank, *World Development Report, 1980,* August, 1980.

[a]The average growth rates for the country groups in the table are weighted by country GDP in 1970 dollars.

[b]Gross domestic product (GDP) measures the total final output of goods and services produced by an economy.

[c]All branches of economic activity other than agricultural, industrial, and manufacturing are categorized as services.

Table 16. Comparative growth of merchandise exports[a] 1970–78 (*Average annual percentage growth rate*)

Low-income countries		−0.8%
Industrialized countries		5.7[b]
Newly industrialized countries		8.9
Ivory Coast	8.5%	
South Korea	28.8	
Taiwan	9.3	
Singapore	9.8	
Hong Kong	4.8	
Brazil	6.0	
Mexico	5.2	
Argentina	6.8	
Colombia	1.2	

Source: World Bank, *World Development Report, 1980,* August, 1980.

[a]The growth rates are in real terms and are calculated from quantum indices of exports.

[b]Only one country exceeded 9%—Japan at 9.7%.

this disparity. Are there certain factors that can be identified as hastening the development process? There are indeed guidelines that governments may find useful to bear in mind in their own planning.

The process of development is not mysterious. It is generally thought that in order for a country to develop rapidly it must industrialize, since it is the industrialized countries that appear to be the wealthiest. To industrialize, a country must have money invested on a vast scale. This investment capital can be obtained through foreign businessmen investing in the country, by borrowing in the international capital markets, or through earnings of foreign exchange as a result of exports in hard currencies.

In today's world, the developing countries, for the most part, dislike foreign investment because they remember how such investment so often led to interference in a country's affairs. They also see foreign investment as a method of transferring outward control of the country's sources of wealth for inadequate compensation. There is, therefore, an increased tendency, quite understandably, to want to nationalize production, particularly if it involves the exploitation of mineral or hydrocarbon deposits, which have somehow come to be considered a particular kind of national asset to be owned invariably and developed in the national interest by the government.

The United States and other industrialized nations have been recently confronted with a new and growing challenge in the international marketplace from a group of developing nations. The trade competition from this group has been strongly felt by many U.S. exporters, who, as a result, are finding it more difficult to maintain their foothold in certain world markets. The rapid economic growth of these countries during the past decade has been startling in contrast to the growth of both the industrialized countries and other nations in the process of industrial development.

Between 1970 and 1979 this group of advanced developing countries, often referred to as the newly industrialized counties (NICs) and including Brazil, South Korea, Taiwan, Singapore, Mexico, Nigeria, Colombia, Egypt, Hong Kong, Argentina and the Ivory Coast, has experienced significantly large comparative productive growth rates. This growth, measured in terms of real Gross Domestic Product (GDP)—the traditional indicator of national productivity—has occurred during the recent eight-year period at an annual rate of 5.7 percent for the NICs, as compared to 3.6 percent and 3.2 percent for the developing and industrialized countries respectively.[1]

Table 17. Non–oil-exporting LDCs: external sector developments, 1972–80 (*In billion of dollars, end of period*)

	1972	1974	1976	1978	1979	1980
Current-account deficit[a]	$10.8	$ 36.9	$ 32.9	$ 35.8	$ 52.9	$ 68.0
Increase in official reserves[a]	6.4	2.1	12.8	18.0	11.6	8.8
External debt outstanding						
World Bank:	62.1	94.8	139.0	211.6	246.4	279.5
Augmented:[b]	81.0	115.6	194.4	273.4	295.8	380.0

Source: [a]International Monetary Fund
[b]World Bank and B.I.S. data.

Undoubtedly, the single greatest contributing factor to this productivity phenomenon among the NICs is their rapid export expansion drive. Of immense importance to the United States is the resulting competitiveness of these nations in world markets and the expectation that their competitiveness is likely to grow further in the next decade, as they seek to build their internal economies through exports. This, of course, will place increased pressure on U.S. exporters in retaining their existing share of the international market.

As developing countries increase their indebtedness to hasten their industrialization through importation of capital equipment, they are increasingly under pressure to expand their exports. Total developing-country debt is reported in March, 1981 to be well over $500 billion (see Table 17). The question arises as to whether, and to what extent, the U.S. Federal Reserve will decide to purchase at sometime in the future any portion of this debt. Under the Depository Institutions and Monetary Control Act of 1980, the Federal Reserve may now legally do so.

What factors have caused certain developing countries to be well on their way to becoming developed while others appear to be unable to extricate themselves from poverty? Wealth of natural resources helps, of course, but this is not the only determinative. Libya, Nigeria, Iran, Iraq, Indonesia, Guatemala, and probably others have great resources of oil yet cannot be considered as developed or even as rapidly developing nations. South Korea, Taiwan, Singapore, and Hong Kong have progressed rapidly by making use of indigenous assets other than the endowment of nature's resources. Can we find a thread of commonality in the development process among those countries that have been successful?

There appear to be a number of factors that play key roles. They can be set out under some six headings: 1. Political stability; 2. A balanced economy; 3. An ability to capitalize on geographic diversity; 4. Modification of import substitution policies in favor of policies of export promotion; 5. Access to foreign capital or credit; 6. Developing human resources, including a strong work ethic and a priority commitment to education. Each of these factors is well worth detailed analysis.

1. Political Stability

In the past four years a new profession has been created in the industrialized countries under the name of political, or country risk, analysis. Banks and manufacturing firms pay for outside consultants to advise on the risks incurred in establishing branch or manufacturing plants in given developing countries. Foremost among the risks to be evaluated is that of inherent political instability. What are the chances of a violent overthrow of the government? Will key personnel be safe? After the recent events in Iran, in which even diplomats were not safe, increased concern has been noted.

Political stability in the developing countries is often a relative term. The development of democratic institutions is a slow process; it relies upon a contented middle class confident of its economic survival under conditions of constant and rising inflation; it requires a tradition of respect for law, authority, or religious guidance. Tribal conflict, as in Africa or parts of Asia, lack of political experience or public participation in government, as in many former colonies, make it difficult to develop stable governments in certain countries. In Africa the problems are particularly difficult: to satisfy political or economic aspirations of countries in Europe to whom colonial frontiers represented an extension of the European checkerboard, local national frontiers were arbitrarily established without regard to ethnic or language affinities. Political stability in Africa will have to await the development of national rather than tribal consciousness, a change of allegiance that may take generations to complete.

In South America the tradition of government has been quite different. Under colonial rule a viceroy governed by right of conquest and by authority of the Church, which had imposed its own culture on the native population. It is no wonder that a military tradition persisted when the countries of Latin America became independent. Equally to be expected was the continuation of the strong role of the Catholic Church hierarchy, which has, with certain exceptions, generally maintained its conservative tradition in cooperation with the military and the large land owners. As industrialization takes place and a new middle class increases its political power, the structure will change, but only slowly.

Since World War II a new political phenomenon has occurred to which not enough attention has been paid: the rise of labor leaders as a governing class in many developing countries. While if the military tradition has normally, but not necessarily, been of the right—note the difference between the allies of the military in Latin America and those in Egypt, Libya, Iraq, and other parts of the Middle East—labor governments in the developing countries base their ideological support in the class conflicts of nineteenth-century Europe.

With factory conditions poor, wage rates low, and ownership often in the hands of foreigners or nationals educated abroad, labor unions have tended, much like their European counterparts, to solidify their political power through direct confrontation with the traditional, conservative social structure. As a result the labor movement is often feared and distrusted by those very groups that can make the development process succeed—the urban small merchants, for example, who are the seedlings of a native-born middle class essential to any stable society. The influence of the ILO, relations with the socialist parties of Western Europe, and the lack of any real participation or guidance from such U.S. labor organizations as the AFL-CIO have all affected the policies of labor leaders in the developing countries.

In Europe, labor acceded to political power at a time of acute social conflict not generally present in the Anglo-Saxon countries. This timing made it difficult to avoid confrontation with the established social structure and often led to violence. Gradually, the realization will come to labor leaders in the developing world, as it has recently to those in Europe, that workers can quickly become part of the middle class in industrialized societies and are therefore the ultimate beneficiaries, not natural opponents, of political stability. As labor leaders in political power preserve, while adapting, the existing economic order, they may best ensure security for their members in a changing society.

Religious and cultural differences also play an important role. Within the religious tradition of East Asia, for example, there is nothing like the Judao-Christian fervor to spread religion in the name of a "one true God." And Chinese culture has existed for too many centuries to be changed easily by new concepts imposed from the outside. Cultural traditions enhance political stability because they are based on an acceptance of norms of social behavior developed over considerable time.

There is one other interesting factor to take into account in evaluating the prospects for political stability in a developing country: fear of outside interference often leads to the acceptance of a strong domestic government, even though such acceptance may mean sanctioning restrictions on the expression of dissent. Two cases in point: In both South Korea and Taiwan, fear of invasion from the outside has increased prospects for continued political stability, rather than decreased them; a majority of the population, understanding the necessity for a strong government to meet the threat of foreign military intervention, has accepted certain restrictions on individual freedom. More recently increased political stability in Thailand has doubtlessly come about as a consequence of the fear of aggression by Vietnam through Cambodia. Domestic political repression is thus often made acceptable as a response to external pressure.

There are many factors to be considered in an analysis of political stability, but there can be no argument with the statement that political stability is essential to economic development. Capital inflows of credit and investment cease if the political situation is not perceived to be stable. The plight of Argentina under Perón illustrates this point. Indeed, as instability increases, the outflows of capital become intense. This is true today of the situation in many countries of Central America. In the face of domestic unrest business slows, investment is deferred, unemployment increases, both trade and tax receipts decline precipitously; as a result, government becomes even more unstable and vulnerable to attempts to overthrow it by violence.

It is clear that exploitation of national resources by the government is more likely to succeed in an environment of quantitative and qualitative political development.[2] Quantitative political development has as its chief characteristic an increase in the proportion of the population that participates, in some sense, in political life. A government that does not have the support of the populace cannot endure and effectively perform its guiding role in the economy. Iran is a good recent example of what happens to political stability when only a small part of the population benefits from economic development or participates in the nation's political life. Even though the government of the Shah had the physical means for enforcing its will, the feeling of alienation of the general populace caused his government to collapse.

Mexico, on the other hand, illustrates how a government derives strength by assuring that all the interest groups will have the opportunity to provide input into the political process. This is done by the dominant party, called the Partido Revolucionario Institutional (PRI), which owes its very origin to the attempts, prior to its founding in 1928, to promote harmony among various conflicting groups. The uprisings and armed conflict that characterized the period before its existence no longer occur.

A study of the PRI's history indicates that it goes out of its way to form interest associations affiliated with the PRI. This forecloses the possibility of illegal and disruptive opposition by disgruntled members of society. The expansive and inclusive character of the PRI is further maintained by a party organization divided into sectors, each of which competes with the others for members.

The Ivory Coast, in basically the same manner, has opened up its political process. It has done so through the influence of Houphouet-Boigny, its outstanding national figure and president since the country became independent. His policy of conciliation and compromise has given the Ivory Coast political and economic stability. His accomplishments are particularly noteworthy in view of the many tribal groups in the country (perhaps over 50) all with different identities and interests. During World War II, when forced labor and production quotas caused resentment of colonial rule, Houphouet-Boigny organized a movement to express the country's dissatisfaction. His movement grew throughout the entire region and became, finally, the Ivory Coast's only political party: the Parti Démocratique de la Côte d'Ivoire (PDCI). A willingness by the tightly knit elite group at the top of the party to incorporate new groups has recently brought about the acceptance of competition in elections for party posts, especially at the levels of the secretaries-general of the subsections of the PDCI.[3]

As Egypt has moved from a centralized, socialist economy to one encouraging private initiative and less centralization it has shown a GDP growth rate from 1970 to 1978 of 7.8 percent. This growth in productivity has been generated in large part by analogous quantitative political developments that produced political stability and cooperation and have formed the foundation for rapid economic advancement. First, there has been a new acknowledgment of the importance of parliamentary politics, with its implications of greater legitimacy and wider political participation. Implementation of parliamentary procedures in Egypt is beginning to replace the rigid administrative-political organization dominant during the sixties.

Second, participation is being encouraged and supported by the regularization of procedures for competitive politics. In many parts of the country elections have appeared to be fiercely competitive, replacing the more reserved participation characteristic of the monolithic politics in the sixties.

Third, competition is being fostered in the parliamentary committees, which actively debate the government's established and proposed economic policies, and also in the media, which have provided public forums for debate. Unfortunately, recent press censorship threatens a reversal of the movement toward greater political participation.

In addition to quantitative political development, political stability may be further assured by qualitative political development, which may be defined as the tendency of a government to function in accordance with its own laws. This means that the administrative and judicial bodies enforce the country's laws fairly and equitably, that government officials are honest and competent, that elections are conducted fairly, that successions of government occur in accordance with established procedures, and that the legal system operates effectively to accommodate the needs of a developing economy. In Mexico, attempts are being made to reform the traditional Spanish system of elaborate regulation of the economy where the regulations serve no economic purpose. Nevertheless, much still needs to be done to eliminate a sometimes unwieldy and counterproductive system of permits, licenses, and complex procedural requirements that continue to thrive and get in the way of economic efficiency.

Nigeria, despite its vast oil wealth and other valuable natural resources, has not been able to tap and mobilize its wealth effectively due to serious qualitative political shortcomings. The country's recent carefully planned and executed return to civilian rule has been plagued by administrative inefficiency and corruption. The Code of Conduct Bureau, charged with overseeing compliance with strict rules dealing with conflict of interest, has had difficulty getting started. The appointed chairman was found to be overage under the constitution; the federal government took the matter to court to get its appointee confirmed, lost, and appealed the decision. The other eleven appointees fared no better; they were given positions but not assigned offices.[4]

Businessmen in Nigeria find that because of decisionmaking delays and the sheer complexity of the regulations that must be observed it can take two or even three times as long as in Europe to implement investment decisions. Many of these procedures contain internal contradictions that impede the natural development of business. For example, although the government wants to encourage investment, a strange interpretation of the industrial companies' indigenous-ownership decree is hindering the investment plans of some companies. According to this interpretation, companies in a certain Schedule Two (those allowed up to 40 percent foreign ownership) that seek to invest their surpluses in new Schedule Two businesses must take on a new 60 percent Nigerian partner. In effect, the investing company is treated as though it were 100 percent foreign owned. Despite complaints, only moderate government understanding has been shown.[5]

Egypt is another developing country that could greatly benefit from qualitative political reform. Its public administration of economic policy is heavily bureaucratic, control ridden and highly inefficient. Pressures from the World Bank, the International Monetary Fund, such regional organizations as the Kuwait Development Fund and other Arab institutions, and from numerous international banking and business groups have provided a new impetus for more effective management. These pressures should contribute to the development of an environment where bureaucratic performance in implementing plans is more closely scrutinized. Whatever the previous inadequacies of the Egyptian public administration, there is strong incentive in the new bureaucracy for the exercise of greater administrative effectiveness, both to obtain and use resources. This is especially important in that the public sector accounts for 75 percent of the total value in industrial output and for over 90 percent of current investment in industry.

2. A Balanced Economy

There is a tendency in the development process to focus on rapid industrialization rather than on the growth of a balanced economy in which urbanization is kept in check by the capacity of the agricultural sector to develop and absorb an equal share of the working population. There has been a tendency, particularly evident in Africa, for governments to increase taxes paid by agricultural producers in favor of social services for the urban poor. This has often had the effect of making the country's agriculture noncompetitive and/or unprofitable.

A clear illustration can be found by comparing the agricultural policy in the Ivory Coast with that of Ghana, a country impoverished by efforts at rapid industrialization undertaken at the cost of ruining the agricultural sector. As such governmental inequality was applied, cocoa, coffee, and bananas, formerly exported, became noncompetitive in price, and the agricultural production of many countries in Africa therefore decreased. Perhaps even more serious are the price-control policies followed in many agricultural countries. It is bad enough to tax heavily a successful portion of the economy on which the country depends for foreign exchange earnings to pay for transfer payments unrelated to production. It is disastrous for government to set such low prices for over agricultural products as to render it impossible to operate at a profit.

Yet this is exactly what has been done in many developing countries, ostensibly to protect the urban population against price gouging by the agricultural sector. The result, expectedly, is destruction of the agricultural sector. Jamaica, in the case of cattle and sugar; India, in the case of rice; Panama, in the case of meat are but a few examples. An agricultural country that allows inadequate prices for its agricultural products becomes rather quickly a net importer of food. This is happening throughout the developing world, where agricultural production is declining rather than increasing. Near starvation is appearing in many areas where agriculture was formerly sufficiently productive to feed the local population. As the world population is constantly increasing and is expected to double before the turn of the century, such policies are particularly tragic.

The problems of the Fourth World countries are more serious. In the newly independent countries of Africa the failure of governments and their advisors to understand the necessity of favoring agricultural development over rapid industrialization may result in one of the great tragedies of all time. Already starvation is spreading throughout the continent at a time when the population continues to increase. True, in some countries, such as Somalia, Ethiopia, Angola, Uganda, and Chad, the problem was caused by war and/or revolutionary activity. Nevertheless, in many other countries government economic policies must take the blame.

The results for these newly independent African countries are clear. Imports of grain from 1960 to 1978 have gone from 2 million to 12 million tons, a sixfold increase; indebtedness of governments in foreign currencies has increased to the point where even interest payments may have to be rescheduled; the second oil price increase of 1979–80 is taking most of the hard-currency earnings from exports (in Tanzania, for example, 60 percent of exports go to pay for imported oil even though oil needs are relatively small); the real price of products exported (coffee, cotton, cocoa, minerals) has not kept pace with the value of products to be imported; internal distribution of goods is difficult because the road and transport systems are totally inadequate; training of the elite in the United States or in Europe has meant that these educated nationals—if they return at all—have been led to believe that their nation must be modernized along Western lines; domestic schools, which at the time of the missions were devoted to training the students to function effectively in their villages, have now been patterned on the schools for expatriates, where manual labor is a forgotten art; and, finally, regardless of whether government is capitalist or Marxist, agriculture and cottage industry is looked down upon.

It is difficult to quarrel with this analysis, not only for Africa but for most of the poorer developing countries. In these countries, it would seem preferable to concentrate almost wholly on increasing food production by every means possible. Large-scale agricultural development on the American model is not the answer here because as was discovered in the Sudan and in Zaire, distribution is impossible for lack of roads and/or transport.

Above all, indiscriminate taxation of agricultural production should be stopped. Industries to favor should be those that will support and build upon elementary agriculture: bricks, fertilizer, simple agricultural implements, sugar mills, rice processing plants, oil processing, with a trend to value-added transformation of basic agricultural production. Only in this manner will the depopulation of agricultural areas towards the cities be stopped and the chances for rudimentary development reestablished on a sensible basis.*

Analysis of the economic growth of the NICs clearly reveals the mutually beneficial relationship between balanced industrial and agricultural development. A modern and diversified agricultural sector, as in the cases of Malaysia, Thailand, and the Ivory Coast, can contribute actively to industrial expansion. It can assure food supplies for urban factory workers, who will have a larger portion of their wages available for locally manufactured goods. In addition, it will serve to earn foreign exchange to finance the importation of capital goods for the industrial sector and provide the necessary raw materials for agricultural processing industries.

Conversely, when insufficient consideration is given to agricultural development, nations find that high food import costs cut back on the for-

* René Dumont, a Frenchman, is known throughout the world as one of the principal experts on agricultural problems of the developing countries. In 1962, he published a book *L'Afrique Noire est Mal Partie* (Black Africa Off to a Bad Start). In 1980, with Marie-France Mottin, he published a new book *L'Afrique Etranglée* (Africa Strangled), Ed. du Seuil, Paris. In these books, he shows clearly the disastrous effects of economic policies practiced by the African governments following the end of colonial rule. This important book by one of the world's foremost environmentalists should be read by anyone concerned with development policy. It mandates clearly the need for agricultural development before industrialization in the Fourth World.

eign exchange that could otherwise be available for importing the technology and capital necessary for domestic industrial development and export diversification. Furthermore, neglect of agriculture retards industrialization by inflating prices of food and leaving little extra for the domestic consumer to save or to spend on domestic nonagricultural items.

Perhaps worst of all, neglect of agricultural production causes farm workers to leave the land and migrate to the cities, where they add to the unemployment rolls and create new slums. From São Paulo to Lagos and Cairo, these slums are an indication that these nations, to their own detriments, have favored industrialization at the expense of agriculture.

The Ivory Coast is a good example of what exploitation of a natural comparative agricultural advantage can do to establish a firm base for a developing economy. In tropical Africa, a region where most countries have single-crop economies, the Ivory Coast has been successfully diversifying its agriculture since 1960, when it achieved independence. Increases in the production of the traditional exports, coffee and cocoa, have been accompanied by substantial diversification into lumber, palm oil, sugar, rubber, coconut, pineapple, and bananas.

Nonetheless, this country faces the plight of any country heavily dependent on raw materials and agricultural products for export receipts. It is subject to erratic price fluctuations, due to the extremely unpredictable demand and supply conditions prevailing in world markets. There is a necessity to develop a control mechanism in international trade that will stabilize prices by building food stocks in periods of plenty. When the Brazilian coffee crop is poor, or when it is ravaged by frosts, the Ivorian economy benefits. The reverse can also be true.

To a significant extent price fluctuations can be overcome by successful agricultural diversification and modernization, which requires heavy public investment in irrigation and new land development, maintenance of acceptable producer prices, and well staffed and funded institutions for agricultural research, for the distribution of inputs and credits, and for international marketing assistance.

Successful developing countries that lean primarily on their comparative agricultural advantage for export receipts, like the Ivory Coast, have used the foreign exchange earned through agricultural exports to increase imports of equipment and raw materials essential for industrial expansion. Industries that have sprung up as a result are varied and include cement, textile, palm oil, chocolate, soluble coffee, fruit preserves, shoes, and construction materials. It is interesting to note that from 1960 to 1979, agriculture and industry showed a definite trend towards a balance. The primary sector (agriculture, fisheries, and forestry) moved from 43.5 percent to 25 percent of the GDP, while industry rose from 4 percent to 13 percent of the GDP for the same period.[6]

In contrast to the Ivorian experience are the countries such as Burma, which have not pursued development of their existing agricultural advantage through new crop diversification, and have moved too quickly into industrialization without regard for a balance between agriculture and industry. Burma, instead of diverting substantial portions of its export proceeds from the sale of rice toward industrialization, should have used its profits to diversify its agricultural sector, which employs the bulk of the working population.

Also in contrast to the Ivorian experience is Egypt. Even though its agricultural sector is dominant in the overall economy, it has also failed to diversify, but for another reason. The government's policy of setting agricultural producer prices at low levels has stifled agricultural growth altogether. The Ivory Coast, on the other hand, has a policy of paying reasonable and stable producer prices for agricultural products. The comparative growth rates between Egypt and the Ivory Coast in the agricultural sector underscore the policy differences. While the Ivory Coast has shown an average growth rate of approximately 4 percent, the Egyptian rate for the same period is only approximately 3 percent.[7]

3. An Ability to Capitalize on Geographic Diversity

This factor is very much akin to the principle of a balanced economy. The reason why one can have confidence in the future of Colombia is that, unlike its neighbor Venezuela*, which appears to be richer in such natural resources as oil, iron ore, and nickel, Colombia, in its diversity of high mountain ranges and as an unintended consequence of an inadequate road system, has taken advantage of its natural geography. Unlike Caracas, Venezuela, Bogota, Colombia is only one of its country's many growing cities. Medellin, Cali, Cartagena, Baranquilla, Cuchabamba, Manizales are regional centers that are developing their own middle classes, relying on the diversity of products they produce and their self-generated momentums, neither dictated nor controlled from the capital. Regional diversity will thus assure a much faster growth and a much

* Economic development in Venezuela, despite the riches of the country, has to date failed to bring about a better life for the average citizen. The indices of wealth are to be seen, but alongside great poverty and increasing economic imbalance. Unless management and training are improved, new plants and equipment will not function effectively.

more diversified product base. Regional diversity can be an important factor in accelerating both industrial and agricultural development. There are indications that Yugoslavia after Tito may capitalize on its geographical and cultural diversity, patterning its development on Switzerland and West Germany rather than on the highly centralized economies of the other Eastern European countries. If so, we can expect economic development of the country to accelerate and its great cultural diversity to develop new bases for democratic political institutions similar to the Swiss cantonal system.

4. Abandonment of Import Substitution Policies in Favor of Policies of Export Promotion

A policy of import substitution represents an attempt, popular in the 1950s and the 1960s, and unfortunately still today in many areas, by developing countries to reduce their dependence on imported goods by attempting to produce capital goods within the country regardless of whether such products can be produced competitively. As a strategy for growth and development, this policy arose in response to both stagnant prices and widely fluctuating demands for primary products normally exported. By the early 1970s it had become evident that this policy was resulting in a misallocation of resources and continued external dependence in the form of imported semi-finished industrial and capital equipment. Concentration of effort on import substitution policies has resulted all too often in unnecessary cost increases, accelerated inflation, and unproductive use of scarce foreign exchange. In addition, import substitution policies have caused too much reliance on quotas, tariffs, and various other forms of government controls, which tend to slow economic growth. All this lead to inefficient industries, slow growth, and missed export opportunities—in other words, neglect of the principles of comparative advantage.

This is not to say that import substitution has been totally defective as a growth policy. Selective use of substitution can promote development. For instance, local energy and food production can spur domestic development. Brazil has produced alcohol from sugarcane and, as a result, has increased the estimated national ratio of alcohol use to gasoline use from 4.3 percent in 1977 to 19 percent in 1979. Other nations with the potential for sugar crops, root crops, and cereals could reduce their reliance on external sources of energy in the same manner. Mexico has wisely used import substitution policies to create a number of new industries by closing the border on further imports to protect a new industry until it could become truly competitive. It also encourages import substitution by requiring, as in the case of automobiles, that manufacturers match their imports of engines or parts with equivalent dollar amount of exports of the finished product.

Food production would also strengthen the domestic foundation for sustained growth. With respect to grains, only North America and Oceania are not net importers. However, improved management of water systems and pricing policies that do not discriminate against agriculture would help in the reduction of food imports in other areas of the world.

In the 1970s policies of export diversification gradually replaced earlier policies of import substitution in the more advanced developing countries. Such a policy enables a country to benefit from rapidly growing external markets and to overcome demand problems found in the domestic market. Additionally, as foreign exchange earnings are needed to pay for the increased import requirements and high debt servicing associated with economic development programs, strong export earnings become essential. Among the reforms accompanying the new outward oriented policies are formal exchange-rate devaluations and realignment,* comprehensive monetary and fiscal stabilization measures and reforms, and the easing of industrial licensing regimes, import tariff and duties, foreign direct investment laws, and other protectionist devices. Generally, the governments of the NICs have undertaken active roles in promoting exports, through direct financial assistance as well as through the above-mentioned policy changes. The most active countries promoting exports were the Latin American and Asian NICs, which have followed the example of Japan in fostering close business–government cooperation.

Colombia is a good example of improved growth through reduced bias towards import substitution. Between 1945 and 1968, when import substitution was prominent, the average annual increase in GDP was about 4.8 percent. However, between 1970 and 1978, when Colombia began a concentrated effort to become export oriented, the GDP rose to about 6 percent a year. Colombia found that self-sufficiency through overem-

* It is interesting to note that Mexico has refused to devalue its currency even though, as of April, 1981, the peso was clearly overvalued. In order to compensate for its overvaluation, the Mexican government has been preparing a package of fiscal incentives to give exporters rebates of indirect taxes and customs duties and new exporter financing. With inflation at 28 percent (over twice that of the United States, Mexico's principal trading partner,), the peso will become even more overvalued.

phasis on industrialization did not provide optimal use of its resources.

While Colombia's most efficient sectors are food, clothing, footwear, wood/wooden furniture, paper, rubber, nonmetallic minerals, machinery, and textiles, between 1962 and 1967 about 40 percent of total fixed investment was in chemicals and petroleum products. These are capital-intensive industries, which require high foreign-capital imports. During this period employment tended to stagnate although population growth was strong. It is clear that the economy suffered from insufficient expenditure on agriculture and labor-intensive industry.

A turnaround occurred in the late 1960s as nontraditional exports became an important engine for overall growth. These exports grew at a rate of about 25 percent per year between 1965 and 1975 alone. The early 1970s showed the GDP rising at about 6–7 percent per year. How did this happen? First, there was a reduction in those protective policies that benefitted the inefficient industries; and second, there was an emphasis on government policy to promote a more rational allocation of national resources to make better use of Colombia's comparative advantages. In 1960 coffee accounted for approximately 72 percent of total commodity exports. By 1972, however, this share declined to 52 percent, due to the diversification of exports into nontraditional areas such as cardboard boxes, textiles, machinery, and printer materials.

Multiple exchange rates, which are different exchange rates for artificially protecting the prices of different commodities, were narrowed to one rate, with the exception of several commodities, including petroleum exports. Another incentive for export diversification is a tax exemption for a certain percentage of export profits. It began in 1960 in Colombia as a means of stimulating the utilization of excess productive capacity, and was later recognized as an effective incentive for the promotion of nontraditional exports.

In 1967 the tax exemption was replaced by tax credit certificates, which were issued in an amount up to 15 percent of the value of all exports, with the exception of various traditional exports such as coffee and petroleum. These certificates are freely negotiable and can be used at their face value to pay income, sales, and import taxes for a certain period of time after their issuance. Adjusted for the tax-free value and the trading discount, the effective subsidy on exports amounts to 18 percent.

Another government program in Colombia, the Plan Vallejo, has given preferential treatment to exports of manufactured goods by granting exemptions from prior licensing, advance import deposits, and customs duties on imported inputs. Much like the policy exempting export profits from income taxes, this plan was originally intended to promote the use of excess capacity in the manufacturing sector. Later, this proved to be an effective means of promoting nontraditional manufactured exports, by providing duty-free entry of various raw materials, intermediate products, and capital equipment to be utilized in manufacturing products for export.

Special credit facilities in the form of export prefinancing have also been established. Under these facilities, prospective exporters can borrow in a foreign currency, free from exchange risk, for a period of approximately one year, in order to finance production for exports and to eventually repay the borrowing with the income generated from export sales. The interest rate on this borrowing would be significantly less than the going rate at Colombian commercial banks.

The main sources of this type of export financing are the lines of credit obtained by Colombian commercial banks with their correspondents abroad. This credit may also be extended directly by foreign commercial banks with branches in Colombia. This program dovetails with foreign export-promotion efforts, such as the bank to bank guarantee program of the Export-Import Bank of the United States, whereby the United States guarantees loans of U.S. commercial banks to foreign banks to finance U.S. exports.

To further the export effort, the Colombian government in 1967 established a domestic program called the Export Promotion Fund (PROEXPO). It provides exporters with working capital at low interest rates to cover foreign promotion and advertisement expenses. It is funded by a 1–1.5 percent import surcharge.

Brazil is another good example of export diversification. While primary products, such as coffee, sugar, cocoa and tobacco are still very important to the basic strength of the Brazilian economy, they are becoming relatively less important as export diversification of manufactured products is being expanded. Primary product exports in 1964 accounted for 85 percent of Brazil's exports, with coffee alone comprising 50 percent. However, by 1978 the effects of a policy of export diversification were evident and the results were significant in that coffee accounted for only 18 percent of total exports, while exports of industrialized products had grown to 51 percent of the total.[8] It is a measure of Brazil's progress in industrialization, that at the Itaipu hydroelectric project on the Parana River between Brazil and Paraguay, a project that will increase electric power capacity in Brazil by 78 percent, 85 percent of the capital equipment has been manufactured in Brazil.

The fiscal incentives are some of the most effective incentives for expanding Brazilian exports. They have included: exemption from the Imposto Sobre Productos Industrializadas (IPI) federal industrial product tax on exports; a tax credit based upon the IPI for exported products; exemption from the Imposto de Circulacao de Mercadorias (ICM) state taxes on exports; a tax credit based on the ICM for exports; an income tax exemption for profits earned from exports; exemption from the payment of various minor taxes for exported products; and drawback provisions allowing duty-free import of materials used to produce finished export products.

Credit incentives have also played a major role in export diversification by providing financing for export sales as well as for export production. The official direct financing by the Brazilian government of export sales has grown steadily from $8 million in 1969 to $424 million for the first ten months of 1978.[9] Official credits for export production are provided through the commercial banking system as working capital loans in local currency for a one-year period. Since the interest rate for these loans is approximately 8 percent per annum, the subsidy element is great, particularly when one considers that the Brazilian inflation rate reached 110 percent in 1980. Overall, credit subsidies for Brazilian exports have provided a massive stimulus for the diversification of exports and for the presence of Brazilian products in world trade. In 1977, for instance, the average nominal credit subsidy, expressed as a percentage of export f.o.b. values, was 5 percent for the manufacturing sector.[10]

In addition to the economic incentives of the Brazilian government, efforts have also been made by the government to market and promote Brazilian exports. Various agencies are assigned to organize seminars, conferences, and trade shows and to work with exporters, providing them with information on the marketing possibilities for their products.*

Until the early 1960s, Korea, like many other developing countries, followed an industrialization strategy based primarily on a policy of import substitution. However, in the early 1960s, after the completion of a program of import substitution in nondurable consumer goods and their inputs, the Koreans changed their developmental strategy to export pro-

* Brazil is a typical example of a developing country that must increase its exports by all means possible in order to meet its indebtedness. In 1980, Brazil's inflation rose to 110 percent; its trade deficit reached $2.8 billion, largely because of its dependence on imported oil. For 1981, its gross borrowings have been targeted at $13.6 billion. Unfortunately, as Brazil's indebtedness continues to grow, its bankers increase interest charges. In 1981, these will probably be in excess of 2 percent over the LIBOR rate.

motion. The success of Korean economic growth through export trade can be attributed to a variety of programs and policies, of which the most important will be discussed below.

The first step toward export expansion came with the adoption of a realistic exchange rate in May, 1964. Prior to this date, Korean exports were stifled by the overvaluation of the *won,* even though other measures—such as multiple exchange rates, inexpensive credits and preferential tax treatment—existed to compensate for such overvaluation. The exchange-rate depreciation amounted to approximately 50 percent and was reinforced the following year by the adoption of a unitary fluctuating exchange-rate system that would reflect realistic demand and supply conditions in determination of the exchange rate.

The exchange-rate reforms were followed by various export incentive programs. These included reduction in or exemption from various taxes and customs duties, export credits at preferential interest rates, accelerated depreciation on facilities used for the production of exports, and discounts on power and transportation rates. Export industries were entitled to total exemption from the business tax and a reduction of 50 percent on income and corporate taxes. Imported raw materials incorporated in export products were exempted from import duties and the commodity tax.

Additionally, bank credits were available to exporters at an annual rate of 6 percent. This provided a strong incentive for exporting, given that bank credit for domestic transactions was available at a rate of approximately 26 percent per year. Other indirect subsidies included a 30 percent reduction in the cost of railway transportation of export commodities and a reduction of charges for electricity used in the production of exports.

The government also provided marketing assistance through the Korean Trade Promotion Corporation (KOTRA) and assumed a supervisory planning function by formulating annual export targets and a geographic export marketing strategy, specifying recommended quantities of certain products to be directed into various markets, and the appropriate marketing techniques to be used. The government also enacted an Export Products Inspection Law to ensure proper quality of exported goods.[11]

5. Access to Foreign Capital or Credit

In order to achieve industrialization, with the enormous investment of capital required, it is essential that a developing country have access to capital from abroad. The necessary long-term capital funds required can be obtained only in one or more of three ways: by encouragement of investment from abroad either through government grants or through private investment from multinational business firms; by sound financial policies at home, which will establish the financial credit-worthiness of the government and encourage foreign banks to make long-term loans for development purposes; through encouragement of the private sector in the domestic economy, which will encourage private loans and investment from abroad. Each of these methods has been tried in the development process, alone or in combination.

Government economic grants to developing countries may be made directly or through the support of international institutions like the World Bank group or the InterAmerican Development Bank, which, in turn, extend credits to developing countries for special infrastructure projects. In the United States, economic aid has gradually changed its focus over the years. Today the AID programs of the United States focus less on economic projects, since these are thought to be better handled through the U.S. contribution to international institutions, than on the special human resource needs of the poorer developing countries, such as water supplies, irrigation, small-scale agriculture, basic educational needs, medical assistance. The programs have never been popular with Congress.

Other countries have tried various innovations, including the French who allow qualified individuals to substitute participation in special assistance projects for military service. Countries like Guinea that have looked for special assistance to the Soviet Union have been critical of the support received. Recently Canada and Sweden have developed special programs to support management education in developing countries on the theory that economic development must, in the final analysis, depend upon properly trained managers qualified to run complex industrial projects. This would seem to be a useful innovation.

The private investments of multinational firms increasingly include educational programs, so that foreign technicians can be replaced by qualified supervisory personnel recruited within the country. The multinational not only invests substantial capital in the country, erects plants, and trains workers, but also transfers its technology to the developing country. There has been much criticism in UNCTAD that only infrequently have research centers been established in the developing countries so that tomorrow's technology can be nurtured in the developing as well as the developed countries.* This may come in time, but it will depend upon easy access to educational institutions that are themselves centers of research.

Developing countries, unfortunately, tend to forget that it is the country rather than the foreign multinational that benefits most from the investment, regardless of any transfer of earnings abroad. The investments by multinational companies are almost always long-term investments that tend to grow rather than be paid out. The country acquires factories, employment for its nationals, an influx of capital, transfer of technology, and training in management skills. These become permanent investments adding to the wealth of the nation.

The importance of sound financial management to a country's development is obvious. If a developing country's government includes a Ministry of Finance and a Central Bank functioning well, banking institutions outside the country will be disposed to make long-term loans and credit available to that country. We have only to look at the changes in borrowing capacity that occurred in Brazil after 1964,† or in Argentina after 1977, or in Peru in 1980 following the appointment of good financial management within the government.

For reasons that have been given throughout this chapter, the most important factor in attracting foreign credits or investment to a developing country is the encouragement by government of a thriving private-sector economy. Egypt is only just now beginning to recover from the Nasser government's nationalization of private companies throughout the economy. Chile is passing through the same recovery process after Allende; Jamaica, essentially a rich country, can expect to turn its economy around following the election in 1980 of a new government.‡ Na-

*As developing countries reach the appropriate stage of industrialization, the multinational corporation is likely to establish research facilities. In 1980, for example, Dow Chemical established a very large research center in Brazil for petrochemical development.

†In 1981, at a time when Brazil may find it difficult to borrow as much as it needs (its foreign debt at the end of 1980 had reached $157 billion), the government is using a technique successfully used by Italy in the early 1970s, when Italy's own credit could support no additional borrowings. The Italian government used the large state owned corporations' borrowing power to make loans in the Eurocurrency market, as though they were private company loans, and then borrowed from the companies or used their additional export potential. In early 1981, Brazil's government-owned steel company, Cia. Vale do Rio Doce, borrowed $300 million from ten U.S. banks.

‡In March, 1981, as a gesture of confidence in the new government headed by Edward Seaga, a subgroup of the Caribbean Group for Cooperation in Economic Development (consisting of the United States, United Kingdom, Germany, France, the Netherlands, Nor-

tionalized industry tends to be wasteful, bureaucratic, and inefficient. It is much more subject to labor pressures. It is also far less inclined to take business risks because profit is always a secondary consideration. Those developing countries that have succeeded best, Argentina, Brazil, Colombia, Ivory Coast, Taiwan, Mexico, Hong Kong, Singapore, and South Korea, all have good financial management in the government and a thriving private sector.*

6. Developing Human Resources, Including a Strong Work Ethic and a Priority Commitment to Education

The quality of human resources and successful educational efforts have been considered by some as two of the most important factors bearing on a nation's development. This can be illustrated rather quickly by citing the highly industrialized economy of Switzerland. This small country with no natural energy resources except water for generating electricity, and no minerals, has relied heavily on its human resources to create an unmatched precision product industry with the result that its per capita income ranks among the highest in the world.

Two years ago the author spoke in Davos, Switzerland with the Deputy Minister of Planning of Saudi Arabia. The son of a nomad in the desert, the minister had an M.B.A. and Ph.D. from two prestigious U.S. universities. The jump across many centuries in one generation gave him a particularly interesting perspective on current mores.

"We have observed in my country," he said, "the difference in approach between the industrialized countries whose representatives flock to my country in search of business opportunities. The Europeans decry each other's capabilities, have good workmanship, but try to give less for more as though we are incapable of judging; the Americans arrive with more lawyers than businessmen; the South Koreans simply tell us to prepare the contracts ourselves and that the charge will be 20% less than the Americans. Negotiation is simple on this basis and the work faultless.

way, Canada, Argentina, Colombia, Mexico, and Venezuela) agreed to make available to Jamaica $350 million for the 1981–82 fiscal year. This was three times as much as Seaga had requested.

* Malaysia has developed an interesting method of encouraging domestic capitalism. A fund, the Permodalan Nasional Berhad (National Equity Corp.) has had transferred to it by the government minority holdings in several hundred corporations (the government owns all or part of 74 business concerns). Individuals are being encouraged to buy into this mutual fund, which will be the subject of a media campaign to publicize the concept of share ownership in the country's industries.

It seems to us that the European work ethic which was once so strong, passed across the Atlantic to the United States a century ago and has now left there too, across the Pacific to Asia, to Japan, Taiwan, South Korea, Hong Kong and Malaysia, where pride of product is still the norm, as opposed to American products, which are too often hastily made, inadequately assembled, and now rarely properly serviced."

There would appear to be no doubt of the importance of the work ethic in the development process. In the Soviet Union and the Comecon countries there is a desperation expressed in time spent by government intellectuals trying to devise special programs to motivate people to work more productively. But no special program can succeed when the system itself is at fault, where rewards are inadequate and unfairly distributed. Third World countries that have followed the Marxist economic philosophy have all ended in economic failure: Burma, Guinea, Chile under Allende, Argentina under Perón, Brazil under Goulart, Uruguay, Indonesia under Sukarno, and Ghana under Nkrumah have all seen their economies decline. Cuba itself is maintained economically through arbitrary Soviet price support. The latest and perhaps clearest exposé of the failure of the collective system and its destruction of the work ethic has been demonstrated to the world by the sad picture of the workers of Poland. It is not only that man wants to be free; it is that he must have pride in his work and be fairly recompensed for its value—or sooner rather than later he will simply cease to be productive no matter what pressures are applied to make him work.

The governments of developing countries, particularly those in the early stages of industrialization, need to devote much effort to encouraging the adaptation of scientific knowledge and technology within the appropriate level of their industrialization, as well as to modernizing their agricultural sectors. Modern technology requires trained personnel to fill managerial, engineering, and supervisory positions and skilled labor to operate machinery and to implement modernization programs. Efforts to step up technical training geared to meet these needs is critical to the overall development process and cannot be overemphasized. The most successful NICs have succeeded in building an educational base to make possible the gradual industrialization of the country. Brazil, Mexico, Taiwan, and South Korea in particular have been successful at this.

The government of Taiwan has recognized the need for technical manpower and has vigorously pursued the qualitative development of its human resources. In fiscal year 1961, when considerable portions of its budget were being channeled toward defense expenditures, 12.7 percent of the budget was directed towards education.[12] Between 1960 and 1977 the number enrolled in secondary schools as a percentage of age group jumped from 33 percent to 76 percent and for the same period adult literacy climbed from 54 percent to 82 percent. India, in contrast, showed an increase in the first category from 20 percent to 28 percent and increase in the second from 28 percent to 36 percent.[13]

Taiwan, in order to pursue manpower development, has created a special committee within the nation's central economic planning agency. Since the committee projected a sizeable shortage of technical manpower in the late 1970s, a number of vocational schools were built with a concentration on industrial skills. The creation of the National Vocational Training Service for Industry, assisted by the United Nations, has brought a greater push for this effort. The government has also encouraged enterprises to set up their own vocational training programs and has sought to coordinate closely the programs of the educational institutions with the needs of industry.

In addition to these activities, the government has sponsored or supported a number of agencies to train and to effectively utilize its available manpower. These include the China Productivity and Trade Center (to promote improvement of management and quality control and other training activities related to trade expansion and increased productivity), the Metal Industries Development Center (to train technical and managerial personnel at all levels of the metal and engineering industries), and the China Technical Consultants, Inc. (to funnel technical and managerial personnel resources available from large-scale enterprises, into local industry).[14]

Conclusions

In an analysis of the industrialization process there are lessons to be learned both by the industrialized countries and by those developing countries that have been least successful to date. The richer countries have much to learn from the experience of their new competitors, a lesson they must learn if they are not to see the standard of living of their own populations decline. In Europe, as well as in the United States, the factors discussed above as having particular relevance to the developing process need to be considered carefully.

To what extent, we must ask, has lack of political stability harmed Italy since World War II? Hasn't geographical diversity in West Germany, since the elimination of Prussia as the political fulcrum of the country, been of enormous help in rapid regional economic redevelopment? Will the United States now adopt import substitution policies to prevent continued imports of Japanese autos? Will the Reagan Administration expand as it should the prior administration's efforts at export promotion? Will the Congress make a mistake of passing laws in the future to restrict foreign investment for fear of further takeovers from abroad? Have we ourselves learned the importance of making a special effort to educate the gifted? Has seeing how important it is elsewhere in encouraging innovation and developing new technology truly and definitively confirmed for us the advisability of encouraging the private sector in our own country? Is it consistent to encourage the transfer of technology to developing countries and at the same time spend billions to protect backward industries in our own country? How can we perpetuate the work ethic at home when the government appears to make less effort encouraging the creation of new job opportunities in the private sector than it does extending additional employment benefits?

We have observed that because of geographic location, history, cultural patterns or the lack of certain natural resources all developing countries have experienced at one time or another difficulties in overcoming impediments to the smooth functioning of the developmental process. Today the United States needs to revitalize its own industrial economy. In doing so, it can learn much from observing the process of development in other parts of the world.

The lesser developed countries which have not been successful, as well as the developed countries which have recently shown a record of decreased productivity and stagnating growth, can learn from the experiences of the NICs and seek to concentrate on those factors in the development process that they have either neglected or poorly managed. Such an effort by developing and developed countries alike would bring economic rewards not only to those individual countries but also to the entire international economic community that has become increasingly interdependent over the recent years.

This economic global interdependence, as well as the new ease of worldwide information transmission, increasingly dictates that development should progress throughout the world without exception. It is only through such understanding that we may avoid future political confrontations from increasingly deprived and frustrated peoples. Instant communication and observation renders intolerable the coexistence of abject poverty and inordinate wealth. Communications have rendered us all next-door neighbors or will shortly do so. If economic betterment can exist anywhere, it must develop everywhere. Technology must spread; energy solutions must not be contained; methods by which men are motivated to better their own economic conditions must be available everywhere.

It is truly indefensible, for example, that industrialization is held back in certain countries because governments are unwilling to encourage exploitation and production of hydrocarbon resources because they prefer to increase prices or are unwilling to let others more enterprising participate in the development of domestic natural resources. The lesson that we need to learn from recent history is that any policy of enforced scarcity, whether through discouragement of resource development or purposeful failure to motivate human ingenuity and resourcefulness for political reasons, is misanthropic and inherently dangerous.

In economic terms, the Marxist system, based as it is upon repression of the individual's need to self-expression, or in the case of the Soviet empire, the desire for individual national consciousness, has failed. Within the Soviet bloc it will either slowly change towards a decentralization of power with new efforts to motivate individual initiative as in Yugoslavia and Poland, or it will become even more centralized, bureaucratized, and repressive in the future.*

Again in economic terms, those policies of OPEC that are based upon the maintenance of scarcity will eventually also change or have the unintended consequence of forcing human ingenuity to develop the alternatives that are all around us. It is indeed inconceivable that 81 percent of the drilling for hydrocarbons in the free world should have taken place in 1980 in the United States compared to 0.5 percent in Brazil, and 0.010 percent in Australia.

There is another aspect of our interdependence to which we have not paid sufficient attention. It is becoming clear that misused technology threatens the environment on which each of us depend. Not only through nuclear proliferation is man's future threatened, but perhaps more important, through his ability to effect climatic change.

The power to create is also the power to destroy. In a few years man has almost perfected the ability to recreate himself. He has also found the power to destroy himself in a way no one could have foreseen as recently as fifty years ago—climatically. How many of us have reflected upon our historical dependence upon the Gulf Stream, which has given us the rainfall and the seasons upon which our food supplies depend,

* The effect of these growing and inconsistent trends, within the context of international trade, are examined in Chapter 9.

from the plains of North America to those of western Europe? What will happen if the rain forests of northern Brazil are cut down in an effort to feed new settlers in those regions? Who decides on the climatic preservation of man? Was it not only a relatively short time ago that the southern shores of the Mediterranean, now the Sahara, were known as the granary of the Roman Empire? To what extent is the climatic tragedy of the Saheel region of central Africa man's latest attempt to self-destruct through his ability in other areas of the globe to heat the atmosphere through hydrocarbon abuse?

Our ingenuity in developing methods of adjustment among ourselves has not matched our ingenuity in developing the new conditions of life that bring about the need for such adjustments. Adjustments require time. Will the time frame be sufficient to allow for such adjustments between conflicting needs within our geographic spheres? Or will we come to destroy ourselves in a future attempt to prevent our fellow man from threatening the way we live and function in our global area through attempts to develop and cultivate his own land. The challenge of this new perception of our global interdependence is awesome, indeed.

But it is in this context that we must consider the relationship between developed and developing nations in the future. If we fail to create new perspectives to better cooperate, we may also fail to anticipate some rather rapid reversals of roles.

9

The Impact of Trade with Nonmarket Economies

I cannot forecast to you the action of Russia. It is a riddle wrapped in a mystery inside an enigma.

WINSTON CHURCHILL

I need not recite again how troublesome, evil, turbulent a country China is. To mention just one instance—there is the matter of their picture writing.

KABO MABUCHI

No clearer statement of the difficulty of dealing with the Russians and the Chinese can be made than in the quotations above; given the perplexity of a Churchill and the frustration of a Japanese scholar, it is no wonder that it is so difficult for politicians and businessmen today to comprehend what happens in those countries with their extraordinary history, their unique civilizations, their philosophies so complicated and alien to our own.

In this chapter we will analyze the development of U.S. political and economic relations, first with the Soviet Union, then with the satellite countries of Eastern Europe (COMECON), including Yugoslavia, and finally with the post-Mao government of the People's Republic of China (PRC).

Although the Soviet Union (and its satellites) and the People's Republic of China are all Communist countries, the United States does not have, in either its trade or its political relationships, one set policy for dealing with Communist countries. Our dealings and relationships with the various Communist countries are often quite different. But these countries do present some common problems: For one thing, we know less about them than we ought to and than we do about other countries with which we trade; and second, during the next five years there may be very great changes in our relationships—trade and otherwise—with both the Soviet Union (and its Eastern European satellite countries) and the PRC. It will be a measure of our ability and right to act as political leaders of the Western World if we make an honest attempt to understand and aid in the adjustment process almost certain to take place.

Trade relations with Communist nations have always presented a dilemma to Westerners.[1] Should the establishment of economic relations with nations that possess political forms of government not in step with our own be avoided to ensure that we do not promote the political goals of those nations? Or should economic transactions be completely divorced from political determinants? Or can well planned and monitored trading relations be used to ease international tensions and lessen the potential for conflict?

It was not until 1934 that the U.S. government granted recognition to the Soviet Union. Prior to that, trade between the two countries existed only under normal buy and sell types of transactions, with no credit terms involved. A second type of trade, entailing various concessions by the United States, i.e., credits, grants or low-interest loans to enable the USSR to finance purchases from the United States, was at first not allowed at all.[2] It was only after 1934, with U.S. recognition of the Soviet Union, that U.S. government financing became available. This was the origin of the Export-Import Bank of the United States.

It is interesting to note that the Executive Order of the President on February 1, 1934, which established the Export-Import Bank, specified that it was to devote itself exclusively to the promotion of trade with the Soviet Union. This was done by Franklin Roosevelt at the urging of William Bullitt, the first U.S. ambassador to the Soviet Union, and Jesse Jones, head of the Reconstruction Finance Corporation. Jones, as chairman, and the secretaries of the departments of State and Commerce, comprised the Bank's first board of trustees. It is also interesting to note that by express written direction of President Roosevelt, the chairman of the Bank was forbidden to handle any transactions other than those with the Soviet Union. In order to get around this restriction the resourceful Jesse Jones had a second Export-Import Bank approved by Congress in 1934 in order to finance trade with other nations.

During the 1920s and 1930s, essentially normal trade relations existed between the United States and Europe on the one hand, and the United States and the Soviet Union on the other. This situation changed dramatically following World War II and the consolidation of Soviet control throughout Eastern Europe. United States trade policy towards the Soviet

Union and her Eastern satellite nations then underwent a drastic shift. Economic warfare became an integral part of the Cold War policy of the United States. From 1948 to 1963, U.S. exports to the Soviet Union fell by 60 percent while trade between our allies and the Communist nations more than tripled.[3] The continued high trade levels between the Western allies of the United States and the Communist bloc nations is easily explained. The United States, under the Export Control Act of 1949, forbade the export of products that would "contribute significantly" to these nations' economic (as well as military) potential, "in a way that would prove detrimental to the national security and welfare of the United States." To insure that this act would be enforced, the government simply forbade the export of almost all U.S. products to these countries by requiring that the exporter obtain a U.S. government license for export of such products. Clearly, throughout this Cold War period, U.S. policy reflected the view that political and moral goals should take precedence over purely economic goals. Unfortunately our allies in Western Europe felt differently about embargoing most military trade with the Communist nations and so they simply provided many of the goods we refused to sell. Today, when most high-technology products sought by the Communist countries can be equally well produced in Europe or Japan, the continued refusal on the part of the United States to expand trade with the Communist countries does little to impede their development.

It is true, of course, that during the first twenty years of this act, export trade with the Communist bloc was not important to the United States economically, since our trade balance with other nations was largely positive. But by the late 1960s the situation was already quite different. The U.S. share of East–West trade in 1967, 1968, and 1969 accounted for only 0.2 percent of the total. True, this is 0.2 percent of some fairly meager total trade figures of $11 billion to $13 billion, but our allies were clearly making the most of the business transactions available (see Figure 4).

Gradually it became evident that the United States ought perhaps to begin to reevaluate its earlier trade policies towards the East in order to allow U.S. business to participate in this growing market. It was also observed that as a by-product of these economic relations there might come an interesting opportunity to promote the political interests of the United States in the area. With the introduction of a policy of détente in 1971 by the Nixon Administration and until the invasion of Afghanistan,* prior political and moral judgments were relaxed to allow most

*On Christmas Eve, 1979, 50,000 Soviet troops invaded Afghanistan, captured Kabul, the capital, and installed a puppet government.

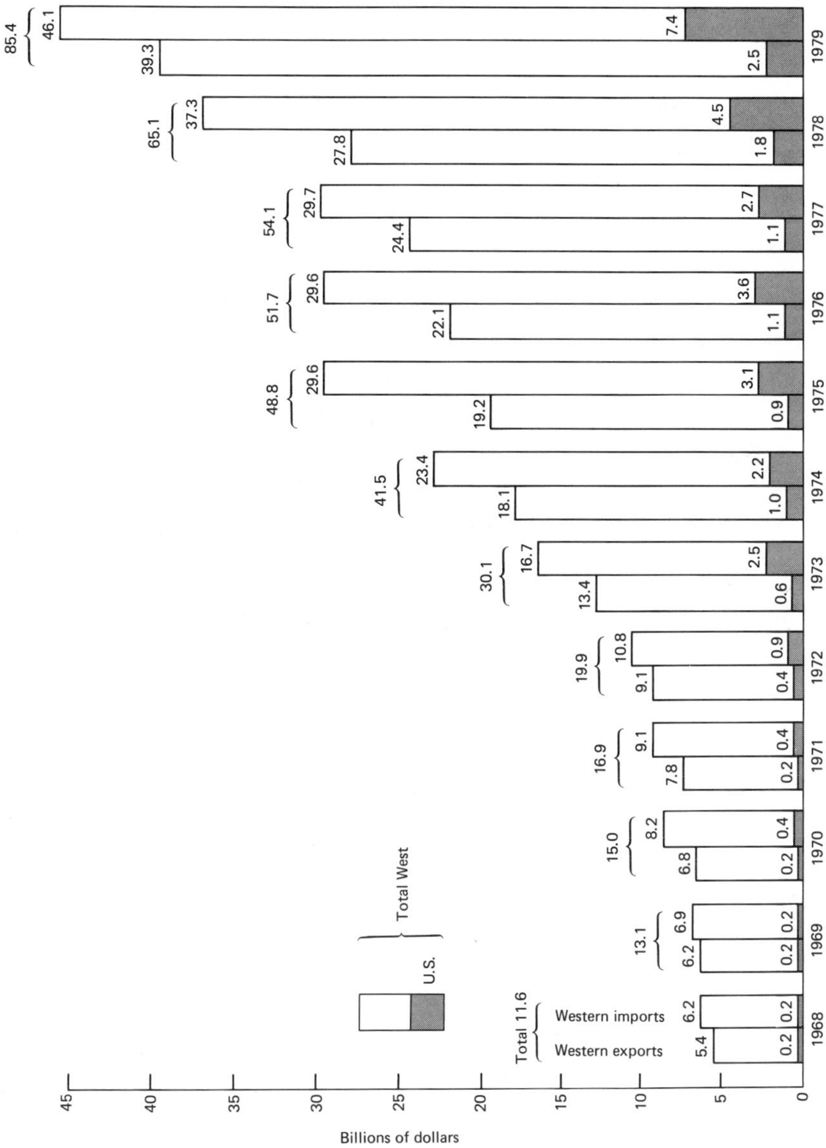

Figure 4. East[a]–West[b] trade and U.S. share

Source: U.S. Department of Commerce, Industry and Trade Administration, Office of East-West Trade Policy and Planning, June, 1979.

[a] East = Bulgaria, Czechoslovakia, East Germany, Hungary, Poland, Romania, USSR and People's Republic of China.

[b] West = Austria, Belgium, Canada, Denmark, West Germany, France, Italy, Japan, Luxembourg, Netherlands, Norway, Sweden, Switzerland, U.K. and U.S.

[c] Figures for 1978 and 1979 released to author by Commerce Department in 1981.

economic interactions. The initial dilemma postulated remained, yet many forces during this period were pushing for a more moderate and calculated approach nonetheless, arguing that economic transactions would generate increased communication between the two superpowers and thereby greatly reduce the chances of conflict. In addition they also argued that another benefit that might come about was a modification of the economic goals of the USSR and Eastern Europe, requiring more imports of Western goods, particularly technology. These arguments plus the general mood of the nation led to a shift in the tone of U.S. trade policy with the European Communist nations.

At the same time a shift took place in political relations with the People's Republic of China (PRC). The PRC has been purposely excluded from the above discussion of postwar, pre-détente East–West trade, as PRC trade with the United States was almost totally embargoed, amounting to less than $1 million prior to 1971. In the 1970s détente became a U.S. government policy, to be applied to both major Communist nations. In 1980 and 1981 changes are again occurring: in the case of the Soviet Union, the relationship is being strained by the Soviet's decision to invade Afghanistan and the threat to Poland; in the case of the PRC, recognition of the government and the beginning of a new trade relationship bode well for increasingly friendlier dealings.

Our purpose here will be to examine in some detail the extent to which the limited policy of détente has liberalized U.S. trade with the Communist bloc. To what extent, if any, have political perceptions on both sides changed? And what auguries for increased trade do we now see in the future? To reiterate, détente was intended to promote the growth of economic and cultural relationships. From the U.S. standpoint increased communication between hostile systems of government would serve to show the peoples within the Communist bloc the benefits of the free enterprise system and gradually "open up" these closed societies to political dialogue. In this chapter we will look closely at those decisions made since Richard Nixon's election in 1968 that have either constrained or promoted U.S. trade, first with the Soviet Union, then with Eastern Europe. We will also examine the evolution of trade relationships with the PRC. A basic premise underlying the entire analysis is that the dilemma postulated at the outset of this chapter regarding political and moral versus economic criteria for determining trade relations can be resolved. Through a coherent and objective analysis of the constraints to trade, both political and economic, coupled with a clear enunciation of actual U.S. goals and national interests in the area, trade can grow to higher yet mutually advantageous levels. This examination will begin with a brief discussion of the structural, economic, and political barriers that presently serve to constrain trade between the United States and the Soviet Union along with its Eastern European allies even under the best of conditions. Next will be examined the difficult question of technology transfer to these countries, taking as an example the sale of energy related technology and equipment to the USSR. There is much to be said on both sides of the argument, and one has the feeling that the government finds it very difficult to determine with consistency just where to draw the line between permissible and forbidden transfers.

Finally, to conclude the section on the USSR and Eastern Europe, we will discuss the practical problems facing the American businessman actually conducting day to day business transactions with the USSR and Eastern Europe. The recent growth of various countertrade and industrial cooperation agreements are relevant here. Are they the wave of the future or perhaps the *only* future for East–West trade? What promise does the unique case of Yugoslavia hold for Western business? For the U.S. government?

The chapter will close with a discussion of the prospects for expansion of trade with the People's Republic of China. Though many obstacles still remain, present U.S. political perceptions of the PRC differ vastly from our attitude toward the Soviet Union, considered to be aggressively seeking military preponderance over the United States. Indeed, to many the "China card" represents a formidable asset to the United States from a policy standpoint. It was therefore to be expected that following the announcement of normalized relations a "China euphoria" would be ignited among American as well as European and Japanese businessmen. Will these expectations be realized? What policies would best promote both U.S. government and private interests in the future?

U.S. trade policy towards Communist nations is in the midst of a reassessment. In the 1970s, as political tensions diminished and the Communist nations appeared to be gradually placing greater emphasis on economic goals related to consumer needs (the tenth Five-Year Plan appeared to be much more cognizant of these needs), a promising atmosphere for the acceleration of trade relations was created. Trade between the United States and the USSR and the United States and Eastern Europe increased dramatically in the period from 1965 to 1976 (see Figures 5 and 6). In 1977 U.S. companies shipped $519.4 million of nonagricultural items to the USSR and agricultural exports boosted the total to $1.62 billion. But in 1979 Western Europe trade with Eastern Europe was $50 billion or over thirty times as great.

In 1978 U.S. exports to the USSR totaled $2.249 billion, a 38.5 percent increase from the $1.62 billion total for 1977. United States imports from the Soviet Union amounted to $540 million, a 130 percent increase from the $234 million figure for 1977. Agricultural exports to the Soviet Union came to $1.686 billion in 1978, a 62.7 percent increase from 1977, reflecting another poor harvest in the USSR. In 1979 United States exports to the USSR totaled $3.4 billion, $2.6 billion of which was agricultural products when again the Soviets failed to meet their target for agricultural growth. In the same year U.S. imports were $700 million.

Recent developments, including the breakdown of détente with the Soviet Union, and the turmoil in Poland, have now made it increasingly

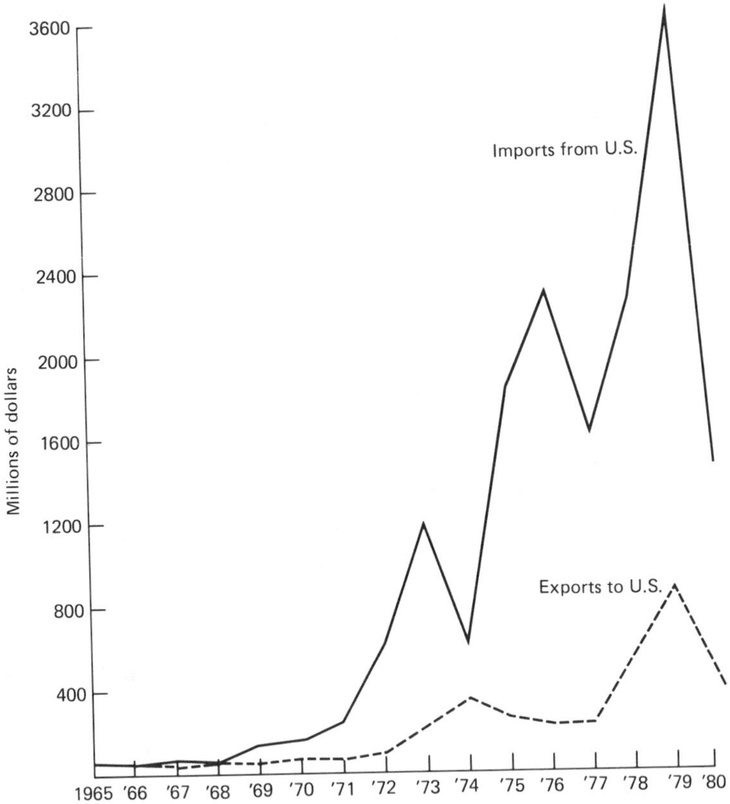

Figure 5. U.S.–USSR trade 1965–1980 (*In millions of dollars*)

Source: For data from 1965 to 1976: U.S. Department of Commerce, *Selected Trade and Economic Data of the Centrally Planned Economies*, January, 1978; for 1977 to 1980: U.S. Department of Commerce, International Trade Administration, released to author, May, 1981.

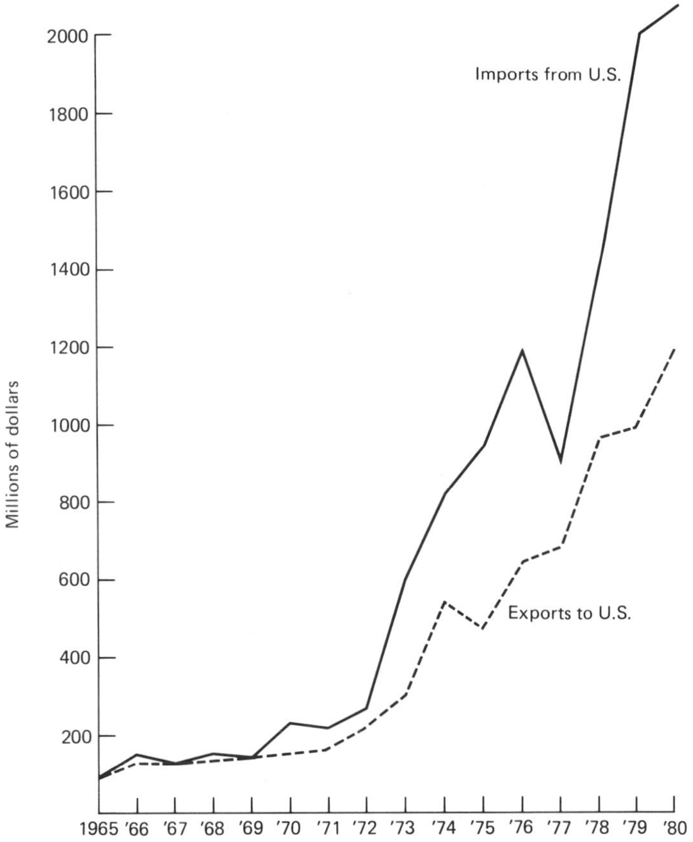

Figure 6. U.S.–Eastern European trade (*In millions of dollars*)

Source: For data from 1965 to 1976: U.S. Department of Commerce, *Selected Trade and Economic Data of the Centrally Planned Economies,* January, 1978; for 1977 to 1980: U.S. Department of Commerce, International Trade Administration, released to author, May, 1981.

difficult to forecast the future trade relations between the Soviet bloc nations and the United States.* Under the best of circumstances the barriers to expansion of trade are great. They fall into three broad categories: 1. structural dissimilarities, 2. political constraints, and 3. economic hindrances. It will be useful to look at each in turn, trying at the

* At the end of April, 1981 President Reagan lifted the grain embargo against the Soviet Union, thereby fulfilling his campaign pledge to do so. The computer embargo remains, however.

same time to interrelate their effects so as to present an integrated picture of a complex trade relationship.

1. Structural Dissimilarities

The structural dissimilarities between Western market economies and Eastern nonmarket economies are immense and undeniably constraining to trade. However, it must be remembered that these special trading difficulties do not make trade impossible, just more difficult for Western firms that prefer the "standard operating procedure" methods of conducting business. This is particularly true of American businessmen who have not found it as essential to engage in foreign trade for the survival of their firms, as is the case for many of their counterparts in Europe and Japan.

The Soviet foreign trade planning apparatus is based on the centralization of decisionmaking. This means that the basic production units all follow a five-year plan developed at the national level in strict and detailed fashion. The Soviet State Planning Commission, GOSPLAN, proposes and formulates five-year plans to coincide with national goals. They are then implemented by the Foreign Trade Ministry and are administered through individual foreign trade organizations. (There is usually one such foreign trade organization for each specific category of goods or services sold.[4]) These plans lay out clearly exact levels and composition of exports and imports; little deviation, except in instances of agricultural disasters, is allowed. The Western businessman is clearly forced to accept the constraints of central planning and negotiate within the constraints of the existing Five-Year Plan. All contracts negotiated with the USSR are signed with the foreign trade organization.

The tenth Five-Year Plan of the Soviet Union began in 1976 and continued through 1980. When compared with earlier plans, this plan seemed to reflect a subtle shift in national goals. Overall, most growth objectives are lower than they have been since 1948, to take into account the results of past experience. For example, national income was targeted to increase annually at an average of 5 percent. The ninth Five-Year Plan had projected an annual increase of 4.8 percent, yet achieved only 3.8 percent.[5] This is, however, not the most significant aspect of the tenth Five-Year Plan. Though the perennial goal of quantitative growth remains, there is a noticeably increased priority placed on improvement of quality and the achievement of more efficient methods of production.[6]

This increased emphasis on efficiency and quality is also seen throughout much of Eastern Europe, where foreign trade is basically conducted along the lines of the Soviet model. These moves have been labeled as "shift(s) from an extensive to intensive development strategy, from quantity to quality."[7] Though at present the shift seems hardly dramatic, it marks nonetheless a significant step towards a different type of economic strategy and may bring about changes that significantly benefit U.S. businesses trading with the USSR and its satellites, as it moves the USSR closer to U.S. economic criteria and goals. However, it cannot be overemphasized that such a shift is still only a proposed one and innumerable factors could force a change of strategies.

Agriculture is the most significant and least predictable factor. Having faced two diastrous harvests in 1970 and 1971 during the ninth Five-Year Plan, the tenth plan attempted to avoid a repetition of that occurrence. Under the tenth plan, agriculture was allotted 27 percent of new investment money in order to meet the yield of 180 million tons of grain envisaged by the previous plan.[8] Unfortunately, this target could not be achieved. In order to achieve these goals, the USSR would have had to harvest over 224 million tons of grain in 1979 and 1980, "and the 1978/79 winter was not at all favorable."[9]

Failure to realize agricultural goals has required the importation of grain, a very costly purchase for a nation with limited reserves of hard currency, earmarked for the purchase of needed Western technology. Along with the shift in production plans to increase productivity through increased investment in agriculture is a drive to modernize technology in most industry and agriculture. This will require the importation of much technology and equipment from the West. The problem of hard-currency shortages, a growing debt, and the desire to import technology will be discussed below. One thing is certain: The U.S. grain embargo, imposed in January, 1980, (and only lifted in late April, 1981) further strained Soviet purchasing power, since the Soviets have had to pay premium prices to ensure supplies.

Aside from the specifics of the tenth Soviet Five-Year Plan, the essentials of which are reflected in most of Eastern Europe, what are the implications of the state foreign-trade monopoly of the USSR and Eastern Europe? Where industry in the U.S. economic system concentrates on the consumer's demands for goods and services, in the Soviet Union most industrial capacity is channeled into the production of capital goods.[10] The purpose there, of course, is to create a much more powerful industrial base. Any expression of a desire to respond to consumer demands has been largely perfunctory.* Overall, the entire Soviet planning system is unbalanced, reflecting the emphasis placed on the development of the military sector.

As one writer on Soviet affairs, Mark Miller, has noted, the "Soviet leaders have relied upon the ability of a highly centralized 'command economy' to concentrate resources on high priority goals in order to achieve results far disproportionate to the general level of development."[12] Therefore, not only does the existence of structurally dissimilar economies constrain United States–USSR/Eastern European trade, but the basically opposing objectives of each economy create further difficulties on economic, and particularly political levels. While the Soviet Union continues to devote between 40 to 80 percent of all research and development funds to the military sector, its population is increasingly demanding consumer goods, which are generally either unavailable or of poor quality.[13]

Though most of Eastern Europe follows the Soviet model in foreign-trade planning and the Soviet lead in the development of Five-Year Economic Plans, there is some variance particularly within Yugoslavia. Attempts within the other Eastern bloc nations, while coming nowhere near those of Yugoslavia, are increasing. Hungary has become a forerunner in attempting to decentralize much of its decisionmaking apparatus and Poland has begun to open channels to selective private enterprises.[14] Even more recently, Poland has decided to allow a few enterprises to sell their produce abroad independently, as does Romania. This deviation does not extend, however, to the independent buying of foreign goods. This is still viewed as unnecessarily disruptive of the long-range goals of the centrally planned economies of the COMECON countries and too costly in terms of the loss of valuable hard currencies earmarked for other purposes.[15]

It cannot be overemphasized that the above modifications are minor and that within most of the Eastern bloc all decisionmaking regarding foreign trade remains highly centralized. The resulting state plan for the economy is supreme and the actual administration of this plan is clearly facilitated by the government's ownership of production facilities and total control of commerce through state-owned institutions. These steps are

* In the Soviet parliament on October 21, 1980, Chairman Leonid Brezhnev stressed the need for improvement in consumer goods production. The shift in policy can perhaps be attributed to unrest in Poland, where the formation of Solidarity was begun with protests over meat shortages. In any case, it is doubtful that such pronouncements will create a consumer oriented economy in the Soviet Union.[11]

only beginnings but, if carefully nurtured through increased foreign trade, may prompt a gradual shift to more independently oriented economies, more susceptible to increased and freer trade relations with the West.

As noted, the deviations previously described are slight when compared with the foreign-trade system existing in Yugoslavia. Following her expulsion from the Soviet trading bloc (CMEA) in 1949, Yugoslavia instituted many unique reforms. Yugoslavia is neither a centrally planned economy nor is its foreign trade a state monopoly. It has developed a system that combines a "socialist market economy, central indicative planning and the self-management of economic units."[16] This system of "market socialism" presents many more opportunities for Western businesses, particularly in light of the willingness of Yugoslavian businesses to engage in trade relations such as joint ventures.

Joint ventures have been allowed in Yugoslavia since 1967. But a law passed in April, 1978 holds out the possibility of an even more promising atmosphere for such types of foreign investment. This law opens many new industries to foreigners wishing to invest jointly with a Yugoslav partner and eliminates certain preexisting requirements on the actual composition of the foreign-equity investment. However, in an attempt to assure the perpetuation of the concept of Yugoslavian worker self-management, the law also places new limits on the foreign partners' decisionmaking powers in such firms.[17] Such foreign industrial cooperation or joint venture arrangements are integral parts of the overall Yugoslav economic planning goals. Thus, the potential for mutually advantageous trade with Yugoslavia appears sizeable.

In dealing with centrally planned economies, such as those of the COMECON countries, Western businessmen must get used to a multitude of special problems that come about from having to deal with a government-controlled monopoly. Western business must first accept the current national plan as law. All trade must be accounted for in the plan and therefore any extemporaneous negotiating would prove entirely futile. These plans also create great problems when an attempt is made to negotiate contracts for periods beyond the year of the existing plan. The Western businessman must also accept the lack of contact with the ultimate consumer of his product that results from this type of dealing.

Although such market access and feedback is an integral aspect of all Western economies, it has no place in the centrally planned economies of the East. Marketing strategies become totally irrelevant here. Although no doubt disconcerting, this particular problem is perhaps exaggerated by most Western business economists. Direct consumer producer feedback is clearly vital to the introduction of new products in the most profitable free-economy markets, but it must be remembered that most Western products, particularly consumer products, are of such superior quality compared to COMECON substitutes that *all* goods are immediately purchased by an increasingly demanding COMECON population. Another barrier to increasing trade with nonmarket economies is the lack of standard commercial information, i.e., prices, costs, competitive products, etc., which forces the Western businessman to forego basic cost-benefits criteria in assessing a profitable market opportunity. Western businessmen must also be prepared to face exasperating and long drawn-out negotiations in order to complete the smallest of business transactions.

Business operations are becoming increasingly difficult for U.S. corporate representatives located in Moscow. The Soviets have recently introduced a tax on corporate profits, which could claim almost 40 percent of company profits. United States businessmen will be required to complete tax forms outlining expenses for all production inputs, including the wages of their staff. In addition, U.S. businessmen will be required to pay a handling charge enabling Soviet employees to be paid through Soviet banks. These measures are seen as a response to IRS actions against Aeroflot, the Soviet airlines. Additional obstacles to U.S. business in the USSR include hikes in office-space rents and curtailment of direct-dial phone service to Western Europe and the United States. Indeed, there are now few incentives for U.S. businessmen to maintain offices in Moscow.[18]

Each of the above problems faced by prospective East-West traders are further accentuated by the highly integrated system of trade within the Eastern bloc and the many economic and political barriers caused by this system. All trade within COMECON is conducted under the direction of the Council for Mutual Economic Assistance. The CMEA was developed as a Communist counterpart to the Marshall Plan, with the original goals of fully unifying the Eastern bloc economies and eventually evolving this bloc into a supranational organization that would coordinate and plan economic policies for the whole COMECON region. These goals were never met and many contend that it was the repeated failure of the CMEA to achieve its economic aims that necessitated the increased trade with the West that now is a regular part of Soviet and COMECON planning.[19]

Through the CMEA the socialist economies of Eastern Europe are closely tied to the USSR. The arrangement has proved mutually advantageous since these countries, with the exception of Romania, are deficient in many raw materials, which the USSR has been able to supply in exchange for the satellites' highest quality consumer goods. However, complete interbloc self-sufficiency has never been achieved.

Furthermore, since there is no pricing mechanism in the COMECON system, the satellite countries have no method other than global prices applied outside of COMECON to determine if they are being overcharged for the raw materials they must import from the USSR, whether sugar, oil, natural gas, or chemical feedstocks. These prices are set at the beginning of each Five-Year Plan to be in effect during the five-year period. On the other hand, the USSR is increasingly torn between continuing shipments of valuable raw materials to its satellite nations or cutting back on shipments in order to export these materials to the West in exchange for desperately needed hard currency with which to purchase Western technology. Further strains within the CMEA are arising from the increasingly independent foreign-trade initiatives being taken by the Eastern nations, who have come to realize that the intraregional self-sufficiency goals of CMEA cannot do what Western technology and equipment can to aid their ailing economies.

In the drive for internal self-sufficiency one of the CMEA's successes was the establishment of the International Bank for Economic Cooperation (IBEC). It is the central bank for the CMEA members, established with the primary purpose of creating a reserve of exchange that can be used to finance all intrabloc transactions.[20] Though trade between members of the CMEA is governed by bilateral agreements, imbalances are settled with the IBEC exchange reserve known as "transferable rubles." One member nation may have a surplus with another member nation, which surplus will be used to settle a deficit with another. Therefore, all CMEA members balance their trade as a whole and not necessarily on a bilateral basis.

As discussed earlier in this chapter, various Western criteria for economic transactions, such as costs, prices, etc., are either unavailable or inapplicable, due to the nature of these nonmarket economies. These structural differences both create and aggravate the economic and political problems of East–West trade. Of those barriers to trade that originated in the Eastern bloc, a majority may have been instituted initially as a consequence of political considerations, but at present all function purely as economic limitations. In the Western countries, particularly the United States, barriers are created by essentially political considerations, and are clearly evident as such. The major Eastern economic hindrances are the external currency inconvertibility of all the currencies of the bloc nations, a severe shortage of foreign-exchange reserves in hard currency, and the growing magnitude of the East's debt to the West. Each of these creates a severe problem for these nations in terms of financing their growing list of desired imports.

The inconvertibility of these Communist nations' currencies makes it difficult for them to purchase goods and services from outside CMEA. As we have noted, exchanges within the CMEA are balanced as a whole and imbalances between two member nations are financed with transferable rubles created by IBEC. However, internationally the inconvertibility of these currencies creates many problems. Western businessmen are quite understandably hesitant to conclude trade agreements under which they will be paid for exports in nonconvertible funds. With such funds, the best they can do is purchase goods from the CMEA members that they may neither desire nor be able to resell in Western markets. The Communist countries, faced with severe foreign exchange shortages, see such purchases as one of a very few alternatives to no trade at all. A Swedish business executive has noted that:

> The Eastern European countries' limited supply of convertible currency is the greatest obstacle to an increased East–West trade and a real expansion can only come about when the currencies of Eastern Europe become convertible. Some countries, for example Hungary—and previously Czechoslovakia—seem to have been in favor of making their own currency convertible. However, the ruble must be made convertible first, but at present the Soviet authorities do not appear to have any plans in that direction.[21]

It appears at this time that strict exchange controls will remain intact, and therefore exchange rates of these nonmarket economies will in no way relate domestic to foreign prices.[22] Currency inconvertibility will remain a hindrance to the liberalization of East–West trade that must be accepted and dealt with by Western businessmen. It is arguable that the present Western system of dirty floats creates an even greater barrier to liberalized trade by creating increased uncertainty.

Overall, currency inconvertibility coupled with continuing imbalance in trade accounts, as the East imports much more from the West than it is able to export, has led to a severe shortage of foreign exchange reserves and resulted in an increasingly unmanageable debt to the West.

The year 1971 saw the beginning of a tremendous surge of imports by Eastern Europe and the Soviet Union (see Figures 5 and 6). Exports from the East did not increase commensurately, and Western credits to help the East finance imports were necessitated, hard-currency indebtedness going from $29 billion to $39 billion in one year. The great majority of this lending came from Western Europe: France, West Germany, the United Kingdom, Italy, Austria, and from Japan. Due to the U.S. government-imposed credit restrictions on the Export-Import Bank's ability to lend and the absence of U.S. government support for private lenders, the United States share of the debt amounted to only about 3 percent in 1975.[23] The U.S. share of the debt also, of course, reflected the general low level of U.S. trade with the East.

The debt did not appear for the first time in 1971, (Romania, perhaps the most externally oriented of all the bloc nations, began buying machinery from the West on credit as early as 1961) but though going back a decade had remained quite manageable. This changed drastically in the early 1970s with the spirit of détente supporting developing East–West trade and the announcement of new Communist growth strategies that required massive imports of Western technology. To view this debt in total world perspective, in 1976 the total external debt of all non-OPEC LDC's was near $180 billion, $75 billion of which was owed to commercial banks. In the same year, the total debt of the USSR and Eastern Europe was stated to be approximately $46 billion, $28 billion of which was owed to commercial banks.[24]

The debt again surged upward following the 1974 recession, when Western governments began to look to the East to boost their exports and balance their foreign oil import bills from OPEC. The only way the East could purchase these goods was on credit. By the end of 1980, the debt was approaching $70 to $75 billion.[25] As would be expected, Eastern estimates place the level of debt much lower. The U.S. CIA has estimated that the total USSR and East European debt as of 1976 was $39.5 billion, while official East European trade statistics have placed it at $25.6 billion.[26] It is in point of fact probably nearer $70 billion as of the start of 1981. Whichever estimate is chosen, the debt is sizeable.

Why is there this enormous discrepancy in debt figures? East European countries, with the notable exception of Poland,* refuse to provide information on their actual indebtedness abroad, and lenders in the West must rely on their own estimates, which vary greatly. Poland's debt to the West (and Japan) was estimated at $27 billion at the end of 1980. West-

* It takes 82 percent of the country's foreign sales to service this debt, obviously an impossibility. Polish loans will not only now have to be rescheduled, but massive new credits will have to be extended if the country is to survive.

ern banks, and, in particular, West German banks, are believed to be financing as much as 47 percent of total East–West trade. All the estimates of the total East European and Soviet debt reflect a variety of types of financing. These include short-, medium-, and long-term loans, official government credits, and private loans from banks.

Recently, the Hungarian government adopted an innovative formula to expand international banking within Eastern Europe. Hungary's Central Bank sponsored the creation in 1979 of the only financial institution in Eastern Europe controlled by Western interests, the Central European International Bank, Ltd. (CEIB). Hungary's Central Bank owns 34% of the shares, with the balance of 66% divided among 4 Western European and 2 Japanese banks. The bank was incorporated under a limited-company law adopted in 1870 during the Austro-Hungarian Empire and never repealed by the Communist regime. It is exempted from all regulatory controls, will not be subject to Hungarian taxes for two years, even has a Japanese loan official on its staff, and has its books audited by an American accounting firm. It makes loans both in Eastern Europe (including the Soviet Union) and in the more advanced developing countries of Africa, Latin America, and the Far East.

The greatest portion of private lending to Eastern Europe and the USSR has been through Eurocurrency funds. This market offers the Eastern nations sizeable loans at favorable terms, terms that are, in fact, comparable to those offered to Western borrowers with good credit ratings. However, even favorable loan terms will not solve the problem created by the massive indebtedness of the Eastern European countries. What alternatives are then available to these countries (including the USSR) to help them level off, if not reduce, an increasingly unmanageable debt without also forcing a decrease in the level of trade? A reduction of imports on the scale necessary to make even a dent in the debt would run counter to the present economic plans of these nations. What options remain? The following section discusses these options and constraints. The two most plausible plans include the expansion of Eastern exports and various types of countertrade or industrial cooperation arrangements.

Exactly how can the West, particularly the United States, continue to do business with the East and under what constraints? The West can aid the East in dealing with its hard-currency debt by recognizing that the removal of various trade barriers will facilitate the expansion of Eastern exports. United States government restrictions on East–West trade are the most severe of any Western nation.

We come now to political barriers to East–West trade imposed by the U.S. government. These barriers include the denial of most favored nation tariff treatment (MFN) to most nonmarket economy goods; restrictions on U.S. government credits; and various licensing requirements designed to protect national security interests.

The denial of MFN tariff treatment to the exports of most Communist nations requires that all imports from those nations face a tariff of the higher, so-called column-one rate. While the denial of MFN has contributed somewhat to the continuation of the unbalanced trade pattern between East and West by raising the price of Eastern exports in the West and thereby reducing the amount sold, the lack of MFN status will be more damaging to East–West trade in the future than it has been to date.*

Historically, Soviet exports to the United States have been primarily raw and semiprocessed materials. Since U.S. tariff rates generally increase commensurate with the degree of processing, lack of MFN treatment has thus far been more of a political and symbolic hindrance than an economic barrier.[27] This pattern is changing however, as the Soviets appear to be promoting increased exports of intermediate manufactures and finished products. The issue of MFN status for the Soviet Union and other nonmarket economies will become an important one if attempts to foster better trade relations with the Soviet Union, Eastern Europe, and the People's Republic of China increase.

The Nixon Administration, as part of its commitment to détente, placed a high priority on reaching a viable trade agreement with the Soviet Union. In October, 1972, a comprehensive trade agreement with the USSR was signed under which President Nixon agreed to seek MFN status for Soviet Union exports. While the agreement included many other provisions to facilitate trade, the issue of MFN was central to the successful realization of trade goals.[28]

This agreement could not be brought into force until Congress passed authorizing legislation. The necessary authority was included in the Trade Act of 1974.[29] This act provided that MFN status and U.S. government credits could not be extended to any country "that denies its citizens the right or opportunity to emigrate" or imposes more than a nominal tax on emigration.† This provision, entitled "Freedom of Emi-

* As of April, 1981, only Poland, Romania, Hungary, and Yugoslavia have MFN status of the Eastern bloc countries.

† This is the so-called Jackson-Vanik Amendment contained in Sec. 402 of the Trade Act of 1974.

gration in East–West Trade," can be waived by the President, subject to Congressional approval by concurrent resolution, if the President finds that a waiver will "substantially promote the objectives" of the act.[30] In January, 1975, the Soviet Union informed the U.S. government that the 1972 trade agreement could not be implemented on the conditions set forth in the 1974 Trade Act.

The U.S. move to politicize trade was not limited to the denial of MFN status; the Export-Import amendments of 1974 (PL 93-636) put a $300 million maximum on Export-Import Bank loans, guarantees, and insurance covering exports to the USSR. Also prohibited was the use of any Export-Import Bank credits for the procurement of any product or service for production of fossil fuel energy resources in the USSR without express Congressional approval. Finally, a $40 million limit was set on loans or guarantees for exploration of energy within the USSR. As is evident from the extent of government-supported credit that Western Europe and Japan have made available to COMECON countries, such credit restrictions have not been accepted by our allies.

An initial attempt at coordination of government credit policies took place in July, 1976, when the Unilateral Declarations on Export Credit Terms were signed by the governments of France, the United Kingdom, West Germany, Japan, Canada, Italy, Belgium, and the United States. These declarations set general guidelines for minimum interest rates and loan maturities for all nations, though the declarations were only for one year's duration. Though the guidelines set were far from all encompassing, they constituted a start towards the coordination of Western credit policies. A beginning that, one hopes, will "limit the tendency for national government to carve out special market shares for their respective nations through the instrument of government supported credit programs."[31] It was further hoped that these guidelines would serve to prompt the United States to ease overly stringent credit restrictions and thereby promote East–West and world trade. It has not worked out this way.

The Jackson-Vanik Amendment (tying the granting of most favored nation status to the liberalization of a nation's emigration policies) together with the limitations imposed on credits have obviously hindered East–West trade, particularly with the USSR. The amendment, in particular, can be said to have hindered trade without accomplishing its goal. Emigration from the Soviet Union fell off dramatically following the passage of the Trade Act and in 1978 was only reaching 1972 levels. (It is interesting to note that the People's Republic of China in order to qualify for a waiver of the Jackson-Vanik Amendment maintains the stated policy of allowing those who have been accepted by a Western nation to emigrate.

The granting of MFN status has been the key issue in trade negotiations with both the USSR and PRC. During the Carter Administration there were numerous meetings held between U.S. and USSR officials to discuss under what conditions Congress might be moved to consider the repeal of waiver of the restrictive Jackson-Vanik Amendment. Waiver of the amendment's requirements ultimately snagged on the question of whether written "assurances" or other documentation would be required. Such a requirement was strongly opposed by the Soviet Union.

The trade accord between the People's Republic of China and the United States concluded on May 14, 1979, included the promise that the administration would seek MFN status for China. The President did so, obtaining such status for the Chinese in January, 1980, after having received confidential "assurances,"* of the PRC's willingness to cooperate in this area. The mood of Congress at the time of the granting of MFN status to the PRC indicates that an evenhanded policy towards the two Communist nations was being pursued. However, the Soviet aggression in Afghanistan removed any hesitation Congress may have had about granting MFN status to the PRC but not to the USSR. Since that time, SALT II has been shelved and détente put in limbo. Thus there currently is no immediate incentive for the U.S. Congress to grant MFN status to the USSR.

United States export controls, most of which date back to the Cold War days, are another inhibiting factor to the expansion of East–West trade. These controls, which were initiated with the 1949 Export Control Act, forbade the export of a wide variety of military and nonmilitary commodities.[32] Prior to the 1969 revision of the Export Control Act, it was illegal to export "goods or technology that would significantly contribute to the *economic* potential of such nation or nations which would prove detrimental to the national security and welfare of the United States."[33] Such wording was used to effectively cover a wide variety of goods, many of which were easily available to the East from other sources, namely Western Europe and Japan. The Export Administration Act was revised in 1969. This revision limited illegal exports to goods

* The assurance with respect to China's emigration policy is interesting. When President Carter asked Vice-Chairman Deng at the White House about the PRC's emigration policy, Deng simply asked him how many Chinese the United States was prepared to accept. There were no further questions asked. (source confidential)

which "would make a significant contribution to the military potential of any nation or nations which would prove detrimental to the national security of the United States."[34]

Many heralded this revision as clearing the way for a more realistic approach towards United States–Eastern trade. Nevertheless, as was later proved, the rewording still left much room for interpretation of "military" potential and for special provisions, which in effect left the granting of an export license to the President. The Carter Administration, for example, refused to grant a license to Sperry Univac (subsequently approved) to export a computer to the Soviet news agency TASS. The President's action in this instance had been politically motivated. He used it to express U.S. displeasure with Soviet actions against U.S. businessmen, to punish the Soviets for their treatment of dissidents within the Soviet Union, and to protest the Soviet-Cuban presence in Africa. True, while U.S. displeasure with Soviet actions was thus made apparent, one questions whether there are not other channels through which such pressure can be exerted without sacrificing exports by U.S. industry. Clearly, if it were a question of military utility for the computer, there is no argument. But in the Sperry Univac case, the product had no military significance and a comparable item could readily be purchased from suppliers in Western Europe or Japan. The policy of expressing the temporary displeasure of the executive or legislative branches of the government by forbidding an export transaction makes it clear to foreign buyers that the United States is not a reliable supplier of equipment.* We are thereby damaging our trade image far beyond the individual transaction.

Also included in both Export Control Acts are cumbersome regulations governing the procedures that a U.S. businessman must follow to export to the USSR and other Eastern nations. These include first gaining U.S. government approval and then securing an export license for the actual export of goods. Once the item is classified as requiring a license, a determination can be made as to whether a general or validated license is required. A validated license brings into play further special regulations. If and when an export has been classified, has been approved, and has received the proper license (generally issued by the Department of Commerce), it is still not allowed to be shipped. Export clearance and desti-

* The Pentagon maintains that any enhancement of the Soviet Union's economic power will further its military power. Further, it sometimes happens, for example, that goods purchased to satisfy specific economic needs at one time may subsequently be put to military use later on. For example, Soviet trucks manufactured in a factory from the U.S., with financing from the Export-Import Bank, were used in the invasion of Afghanistan.

nation-control regulations must now be satisfied. This entails further Department of Commerce approval and a Shipper's Export Declaration to the Collector of Customs to be in turn approved by him.[35] Compared to what a U.S. businessman must face in order to export to the USSR, the procedures faced inside the USSR with Foreign Trade Organizations and Five-Year Plans seem almost less onerous. Clearly, trade with the Eastern bloc countries is seriously hampered by the export controls and export control procedures required by the U.S. government.*

The whole question of technology transfers is one of the most difficult to resolve in terms of how to expand East–West trade without hurting U.S. vital interests. Two questions remain essential to any resolution of the debate. First, does the United States oppose the transfer of technology for fear of losing a competitive advantage in world markets or for the fear that such technology will be altered for military usage, ultimately against the United States or its allies, or for both reasons? The second issue is how much control does the United States possess over the Consulting Group Coordinating Committee (COCOM), the international export coordinating body. To date, it appears COCOM support for U.S. export control measures has been less than assured.

COCOM was established in 1949 to create a collective mechanism among Western allies and Japan to control the export of strategic goods to Communist nations. Member nations include all NATO nations (except Iceland) and Japan. In theory, COCOM is set up to decide which exports should be considered strategic and to restrict the export of these goods. But there is no COCOM treaty nor is there any other type of agreement to regulate the activities of its members. COCOM does maintain a list of items that are supposedly forbidden for export without its approval of an "exception request,"[36] but compliance by member nations is not policed and there are no sanctions. COCOM has proved to be just as cumbersome as U.S. licensing procedures. For example, an application for an "exception request" to export machinery made by the Cyril Bath Company of Cleveland, took over three years for COCOM

* The debate in 1979 over export controls and technology transfers surfaced in two opposing bills in the U.S. Congress as the Congress debated the extension of the Export Control Act. A bill introduced by Representative Jonathan Bingham (D–NY) called for the expansion of sales of U.S. goods and sought less onerous controls over the transfer of technology. Opposing this bill was one introduced by Representative Lester Wolff (D–NY), which called for tighter Defense Department control over U.S. sales, to be implemented when the Export Control Act expired in September, 1979. Bingham's bill did not pass in the House and the 1979 Export Control Act extension created a Commodity Control List, which is to be a list of critical technologies to be compiled by the Department of Defense.

approval. In the meantime, the French are believed to have already exported the same products to the USSR.[37]

The United States fears pressuring COCOM members, lest such actions cause the entire mechanism to collapse. But the United States is increasingly alone in the imposition of such rigid export controls. Fear of pressuring COCOM to apply similar controls, in expectation of the collapse of a nonfunctioning organization, is unnecessary. COCOM is ineffective and has only symbolic value. The United States should therefore decide promptly whether to attempt to make it effective or dismember it. The perpetuation of such an ineffective organ can only be an embarrassment.

The Question of Technology Transfers

The debate over the issue of technology transfers has surfaced most recently over the issue of the Soviet Union's need to import Western technology and equipment in order to develop energy resources. The USSR is currently the world's largest oil producer; the title, however, appears to be slipping away. Lack of foresight in past production methods threatens the Soviet Union with an energy crisis[38] at a time when continued acceleration or, at the very least, maintenance of the level of oil production is vital not only because of domestic needs. The Soviet Union is the principle supplier of oil to most of the Eastern bloc nations. Czechoslovakia relies on the Soviet Union for 92 percent of its oil needs, Bulgaria for 90 percent, and East Germany for 80–85 percent.[39] Clearly, oil is an essential facet of Soviet control over bloc nations. This Eastern dependence on Soviet oil leads into another intricately involved issue; that of earning hard currency.

Presently, over 40 percent of the foreign exchange earned by the USSR comes from the export of oil, mostly to Western Europe. Since hard currency is essential if the USSR is to import the technology required to extract crude oil from the earth, the Soviets may have to continue to cut back production and/or raise the price of the oil sold to its satellite nations. This will obviously aggravate questions of political control and force most of the bloc nations further towards independent economic and ultimately political policies. Thus, a vicious cycle is created that can only be resolved by maintaining production at current levels.

In 1975 the decision was made that in lieu of attempting secondary and tertiary oil recovery, the Soviets would undertake massive exploration projects in Western Siberia with the hope of uncovering new reserves.[40] At this point U.S. willingness to sell its technology became a crucial factor in future Soviet oil policy. The Soviets need vast amounts of energy-related technology and specialized drilling equipment, and the United States is the *easiest* but certainly not the only place to purchase it. Within the Carter Administration, a heated debate took place over whether or not to supply the needed technological goods. The President decided in December, 1978 to allow U.S. firms to sell to the Soviet Union the equipment it so desperately needed.

What were the U.S. national interests in this situation? Should the twenty-two licenses have been denied in the hope of watching the Soviets edge towards an energy crisis, which might be followed by a break in Soviet control over the satellite nations? Or would such a crisis have aggravated the already unacceptable level of world inflation by forcing the Soviets to buy oil in a competitive world market? Within the administration and the Congress the most vehement opponents of the President's decision were National Security Advisor Zbigniew Brzezinski and Senator Henry Jackson, both of whom argued that the United States had economic leverage here and that it should be utilized to obtain political concessions. Supporting the President were the secretaries of State, Treasury, and Commerce, who all argued that it was in the country's national interest to remove energy-related products from the control list, as the continued development of all energy sources represented a vital global goal. They also noted that the goodwill promoted by allowing the Soviets to purchase the equipment would further successful completion of a SALT II treaty.

The debate over technology transfers continued within the Carter Administration during the rest of its tenure and has certainly not ended with the election of President Reagan. It can be claimed that energy is unique and that other technological goods must continue to be controlled for purposes of military and economic competitiveness. Increasingly, it appears unlikely that the Soviet Union will be able to develop an indigenous base for technological development outside of its extraordinary achievements in nuclear and space technology and those products directly related to armaments. Supporters of continued and more rigid export controls contend that, because of the disproportionate amount of money the Soviets spend on military goods, consumers in the Soviet Union are becoming increasingly dissatisfied. They argue that the United States, by giving the lagging domestic economy of the Soviets massive infusions of needed technology, enables the Soviet government to continue to increase its manufacture of weapons.

Those who argue the other side contend that what the United States doesn't sell, its allies will, and U.S. firms will be forced to sacrifice a sizeable amount of business. The debate continues. Are technology transfers what Lenin was referring to in his famous statement that "The capitalists will sell the Soviet Union the rope by which they will be hanged"? Conversely, one can ask, is continued economic interaction, including technology transfers, the best way to assure the continuation of the détente process, that process in turn eventually bringing about a change in attitude of the leaders of the Soviet Union? We must never forget that the present Soviet leaders suffered through the German invasion of 1939–1945, six terrible years of war and its aftermath, and have a paranoia about new attacks if they should ever weaken their military superiority over the West. History continually teaches that political relationships change: France and Germany, Egypt and Israel are but recent examples.

It seems clear that the Reagan Administration will take a much harder line on the question of technology transfers to the Soviet Union. Democratic administrations and Democratic Congresses have been more disposed to technology trade-offs in return for changes in Soviet immigration or human rights policies, whereas Republican administrations have tended to focus more on countering Soviet arms buildups or military adventurism. Both the USSR and the United States may now see the necessity, if conditions in Poland worsen, to limit their economic relations even further. Should there be a Soviet "takeover" in Poland, then the entire Western world can be expected to sever trade relations with the Soviet Union. This would mean the end of West German financing of the gas pipeline between Western Europe and the Soviet Union and probably the end of Japanese negotiations for development of the Siberian gas fields.

The Practicalities of East–West Business Transactions

A growing emphasis is being placed by Eastern nations on various types of countertrade and industrial cooperation arrangements, as a temporary solution to the problem of how to continue importing the desired Western technology and equipment without aggravating the existing debt problem. Definitions of the terms countertrade and industrial cooperation are often conflicting and ambiguous. However, for the purpose of this book, countertrade is defined as the practice of avoiding the hard-currency cost of importing a product from the West by simultaneously negotiating a balancing purchase by the West from the East. Such arrangements can take various forms, i.e., barter deals, counterpurchase arrangements, and (as will be discussed in detail below), compensation or buy-back arrangements. Industrial cooperation has been best defined by Carl H. McMillan as "constituting arrangements whereby individual producers, based in East and West, agree to pool some assets and jointly coordinate their use in the mutual pursuit of complementary objectives."[41]

Many predict that the new future for East–West trade, if not its only future, will be in these methods of exchange, rather than the normal buy and sell types of trading relationships. Countertrade mechanisms and industrial cooperation agreements offer obvious advantages to the hard-currency starved nonmarket economy nations, who need to import Western technology and equipment but don't have the funds to pay for them. In the Soviet Union, industrial cooperation has been established under the Ministry of Foreign Trade in two separate units, the "Main Administration for Compensation Projects," and the "Main Administration for Scientific Industrial Cooperation," to coordinate projects.[42]

The crucial question for Western businessmen to decide is whether or not they will accommodate this form of business transaction, and if so, how will they do it. Typical examples of countertrade transactions were those entered into by International Harvester in Poland and Hungary, which enabled the American company to "sell goods it would not otherwise be able to sell" and the transaction entered into by General Electric for the sale of steam turbines to Romania in 1981. The 1973 countertrade transaction between International Harvester and Poland included the sale to Poland of the basic design and technology for a crawler tractor and the promise by International Harvester to buy back tractor components manufactured by the Polish plant. Poland's shortage of hard currency was therefore unaffected and it appears that International Harvester was satisfied with the tractor parts. (In this instance countertrade was mutually beneficial, but this may not necessarily always be the case.)

Western European and Japanese firms have also been quite successful in establishing trading relationships under such arrangements, and U.S. businesses could easily follow suit if they chose to enter into types of transactions so alien to normal U.S. business practices. The General Electric countertrade transaction with Romania is particularly interesting because the American company was able to require that the components to be furnished by the Romanians under countertrade agreements meet specifications established by GE. Though many types of industrial cooperation and countertrade agreements have been tried, two of the most promising and popular are joint ventures, including joint third country ventures, and compensation agreements.

Joint ventures are especially attractive to nonmarket economies where the state owns, or, as with Yugoslavia, the workers own all production facilities. Each East European nation has, however, specific, often quite differing laws pertaining to joint ventures. Yugoslavia, Romania and Hungary have been the most active in entering into joint ventures with Western firms. Poland, though somewhat more restrictive, has recently adopted legislation permitting and delineating the scope of joint venture activity.[43]

These five countries, Yugoslavia, Romania, Hungary, Poland, and Bulgaria are, as of March, 1980, the only Communist nations that permit a Western firm to hold a participating interest in a given project. Other nations have mechanisms for various types of industrial cooperation; in these, however, no joint investment is allowed.[44] The philosophical problem is an interesting one since under Communist doctrine all means of production must belong to the state, or, in the case of Yugoslavia, to the workers in the enterprise. The means used to get around the doctrine is a contract permitting what would not be allowed through equity ownership.

Yugoslavia has had joint venture legislation since 1976, preceding all other Eastern nations in this regard. This nation's unique economic system, a socialist market economy where the means of production are owned by the workers and not the state, makes it perhaps the most favorable Eastern country for Western business and it has attracted a great deal of Western interest in joint ventures. In Yugoslavia the two parties negotiate a contract that delineates the specifics of the joint venture, such as the division of profits, management, etc., and a partnership is formed without actually issuing any stock in the enterprise.[45]

Joint third country ventures have also become popular, particularly with Poland. These typically involve bidding and subcontracting by the East–West partnership for projects in third countries. Such third country ventures offer several advantages to both the Eastern and Western partner, the most outstanding of which is that full risk in such large-scale projects is shared. For Western firms, the major benefit is that the Eastern partner is usually able to deliver goods and equipment at attractively low prices without regard to inflation, making it an excellent bidding partner. This is made possible because prices in the Eastern countries are fixed during the five-year planning period. Workers in these countries do not get pay increases to reflect inflation since the state recognizes inflation only as a foreign phenomenon, inapplicable at home.

Overall then, joint ventures offer many advantages to those choosing to enter into such types of business deals. Eastern nations acquire continued access to Western technology, capital, management, and technical expertise without aggravating the problem of a foreign exchange shortage. For Western firms, there do exist many logistical problems such as the need to delineate carefully actual management control, estimates of how much profit may have to be reinjected into the nonmarket economy, accounting methods to be used in determining distribution to the joint ventures, and so on. In more general terms the problem of international marketing of the product must be carefully worked out so that the product resulting from the joint venture using U.S. technology does not then compete with the same product manufactured in the United States, since a clear dilemma would then arise as whether this type of increased competition is beneficial to U.S. interests.[46]

Another increasingly popular form of countertrade is the compensation agreement. This consists of the negotiation of two separate contracts. The first consists of the East's purchase of a Western plant, often a total production line, with payment to be received over a period of time. The second contract is the agreement by the Western firm to buy the product of the plant, or some other product. This form of import financing obviously guarantees that the nonmarket economy will balance exports and imports.

Sizeable problems arise for Western businesses that engage in such practices. They may be exposed to charges of dumping or, more important, they may face problems of quality control, particularly if they have not insisted on the right to inspect any products to be exported and to reject those that do not meet their standards of quality. It is understandably difficult in nonmarket economies to perceive or respond to the Western demand for quality consistency. As the supply of consumer goods never approaches the demand within Eastern countries, a product is sold regardless of its quality. The excess resources necessary to produce manufactured goods that satisfy Western standards is viewed by Eastern countries as wasteful and cost prohibitive. Therefore, long-term compensation arrangements involving the exchange of Eastern manufactured goods are very risky undertakings.[47]

There are, however, methods by which such compensation agreements can be utilized successfully. One clear case is where exceptional quality is not a requirement, as with raw materials or semi-processed goods. Another is if the Western firm can retain control over quality during the production process. When Levi-Strauss Co. recently entered into a compensation agreement with Hungary, the problem of quality of the end product was avoided by delineating in the initial agreement that quality control of the production of the jeans would remain under the direction of Levi-Strauss. A certain percentage of the jeans are to be sold in Hungary and Levi-Strauss agrees to buy back a certain percentage for export to Europe.[48] In another instance, Pepsico Incorporated instituted a type of compensation agreement with the Soviet Union in 1974 under which the American firm received exclusive rights to import Soviet vodka, that it then distributes in the United States, in exchange for Pepsi-Cola concentrate to be marketed in the Soviet Union.

It is expected that the countertrade phenomenon will gain momentum. In 1978 Poland predicted that by 1980, 40 to 50 percent of its exports of electrical products and machinery to the West would be via countertrade arrangements; the Soviet Union estimated that 38 percent of United States–Soviet trade turnover from 1976 to 1980 would be through countertrade practices.[49] Clearly, countertrade shows no signs of diminishing. Neither, therefore, will the problems it generates. These include those discussed above—the impact in the West of imports generated from such deals, quality control, and problems with delivery and after-sale service of goods.

A fundamental problem with the growth and promotion of such trade practices also arises for the Eastern nations, because of the basic premise upon which countertrade is based. Most industrial cooperation deals and compensation buy-back schemes provide the Eastern nationals with only a quick solution to the necessity of earning foreign exchange: they are given access to Western markets but they do not establish any type of long-term export base. Products offered to the West are not necessarily those that can be successfully marketed to the West. Furthermore, the nature of the transaction may further aggravate the East's long-term economic picture by "being self-defeating to the extent that Communist exporters forego the development of marketing skills and abdicate control over the pricing and destination of their products."[50] As was recently pointed out by an outstanding Hungarian central banker, Janos Fekete, "when times are good you are receptive to selling our products in your markets but when times are bad our products are the first to be let go."

Yugoslavia's unique system of market socialism could prove the exception to the foregoing conclusions. In that country, incentives may well increase the potential for mutually advantageous compensation agreements and joint ventures with the West. Yugoslavia considers itself the leader of the so-called nonaligned nations, those nations nonaligned to either of the superpowers politically or to any previously developed types of economic system.

The Yugoslav economy is based on a type of "market socialism" wherein the means of production are owned collectively by the workers in the enterprise. There is a free flow of labor, and a free exchange of goods and services. These self-managed, worker-owned means of production account for over 82 percent of the total GNP of Yugoslavia.[51] The personal incentives offered through such a system have led to an impressive postwar growth rate: from 1945 to 1975 GNP has increased an average of 6.5 percent annually.[52] The economic potential of Yugoslavia should continue to compare favorably with that of all other Eastern bloc nations.

This is not due, it should be noted, to possession of abundant natural resources or raw materials, a highly educated population, or access to capital, but rather to the creation of an effectively functioning economic system when compared to that of other COMECON nations. According to accepted indicators of a country's level of development, i.e., gross domestic product per capita, distribution of labor force, etc., Yugoslavia is still classified as a developing country on the same level as Greece, Turkey, Spain, Portugal, Hungary, and Romania.[53] Nevertheless, the United States is currently Yugoslavia's fourth largest trading partner. From 1976 to 1977, for example, U.S. trade (two-way) with Yugoslavia increased by 48 percent.[54]

Further, there are many indications that trade and industrial cooperation agreements between the United States and Yugoslavia will increase despite the difficulty in financing hard-currency imports. During the 1960s almost all Yugoslav trade was oriented to the West.[55] But in the 1970s, Yugoslavia appeared to be reversing her trading trends of the 1960s and to be increasing her trade with the Eastern bloc. In 1976, for example, over one-third of all Yugoslav trade was with Eastern nations. True, trade with the West still accounted for over one-half; this, however, represented a significant drop from the 1960s.

Reasons for this shift are interesting: Yugoslav exports to the West declined as a result of the recession of 1974 in Europe and the United States (in times of recession imports from the COMECON countries are the first to decline because the quality of their products tends not to be as good as that of Western countries). On the other hand, Yugoslav goods continued to be attractive to Eastern European nations because even the limited exposure to Western quality standards in Yugoslavia made such goods compare favorably in quality to those available from other COMECON countries. It appears at the present time that the Yugoslav trade patterns of the 1970s may be shifting back toward trade with the West, and, as European Community protectionism grows, particularly with the United States. This shift is attributable in some degree to the fact that the other Eastern nations do not have desirable exports for Yugoslavia to buy. With an increasingly positive trade balance with the Eastern bloc countries, Yugoslavia now trades with Poland, Hungary, and Romania in dollars and no longer in "transferable rubles," for which it has no need.

As discussed earlier, this socialist market economy has allowed basic production decisions, i.e., output, investment, prices, etc., to be determined by the firm rather than by political central planners. It has also allowed a system of bonuses to plant managers and workers to be maintained. These moves have created an environment that is conducive to increased productivity because they have provided incentives not found in other COMECON countries. These factors have encouraged industrial cooperation arrangements between Yugoslavia and Western firms. Yugoslavia sees the promotion of industrial cooperation as an effective means of combatting a growing trade deficit. This deficit is a result, in part, of the national Yugoslav policy of maintaining stable exchange rates, even as the nation encounters double-digit inflation. Such monetary policy has obviously increased foreign imports while making Yugoslav exports less competitive in the world market.

Foreign investment was legalized in Yugoslavia in 1967. Since that time over 200 joint ventures have been entered into by Yugoslav and Western firms. These account for over $323 million in foreign investment. The largest U.S. investment in Eastern Europe was made by Dow Chemical Company in Yugoslavia.[56] This was a $700 million investment to build a petrochemical complex on the Yugoslav island of Krk, Dow contributing 49 percent of the equity investment.

In 1976, new legislation was passed in Yugoslavia opening up new industries to joint venture opportunities but placing several new limitations on the decisionmaking authority of the Western partner. (These limitations were imposed to maintain the basic concept of worker self-management and to assure that it is no way diminished in the joint-venture process.) As well, new controls were announced on the repatriation of profits and markets for export. Overall, joint ventures with Western firms have served to strengthen Yugoslavia's economy and increase exports. Such cooperation, it is hoped, will also serve to help alleviate unemployment and aid some less developed regions of this very Balkanized nation. Tax incentives and federal coordination of joint venture proposals are expected to further these aims.

Beyond economic gains and risks, U.S. trade policy with Yugoslavia could effectively support U.S. political goals in the area. Yugoslavia presents a dangerous socialist role model in economic and political terms for the USSR and other Eastern European nations. A rising standard of living, increased consumer welfare, larger amounts of repatriated earnings of Yugoslav workers abroad (which earn 12 percent interest in hard currency when deposited in Yugoslav banks) and greater personal liberties all serve to make it the envy of other Eastern bloc nations. Increased U.S. trade, either bilateral or through various types of industrial cooperation and countertrade, can only serve to enhance this success. It is clear that in terms of political and economic goals Yugoslavia and the United States have much to gain from closer economic collaboration.

Countertrade practices and industrial cooperation arrangements with Yugoslavia and the rest of the Eastern bloc countries can be expected to increase. In view of continued hard-currency shortages, growing debts to the West, and the expansion of imports due to increased needs and desires for Western goods, particularly Western technology, countertrade and industrial cooperation appear to be two of the very limited number of options for Eastern nations to pursue for the attainment of domestic economic goals. It is doubtful that these Eastern nations will be able to expand exports to generate sufficient hard currency or to develop other preferable types of financing arrangements in the near future. Therefore, countertrade and industrial cooperation appear to be the wave of the future, but only for as long as Western firms will negotiate transactions on this basis.

To reiterate, for Western firms such arrangements offer advantages and disadvantages. They are able to gain market access that may otherwise be unattainable. Raw materials and often cheaper manufactured components may also be secured with price guarantees over a period of time. Yet, many problems remain, most of which reflect issues faced in all East–West trade transactions. Is the transfer of technology (continued transfer in the case of joint ventures) in the nation's best interest, strategic and commercial? If so, should the United States encourage joint ventures as opposed to the simple buying and selling of technology? The transfer of technology through joint ventures is more complete and self-perpetuating than it is through a licensing arrangement. Under this form of business transaction the East is guaranteed continued access to the most recent know-how and technical expertise, since the Western firm, in good capitalist fashion, will be disposed to use in a joint venture its most advanced production methods. The questions are not simple because countertrade invites problems of unfair wage competition and charges of dumping, particularly if countertrade involves unrelated products brought back to the United States for sale in competition with products manufactured here.

If East–West trade should in the future begin to grow again, the United States and all Western nations should carefully reassess existing policies that work on the assumption that countertrade affects the competitiveness of similar products manufactured domestically. There are competing factors here. Domestic employment may be seriously risked when we encourage exports of competitive countertrade products but these countertrade agreements, one must not forget, have also been a source of increased employment at home.

What is the prognosis, as of April, 1981, for increased bilateral trade between the United States and the Soviet Union? It will entirely depend upon how political relations develop between the two countries. We can expect a consistent hard-line policy towards the Soviet Union under the Reagan Administration, with the continued lifting of the grain embargo dependent upon progress at least in the Polish crisis. President Carter's reaction to the Soviet invasion of Afghanistan was severe: a trade embargo on agricultural products and high-technology goods, fishing limitation, cancellation of economic and cultural contracts. The effect of these steps was limited because our allies did not follow: the Soviet Union was able to purchase wheat from Argentina, Australia, and Canada, and technology from Western Europe. At the beginning of 1981 the Soviet Union began negotiating a very substantial transaction with West German bankers looking to finance a gas pipeline from Siberia to Western Europe—in view of the unreliability of Middle Eastern oil in the minds of the Europeans, this Soviet move represents an appealing investment to Western Europe. The United States, although it did not cut off all trade, has been made to look like an unreliable supplier to Eastern Europeans. Inconsistent application of the limited embargo has also hurt our image abroad. Why, for example, was the Caterpillar Company granted permission in March, 1981, to go ahead with an $80 million contract to sell pipe-laying equipment to the Soviet Union for this gas contract when other less-sensitive projects were held up?

Trade with the People's Republic of China

We come now to a discussion of trade with the one-quarter of the world's population living within the People's Republic of China (PRC). Recent political changes in that country since the death of Mao Zedong (Mao Tse-Tung), particularly the decision of the new rulers to modernize the country as rapidly as possible, have meant that for the first time in some thirty years trade between the industrialized nations of the West and this vast market can be resumed.

The recent announcement of the normalization of relations with the People's Republic of China; the perpetuation of the Sino-Soviet split; and the new rapid drive for modernization as enunciated by China's new, pragmatic leadership in March, 1978 will all serve to increase Western trade with this Asian giant. However, the initial grandiose visions of marketing products to "400 million customers" (who now number nearly 950 million) are beginning to wane as some realities of the China trade potential come into focus.[57] United States–PRC trade was practically nonexistent in 1971. By 1977, total two-way trade between the two nations had reached only $931 million. By 1978 the figure had leapt to nearly $1 billion with a $500 million surplus for the United States. For 1979 U.S.–PRC two-way trade had come up to $2.3 billion. In 1980 this figure was about $4.3 billion.* This is still substantially below the levels reached in bilateral trade between the PRC and the Western European nations and Japan.[58]

Many of the limits to the expansion of United States–PRC trade, particularly those resulting from U.S. government restrictions, are similar to those faced by U.S. businessmen in dealings with Eastern Europe and the Soviet Union, as outlined earlier in this chapter. Yet there are also many constraints unique to trade with the PRC. The direction of China's future policies regarding foreign trade has not yet been determined by the country's leaders, largely because the leadership itself is still struggling to determine its own policies and priorities.

Other unique constraints to be examined include the historic Chinese aversion to accepting credit from foreign nations. Why this aversion? As the Chinese see it, Britain, France, Japan, and the United States have each, at one time or another, extended credit and used such credit to occupy ports, seize territory, establish extraterritorial courts and police

* In 1980 the National Council for United States–China trade reported that United States exports to PRC had reached $3.4 billion, while imports from the PRC had been $900 million.

jurisdiction; the Japanese extended credit and occupied much of the country; the Soviet Union extended credit and took away much of the productive facilities of Manchuria. Thus, from the Chinese point of view, one can understand why there exists a reluctance to engage in new credit transactions with the industrialized nations.

Finally, the success or failure of the drive for four modernizations (agriculture, industry, science, and defense) will be determined in part by the ability of the PRC to remedy a chronic lack of technical expertise. The Cultural Revolution, in effect, wiped out one whole generation of the educated professional class, without whom no modern nation can function. Let us now analyze these constraints in light of what the PRC wants and needs from the West and whether the government will have the necessary courage, in the face of past experience, to negotiate massive new borrowings for industrial modernization.

Uncertainty about the future direction of PRC domestic and foreign policy will constitute the most severe limitation on future United States–PRC trade relations. It must not be forgotten that the revolution orchestrated in China after World War II by Mao Zedong was an *agricultural* revolution not at all similar to the uprising of the *urban* proletariat in the Soviet Union in 1917. Since the death of Mao, and Zhou En Lai (Chou En-Lai) in 1976, the future economic goals of China have been hotly debated within that country. Most of the disputes and decisions can only be speculated on by the West.

Some tendencies are becoming clear; however, of these, those that appear to be contrary to the fundamental tenets of Maoist philosophy pose a special problem. How far can the emerging leadership, if one is indeed emerging, deviate from Maoist doctrine and still maintain some legitimacy* with which to govern this vast nation? This question must be seriously considered by businessmen involved in major PRC projects since foreign trade is a major issue in the present debate. Mao advocated self-sufficiency as the primary goal of China's economic growth. The present leader Deng Xiaoping (Teng Hsiaoping), contends that foreign

*Westerners should understand the trial of the Gang of Four as a means whereby the new leaders sought to establish the legitimacy of the new policies: Mao's wife and her collaborators had been responsible for the Cultural Revolution and had perverted the efforts of Mao and Zhou En Lai to modernize the country. Deng Xiaoping would now lead the country back to the correct path. The trial legitimized Deng's power as the successor to Mao and ended the claim of Hua Guofeng (Hua Kuo-feng) to the succession. Deferment of execution of Mao's wife for two years following her sentence on January 23, 1981—insisted upon by Deng against the recommendation of his colleagues—makes clear to her followers that she remains hostage for their continued good behavior.

trading relationships are only a temporary necessity, engaged in for the achievement of a higher level of economic development and ultimately the self-sufficiency advocated by Mao.

Maoist philosophy also placed primary emphasis on the achievement of a basic standard of living for everyone and the supreme importance of ideology. The themes of *equality, ideology* above all else and *national independence* remained pillars of all post-1949 policies. For the PRC to achieve true equality in China, Mao felt that "three major differences" in Chinese society had to be eradicated—those that distinguished intellectual from manual laborer, urban from rural dweller, and industrial from agricultural worker.[59]

In order to reduce these disparities and achieve a more egalitarian standard of living for all, Mao promulgated strict policies limiting urban migration and instituted programs to "reeducate" party officials, who were forced to attain the necessary perspective on the benefits of rural life by being sent back to the farms. In the decade prior to Mao's death, particularly during the Cultural Revolution (1966–69), intellectual achievement was discouraged in favor of ideological purification. Clearly, the issue of foreign trade was unimportant.

Prior to his death in September, 1976, Chairman Mao appointed Hua Guofeng as his successor. While Hua had risen rapidly through the party ranks as a result of the Cultural Revolution, his present policies do not reflect such a background. The struggle for power after Mao's death was chiefly between the Radicals of the Gang of Four, who supported a strict interpretation of and adherence to Maoist ideology, and the Pragmatists, who were led by Deng Xiaoping. He was joined by then Chairman Hua.

The Pragmatists are currently making policy. However, the present ruling elite is far from secure, and the results of their programs will likely determine the longevity of their rule. Because of their insecurity, it is difficult to determine the precise goals of the present leadership. The present Politburo is split. About half are devotees of the values of the Cultural Revolution and began their rise to power during that upheaval, as had Hua. The other side of the split can best be characterized in the person of Deng Xiaoping, who was forced into a "re-education" process as the result of the Revolution. For a time neither side was represented in the supreme ruling body.[60] Since 1980, the goals of Deng clearly appear to be dominating the economic planning process. While the present program for modernization was introduced by both Hua and Deng, Deng will now clearly be held accountable for the alterations in the overall program that have had to be made as grandiose goals become difficult to justify to people increasingly reluctant to accept new sacrifices at a time of new aspirations.

Deng is seventy-six years old; age will clearly be a factor in determining the ultimate fate of PRC modernization. Deng has attempted to decrease the chances of his vast economic plans becoming diverted following his death by placing the PRC on an unchangeable course towards modernization. How unalterable his long-term plans and commitments are is questionable. Daily alterations of the PRC's modernization goals will continue to appear well into the next decade as this nation adjusts to the realities and costs of modernizing (i.e., hard currency requirements, additional domestic sacrifices, and perhaps even further adjustments in leadership and policies).

The goal of transforming the PRC into an industrial world power by the year 2000 will require massive purchases by the PRC of Western technology and equipment. By most estimates, the PRC's present external debt is near $2.5 billion. This is presently quite acceptable, since the PRC possesses hard-currency reserves of over $2.5 billion plus gold holdings valued near $4 billion. However, the PRC is slowly realizing that future export earnings will not cover escalating costs and that other avenues to foreign exchange must be explored.

The present PRC budget counts heavily on revenue from tourism and particularly on an increased flow of repatriated earnings from Chinese living abroad. Gains in earnings from tourism will come slowly since China presently lacks adequate facilities for any sharp increase in this source. Negotiations are underway with several Western countries, including the United States, to aid the PRC in the development of its tourist trade. Here, U.S. technological expertise has the advantage in an unexpected field. The Chinese have always been very "label" conscious. To them, a beautiful silk shirt is fine, but it is not an "Arrow." Similarly a hotel for tourists, to be acceptable in their eyes, should carry the name "Hilton," "Intercontinental," "Sheraton," or "Ramada."

The PRC currently has about 30,000 hotel beds, yet accommodates only some 100,000 tourists a year. In comparison, Hong Kong, with 24,900 hotel beds, handles over 1.7 million tourists annually. It is evident that much must be done to boost a lagging yet potentially highly profitable industry. As of April 1, 1979, the PRC had signed deals with Western companies, most notably Intercontinental, Western International, and Ramada Inn, for the construction of over 35,000 hotel rooms.[61] As with all contracts negotiated during the "no-holds-barred" modernization phase, these are also being reassessed, but it remains a safe bet that pro-

Table 18. Expenditure and income projections under the 1976 ten-year plan[a] in the People's Republic of China (*In billions of dollars*)

Expenses		Income	
Total expenditures in hard currencies on modernization plan	$230[b]	Export Revenues (1978–1985)	$175
		Tourist Revenues	8
		Remittances	12
		Oil (?)	
		Debt Service (?)	
	$230		$195

Source: Author's discussions with officials of PRC in 1978.

[a]This current plan ends in 1985.

[b]The total capital budget of the PRC is $600 billion.

motion of tourism will remain a high priority when the modernization reevaluation concludes.

The phenomenon of the flow of foreign funds to support relatives in the PRC from those Chinese who have emigrated abroad is not matched by any other nation. These flows are expected to increase greatly as a consequence of the PRC's improved relations with the Western world. These repatriated earnings are expected to serve as a primary source of foreign exchange/hard currency for future modernization projects.

In terms of the repatriation of foreign workers' earnings, the Chinese rank first, followed by Italy, India, Egypt, Yugoslavia, Turkey, and Portugal. The importance of repatriated earnings (as well as tourism) to the PRC is shown in Table 18. Still, this ten-year plan projected a shortage to be made up by foreign borrowings of $35 billion.

The successes or failures of the modernization program will partially determine whose hand continues to rule. One likely scenario is that modernization may become too costly; costly in sheer economic terms of hard currency, in terms of the domestic sacrifices required, and in terms of just how much Mao's fundamental doctrines of self-sufficiency and distrust of foreign influence must be muted in order to partially legitimize some very Western goals. Were all these sacrifices and costs to become prohibitive, it appears that Party Chairman Hua, who is after all Mao's chosen successor, and the followers he acquired during the Cultural Revolution, may try to seize power, abandon modernization plans, and seek to reaffirm Mao's basic revolutionary values.[62] Such a shift in policy would virtually halt all foreign trade, particularly that involving large industrial projects. All trading relationships established during this present drive towards economic growth must take into account the very unstable current leadership within the PRC.

As seen, historically, the PRC has not viewed foreign trade as an integral aspect of its economic system. This reflects two central themes that are at the root of Chinese foreign-trade policy, the themes of self-reliance and trade on the basis of equality and mutual benefit.[63] However, as we have seen, following the death of Chairman Mao and the ensuing struggle for power, the theme of self-reliance began to be subverted. The economic plans devised to spur China's modernization required interaction with other economies to assure China's economic development.

About 83 percent of China's trade in 1977 and 1978 was with non-Communist nations,[64] led by Japan and followed by Hong Kong and the United States in that order. China's main exports are food, textiles, and petroleum. Leading imports are industrial goods and grain. The portion of imports represented by technology and related equipment will become increasingly dominant. The PRC sees Western technology as indispensable in achieving the enormous goals of modernization set by the post-Mao leadership.

It might be interesting here to note some recent agreements between the PRC and Western nations. In August, 1978, Japan and the PRC signed a treaty of peace and friendship that included a $2 billion loan, which the PRC will use to import goods from Japan. The loan, in dollars, is for five years at an interest rate of 0.625 percent above the London interbank rate (LIBOR). The Japanese transaction followed earlier British and Italian trade agreements in early 1978.

In December, 1978 the PRC signed a seven-year trade agreement with France that calls for $14 billion in trade between the two countries, including the sale of two French-built nuclear plants to China. Credits for $6.8 billion were extended by France over a ten-year period bearing an annual interest rate close to the 6.5 percent accorded by Japan to China.

Also in December, 1978, $61.2 billion of British export financing was arranged with seven British banking groups. Under this arrangement the British banks will make deposits at the Bank of China instead of conventional loans to that bank. Maturity of credits will be two to five years from dates of drawdowns with interest at a flat 7.25 percent and credits insured by the British government.

The goal of transforming the PRC into a modern industrial state by the year 2000 can be realized only by a massive infusion of Western technology supported by favorable financing arrangements.* The PRC's historic dislike of any type of foreign dependency, particularly economic, has, of necessity, been temporarily quieted—one hopes until sufficient energy-production equipment and capital have been acquired to allow full exploitation of on- and off-shore oil reserves, which to date have proved unexpectedly disappointing. It remains clear that this is only a question of expediency. The desire to achieve self-sufficiency still colors all Chinese economic transactions.

The PRC's foreign-trade planning apparatus is similar to that found in the USSR and Eastern Europe. The State Planning Commission is the nation's central planning group and controls the Ministry of Foreign Trade. As with the other Eastern nations, economic goals are established through five- or ten-year plans and are administered through various trade corporations, each of which is responsible for a specific category of goods or services. All foreign contracts are negotiated through the foreign-trade corporations.

As is the case with the USSR and Eastern Europe, this lack of contact with the end-user creates many problems for foreign business executives. However, one significant difference in the PRC's foreign-trade planning is that a greater degree of decentralized planning is allowed here than in the USSR and Eastern Europe. Though the state still controls the ultimate decisions, the ultimate plan is usually a combination of decisions made at various levels.[65] And, since February, 1980, there has been an increased bureaucratic layer of contract approvals.†

Another unique feature of the Chinese foreign-trade system is the semiannual Guangzhou Canton Trade Fair, officially known as "The Chinese Export Commodities Fair." This is sponsored by the foreign-trade corporations and is held every spring and fall. The fair attracts over 26,000 foreigners and over 40 percent of China's export trade is conducted there. It is designed to display and promote Chinese exports, but foreign imports are also purchased by the foreign-trade corporations. At

* At the end of 1980, it had become clear to the leadership in the PRC that the modernization projects entered into previously were far too ambitious and most have been cancelled.

† The author has observed that the older the civilization the more entrenched the bureaucracy. The type of government has little effect on this phenomenon. From this standpoint the PRC of 1981 may not differ appreciably from China under the rule of the Dowager Empress at the time of the Boxer Rebellion in 1900. Other examples of relatively ancient civilizations with problems of entrenched bureaucracy regardless of form of government may be cited: Egypt, Iran, Russia, France, and, of course, Italy.

the spring 1978 fair, total deals negotiated were estimated at $2.3 billion. It is calculated that the U.S. portion of this figure was about $30 million in orders and $55 million in purchases.[66] These figures are not as high as had been predicted and may signal further signs of a slowdown of the present Ten-Year Plan and its modernization goals. The present Ten-Year Plan (1976–85) was so ambitious in its aim of setting the PRC well on the road to modernization that it had to be scrapped in 1979.

Mao's fundamental doctrine of self-sufficiency was clearly opposed to foreign indebtedness, be it economic, political, cultural, or, worst of all, ideological. Though this attitude probably remains ingrained in the Chinese psyche, the increased drive to acquire Western technology has made it impractical if not impossible to continue Mao's concepts of financial policy. There is no way the Chinese can obtain needed technology unless they enter into various types of credit arrangements including loans, government lines of credit, or even barter arrangements. But the current willingness of the PRC leadership to enter into such arrangements represents a strong shift in policy and it is unlikely to be a permanent change. Credit arrangements should be viewed as clearly short term and extremely tenuous. As can be seen in Table 19, the PRC has not been experiencing a foreign-exchange shortage or debt problem. This is due to the prior policy of balancing imports with exports and maintaining a low level of foreign trade. This situation is changing as the PRC begins its capital expenditure development program in earnest. The scale of imports required, even though much reduced, will necessitate important new credit facilities. It has been estimated that in order to achieve development targets, the PRC may need to import between $55 and $85 billion worth of capital goods.[67] These figures are, of course, very subjective. Politically, the trial of the Gang of Four was intended to discredit Mao's management ideas and raise support for Deng's plan allowing for more free play in the market.

Negotiations with Beijing (Peking) over the terms of loans have often been difficult. The Chinese government still remembers early loans from the USSR to which political strings were attached and has little confidence that the West will not eventually insist on similar conditions. The avoidance of such infringements on national sovereignty is a high priority now with the negotiation of all new loans, and the PRC is carefully negotiating loans that are free from all unnecessary conditions. Recent loans negotiated with British banks and the Union de Banques Arabes et Francaises (UBAF) reflect this desired simplicity. Loans negotiated with the British banks include $100 million each from Midland and Standard

Table 19. The foreign debt position[a] of the People's Republic of China (*In millions of dollars*)

	1970	1971	1972	1973	1974	1975	1976	1977
Short-term credits[b]								
Drawn	275	240	240	530	840	920	225	470
Repaid	325	305	175	230	655	830	935	260
Net	−50	−65	65	300	185	90	−740	240
Interest[c]	30	30	15	20	50	65	95	25
Outstanding	325	260	325	625	810	900	190	430
Medium-term credits[d]								
Drawn	0	0	0	0	215	560	285	60
Repaid	0	0	0	0	0	0	20	215
Net	0	0	0	0	215	560	265	−155
Interest	0	0	0	0	0	0	5	65
Outstanding	0	0	0	0	215	775	1,040	885
Totals								
Drawn	0	0	0	0	215	560	285	60
Repaid	0	0	0	0	0	0	20	215
Net	0	0	0	0	215	560	265	−155
Interest	0	0	0	0	0	0	5	65
Outstanding	0	0	0	0	215	775	1,040	885

Source: CIA Report, December, 1978, p. 22.

[a] All data are estimates based on contract terms, delivery schedules, and trade statistics and are rounded to the nearest $5 million.

[b] Six- to eighteen-month credits for grain, for Japanese fertilizer in 1970, and for Japanese steel in 1975.

[c] Estimated at 8 percent per year for 1970–74, 10 percent for 1975–76.

[d] Five-year credits for complete plant purchases.

Charter and $175 million from Midland and International Banks (MAIBL). The loans from UBAF totaled $500 million. These loans have relatively short-term repayment periods and payment is to be made in a single sum. The time frame is three and one-half years for the UBAF loan and five years for the British.[68] Again, such agreements reflect the PRC's desire to avoid entangling arrangements with foreigners.

Since November, 1980 the PRC has been a member of the IMF and IBRD. In May, 1980 the PRC also became a member of IDA. Chinese leaders realize that loans from international institutions are apolitical and hence quite different from normal government-to-government credits, which necessarily imply continued bilateral political relationships. Following the announcement of normalization, and the granting of MFN status in January, 1980, contracts have greatly accelerated between major U.S. corporations and the PRC. Several of the largest include a

Pan American World Airways $500 million contract to build and operate hotels in the PRC (a promising move for the PRC tourist industry), a Bethlehem Steel Corporation $100 million contract to develop an iron-ore mine and Coca-Cola's exclusive rights to sell in the PRC. But the PRC's firmest hopes for foreign exchange rest on the development of onshore and offshore oil reserves.

The PRC has recently been producing about 2 million barrels of oil per day. It is hoped that new reserves onshore and offshore will materialize that will place the PRC among the world's largest oil producers. Unfortunately, the PRC's oil reserves are not as extensive as originally thought. In addition, the Chinese economy is not sufficiently industrialized to use energy efficiently. Thus, most of the oil production is used for domestic consumption. It is expected that throughout the 1980s, barring any significant finds, the PRC will continue to use up its surplus oil, forfeiting sorely needed foreign currency. The PRC recently cut back a $5 billion Baoshan Steel complex and indefinitely suspended Japanese petrochemical contracts worth $1 billion, both of which are energy intensive and would require massive imports.

Both oil exploration and oil production require vast expenditures, which the Chinese have wisely decided would be best incurred by the foreign petroleum industry giants. To this end, the PRC has been negotiating with many Western oil companies to begin exploration. French and British companies have already begun oil surveys in the Yellow Sea. And massive contracts have been under negotiations with U.S. companies* to explore the South China Sea. Unfortunately, relations between the United States and the PRC have been complicated by additional political problems: the election of President Reagan (the Chinese are concerned about his attitude toward Taiwan) and the efforts of the conservative Maoists in the Chinese government apparatus to sabotage the PRC's economic relations with the outside world.

Of necessity, exploration and ultimate drilling and production deals will be quite costly to the PRC in terms of foreign exchange. To help alleviate this problem and some of the financing problems with other needed imports, the Chinese, like the East European nations, are beginning to promote various forms of countertrade and industrial cooperation arrangements in order to accelerate export earnings. They hope to arrange buy-back deals or compensation agreements with the oil companies that will consist of payment for technology and equipment to

*Twenty-two U.S. oil companies have been declared eligible by the PRC for contracts.

be made through the deliveries of crude oil at fixed prices over a period of time.[69] This assumes that exploration and development made possible by Western technology and equipment will indeed be successful. It must also be kept in mind that domestic energy requirements may preempt much of the crude oil discovered.

Other types of countertrade presently being promoted by the PRC include schemes to develop various tax-free export-processing zones, where raw materials or certain semi-manufactures would be imported into the PRC for further processing or assembly and then be reexported. The Chinese are also showing an increased interest in entering into types of joint ventures where the West supplies technology and equipment or even entire factories and the PRC supplies the raw materials and labor. As with the USSR and Eastern Europe, such arrangements with nonmarket economies raise many problems, particularly when the end product is to be manufactured goods. Here again the most difficult problem is quality control.*

These types of arrangements and other bilateral trade agreements are hindered by U.S. government restrictions. Normalization did allow the successful completion (ignoring textile problems) of a bilateral trade accord between the United States and the PRC, which included the resolution of the long-standing problems of U.S. claims† and frozen assets. (Tariffs on imports from the PRC were, prior to the granting of MFN status, approximately 300 percent higher than those for countries receiving MFN treatment.) Export-Import Bank support is also now available to finance U.S. exports to the PRC.‡

The issue of technology transfers has yet to really surface with regard to the People's Republic of China. One potential problem is the recent Chinese request to purchase a highly sophisticated satellite to establish a better network of communications over its vast territory. However, the satellite required could also prove to have great military value to the PRC

* Western firms can expect fewer problems regarding quality control in the PRC than in Eastern Europe. Chinese workers have traditionally had a reputation for excellent workmanship in their work.

†The 1979 agreement between the United States and the PRC provided that the 579 claims of U.S. citizens worth $197 million would be settled by the payment of $80.5 million, payable over five years.

‡Former Vice-President Walter Mondale promised the Chinese, when he visited them in 1979, a $2 billion line of credit to be made available through the Export-Import Bank. But as of May, 1981 these funds had not been appropriated by Congress. The Bank, which had no funds available for this commitment then, has even fewer funds now. Yet in June 1981, Secretary of State Alexander Haig spoke again in Beijing of this line of credit as though it were in place.

in terms of the inherent technology. The United States has apparently resolved the dilemma by deciding to deliver the satellite to the Chinese in space, where they would be unable to translate the technology for military purposes, but would still be able to greatly modernize their entire communications network. The United States and China already in 1980 established a cooperative effort to monitor space activity in the Soviet Union.

Disregarding this rather unique solution to this satellite problem for the moment, there appear to be several reasons why the problem of technology transfers to the PRC has not become overwhelming, as it has so often with the sale of technology to the USSR. There is a wide discrepancy in the level of military and economic development between the PRC and the USSR and, coupled with a history of nonaggression unless pushed to the wall, the PRC obviously presents less of an overall economic and military threat to the United States. The issue is also colored by the present euphoria over trade with the long-silent PRC, a euphoria that has permeated all sectors of the U.S. government and business community. Can these high expectations be realized? And even more important, will overexpectations blind the United States in the development of coherent, well-formulated trade policies with the PRC? Normalization did allow the successful negotiation of a bilateral trade accord that included resolution of the outstanding issues (economic) between the United States and the PRC. However, completion of this accord should not make American businessmen think that development of trade relations with the PRC, despite the best of intentions on both sides, will be easy.

As noted, the success or failure of the PRC's domestic development is unfortunately very much dependent on first locating and developing the PRC's oil reserves and second, accelerating the export of oil. Since this oil is not expected to materialize on the scale hoped for, the entire modernization process has been drastically altered. Such an alteration has undoubtedly further weakened a very shaky governing coalition. The possibility of the PRC's not becoming an oil giant in the near future has been acknowledged by Chinese leaders. There are innumerable factors that make the PRC's future as a leading oil exporter very tenuous.[70] Will it be able to generate sufficient capital internally or externally from credit arrangements to pay for the equipment and technology to extract the oil? Are the reserves there to exploit? Can the PRC develop or import sufficient technical expertise to conduct its modernization projects[71] in view of the effects of the Cultural Revolution on the development of human skills? Finally, the most debatable factor is the future of the present leadership. Will Deng Xiaoping have the time to put in place a group of trained younger leaders to assure the continued technological development of the country in a period of political as well as economic transformation on a vast scale?

The problem of sufficient technological expertise is vital to the future of PRC modernization in all sectors, not just oil, and the virtual absence of technically trained persons available for the modernization program must be resolved as soon as possible. The Cultural Revolution (1966–69) halted all technical education in lieu of political indoctrination and has left the PRC with a real scarcity of trained personnel. An historic aversion to all foreign influence makes the large-scale importation of foreign technology difficult and practically prohibits the possibility of bringing foreign technicians to the PRC on the scale necessary to implement these programs.

The long-revered principle of self-reliance has led the PRC to attempt to resolve this fundamental problem by sending vast numbers of scholars to U.S. technical institutions for a quick education in the necessary technology-related skills. Internal educational reforms have also been undertaken in order to create, a contingent of first-rate scientists and technicians by the end of the century. Ideally, such plans will be supplemented by inviting Western scholars of Chinese origin who can lecture in the PRC. All these attempts to remedy the failure to educate the generation of the Cultural Revolution were developed to minimize the actual presence of foreigners within the PRC.

The problems of sufficient capital, adequate credit arrangements, actual oil reserves, and lack of technical experts will all interact to delineate the future of China's present modernization program. However, the question of political stability remains the ultimate denominator that will determine what China's future will be in terms of economic world power.

The present cautious reassessment of modernization goals should not be taken as a signal by the West of a shift back to isolation by the PRC. In fact, such a moderation of economic plans should be an encouraging sign for U.S. businessmen. More realistic goals are more easily accomplished, adding a note of certainty and stability to business relationships. In contrast, the lack of onshore and offshore oil reserves, the recent bad harvests caused by droughts,* the inability of the Chinese to solve the

* In 1980–81, the Chinese had the worst floods of the last quarter of a century in Hupei and severe drought in the whole area immediately to the north, particularly in Hubei province. As a result the PRC government was forced to appeal to the United Nations for

problem of producing adequate numbers of people with technical expertise and the overall political instability of the nation should all be monitored carefully as future potential restraints on the PRC's project-development programs. The immediate short-term outlook for U.S. trade with the PRC is good,* but hardly promising enough to warrant euphoria.

In the long-term, the picture is less promising and must be watched closely for potential danger signals. The PRC is facing nearly $12 billion in trade deficit and still has not found the hoped-for oil. Clearly, the U.S. trading posture should reflect overall political concerns in the area, and these political concerns are closely tied to the Soviet Union. Does the United States wish to promote the growth of United States–PRC trade and the concomitant growth of the Chinese economy as a counter to Soviet power in the area? Or does the United States wish to promote relations with both powers in order to utilize the now familiar term of "triangular diplomacy"? In fact, even if the United States so desired, can evolving policies towards the PRC be divorced from those with the Soviet Union? And what of our relations with Taiwan?

In geopolitical terms these problems must be examined without being colored by an unsubstantiated euphoria over trade possibilities. In the United States, both businessmen and congressional leaders have a tendency to look upon future commercial relationships with the People's Republic of China much as, more than a century ago, British businessmen and political leaders in the House of Commons looked upon the teeming masses of India and China "who, were they to buy enough Lancashire cloth for one shirt apiece, would bring prosperity to England."†

A final word of extreme caution—it is important to remember some lessons from history. Countries that have lasted as such for thousands of years reflect two rather special characteristics that to our detriment, we tend to forget: the first is that such societies survive by remaining quiet in times of revolt. This has been as true of Egypt and Iran as it is of China. In China's long history there have been many tales of wars but never of battles, for if generals met and one was obviously the stronger, the other quietly faded into the vast countryside. This was as true during

massive disaster assistance. Large purchases of grain will have to be made in 1981 from the United States and Canada. This will require further downward revision of China's modernization program owing to an even greater scarcity of foreign exchange.

* Bilateral trade in 1981 is expected to rise to $6 billion, compared to $4.3 billion in 1980.[72]

† Indeed, Britain's trade relationships with India and with China in Victorian times did maintain the prosperity of British mills.

the so-called Civil War ending in 1949 as it was before under the Japanese occupation, or the revolt against the Mandarins or the Mings in earlier times. During the Cultural Revolution educated Chinese sought refuge in anonymity. Today Mao's followers sit in the Politburo and throughout the ministries quietly waiting for the new leadership to make mistakes, or go too far, or promise too much to the masses whose aspirations for a better life they have now awakened.

Second, and similarly, in old cultures a vast bureaucratic apparatus has been developed over centuries of rule. If the Shah failed in Iran, history may well blame not the religious leaders who overthrew him but the entrenched civil servants who resisted through inaction all his efforts at modernization. China is no different. Whether under the old Mandarinate system or under Chou En Lai's state bureaucracy, the same reluctance to change will cause the civil servants to give their approval to directives from above, and then do nothing.

It is with this historical perspective in mind that China's current drive for modernization must be examined. As Americans we must be careful not to make the same faulty analysis in China—that we made in Iran.

10

U.S. Productivity and Competitiveness in International Trade

> And he gave it for his opinion, that whoever could make two ears of corn or two blades of grass grow upon a spot of ground where only one grew before, would deserve better of mankind, and do more essential service to his country, than the whole race of politicians put together.
>
> *Gulliver's Travels*

For many years, U.S. products were renowned the world over. Their workmanship was good, the price was fair, and the product maintenance made available by U.S. companies, particularly those with well-established after-sales service, was esteemed worldwide. Today unfortunately, this is no longer so. U.S. products are not only barely competitive in the global marketplace, but, in many instances, are not even competitive in the United States.

To better understand this discouraging phenomenon, we will examine certain key industries in the U.S. market, including the manufacture of automobiles, tires, aircraft, microprocessors, robots, chemicals and petrochemicals, transportation equipment, pharmaceuticals, nuclear plants, and project engineering. These are all industries where U.S. engineering skills and advanced technology have been the key to America's competitive edge in the past.

Older industries, such as textile, steel, or shoe manufacture, will not be considered here. U.S. technology in these areas is no longer thought to be more advanced than that of other countries, and wage rates play a preponderant role in determining price competitiveness in these areas. Since the United States is becoming a relatively low-wage country (but only by comparison with Western Europe and Japan, where wages are rising faster than in the United States), it may, in the course of time,

Table 20. Comparison of combined total assets of the 10 largest foreign and the 10 largest U.S. nonpetroleum industrial companies (*Ranked by 1976 sales*)

	Combined total assets (*In billions of dollars*)			Percentage increase over 1965	
Year	U.S.	Foreign	U.S. Foreign ratio	U.S.	Foreign
1965	$ 45.1	$15.6	3:1	—	—
1970	65.9	33.2	2:1	46%	113%
1973	89.4	54.0	1:7:1	98	246
1976	113.6	76.2	1:5:1	152	388

Source: Figures derived from data presented by *Fortune.* See Lawrence G. Franko, "Multinationals: The End of U.S. Dominance," *Harvard Business Review,* November–December, 1978.

become competitive again in these old, mass-production industries.* The question addressed here is to what extent we are competitive today, and to what extent will we be competitive tomorrow, in the high-technology industries in which, for many years, we were the pioneers.

The attributes of product quality, price, and service are interrelated. Quality depends on manufacturing controls, the competence of the working force, and the excellence of the machinery and equipment. Service depends on the quality of the marketing and servicing organization, the attitude of management toward foreign sales, the strength of the dealer organization, and in most cases the type of marketing and distribution relied on. Larger companies with established marketing and dealer organizations are thus likely to be better placed to service the market. Table 20 shows the changes that have recently taken place in company size in the United States and other countries. This indicates that U.S. firms are likely to face increased competition in the future. Two additional factors weighing against future U.S. competitiveness should be noted here: the anti–big-business attitude prevalent in the United States right now, and the lack of any system of sales and distribution that might help the nation's smaller high-technology manufacturers the same way the Japanese do via their trading company system. In 1980, Congress, at Senator Adlai Stevenson's instigation, began to focus on this problem by considering legislation to encourage the creation of trading companies.

We have become less competitive. Why? The price of a product ulti-

* Indeed, as of 1981, the U.S. shoe industry is again able to compete with the French and the Italian industries.

mately depends upon worker productivity in a high-wage economy, such as that of the United States or Western Europe.

Since productivity is defined as output per unit of input, the outputs defined in terms of gross national product (GNP) or gross domestic product (GDP) must be divided by a measure of input, such as man-hours of labor. In the United States, productivity statistics are kept by the Department of Labor's Bureau of Labor Statistics (BLS). The BLS data deducts from GNP all output produced outside the United States, by the government, by nonprofit institutions, and in private homes. The resulting total is then divided by the labor input as measured in total man-hours.

Under this definition, national productivity includes the service sector. Although we pride ourselves on the fact that the United States is rapidly becoming a post-industrial or service economy—indeed more than 60 percent of the U.S. workforce is now employed in supplying services—the service sector does not produce any tangible goods, although it does adversely affect the cost of goods. The export of services as such is, of course, a positive factor in the U.S. trade balance.

Productivity is thus a measure of the generation of a nation's wealth. What has been the recent performance of productivity in the United States?

Analysis of U.S. Productivity Decline

The long-term statistics indicate a steady decline in growth of the economy's overall productivity. Figure 7 shows U.S. productivity in manufacturing industries for the years 1967 to 1978 compared with that of France, West Germany, the United Kingdom, Canada, Italy, and Japan. Figure 8 shows labor productivity growth in the U.S. private domestic economy.

Figure 9 shows the U.S. slump in productivity and the large decline that took place in 1979. Since productivity generally declines during recessionary periods because workers are not laid off as fast as orders slow down, it must be expected that 1980 figures will show a further productivity decline in the United States until there is a rebound in the economy.

As relative productivity declines, exports tend to decrease, which in turn tends to reduce the value of the dollar. When this happens, inflation increases as the cost of imports rise. At the same time, productivity directly affects the rate of domestic inflation because the cost of products increases as productivity decreases. Figure 10 shows how closely the

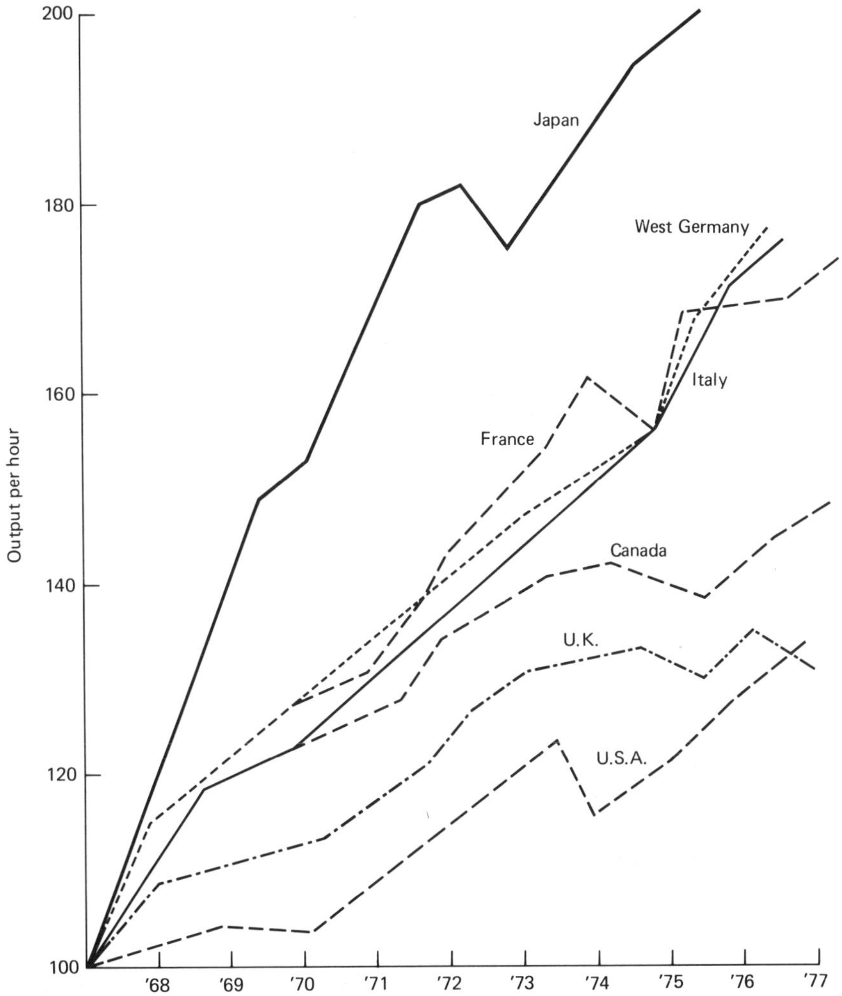

Figure 7. International indices of labor productivity[a] of manufacturing workers, 1967–1977

Source: "Why is U.S. Productivity Slowing Down?" *Harvard Business Review,* April, 1979; and U.S. Department of Commerce, International Economic Indicators.

[a] Productivity is normalized to 1967 figures.

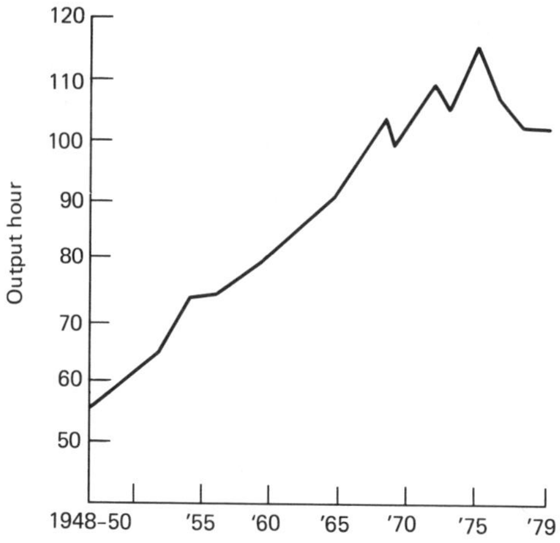

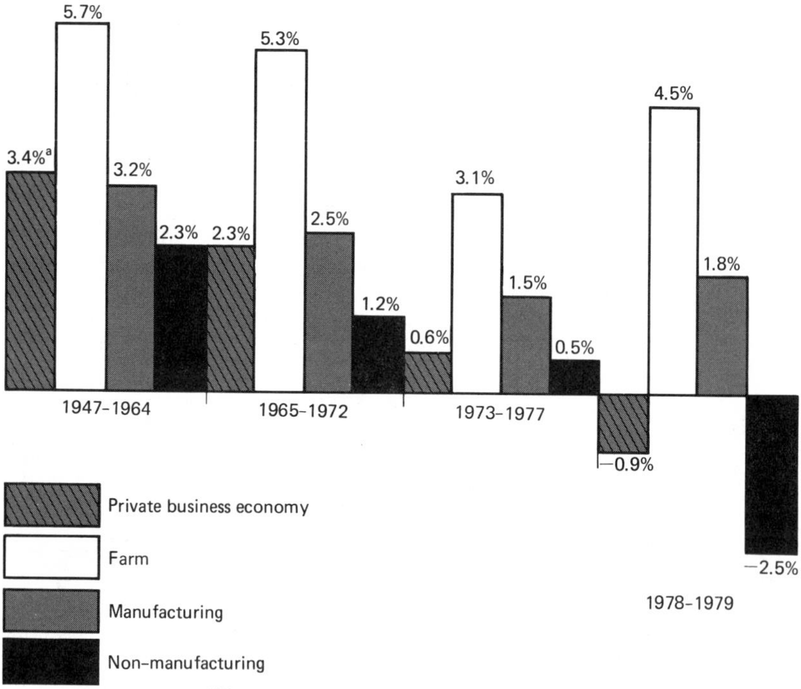

Figure 8. U.S. labor productivity growth; above, of private business 1948–1979; below, private domestic economy.

Source: From data released by U.S. Bureau of Labor Statistics, *The Washington Post,* April 27, 1980.

[a] Percentage of productivity growth measure as average per year.

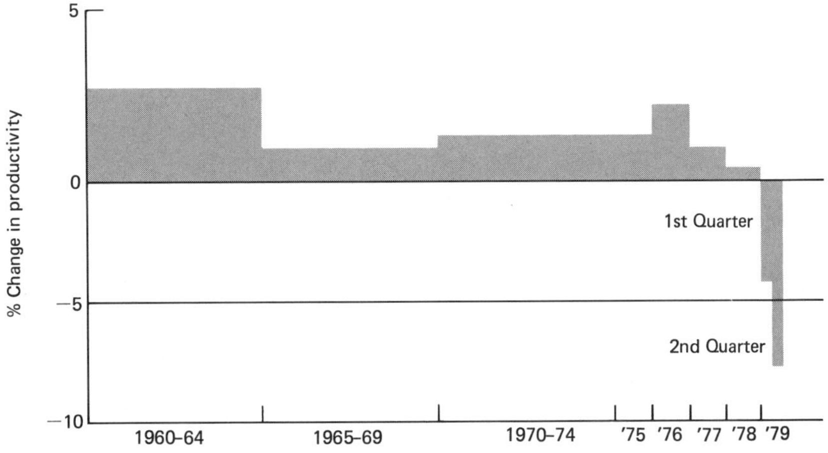

Figure 9. The U.S. slump in productivity *(of private nonfarm business sector)*

Source: From data released by OECD, in Christopher Lorenz, "Now America Needs Its Own Miracle," *Financial Times* (London), November 21, 1979.

"productivity gap"* in the United States parallels the climb in the consumer price index (CPI). This is attributable to the fact that the CPI combines the increases in compensation per hour with the decreases in output per hour. Assuming that wages will increase in 1981 while productivity decreases, it appears obvious that the CPI will continue to advance above the 1979 and 1980 levels, at least to the extent that the cost of labor affects this index.

If productivity in the United States continues to decrease relative to that of other countries, this will also affect the value of the dollar compared with other currencies. To continue to sell our products abroad, we will have to reduce their prices by reducing the value of the dollar.

Measures taken by the Federal Reserve in October, 1979 increased U.S. interest rates, thereby maintaining the dollar's strength. The high rates caused foreigners, particularly the OPEC countries, to keep their excess liquid reserves in dollars—principally U.S. government obligations. Rising U.S. interest rates, however, have also increased domestic inflation and the cost of U.S. products, caused production to decline, increased the likelihood of a severe recession, accelerated the decline in productivity, and encouraged other industrialized countries such as West

* The "productivity gap" is tracked by Science Management Corporation of Moorestown, New Jersey, a productivity improvement consulting firm.

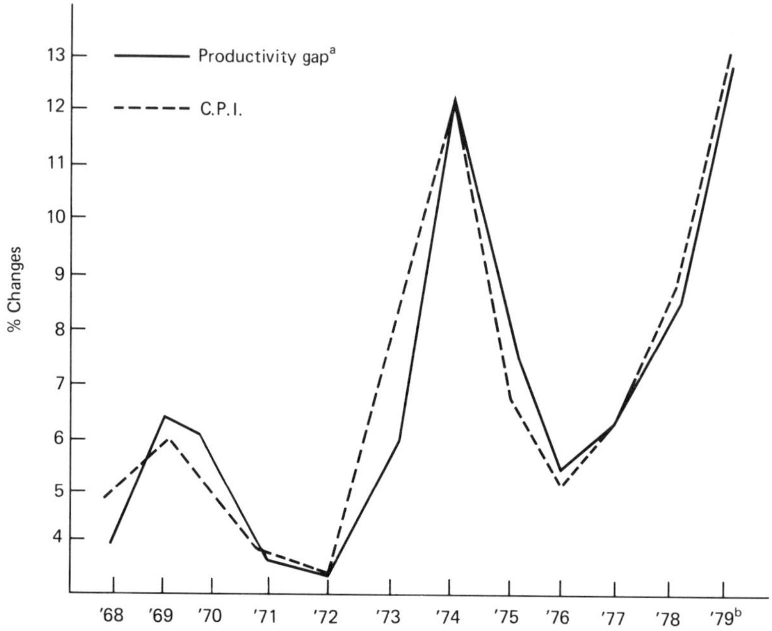

Figure 10. The productivity gap

Source: From data released by the U.S. Bureau of Labor Statistics, *The New York Times,* October 14, 1979.
[a] The Bureau of Labor Statistics determines the productivity gap by determining the percent changes in output per hour less changes in compensation per hour.
[b] Based on 1979 2nd quarter statistics.

Germany and Japan to increase their own interest rates to prevent their currencies from declining further relative to the dollar. Raising interest rates to protect the value of a currency is a policy of despair.

Other industrialized nations must earn dollars to pay for their oil. If their currencies decline, their products become more competitive in the international marketplace, but their cost of imported oil increases. Because West Germany and Japan are almost totally dependent on imported oil, they cannot allow the dollar to gain additional strength versus their currencies. If we are not careful, the actions of the Federal Reserve may result in an interest-rate war that will only end in benefiting OPEC. The OPEC countries are understandably delighted to receive 12–20 percent in interest on their excess funds in U.S. dollars, which only earned 7 percent a year earlier.

In any country, growth of the economy results in an increase in the standard of living of its citizens. That is why government economists everywhere strive for continued periods of growth. Growth, however, depends on increases in total man-hours worked within the country, and increases in productivity.

In the post-World War II era, U.S. growth came principally from increases in the work force. In the 1960s, the wartime baby boom led to substantial increases in the number of young men and women working for the first time. In the 1970s, women and minority groups were substantially added to the work force. In the 1980s and 1990s, as the workforce stabilizes and then declines, increases in hours worked will cease, and it will be necessary for productivity to increase substantially if the U.S. standard of living is not to decline. This means that in the next two decades we must find a way to materially increase the output of the worker. The Japanese, who have a shortage of skilled labor, accomplish this by constantly upgrading the productivity of their workforce by giving each worker who is capable of assuming more responsibility access to the machines or machine tools that will enable him to produce far more than he previously was able to. There are other facts worth noting in the Japanese business system: in approximately five hundred of the largest companies, there is a guarantee of employment. There is also a bonus system that gives workers up to an extra year's salary if company results warrant it. Finally, workers are motivated to set aside savings out of their current income because of the inadequacy of the retirement system.

In the United States do the social security and medicare/medicaid programs discourage the growth of savings? The answer is probably yes. In any event, the savings rate in the United States is minimal compared to that of Europe and Japan (see Figure 11).

If retirement benefits are indexed, as they are for government employees in the United States, then government employee incentive to reduce inflation is eliminated. In countries such as the United States, where the bulk of government tax receipts comes from graduated personal as well as business income taxes, the government is the greatest beneficiary of increased inflation because the taxpayer is automatically put in a higher tax bracket without any increase in real income. For example, in 1980 the government expected to balance the budget not because its expenditures were to be reduced but because taxes would increase through the effect of higher wages granted to meet rising inflation. In 1981, the Reagan Administration did not propose that Congress cut the 1980 federal

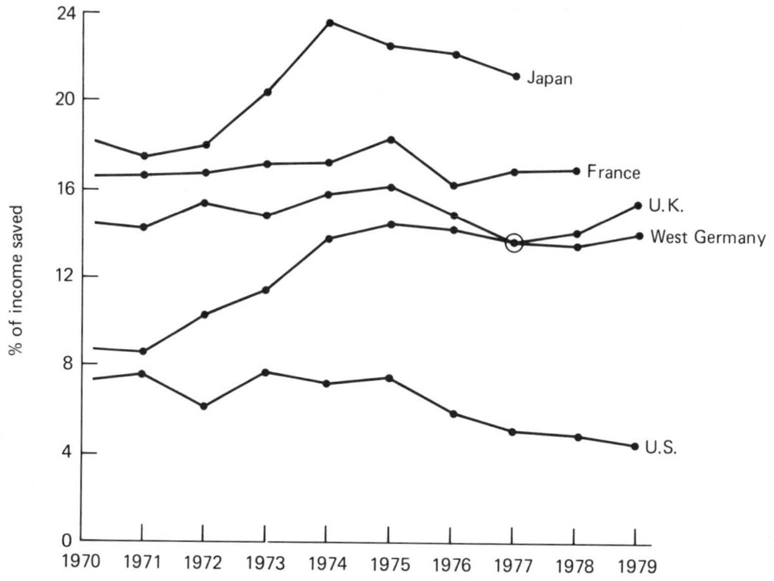

Figure 11. Personal savings rate 1970–79

Source: From data released by the U.S. Department of Commerce, *Fortune Magazine,* April 7, 1980.

budget but only that a portion of the increases proposed by President Carter be reduced.

It is difficult to understand why U.S. labor unions, representing members who are certainly in the middle class and therefore increasingly hurt by the effects of higher taxes and declining real wages, have not seen the need to boost productivity to justify increased wage demands. When unions insist that management employ more workers, the effect is exactly the opposite, since it reduces rather than increases worker productivity in the plant. It is the antithesis of the Japanese system of upgrading worker productivity. In the United States high-technology industries employ highly skilled workers at above-normal wages, few plants are unionized, and productivity is constantly increased as men adapt to new machine technologies.

It is clear that increased productivity must become a national priority if we are to maintain our standard of living. In continental Europe, the United States is often compared to the United Kingdom, where for years social programs and the quality of life have become the chief national concern of government. But Great Britain found oil in the North Sea, and the discovery has given the country twenty years of increased revenue that will either be invested wisely for the creation of future wealth within the country or lost forever in shorter work hours and lowered motivation. In the United States, we may have to meet the same challenges out of our own resiliency as a people. Whether we succeed may well depend on whether we make the necessary effort to increase the productivity of our work force.

As inflation grew in the United States in late 1979 and early 1980, we began to see extraordinary attempts by the U.S. government to reduce inflation by first trying to talk the country into a recession and then by creating it through raised interest rates and curtailed consumer credit. How much better it would be to reduce inflation by taking steps to increase productivity so that wage increases will not create what economists call cost-push inflation. From 1959–68, for example, annual compensation increases exceeded increases in productivity by only 1.7 percent. In 1970–78 the figure became 6.6 percent per year, which matched the annual inflation rate for the decade.

A simple example of how increased productivity can control inflation despite wage increases can be seen in a comparison of France, West Germany, and the United States over the five-year period from 1973–77. In France, wage increases exceeded productivity boosts during this period by 54 percent, so that inflation was high; in the United States the figure was 37 percent; and in West Germany, where inflation was low, the figure was 21 percent. As a result, the German mark increased in value relative to the dollar, while the French franc decreased in value. The effect of the exchange-rate adjustments evened out as follows: France—39 percent, West Germany—39 percent, and the United States—37 percent. Adjustments in flexible exchange rates thus compensated for this nation's failure to maintain its productivity ratio relative to wage increases. We shall see how the productivity gap affects the value of the dollar in 1981 unless offset by continuing high interest rates.

If increased productivity is to have the highest national priority, as we have indicated it should, what steps can be taken? What brings about increases in productivity in an industrial society? Is it more innovation, higher research expenditures, more infusion of capital into business ventures, changes in the tax system, greater concentration on the educational process, better allocation of national resources, better planning, or bigger companies to permit more economies of scale?

Factors Affecting U.S. Productivity

Because of the complexity of this subject and the somewhat contradictory emphasis that has been placed on various factors by the experts and study groups that have analyzed the subject, a more pragmatic approach will be followed here. The factors that affect productivity in an industrialized society will first be discussed. In so doing, analogies will be drawn wherever possible to the experience of other countries, where recent trends have been more favorable than ours, (i.e., Japan, West Germany, and France). Then, we will analyze the experience of certain key U.S. industries in recent years. Finally, we will offer some possible solutions to the productivity problem.

Some very capable economists have devoted considerable effort to dissecting the problems of productivity. John W. Kendrick, professor of economics at George Washington University and former chief economist for the U.S. Department of Commerce, and Edward F. Dennison, associate director for National Economic Accounts of the U.S. Department of Commerce, for instance, have written excellent treatises on the subject. Our own interest, however, is in focusing on the policies of governments, businessmen, and labor leaders that have led to the current decline in productivity. The economists can show us where we have been and indicate some of the reasons why we have come to where we are today. Our guides for the future, however, will have to be political leaders who understand the need for remedial action, along with innovative business leaders and engineers who have the foresight to take advantage of new opportunities that the government may make available.

In our mixed economy, it is not the government that creates new jobs, nor is it the large multinational corporations, since employment in the Fortune 500 as a whole has not increased in the last ten years. Rather, it is the small business enterprises, often those in new fields, using new technologies, that lead to the creation of new industries for the future. These are the industries, as Figure 12 shows, where productivity tends to be highest. Productivity gains in high-technology industries have also led to relatively high increases in employment.

Parenthetically, it must be repeated here that we are interested in the analysis of productivity in the manufacturing industries. In the United States about 67 percent of those in the U.S. workforce are in the service industries, according to BLS, compared with 22 percent in manufacturing, less than 8 percent in construction and mining, and only 3.4 percent

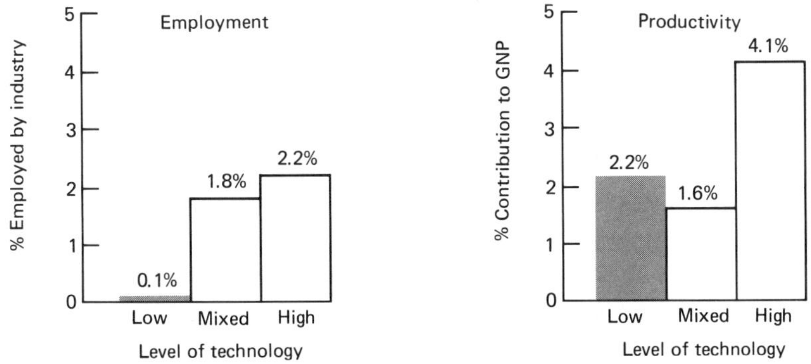

Figure 12. Productivity and employment—high-, mixed-, and low-technology industries in the U.S.

Source: IEEE Spectrum, October, 1978, p. 46.

in farming.* The productivity of the American farmer is justly celebrated. It is hard to imagine how fewer farmers could in fact produce more.

Figure 13 shows Denison's analysis of the various elements that he believes account for increases in productivity in the United States. Almost half come from what he calls technological innovation, or the practical results of advances in knowledge. Whether the chart is complete or whether the emphasis on economies of scale is correct is debatable. The importance of accelerated innovation seems clear. More stress should be placed, however, on the need for capital input, particularly when, as now, inflation makes the replacement of equipment much more expensive to business than was the case when inflation ratios were considerably lower. Analysts can reasonably differ in stressing the various factors noted. Let us briefly analyze the various factors that may be thought to have caused the recent decline in productivity in the United States.

The Decline in Technological Progress

In part, the recent decline in U.S. productivity comes from a slowdown in technological progress. Total expenditures for research and develop-

* It has been estimated that "in 1970 manufacturing involved 26.4 percent of the employed labor force; in 1977 that portion amounted to 22.8 percent. . . . In 1970 [the service sector] . . . had grown to 66.5 percent. In just seven years the goods-producing part of the employed labor force (agriculture, fisheries, forestry, mining, construction, and manufacturing) fell from 37.7 percent to 33.5 percent. On its previously shrunken base this amounted to a 11.1 percent downward shift."[1]

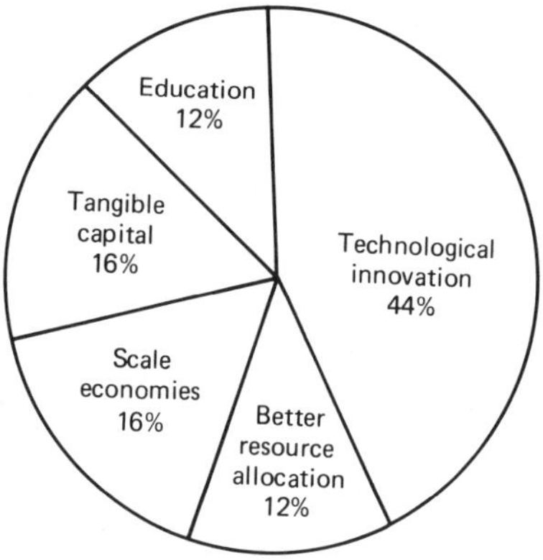

Figure 13. Elements affecting productivity gains

Source: IEEE Spectrum, October, 1978, reprint from Brookings Institute Analysis.

ment (R&D) fell from 3.2 percent of GNP in 1964 to 2.3 percent in 1977.* When adjusted for inflation, this decline is considerable. The Organization for Economic Cooperation and Development (OECD) pointed out in its 1979 survey of the U.S. economy that one of the four principal reasons for the decline in U.S. productivity in recent years was a reduction in R&D.

Figure 14 shows R&D expenditures as a percentage of GNP over the last few years. Figure 15 gives the U.S. R&D trade balance. Figure 16 shows government R&D expenditures over a selected period. Figure 17 gives an estimate of the number of scientists and engineers engaged in research activities.

Of particular interest in terms of technological progress is a comparison of research efforts in the United States and Japan. Even in the early period following the signing of the San Francisco Peace Treaty with Japan in 1951, Japanese efforts to modernize their technology compared very favorably with that of the United States. The effect of this effort is clearly demonstrated by Figure 18 which shows the development of the trade balance between Japan and the United States.

* The question of comparative research expenditures was examined in detail in hearings held before the Subcommittee on International Finance of the Committee on Banking, Housing, and Urban Affairs jointly with the Subcommittee on Science, Technology, and Space of the Committee on Commerce, Science, and Transportation, U.S. Senate, 95th Congress, 2nd session. See Part 7, "Oversight on U.S. High Technology Exports," May 16, 1978.

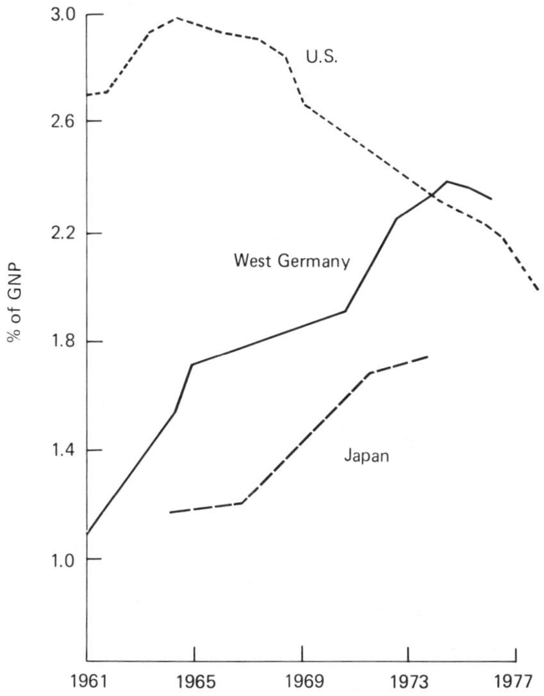

Figure 14. Research and development expenditures as a percent of GNP[a]

Source: U.S. Congress, Senate, Committee on Banking, Housing, and Urban Affairs, Subcommittee on International Finance, *hearings,* Part 7, May 16, 1978.
[a] Computed into these figures are defense-related R&D expenditures, with limited commercial transferability. U.S. R&D expenditures for defense add up to about 50 percent of the total U.S. R&D costs. West Germany defense-related R&D costs equal 11 percent; Japan, 2 percent.

The decline in our research effort is also evident in the fall in the number of patents issued to U.S. inventors compared to foreigners. Obviously certain patents are far more important than others, but this numerical decline seems to indicate a falloff in U.S. inventiveness in recent years compared with the Europeans and the Japanese.

The Decline in Labor Quality

Reference has already been made to the labor situation in Japan and the continuous attempts by the Japanese to upgrade the workforce to make up for a shortage of skilled workers. This has not been the practice in

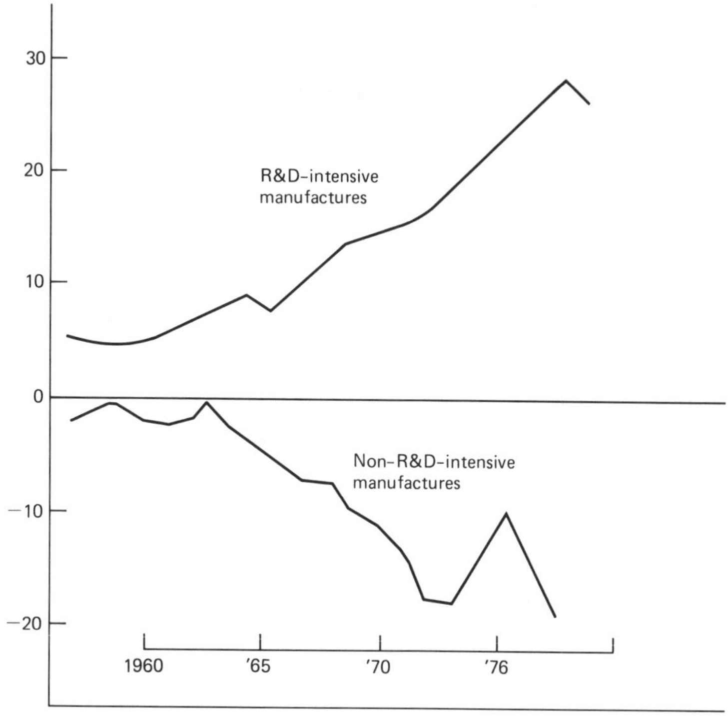

Figure 15. U.S. R&D trade balance[a]

Source: Computed from National Science Foundation Indicators, "Science Olympics," Business Brief, *The Economist,* May 20, 1978, pp. 86, 87.
[a] Exports less imports.

the United States. Government policies have been consistently directed at increasing employment rather than increasing the productivity of the workforce.

While unemployment figures have varied over the last decade, employment totals have increased consistently since the end of World War II. This is quite a remarkable achievement. The composition of the workforce has, however, changed, and this has affected productivity. The workforce today includes many more women, younger workers, blacks, and minorities. One of the structural problems in the U.S. education system is the lack of technical high schools to train potential industrial workers for jobs that are increasingly demanding more technical skills.

There is also a need, not presently being met in the United States to

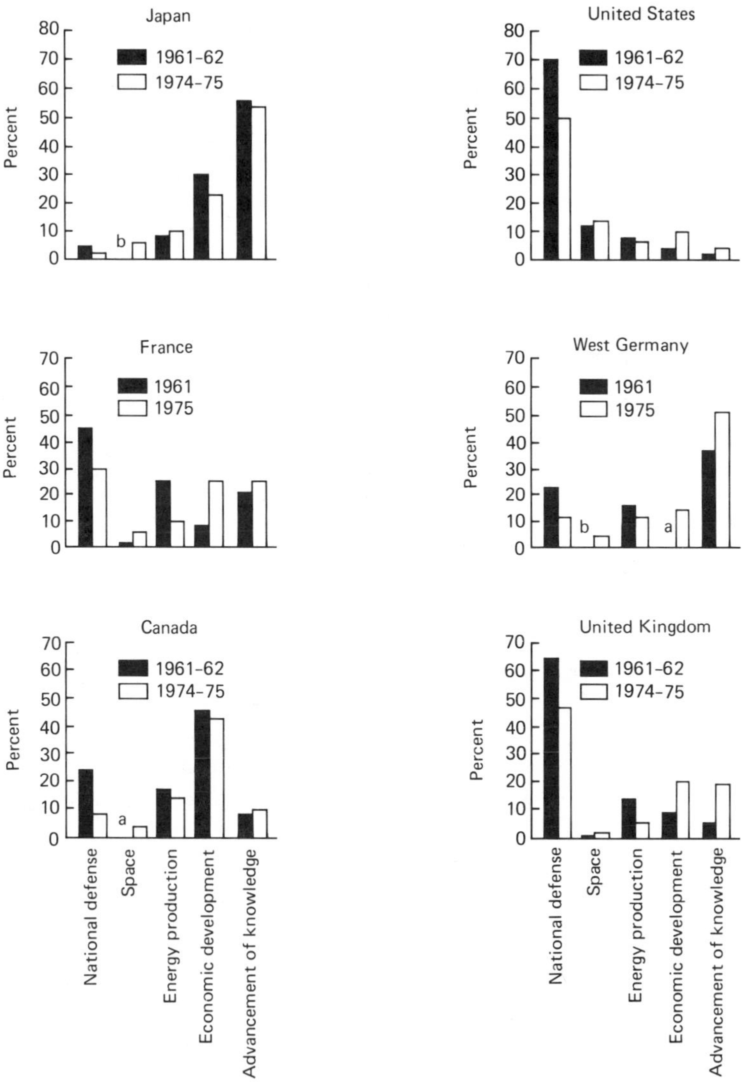

Figure 16. Government R&D expenditures (*Estimated distribution among selected areas*)

Source: U.S. Congress, Senate, Committee on Banking, Housing, and Urban Affairs, Subcommittee on International Finance, *hearings,* Part 7, April 16, 1978.
[a] Figures are not available.
[b] Figures represent less than 0.5 percent.

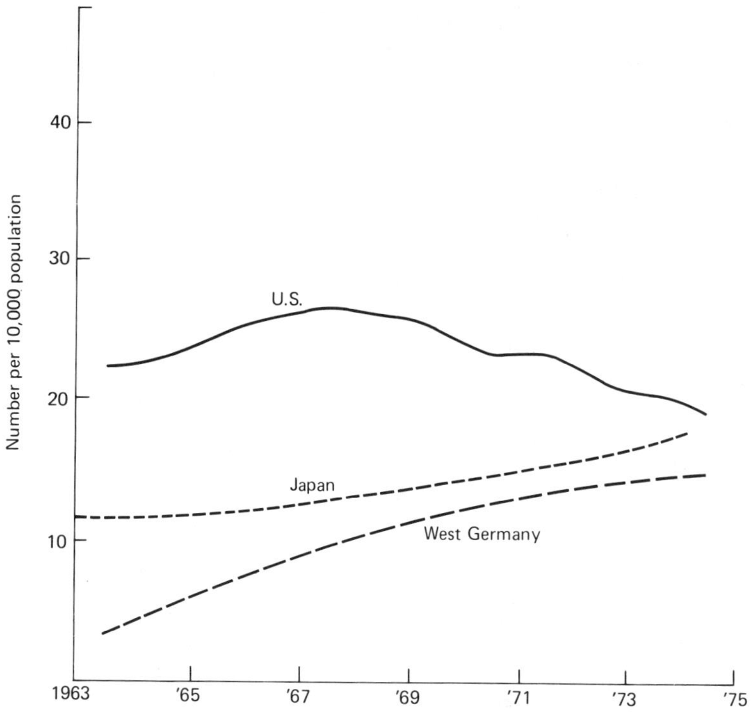

Figure 17. Scientists and engineers engaged in research and development

Source: U.S. Congress, Senate, Committee on Banking, Housing, and Urban Affairs, Subcommittee on International Finance, *hearings,* Part 7, May 16, 1978.

any great degree for greater worker participation in discussions immediately affecting his job. In Japan, two-thirds of the nation's larger enterprises have consultative committees to discuss not only matters affecting health and safety but also such issues as layoffs, transfers, and plant discipline. Paralleling these committees are about 600,000 quality-control groups composed of workers and foremen. This system has made it possible for Japanese automobile plants to employ one-third the number of inspectors needed in the U.S. auto industry. In addition, Japan has a very effective system of middle-management consensus decisionmaking called *ringi* which, while cumbersome, enables managers to feel that they have participated in plant decisions and that once these decisions are reached, they can be implemented quickly and without recrimination.*

* See Denison and Chung, *How Japan's Economy Grew,* p. 85: "Management is a key element in efficiency. . . . A characteristic feature of management in large Japanese

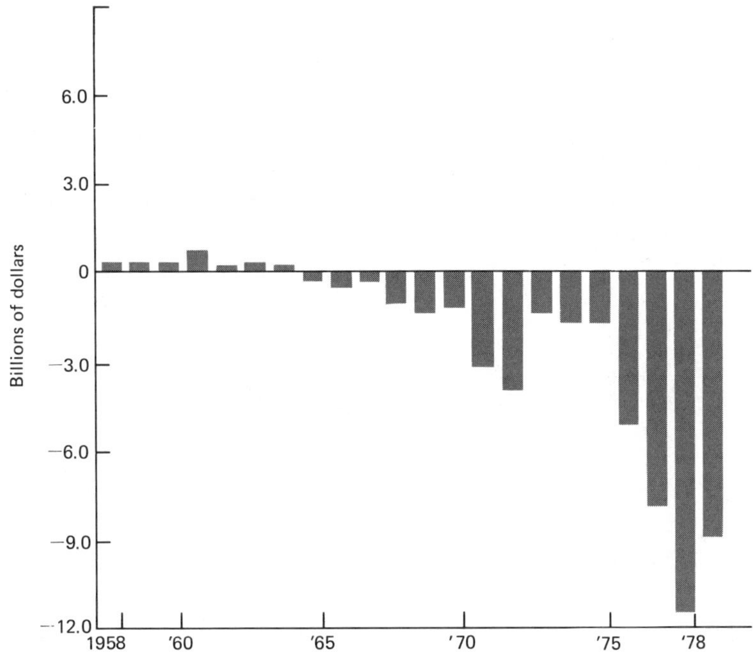

Figure 18. U.S. trade balance with Japan

Source: U.S. Congress, House and Senate Joint Economic Committee, *U.S. Trade Relations,* hearings, October 10, 1979.

Changes in the Availability of Natural Resources

A study released in January, 1980 by the Worldwatch Institute finds that current high rates of inflation are due at least in part to a global depletion of natural resources. While the aim of the organization is to persuade people to conserve and reduce their standard of living voluntarily to make scarce resources last longer, it highlights, nevertheless, a worldwide phenomenon that can only result in price increases for commodities, whether food, meats, oil, copper, wood, fish, or cereals.

Changes in Resources Allocation

The question here is economic efficiency. In the past in the United States, there was a continuous flow of labor from the farms to industry. Since

firms is decision making by consensus. . . . Although it may delay decisions, good or bad, it is said to facilitate wholehearted implementation by all concerned.

industrial wages have traditionally been higher than those for hired help in agriculture, this has had the effect of statistically increasing productivity. Now that employment in agriculture has stabilized, this factor is no longer significant.

Resource reallocation can also take place geographically. In the last few years, New England, and in particular Massachusetts, has seen a significant reallocation of resources as a result of new and more favorable tax and finance legislation resulting in an influx of high-technology industries. Highly skilled labor that can no longer command high wages in the textile industry—because the industry has moved to the Southeast—now finds that the electronics industry is willing to pay high wages for workers who have been trained to use complex machinery and who are careful with their tools. The rebirth of Massachusetts within the last few years illustrates what can be done to increase productivity and the standard of living of an entire region when local government, industry, and the workers themselves create an atmosphere of cooperation rather than confrontation.

Volume Changes

An important factor contributing to productivity is economies of scale or volume changes. Most important for productivity growth is production at full capacity. In a recessionary period, productivity tends to decline rapidly because management reduces production schedules in advance of any cuts in the workforce. Stop-go economic policies, of course, make it difficult for business to plan ahead and result in plants not producing anywhere near capacity. At the same time, such conditions make it unlikely that businessmen will increase investment for plant and equipment.

The Net Government Impact

The government sector employs one out of every six workers in the United States.[2] Efforts to measure productivity in government have not been overly successful; there has nonetheless been a tendency for the size of government to grow continuously. Efforts were made both by the Carter Administration and by Congress, at Senator Proxmire's urging, to look at the problem more closely to see what could be done to increase productivity and efficiency in government. The Joint Economic Committee (JEC) held hearings in May, 1979 and concluded that if overall federal productivity could be increased by only 10 percent, personnel costs could be reduced by more than $8 billion without a cutback in services.

Aside from the failure of an ever-larger government bureaucracy to demonstrate a commitment to the kinds of productivity standards that the private sector must meet to survive, the impact of government regulations on the productivity of the private sector itself must be considered. Just as a business cannot function effectively if its management has no clear objectives, the government must be judged by the same standards to the extent that it feels compelled to interfere in the economic process. In the United States, particularly in recent years, very little attention has been paid, as a matter of national policy, to making domestic industry either more productive or more competitive in the international marketplace. The focus of government in the United States has therefore been quite different from that in Japan, West Germany, or France. In the United States the focus has been on business regulations; in these other countries government has been much more concerned with guaranteeing that domestic industry remains internationally competitive.

The tendency of U.S. government regulation has all too frequently been to decrease productivity or increase costs. Price regulation of natural gas prior to 1979 kept that industry from developing the energy equivalent of untold TVA systems within the United States while encouraging the export of jobs, materials, and technology toward such countries as Algeria and Indonesia. Productive capacity increased in these countries with the result that we now import oil or gas from them at constantly escalating prices. In its planning for energy, the government has also alternately encouraged public utilities to shift from coal to oil, and more recently back to coal. We have seen the government encouraging a new $12 billion coal-development program while at the same time tacitly encouraging the nation's railroads to increase the cost of transporting coal from the mines to the consumer. It is almost impossible to expect business to plan under these conditions. The cost of excess regulation should also be addressed: in energy, under the Environmental Protection Agency (EPA), through the Occupational Safety and Health Administration (OSHA), through the export-licensing process, under alternate dollar-decline and dollar-support policies, and, more recently, in the government's efforts to control inflation by first forecasting recession and later accelerating it by tight-money policies and credit controls. Fortunately, increasing attention is now being paid, particularly in Congress through the bipartisan efforts of the Joint Economic Committee, to the necessity of encouraging increases in productivity. It also seems clear that the Reagan Administration intends to eliminate excessive government regulation of business wherever justified.

The Decline in Capital Investment

Since World War II, attempts have been made to increase U.S. employment by "priming the pump" whenever a slowdown in economic activity was feared by government economists. This was done through increases in the money supply, the lowering of taxes, or otherwise adding to the purchasing power of the consumer. This has resulted in increased inflation. A better program might have been to forego stimulation of consumer spending and focus instead on increasing the rate of consumer savings, thereby motivating savers to invest their funds in business enterprises so that these in turn could innovate and modernize.

As mentioned earlier, Figure 11 shows how the savings rate in the United States has been shrinking. Figure 19 demonstrates the changing patterns of U.S. savings by relating the savings rate to the increase in

Figure 19. The changing pattern in saving[a]

Source: Morgan Guaranty Survey, February 1980.
[a] Saving equals the difference between the increase in financial assets and the increase in debt, net of tangible investment.
[b] Data for 1979 are the average of the first three quarters.

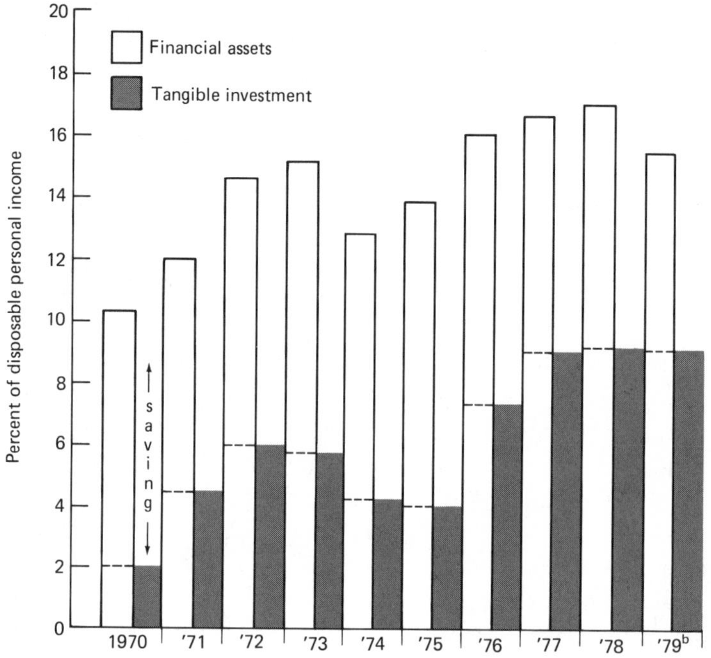

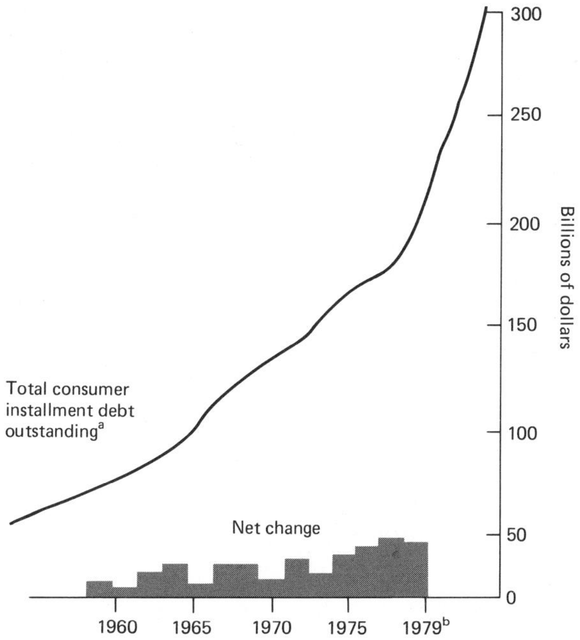

Figure 20. The pace of consumer borrowing (*In billions of dollars*)

Source: Federal Reserve Board, reprint from *The New York Times,* November 11, 1979.
[a] Consumer Installment Debt excludes home mortgages.
[b] 1979 figures reflect through September.

personal debt. Figure 20 brings the role of personal finance into focus by showing the growing level of private installment debt. Figure 21 then compares the growth of personal income in the United States with that of West Germany and Japan. The trends indicated by these figures are clear: the U.S. rate of savings has declined to the point where it is essentially no longer a factor in capital formation. By comparison, the savings rate in West Germany is 15 percent, in France 17 percent, and in Japan 23 percent. The comparable figures are set forth in Figure 22. Thus, the rate of investment in these other countries is currently much higher than in the United States.

Figure 23 shows the growth in capital formation among the United States, Canada, Japan, the United Kingdom, and West Germany in recent years. Were it not for the fact that capital markets in the United States have been particularly well developed and have no difficulty buying and

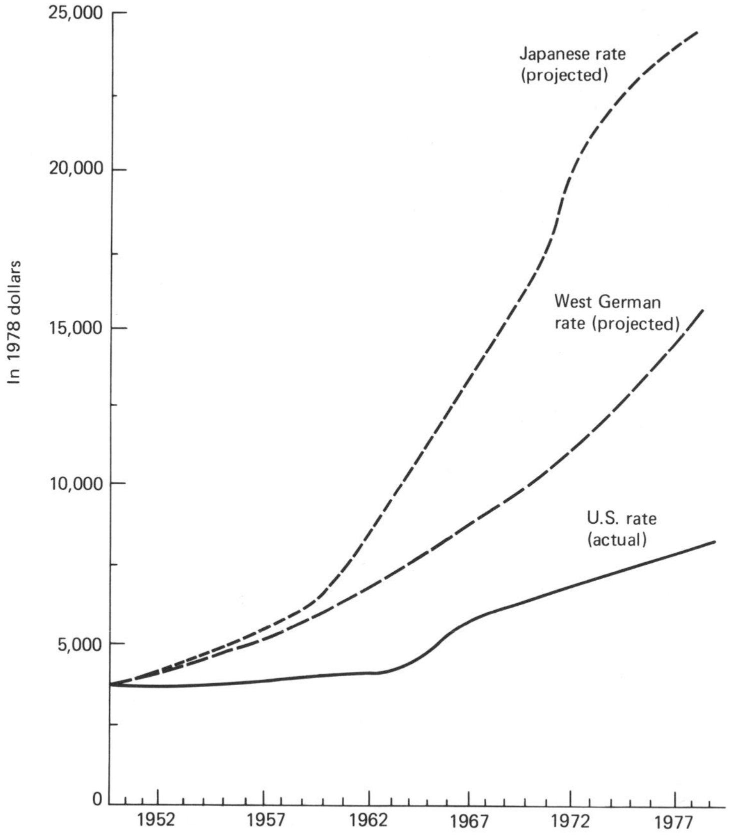

Figure 21. Real per capita disposable personal income

Source: Dept. of Commerce, Dept. of Labor.

selling securities and do not have exchange controls of any sort, it is likely that the flow of investment funds to other countries would have accelerated far more than has been the case until now. Nevertheless, there are disquieting signs even here. In the 1960s approximately 70 percent of all transactions on the New York Stock Exchange were for individuals and 30 percent for institutions. Today, in 1981, the reverse is true. This means that 70 percent of the funds flowing into companies listed on the exchange comes from institutions, which unfortunately also means that the smaller, high-technology company may be penalized, because institutional investors are generally more reluctant to invest in the smaller, less seasoned companies.

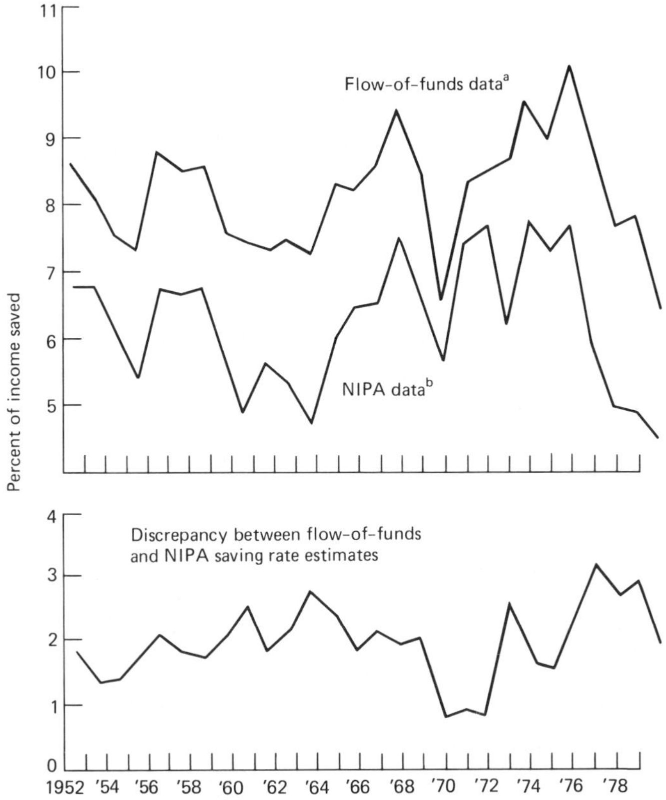

Figure 22. The shrinking saving rate

Source: The Morgan Guaranty Survey, February, 1980.
[a] Flow-of-funds data for 1979 are averages of the first three quarters.
[b] NIPA = National Income and Products Accounts.

Might it be that the Securities and Exchange Commission (SEC), in insisting on negotiated brokerage commissions, has performed a disservice to the development of new, technology-oriented companies by encouraging people to invest through an institution rather than directly through the research-oriented brokerage firms, many of which did a highly creditable job of ferreting out new ventures? The answer in time may be the development of new, strictly venture-capital management firms organized for the sole purpose of finding and financing new innovative businesses. This is probably the greatest need today in the U.S. capital markets.

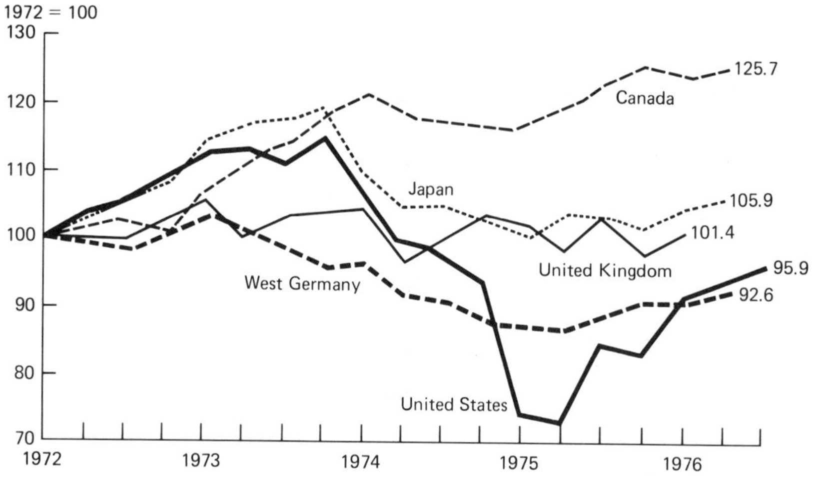

Figure 23. International investment trends (*Private capital formation*)

Source: U.S. Congress, Senate, Committee on Banking, Housing, and Urban Affairs, Subcommittee on International Finance, *hearings,* Part 7, May 16, 1978.

Of great significance in recent years has been the reversed uptrend in the capital-labor ratio. While invested capital grew 2.6 percent faster than the workforce from 1950 to 1972 (3.3 percent from 1947 to 1967), this ratio declined to 0.3 percent during the period 1973–77 and turned negative from 1977 to 1980. Equity investment has declined because it is simply no longer profitable to invest under current inflationary conditions in the U.S. capital markets. If we allow for a decline in the value of money since 1972, the value of securities listed on the New York Stock Exchange has decreased since that date while the value of almost every other investment has gained substantially.

What is the situation with corporate earnings today? Table 21 shows a continued steady decline in corporate profits during 1978 and 1979, and into the first quarter of 1980. It must be expected that profits in the same constant 1972 dollars will decline even further for 1980 as a whole. Given the current inflationary psychology and the inability of business to use replacement accounting before paying corporate income taxes, it is likely that business enterprises may report a real net loss for 1980.

The government may not understand what the stock market is saying because the tax take will continue, but the investor is not making equity investments as he did twenty years ago. And if money does not continue

Table 21. Corporate profits (*1978 through first quarter 1980*)

	1978				1979				1980[a]
(Quarters)	I	II	III	IV	I	II	III	IV	I
Pre-Tax Reported Profits	$177.5	$207.2	$212.0	$227.4	$233.3	$227.9	$242.3	$243.0	$257.1
Inventory Val. Adjustment	−23.9	−25.1	−23.1	−28.8	−39.9	−36.6	−44.0	−46.0	−63.2
Capital Cons. Adjustment	−12.4	12.6	−13.8	−13.8	−14.5	−14.7	−17.6	−20.1	−22.1
Pre-tax Economic Profits	141.2	169.5	175.2	184.8	178.9	176.6	180.7	176.4	171.8
Tax Liability	70.8	84.7	87.5	95.1	91.3	88.7	94.0	96.1	101.7
After-Tax Economic Profits:									
Current Dollars	70.4	84.8	87.7	89.7	87.6	87.9	86.7	80.3	70.1
Constant 1972 Dollars	47.9	56.2	57.2	57.3	54.7	53.7	51.9	47.1	40.2

Source: "Synopsis of the Economy," *Economics* (newsletter), H. C. Wainwright & Co., June, 1980.

[a] Preliminary first quarter 1980 figures for corporate profits indicate a continued decline in after-tax economic profits in constant 1972 dollars. Increased pre-tax reported profits notwithstanding, a record adjustment of $85.3 billion in undercosting of goods sold (IVA) and underdepreciation of fixed assets (CCA), combined with a tax liability of $101.7 billion, brought constant dollar after-tax economic profits to the lowest level since second quarter of 1975.

to flow into industry, productivity will surely continue to decline. Investors may not be mathematicians, but they understand that the government's tax take increases with inflation while the investor and his investment both carry the penalty.

Two corrective steps should be taken here: (1) the depreciation allowance should be permitted to rise to match the increase in replacement costs; (2) the tax on inventory profits should be eliminated, since this is only a fictitious profit.

Two final comments need to be made with respect to capital investments. In recent years there has been a very noticeable change in U.S. capital stock expenditures away from the purchase of new equipment for increased productivity toward the meeting of government regulations that do not affect productivity. About 9 percent of capital investment now goes toward meeting environmental regulations.

In Japan, businesses have been allowed in certain cases a one year write-off to meet the country's environmental requirements. Why not use the same principle in the United States? It might even ensure that environmental regulations were reviewed more carefully before being adopted.

Finally, we need to call attention to the shift in recent years away from the equity market and into short-term corporate borrowings to finance capital expenditures. In part, this is the result of tax policies that permit the deductibility of interest but not corporate dividends. It is also partially the result of business efforts to maintain corporate earnings per share by further leveraging the share of capital represented by equity. Regardless of the reason, the actual result has been to reduce the ability of business to face the effects of business cycles.

With the equity market in its current condition, businesses are increasingly being forced to raise money through short-term borrowings rather than through the issuance of share capital. Since the economic recovery began in 1975, corporate debt in the United States has risen by 36 percent to more than $1 trillion, while total debt has surged by 42 percent to nearly 14 trillion.[3] If the necessary funds are to flow into new business capital, where these funds are desperately needed, the financial community must make a concerted effort to explain to the Congress the necessity of making it attractive for people to invest their savings in the equity market, particularly in smaller, high-technology companies.* If funds

* According to given testimony before Congress in March, 1978, by Dr. Frank Press, director of the President's Office of Science and Technology Policy, as recently as 1968, 300 to 400 high-technology companies were founded, but in 1976—the last year for which data

that are needed to fuel corporate economic growth are diverted away from corporate equities into the short-term money-market funds, to stamps, precious metals, arts, or real estate, U.S. productivity can only deteriorate further.

Indeed, given the French government's policy to subsidize equity investments in the private sector, it is likely that U.S. investors may leave the U.S. equity market to invest in France, West Germany, or Japan, where government, the business community, and the public all seem to understand better than we do the importance of motivating increased investment in business plant and equipment.

Better access to capital has to be the principal need of U.S. industry today. We should be aware of what Japan, West Germany, and France are doing in this area. In Germany, relations between business and the banks have been very close. In France, government has recently encouraged much greater banking support for innovative or high-technology firms. In Japan a number of steps have been taken. The effective rate of taxation has been reduced through the introduction of tax credits, deductions, and investment incentives. Tax exemptions have been allowed on capital gains from securities investment to foster such investments. Although individual banks are permitted to own only up to 5 percent of a company's stock, companies are allowed and encouraged to join with banks and insurance companies in an informal grouping of capital and industrial firms. Last, banks, especially long-term credit banks like the Industrial Bank of Japan, are playing a key role in helping Japanese firms raise massive amounts of capital rapidly and easily for key industrial investments, such as the recent case of integrated-circuit production.

The Decline in Educational Standards

During World War II, Albert Speer, the German minister of war production, sent recruiters to hire French foremen for work in German plants. The reason—the technical education and initiative of the foremen in France were the best in Europe. In the United States the graduate schools in medicine, law, and business are the finest in the world. But our technical high schools are nowhere near as good as those in Japan, France, or West Germany.

was available—the number was zero.[4] On the other hand, the venture capital fund concept has been helpful in the U.S. and has grown. The concept of the Small Business Investment Corporation (SBIC) encouraged by the government a few years ago to funnel investments in smaller companies has also been useful. Consideration should be given to expanding the concept.

We have mentioned the effect of demographic changes in the United States on productivity, noting that as the population declines in the 1990s and afterwards, we will have to step up our efforts to increase individual productivity so that despite the smaller workforce our national production is not diminished. One of the first steps we must take to accomplish this goal is to provide a continuing education program for our manufacturing and service industry workers so that individual productivity will continue increasing throughout their years of employment.

If the scale of education is to be raised at the theoretical graduate school level, it must also be improved at the practical level of the technical high school so that we can upgrade worker responsibility as the Japanese have managed to do so well. There has to be a much better fusion between the theoretical education at the graduate school and the practical application at the foreman level on the shop floor. In Japan this better cooperation has been accomplished through closer contact between management and workers on such matters as quality control and work methods. There is no reason why we cannot encourage the same in the United States at the company level.

Other Factors Resulting in the Decline of Productivity

These are the so-called residuals referred to by Denison. They include restrictive work practices, payment for work not performed, absenteeism, the effects of crime, the loosening of the work ethic, and, finally and perhaps most important, the value of management. These items have never been a particular problem in the United States, the way absenteeism is in Sweden or in Poland. Has there been a recent increased effect of these factors on productivity decline? Undoubtedly, there has been a loosening of the work ethic. But then this is also true of parts of Europe. Curiously enough, the work ethic has tended to move from Europe to the United States and now from the United States to the developing countries of Asia. Worker motivation, however, is still strong in the United States.*

The National Center for Productivity and Quality of Working Life,

*Lester Thurow of M.I.T. has indicated however, as recently as June 22, 1981, that there was an average turnover per month in United States manufacturing companies of as much as 4% per month—this kind of turnover record makes clear the necessity of remedial action because business will not train its employees adaquately if it is so likely to lose them.

created by Congress in 1975, has concentrated its efforts on increased productivity in four areas: 1. producers' lack of information about the needs of customers; 2. neglect of industrial marketing of innovations in management education; 3. a tendency for decisions on innovations to be made by conservative financial heads of large companies who resist innovation when quick returns on investment are not apparent; 4. the inability of small firms to raise capital for new projects. Each of these has been discussed above in one way or another under the categories of quality of management, educational emphasis, or the need for operational capital.

Having outlined the principal reasons behind the decline in productivity in the United States in general terms, it is important to analyze individual industries before considering what steps might be taken to increase productivity and render the country once again fully competitive in the international marketplace.

Productivity Analysis by Industry

Because the following industries were, or still are considered key, high-technology industries in which the United States has historically been in the forefront of technological improvement, we will look more closely at their current situation. Many other industries could, of course, be examined. Those chosen, however, illustrate the various factors inherent in the decline of U.S. competitiveness. The purpose here is not to single out any industry or its management for recrimination but to indicate the extent to which a structural problem truly exists in the United States that will be solved only by a change in attitude on the part of business, government, and labor alike.

Automobiles

In 1979, the United States was a net importer of $10.5 billion worth of automobiles. Appalling as this figure is, in 1980 the net imports of automobiles were in excess of $13 billion. When we consider that historically one out of every seven Americans depends for his livelihood on the automobile industry, it is clear that we are facing a very serious problem.

It is interesting to note the reluctance on the part of Japanese manufacturers to establish plants in the United States. Despite years of inactivity on the part of U.S. manufacturers, the Japanese believe that once these manufacturers make the decision to come in with competitively-priced models, they will quickly regain their traditional share of the market despite the three-year lead-time usually required for company retooling and product engineering. Germany's Volkswagen, meanwhile, has taken the opposite tack. The company is currently building its second assembly plant in the United States.

By the time U.S. manufacturers are ready to recapture the market, dealer organizations of foreign manufacturers will be functioning smoothly in the United States and the importation of parts from abroad will have been standardized. This will make competition with such foreign firms even more difficult.

The lesson from the automobile industry fiasco is that big business can sometimes be as arrogant and mistaken in its policies as government. Given the current situation, should the government support the automobile industry or any particular companies such as Chrysler in order to give a private company time and money to reestablish its competitive position? If Chrysler, why not Ford or International Harvester, or suppliers of parts that will no longer be needed?

In the Chrysler case, the government painfully decided the answer was yes, but the Congress established conditions requiring participation by banks, dealers, employees, and stockholders. The executive branch later recommended that these requirements be essentially waived. In 1975, when the question of government support for a mismanaged private company came up for discussion at a management seminar for presidents of multinational companies, only the Americans favored such action. The Europeans and the Japanese pointed out that this would let government anticipate corporate decisionmaking to avoid the need for further bailouts and that business was thus accepting government control. After the Chrysler support package, how can banks or business ever complain again of government interference in their affairs?

The Tire Industry

The troubles in the tire industry are similar to those plaguing the auto makers, but they occurred earlier. After World War II, the United States essentially controlled the worldwide production of automobiles. The tire manufacturers, instead of concentrating on making better tires, followed the auto companies abroad and established plants in strategic locations in various regions where U.S. automobiles were being sold. Management apparently preferred to invest outside the United States rather than spend money on researching and developing a better tire. Unfortunately, the tire makers ignored the revival of the European auto industry.

European motorists drive smaller cars, faster, over roads more winding and rougher than the American highways. Michelin, the family-owned French company, started a research plan that eventually led in the 1940s to the invention of radically different radial tires to accommodate European driving conditions. Michelin also had the advantage of being integrated into the European automobile industry. With a 53 percent interest in France's Citroen, Michelin foresaw that an enormous sum had to be spent on research and development. Such expenditures resulted in the invention of the steel-belted tire in 1960.

In the 1960s, Goodyear and Michelin were following diametrically opposed strategies—both closely linked to the broader geopolitical designs of their home nations. As France dismantled its colonial empire, President Charles de Gaulle exhorted French industry to strive for greatness through technology. At the same time, U.S. multinationals started to establish plants in Europe, Africa, Asia, and Latin America that utilized less than the latest in advanced technology. But the billions of dollars they invested in setting up the manufacturing operations around the world drained surplus capital from research and development.

As U.S. companies created a global network, Michelin poured hundreds of millions of dollars into radial-tire development and into building new radial plants in its home territory of Europe. The radial tire began to sweep Europe in the 1960s, and the U.S. tire manufacturers, stuck with a conventional tire, lost markets to Michelin.

In 1966, Michelin started selling some of its "x" series radials in the United States under a Sears label. Yet, not until 1969 did General Motors alter the suspension system of some car models to accommodate radials. Ford quickly followed, using steel-belted radials on its luxury Lincoln Continental.

As demands increased, Michelin built a new tire plant in Greenville, South Carolina. None of the U.S. tire companies had predicted or planned for the age of the radial. In 1973, only Uniroyal had a U.S. radial plant in operation. Today, largely as a result of this negligence, the United States is the world's leading tire importer. Americans spend $1 billion a year on foreign tires. One passenger car tire out of two sold in the United States is a radial, compared with one out of twenty-five in 1970.

Michelin, as a result of its progressive research plan, has moved into fourth position in tire sales even in the United States. Firestone's volume has waned, the company has lost millions of dollars, damaged its popular name, and been forced into a merger with another company. Since 1970, more than 91,000 American workers in the tire industry have lost their jobs.[5]

Aerospace

The aerospace industry has been synonymous with U.S. technology at its best. Boeing, McDonnell-Douglas, General Dynamics, Northrop, and Lockheed have for years been in the forefront of advances in aircraft manufacture. Yet here, too, formidable competition from abroad has appeared. In 1976, Airbus Industries, a European consortium consisting of French, German, Dutch, and now British stockholders, sold its first plane to Lufthansa. There are 88 of these planes now in service on 33 airlines around the world, and Airbus has passed, in total orders, all other companies except Boeing. By May, 1980, the company had received 257 firm orders and 147 options, 404 planes in all for the two versions of the plane, the A–300 and A–310. There is no doubt that the plane is fully competitive with what the United States has to offer on competitive routes. In 1979, France has to offer on competitive routes. In 1979, France alone shipped $25 billion worth of aeronautical products.

What does this suggest for future competition in international trade? In 1979, U.S. export sales in aircraft amounted to $9.7 billion. In the first quarter of 1980 this was $2.8 billion, or $11.2 billion at an annualized rate. It is essential that the United States continue to be competitive in aircraft sales abroad. But there are problems.[6] First, the nation's preeminence in commercial aircraft is in part attributable to Defense Department support for military aircraft research and development (R&D). Commercial aircraft development has in many cases resulted from support from the U.S. government in the past. But military research is no longer being done on manned aircraft to the extent it once was. Today, major R&D funds are being used to study and improve missile technology, which currently has no passenger or transport potential.

Second, the competition in aircraft development abroad comes from state-owned companies. This represents a serious problem for the United States. The airframe for the Airbus consortium is built by Aerospatiale, a French firm that belongs to the French government. Just as losses on the Concorde were made up by the French and the British governments, the cost of developing the Airbus frame was made up by the French government. The French argue that the Boeing designs came from Defense Department research budgets. But this is not quite the same as having the leading aerospace industry under government ownership. The 1970–71 Boeing financial disasters, which stemmed from the company's inability to market the 747, almost caused the company to fall into the hands of its bankers. Had the worst happened, would the U.S. government have come in to save the company? If the recession and the increased price of fuel now cause the 767 and 757 orders to be deferred a year or two, or to be abandoned, Boeing may again find itself on the edge with perhaps less hope than it had in the past that the government will see its survival as a government responsibility.

Will Boeing become another Chrysler? Boeing's management is very aware that despite substantial firm orders and a good current cash balance the 747 experience *can* happen again. How can U.S. industry, which is not directly subsidized, face the state competition represented by Aerospatiale and the Airbus consortium? Without government financing support for its export sales to match foreign competition the U.S. aircraft industry may well go under.

To make the problem more complicated, there are incestuous relationships within the Airbus consortium that make the transfer of technology abroad more likely in the future. The plane is assembled in various stages in Bremen, West Germany, and Toulouse, France. Final subassemblies are shipped from Bremen to Toulouse in American-cannibalized Boeing stratocruisers. The German partner is a combination of the old Messerschmitt company (MBB) and a German-Dutch partnership called VFW-Fokker. United Technologies owns a 26 percent interest in VFW. On the other hand, Boeing had until recently, an 8.9 percent interest in MBB, which also builds satellites supported by German, British, Italian, French, and U.S. subcontractors.

Computer Hardware

In 1973 a high-level Japanese trade and investment group organized by the Ministry of International Trade and Industry (MITI) and including industry leaders, bankers, and a representative of the Japanese trade unions, visited Geneva to spend a day at the Center for Education in International Management to discuss Japanese plans for investment and trade in Europe. Before talking about Japanese prospects in Western Europe, the group announced that they wanted to describe the Japanese economy as they saw its development by the year 1980. They first pointed out that they had had to physically relocate their textile industry because textiles were principally exported to the United States where severe rumblings in Congress had threatened a curtailment of Japanese imports through legislative action. To accomplish the same ends, the Japanese had decided to move their plants to Taiwan and South Korea and to continue exporting to the United States from there. As they explained it, they would henceforth ship equipment and material to be finished and then exported rather than perform the manual labor in Japan, where there was a skilled labor shortage anyway. They then said that Japan would have to get out of heavy chemicals because despite one-year tax write-offs to encourage the industry, it appeared to be foundering.

Finally, they stated that by 1980 it was probable that the steel industry—which they recognized was the finest in the world—might eventually have to be moved (other than specialty steels) to developing countries with abundant supplies of coke and iron ore. When pressed, the Japanese group said that Japan in 1980 would resemble Britain in 1880 with a strong position in international banking and insurance but with a workforce trained to use Japanese computers and electronic equipment.

Considering that Japan had no computer capability in 1973, one might have questioned the group's claim that by 1980 the leading manufacturers of computer hardware would be either American or Japanese. When asked how they proposed to bring this about, the Japanese explained that they would use competition to motivate the private sector to solve the problem. They stated: "We will select seven high-technology companies and invite them to bid on computer manufacture. Each will submit plans and budgets. Out of the seven we will select three and suggest that their budgets be funded by the government, since our study of IBM has clearly indicated the extent to which the industry is capital-intensive. We will not question the budgets submitted but will advise the companies that by 1978 one of them may be eliminated and by 1980 probably a second one. By then, we will have succeeded, and competition will no longer be necessary."

It is now 1981, and both Hitachi and Fujitsu have succeeded not only in manufacturing computer hardware in Japan but also in exporting their products to the United States. In the meantime, the U.S. Department of Justice has been trying to break up IBM under the antitrust laws. How different is the sense of national priorities in the two countries! In Japan competition is used as a way to develop products deemed essential to the nation. In the United States, competition is deemed essential to benefit the entrepreneur who might otherwise not be able to penetrate the market. (In the one country, the individual or the business is subordinated to the national need; in the other, the individual is protected by the government against the power of his competitor regardless of public goals.)

Are we modifying our point of view in the United States? The recent joint research program President Carter suggested to the automobile industry comes close to the Japanese plan to develop the computer industry. We shall see the sequel in our analysis of the semiconductor industry.

Semiconductors

The United States has certainly had the lead in the development of semiconductors. Companies like IBM, Texas Instruments, National Semiconductor, Motorola, and Intel have kept the country in the forefront of technological advances, in microprocessors and high-density memory circuits, also described as very large scale integrated circuits (VLSI). Chips have become smaller and smaller, and their capacity for storage of information has been continuously increasing.

The industry has two problems on the horizon: declining world market share in the face of government-subsidized and protected Japanese competition, and an inability to find properly trained engineers.* In part, the two problems are indirectly linked. When U.S. companies first developed their semiconductor capability, the Japanese government, through its trading company network in the United States, recognized that this industry would revolutionize the entire electronics industry. From that point on, the Japanese government began to give substance to the Japanese dream expressed in Geneva in 1973. Given the Japanese educational system (structured to train a high percentage of students in computer technology and use), it was hoped that every citizen capable of using a computer terminal would have one in his home for problem solving use by sometime in the early 1980s. VLSI technology was thus given the highest priority by the government. Funds were made available to purchase the technology on a one-payment basis, regardless of cost. In addition, the government set up a special research foundation and invited three companies to join, with the government paying for the cost of research. Each of the three companies was allowed to keep the patent

* Continued development of this industry is of immense importance to the revitalization of U.S. industry as a whole. International competition can be expected to grow. The industry is well aware of the stakes. In March, 1981, its association published under the title "The International Microelectronic Challenge," an analysis that is relevant to other U.S. high-technology industries as well.

rights on any new developments. This has proved highly successful. Japanese companies have significantly advanced electronics technology, particularly in the area of telecommunications. Japanese semiconductor competition in the future can thus be expected to grow substantially.

The other difficulty can be laid in part at the U.S. government's door. In the United States, no one in government foresaw the national need for computer software engineers to use the new electronic technology. Thus, today there is a shortage of persons qualified to develop and use the software systems required by the advances in computer hardware. There is a desperate need for highly specialized engineers who can develop software packages so that the computer hardware already developed can be used to increase productivity in almost every industry in the United States. Unfortunately, electronics engineers increase at the rate of only 4.5 percent per year, while the demand for their services is increasing at the rate of 17 percent per year. In 1971 a total of 12,200 degrees in electronical engineering were awarded in the United States. By 1976, this number had been reduced to 10,000. In the meantime, the government has been funding the training of additional sociologists for its social programs! Suddenly, everyone who is now qualified wants to study computer sciences. But school facilities are not increasing because the faculty has accepted, in many cases, generous offers to join an industry that is very short of qualified engineers and willing to pay almost anything to get them.

Robots

Perhaps the most innovative development of this business generation will turn out to be the use of robots to perform manufacturing duties that employees in the industrialized countries are reluctant to do. Japan is currently using numerous robots to reduce the number of dull, repetitive jobs that are prevalent in auto manufacture. At Toyota, the third shift is managed by robots, and, indeed, the performance of Japanese cars is in large part the result of having such tasks as welding and nut tightening handled by machine-controlled tools and not by workmen, thus assuring standardization and quality norms. Again, the Japanese have acquired this technology from such U.S. firms as Condec's Unimation Division, which finds it difficult to sell its system in the United States because of governmental pressures to employ more workers—particularly those who, for lack of training or education, are unable to take on any but the most simple tasks.

It is worth noting that modern mass-production methods were invented by the U.S. auto industry. As workmen in the auto plants became both better paid and better educated, two problems became apparent: 1. an educated man was unwilling to spend his working life in a routine mechanical job endlessly repeating the same function on an assembly line; 2. periodic salary boosts also require that his job be upgraded wherever possible to justify the cost of pay increases.

Volvo in Sweden has tried to solve the first problem with limited success by terminating the assembly line and substituting a team approach where members can rotate functions and time on the job. The Japanese are turning to the use of robots, while the U.S. aircraft and computer manufacturers have turned increasingly to the use of computer-controlled machine tools.

At IBM, for example, computers for many years have been manufactured by tools controlled by computers. This means that a worker watches dials and gauges rather than performing a physical act in the manufacturing process. It means he must have the technical competence to ensure proper control of the equipment he is using. It also means that he will produce by himself many times what his predecessors were able to in the past, and, hence, his increased output justifies the much higher pay awarded for what is now an engineer's function. Since car assembly is particularly labor-intensive, it is one industry that lends itself in a particularly rewarding fashion to more automation. Also, as government safety regulations increase, particularly in the United States, the rise of robots means that jobs dangerous to man can increasingly be done by machine.

At Fiat in Italy, the Robogate is the first generation of automatic assembly systems that can weld and assemble two different models on the same production line. Nissan in Japan has gone even further and is turning out 45 variations of two models on the same automatic assembly line. In the body-assembly shops 96 percent of the welds are done by robots. In due course, this will mean that one man at the factory will produce the equivalent of 81 cars per year, compared with the current equivalent of 45 in the Japanese auto plants. By comparison, productivity at the Austin plant at Longbridge, England, is currently 16 cars per man per year.[7]

It would seem that the UAW in the United States should be more concerned with increasing the pay of its members by "upgrading" their performance than in increasing membership in the union by requiring the companies to employ additional workers. In Japan the shortage of skilled workers makes boosting productivity a national policy because this will not result in a loss of jobs. In the United States it is time to realize that we should be more concerned with creating new jobs as a result of new technologies rather than by insisting that additional people be added to current production. Our current thinking will only mean reduced national productivity and hence a reduced national standard of living.

Chemicals and Petrochemicals

The chemical and petrochemical industries have been star performers for many years in the U.S. balance of trade. In 1979 net exports of raw materials and chemicals from the United States amounted to nearly $18.8 billion and in 1980 over $24 billion. Yet, in the future the United States may see the rate of exports in these industries reduced substantially.

The problem is threefold and comes, of course, from the fact that so many chemicals depend on oil and gas feedstocks. In the past, the low price of oil and gas in the United States and their ready availability meant the rapid development of this industry and its strong trade position. But now, as the price of oil and gas continues to rise in the United States, the cost of petrochemicals will also increase. Second, because of price ceilings on oil and to a lesser extent on natural gas, we may find ourselves in difficulty under the newly negotiated Multinational Trade Negotiations (MTN) Subsidies Code, since the Europeans have already threatened to claim that U.S. petrochemicals are subsidized because domestic oil and gas prices are subsidized in the United States. Third, and perhaps more important, the oil-producing countries are increasingly passing from crude oil production to refined products and from refined products to petrochemicals and eventually chemicals. In Ecuador, gasoline is only a few cents a gallon, in Colombia and Venezuela not much higher. With low production prices it is only a question of time before competition in the petrochemical and chemical industry increases.

Competition will come not only from the OPEC country petrochemical plants of the future but from Eastern European countries. Increasingly U.S. multinationals have participated in joint ventures in the COMECON countries to supply Western Europe. Dow-Ina in Yugoslavia is a case in point. So here again the United States, if it is to remain competitive, must increase the productivity of its plants and its technological lead. This will be difficult since plants in the OPEC countries will be new and will have the latest technological innovations, including many from the United States itself.

Drugs and Food

The pharmaceutical industry, like the chemical industry, has been one of the most technologically advanced industries in the world since World War II. The medical advances that took place during the war as a result of government funding, and the enormous grants for research since that time, have maintained the U.S. development base. In addition, as U.S. pharmaceutical companies spread their activities to other countries, they used capital funds to develop research facilities in England, Italy, and France, where government grants were not so readily available but where highly trained and well-qualified researchers in biology, chemistry, and medicine could be found.[8] As a result, the U.S. industry gained a true international base of enormous value in its research efforts.

Unfortunately, however, U.S. government policies in the Food and Drug Administration have often denied drugs to U.S. users although they have been successfully administered for years in other countries.* This has raised the cost of drugs in the United States by reducing competition and has increased the cost of the research effort of U.S. pharmaceutical companies, thereby reducing their competitiveness. There is obviously a need to establish one standard of drug evaluation that is applicable to all countries. Such a move would help U.S. companies maintain the competitive edge they have held over the past thirty-five years.

In food distribution, another area where U.S. companies have led the rest of the world, a modularization of shipping containers could reduce food wastage, raise truck capacity utilization, and increase productivity in warehousing. This would require, however, that grocery manufacturers, truckers, retailers, and wholesalers agree on container standards, and no such agreement has yet occurred.

Transportation Equipment

If one is concerned about reindustrializing the United States, one needs only to take the train from New York to Washington and look out of the window. Newark, Elizabeth, Trenton, Philadelphia, Wilmington, Baltimore—all reflect the extent to which industrial plants in the core cities of the Northeast need rehabilitation. Less noticeable is the fact that the Northeast corridor railbed is being rebuilt with French machinery that

* The Food and Drug Administration has often been accused of taking unnecessary time to review new drug applications. Under the Reagan Administration, it will now review its new drug approval process.

can lay rail more efficiently and at less cost than that available in the United States. In Washington, D.C., the subway cars were built in Italy; in Philadelphia, they came from Japan; in Atlanta, Georgia, from France. Why? During the past five years, four U.S. companies have dropped out of the railroad car business. Only Budd is left, and that company was recently purchased by a German steelmaker. All this has been complicated by the uncertainty of federal program funding for mass transit, which is hard to believe at a time when the federal government is urging conservation of gasoline. One also wonders why the United States has been unable to focus on one standard subway car. Surely, a government research grant should have been used to develop such a car. Even in Washington, the supposed home of the standardization efforts, subway cars are different from those anywhere else—presumably to save money by allowing for narrower tunnels.

Radio and Television Manufacturing

Everyone is familiar with the lead position RCA held in this industry before it reduced its research efforts and used its capital to diversify into car rentals, publishing, food processing, real-estate brokerage, and home furnishings. For many years the industry was seen as one of the great growth areas in the United States, yet today only Zenith, of all the pioneering manufacturers, still concentrates on television-set production. Recently, however, it has acquired some new and formidable competitors in the U.S. market.

The significance of this new source of foreign direct investment extends beyond the radio- and television-manufacture industries. In 1975, Magnavox, which found itself unable to compete effectively in its own domestic market, was acquired by Phillips of Eindhoven in the Netherlands, one of the great electronic giants of Europe. At about the same time, Matsushita, the Sears Roebuck of Japan, acquired the consumer television division of Motorola, a high-technology company that was better at research and manufacturing than consumer marketing.

Both of these new subsidiaries thus became the U.S. marketing arm for their respective foreign parents. And because they were both strong in research and manufacturing, they could use their U.S. plants to assemble components made outside the United States. In this way, the Europeans and Japanese did to the United States what we had so frequently done to them during the postwar period: they established a marketing position by acquiring a manufacturing-base company, then equipped it from the parent company, and used it to assemble components manufactured at the parent company's plants according to the latest technology available.

Most of the large consumer-oriented U.S. manufacturing companies, and many smaller high-technology firms have found it advisable, as part of their marketing strategies overseas, to establish regional manufacturing plants that also service customers throughout the region. The experience of firms such as Caterpillar, J. I. Case, Becton-Dickinson, and others with which the author is familiar, is that exports from the United States to those countries where such assembly or manufacturing plants have been established tend to rise faster than in other countries, because equipment is first shipped from the United States, then components, then service parts, and then the cycle is renewed as products are added. Contrary to what is generally throught by labor writers, exports from the United States increase rather than decrease.[9] The reverse, unfortunately, is equally true. Volkswagen has increased German employment by establishing an assembly plant in the United States. Philips and Matsushita have done the same for television sets. In many areas, of course, as generally in South America, the border is closed to competitors as soon as a manufacturing plant is established. This becomes then the only way to enter the market.

As for Magnavox and Motorola television, both these newly-acquired subsidiaries will transfer U.S. currency to their parents via service fees and dividends in much the same way that the United States today receives some $45 billion worth of service income toward its balance-of-payments deficit. The process should in no way be criticized because U.S. employment would have been reduced if Motorola and Magnavox had been unable to stay in the television-receiver business. But it is ridiculous for this nation to be complacent about such a process, which must ultimately transfer wealth from the United States abroad. Britain has proved that one can live for a long time on the wealth accumulated by prior generations. But in the course of time, any nation will be affected by a reduction in its wealth because this must ultimately reduce its power.

The Nuclear Industry

Perhaps the saddest report is what has happened in the past decade to the U.S. position in nuclear energy. Whether for subjective reasons of fear or guilt or both on the part of successive administrations we have abandoned to others a technological lead that we may never be able to regain and that will cost us dearly in the future.

There is no doubt that we are living in a nuclear age. As a consequence of carefully designed efforts under Presidents Roosevelt and Truman to create a capacity for both war and peaceful uses of the atom, we entered the atomic age in a position where other nations had to rely on our technology. But through bureaucratic abuse and lack of leadership, we have since abandoned not only our lead-time of twenty-five years but may now be behind France and the Soviet Union in the design of nuclear plants for energy-generating purposes. Future generations of Americans may well ask why the United States dissipated its technological lead in nuclear energy for the supposed fear of proliferation when our only strength in controlling what others might do came from the fact that others had to depend on our help for nuclear-plant design, construction, and fuel supplies. Today all that is unfortunately gone.

In 1977, when President Carter realized he could not persuade other countries to go along with his nuclear policies, he suggested the International Nuclear Fuel Cycle Evaluation Conference in Vienna. He then decided that Washington would not permit the commercial reprocessing of spent nuclear fuel in the United States. That technique not only recovers reactor fuel but also produces plutonium, the chief ingredient of nuclear weapons. The administration argued that uranium reserves were too abundant and the proliferation risks too high to justify the process. It also decided not to go ahead with the development of breeder reactors, at least those based on plutonium, because of the risk of proliferation. And it asked other nuclear powers to stop selling reprocessing technology to Third World countries and to reexamine their own needs for the process.

The European countries thought the U.S. policy a naive strategy to defend the interests of the U.S. nuclear industry. The French, with no oil, little coal reserves, and a finite supply of uranium saw the absolute necessity of quickly moving ahead toward nuclear energy. "To Paris, breeder reactors and reprocessing of spent fuel looked like the legendary perpetual-motion machine to energy independence. Furthermore, to defray the enormous if undisclosed cost of a full-cycle nuclear power development program, the French wanted to contract with other countries to reprocess their fuel." [10]

France has already built a commercial breeder reactor and is rapidly developing new technology for the future. In fact, the French are so far advanced that Paris is able to flex its muscles for a virtual renegotiation of the Euratom Treaty that was to have made nuclear development a Common Market undertaking. If the French system proves correct, the United States could well end up importing breeders from France.

What has the United States gained by its attitude on nuclear power? By allowing its position of leadership to pass onto others it has not in any way reduced the chances of proliferation. But it has given up a whole industry that would not only have helped its position in energy but also ensured substantial exports of plants and equipment and protection of its technological lead in an industry that must play a greater role in the future of mankind.[11]

Construction and Engineering

During World War II, U.S. engineers became known the world over for their skill at building roads over any terrain, building airfields in jungle regions, and building ports where nothing had existed before. After the war, U.S. engineering firms used this experience to become construction specialists throughout the world. Bechtel, Fluor, Ralph M. Parsons Co., Dravo, Raymond International, and Morrison-Knudsen subsidiaries can be found throughout the world. Recently however, their share of international bid contracts has declined greatly. In the Middle East the United States has dropped to twelfth place in obtaining contracts after South Korea, Italy, West Germany, Japan, France, Brazil, Yugoslavia, the United Kingdom, India, Taiwan, and the Soviet Union. Out of 220 construction contracts awarded in 14 Middle East countries during the thirteen-month period ending June, 1979, U.S. firms were able to obtain only seven jobs, $346 million out of a possible $21.8 billion, a scant 1.6 percent share.[12] What is the reason for this appalling record? Many reasons have been advanced by the engineering firms working in the area: (1) U.S. products are not competitive because quality control is poor and delivery is unreliable; (2) there is little government assistance compared with that given by other governments, perhaps because imported oil from the area is payable in dollars and therefore not in a foreign currency that must be earned; (3) the U.S. government has legislated the application of U.S. moral standards (antibribery), human rights, environmental standards, and tax rules; (4) U.S. engineers must receive in salary two to four times that given a German or British engineer as a result of paying full U.S. taxes even though they live in the Middle East;* (5) differ-

* It is now highly likely that Sections 911 and 913 of the Internal Revenue Code will be amended to solve this problem.

ences in freight costs (freight rates may be very much less from Japan to the Middle East than from the United States to the Middle East); (6) U.S. technology is no longer superior (for example, 64 percent of the cement plants currently being built in the United States use Japanese technology); (7) for many other countries, the government either owns the construction firm or acts as a partner for the firm in negotiating contracts in the Middle East; and (8) the United States has no government agency ready, as other countries do, to back construction firms with government insurance against political risk, or supply performance bonds and advance payment bond coverage. Whatever the reasons, the upshot has been that instead of concentrating on landing engineering and construction contracts in the Middle East, the United States has turned to selling arms to pay in part for imports of oil.[13]

Can anything be done about this problem of declining productivity in the United States? Many competent people are beginning to focus on the question. Various causes have been advanced, but solutions are harder to enunciate. Let us look at some of the recommended steps under three headings: the role of (a) government, (b) management, and (c) labor.

The Role of Government

Many Americans feel that if anything constructive is to be done it can only be done through government action, while others believe that the government is incapable of taking any constructive action, particularly in an area that concerns the private sector. The answer must probably be found somewhere in between these extremes. The government can and should create an economic climate where the private sector in our mixed economy can function most effectively. The government can encourage national goals as we have found the governments of other countries doing; it can also exercise great forbearance in avoiding legislative or regulatory action that reduces productivity and/or innovation. There thus appear to be a number of constructive steps that can be taken by the government.

1. The declaration of national goals

The credibility of government in its declarations is understandably not high. Those few attempts thus far made have tended to be either public-relations plays (WIN—Whip Inflation Now), or cosmetic alterations. If the reindustrialization of the United States is to be an important national goal, it should be a clearly stated government policy, and it should be continually reported upon and monitored so that the media and the public can judge what progress, if any, is being achieved. Studies conducted in 1980, by the New York Stock Exchange and by Union Carbide, clearly show that the public is more aware than the government that something is very much amiss in the U.S. economy (90 percent of those interviewed in the NYSE study were dissatisfied with current policies) and that the President and Congress have failed to understand and control the problem (78 percent of those polled). Fully 87 percent agreed that drastic steps to strengthen the economy were needed. If the current sluggishness deepens, this figure will rapidly reach 100 percent. It would be helpful to have a clearly enunciated national policy statement by the executive branch, and if possible the Congress, to the effect that the necessity of modernizing U.S. industrial plant and equipment has become a national priority.

2. New concepts for the role of the Office of Management and Budget and the Joint Economic Committee

It is not enough to make declarations of policy if they are not monitored and accounted for. The federal government must have an agency or agencies charged with reporting on the progress achieved or there will be no progress. Under the past few administrations, the Office of Management and Budget has acquired a degree of power that was never intended at the start. Power implies responsibility and accountability and a degree of expertise that has not always been apparent. Why not also give this agency within the Office of the President the responsibility for monitoring the effectiveness of this national policy goal for the executive branch? In the Congress, the Joint Economic Committee has done some excellent work in the area of productivity analysis, and on a bipartisan basis. It may be advisable to rely on this already effective legislative group to ensure that the legislative branch of government will also give priority to this declared policy goal.

3. Encouraging savings and capital investments, and reviewing our Social Security concepts

We have already shown what has happened to the savings rate in the United States. Our economists have led us to believe that it is the government's duty to look after its citizens and to take care of their education, their medical bills, and their care during old age. Perhaps it indeed should be. Unfortunately, however, with inflation brought on in part by heavy government expenditures to accomplish these laudatory aims, the retirement program of the Social Security system now faces bankruptcy. Is it really wise to encourage people to believe in their government's promises to look after them when the fulfillment of such promises means borrowing from future generations? Isn't it better, as in Japan, to promise low government retirement benefits and encourage the workers to save and invest their savings in the country's economy, in order to provide retirement income?

In part, the Japanese system works because of a guarantee of lifetime employment that comes with working for the larger companies. As a result, as workers get older, the nature of their employment changes along with their salaries. But because of the system, the rate of savings is very high. In West Germany, people save and invest because they remember that those who did not were wiped out twice in two successive generations, in 1923 and in 1948, and as a result, they fear inflation above all other potential calamities. In France, under an interesting four-year plan introduced in 1978 by Economic Minister Rene Monory, French investors are given the right to deduct as much as $1,200 worth of stock from one year's taxable income. Thus, the government, in order to increase investment in the private sector, has used the tax system to encourage savings and investment.

Why shouldn't the same idea be tried in the United States? In time it might even bring the individual investor back into the equity market. For instance, in France, more than 1 million taxpayers have claimed rebates under the stock-purchase exemption, and authorities believe that more than one-half of these are new investors with a stake in the private-sector economy. For French industry, the system has meant an annual increase of $2 billion in new investments channeled into the private-sector economy. It is curious that France—the country after the Soviet Union where more of the gross national product is controlled or owned by the state than in any other industrialized nation—should use the tax incentive to increase private investment!

Why should we encourage private investment in the United States? For one thing, the average age of U.S. manufacturing plants is twenty years, compared with twelve in West Germany, and ten in Japan. If we can increase the rate of return on investment in the United States by as little as 2 percent of GNP, Kendrick has estimated that $35 billion would go to new business investment, thus raising the proportion of savings going into business investment to what it was in the mid-1960s.

4. Changes in the tax laws to encourage increased productivity and competitiveness

The consideration of changes in the tax system always raises delicate and difficult questions, because any change results in cash benefits to one group of taxpayers at the expense of the mass. Yet no system is entirely without bias, and in addition to raising revenue needed by the state, any effective system must be tailored to the accomplishment of national objectives. The case for raising the proportion of income devoted to savings and hence to investment rests on the view that the U.S. tax system is biased against capital formation, both in its structure and in its application, compared with that of the other industrialized countries. There is good reason, therefore, to consider reducing the bias in the U.S. tax system in any of several different ways.

It has been said, for example, that savings are effectively taxed twice.

> For the most part, neither the part of income which is saved nor the return on such saving is excluded from the base of the income tax, the principal source of tax revenue. Since saving is the capitalized amount of the future income purchased by the saving, this characteristic of the income tax subjects the part of current income used to buy future income by a double tax, whereas the part of current income used to buy consumption goods is taxed only once.[14]

In addition, certain nonincome taxes, such as capital-gains taxes, increase the disincentives to savings. The same thing is true of inheritance, estate, and gift taxes. In 1961 the Mexican government discovered that by doing away with the inheritance tax the flow into investment was so great that it more than made up for the resulting cutoff in U.S. aid of $40 million per year.

What might be done to eliminate, at least in part, the antisavings bias of the U.S. tax system? One recommendation has been to repeal the income tax on corporations and attribute corporate earnings directly to the shareholders as though the corporation were a partnership; and a second has been to exclude current savings from the individual income-tax base while fully taxing returns from investment and repayments of principal.[15] Revenue losses might then be made up by a value-added tax or by increasing taxes on personal income less net savings.

There are, of course, many other ways to remove the antisavings bias, including accelerating depreciation charges, adjusting the depreciation of fixed assets to account for replacement costs, reducing corporate income-tax rates by decreasing the normal or surtax rate of tax, eliminating the double taxation of corporate dividends, increasing the investment tax credit, or adopting some scheme such as the 10–5–3 depreciation schedule recently suggested in Congress.* It might also be interesting to consider what the Japanese tried several years ago: to give business a one-year tax write-off for expenses incurred in meeting environmental regulations.

In terms of capital gains taxes, why not a rollover provision similar to the one allowed on reinvestments in a personal residence? Also, particular attention ought to be paid to revising the capital gains tax to favor investment in the new high-technology companies generally considered riskier investments.

Obviously, many other suggestions can be made. In Sweden the tax rates are high, but the effective rate is very low because inventories can be written down as management decides to do so. In Japan, exporters can set up reserves essentially without fear of review by the authorities. In Mexico, the government decided some years ago to exclude from audit any company that was 51 percent Mexican-owned, engaged in a business that might be related to the development of the country's infrastructure, and not paying cash dividends of more than 10 percent of its earnings. Their reasoning was expressed as follows: "We must increase employment to meet the increase in the population. Private business if it reinvests 90 percent of its earnings will expand productive facilities and hence employ more people faster than the government might do if it taxed these earnings and increased government employment."†

Of course, research and development expenditures should be freely deductible from taxable income if research efforts are to be accelerated in the United States. Perhaps certain research expenditures should be eligible for tax credits rather than deductions.

Finally, unless the Reagan Administration manages rapidly to decrease the inflation rate, the accounting rules ought to be revised to include inflation-accounting principles so that businesses are taxed at current rates on real, rather than inflated, earnings. Business must be allowed to take replacement costs into account in valuing inventory, plant, and equipment. One of the salutary effects of inflation accounting is that it tends to penalize concerns that do not modernize their plant and equip-

* Another interesting approach to the suggestion that unearned income be taxed separately from earned income—so-called "separate stacking"—to give the wage earner more incentive to invest.

† This was the famous concept developed by Ortiz Mena and his team of young economists when he was first appointed as Minister of Finance in the early 1960s when Mexico had just been through a wrenching devaluation. Ortiz Mena succeeded in reestablishing economic growth by motivating the private sector.

ment. In the case of the Ford Motor Company, for example, inflation accounting applied to 1979 earnings (which management reported to be the third highest in history at $9.75 per share) would have meant a reduction to $1.78 per share, hardly enough to support a dividend of $3.90 per share, or to offset the damage created by poor management decisions, that would show up in 1980 sales and profit figures.

The new inflation-accounting ruling recently adopted by the Financial Accounting Standards Board (FASB) help illustrate the problem caused for business by constantly increasing inflation. It will not, however, bring about a solution to the problem because corporate income taxes are still not reduced to take real earnings into account. The new FASB method, however, should be particularly helpful to management in deciding which capital projects to support and which to set aside, thus during periods of inflation favoring less capital-intensive investment or service-oriented businesses where earnings per dollar invested are high.

5. Action to eliminate disincentives to business from overregulation; modification of the application of antitrust laws outside the country

There is no question but that in the past ten years government regulation of business has increased enormously. The need for government to do something about energy has resulted in the creation of a vast new bureaucracy, the Department of Energy, with more than 18,000 employees and an annual budget currently of $13 billion. Many other new agencies have been created and are still being created: the Environmental Protection Agency, the Department of Education, the Office of the U.S. Trade Representative (USTR), the Office of Safety, Health and Accidents, and many more still in the legislative process. If a problem is perceived, sooner or later Congress will create a new bureaucracy to cope with it and give it the funds with which to operate.

Unfortunately, doing away with an agency that has outlived its usefulness becomes almost impossible. President Carter vowed to reduce the bureaucracy but instead added thousands, directly and indirectly through contracts, to the federal payroll. It was only recently that such agencies as the Mexican American Claims Commission, which was created to pass on claims arising from the Mexican War in 1846, ceased its activities. It would seem as if successive, well-intentioned presidents have been able to do nothing about the problem, probably because it is easier to create the new rather than repair the old. But the old remains, creaky and unnecessary, but staffed with the same number of personnel and costing ever more money. The Carter Administration and the Congress had sought to deregulate airlines, trucking, railroads, and banking. While it is too early to judge the effect of these steps or of new programs adopted by the Reagan Administration toward deregulation of basic industries, it is highly likely that all such steps will result in cost savings and increased competitiveness.

Without accountability through strict federal budget controls, the situation can only worsen, as each new administration creates new agencies to cope with new problems. A case in point is the reorganization of the international trade agencies. To avoid creating a new Department of International Trade, functions performed by the Departments of Treasury, State, and Commerce were transferred to the Executive Office of the President, to the Office of the U.S. Trade Representative (formerly the Special Trade Representative's Office).

Because of its new responsibility for trade policy, the USTR is now seeking an international presence (i.e., its own employees located abroad to supplement Commerce Department staffs outside the United States, thus duplicating what other agencies (State, Commerce, Treasury), are currently already doing. The result is that in its effort to increase trade without creating a Department of International Trade, the U.S. government may end up in an incomplete consolidation of four agencies functioning in place of three, thus adding considerably to public expenditures without any commensurate benefits. It is hoped that the Reagan Administration, which has declared itself dedicated to reducing the size and cost of government, will abolish the USTR and either transfer its functions preferably to an undersecretary of commerce responsible for all aspects of international trade or to an independent, cabinet-status, Department of International Trade.

What do we mean by disincentives to business, and what is the principal impact of those disincentives? In the context of our discussion here, the disincentives to business are of two kinds: 1. those that affect productivity because they increase the cost of a U.S. product and hence make it less competitive for sale in international trade;* 2. those that directly affect the movement of goods in international trade to the disadvantage of a U.S. business concern. We have already referred to the many government regulations that tend to reduce productivity and/or increase the cost

* It must be admitted that government regulation can in certain instances encourage essential research and therefore aid competitiveness. A typical example was the early introduction of auto-emission standards in Japan, which later gave the Japanese an advantage in foreign markets.

Table 22. General Motors expenditures to meet government regulations[a] (*In millions of dollars*)

	Safety	Pollution	Other	TOTAL
1979	$512	$601	$830	$1,943
1978	466	446	706	1,618
1977	423	247	590	1,260
1976	354	188	478	1,020
1975	347	185	406	936

Source: General Motors 10–K, 1979

[a]General Motors reports that the equivalent effort of 26,600 full-time employees was required in regulatory compliance in 1979, or an increase of 1,800 over 1978.

of manufacturing in the United States. The growing cost of meeting government regulations is illustrated in Table 22, which uses the example of General Motors. The regulations mainly deal with energy costs, the cost of meeting environmental or health and safety regulations, or those that deal with consumer protection. The pertinent legislation is the Clean Air Act of 1971, the Federal Water Pollution Act of 1976, the OSHA Act of 1970, the Toxic Substances Act of 1976, the Consumer Product Safety Act of 1976, and the Employment Retirement Income Security Act of 1974.* In 1978, the White House's Council on Environmental Quality (CEQ) even sought to apply extraterritorial effect to executive orders on air quality, thus in effect requiring that U.S. regulations on environmental matters have extraterritorial application. Regulatory disincentives that reduce the ability of U.S. firms to compete abroad are more complicated in that they are of many different sorts covering a wide spectrum of controlled authority.[17]† They may be briefly summarized here to give an idea of their extent.

A. The arbitrary use of export license requirements to prohibit exports of U.S. products applies primarily to sales to the USSR. In 1979, for instance, during a period when détente was still recognized as part of government policy, Sperry-Univac was refused an export license for a computer system ordered by Tass, the Soviet news agency, as a way of telling the Russians that their handling of dissidents within the Soviet

* In just one industry, coal, some 16 major federal laws affecting coal mining have been enacted in the past ten years.[16]

† The Carter Administration was aware of the growth in disincentives to exports and initiated interagency studies to see how they could be reduced. It is hoped that the Reagan Administration will accelerate this effort.

Union violated U.S. standards of human rights. At about the same time, oil-drilling equipment and technology to be exported to the USSR by Dresser Industries was also held up, then subsequently released. More recently, as an indication of our displeasure over the Soviet invasion of Afghanistan, we partially halted the shipment of grain and certain high-technology products, even though such products could generally be purchased by the Russians in Western Europe. Now the embargo on U.S. grain to the USSR is to be relaxed.* Whether or not these steps to control exports are helpful in accomplishing the political ends they seek is highly questionable. Similar types of economic sanctions of one sort or another against South Africa, Rhodesia (before it became Zimbabwe), Chile, and Argentina have largely penalized U.S. exporters rather than the importing country. Licensing in the United States may affect as much as 10 percent of exports, an unusually high figure.

B. In 1978 amendments to the Export-Import Bank Act of 1945 placed severe restrictions on Export-Import Bank financing of exports to South Africa. The act also prohibits Eximbank from lending more than $300 million for fuel projects in the USSR. Section 402 of the Trade Act of 1974 (the Jackson-Vanik Amendment) bars all Eximbank financing to Communist nations that restrict emigration. Only Poland, Yugoslavia, Romania, Hungary, and more recently, the People's Republic of China, have been cleared as satisfying the provisions of the act. One result of such restrictions on financing is that West Germany exports five times as much in dollar value to the USSR as the United States. Moreover, since Congress reviews any Eximbank direct loan financing in excess of $100 million, Congress may stop a specific financial transaction. One example of such a case was the proposed Mexican gas pipeline financing in 1977. For human rights reasons, the President halted any Eximbank direct credits for exports from the United States to Chile.

In any event, the amount of support given by the Eximbank for exports does not compare favorably with that given by other countries. Government support covers 50 percent of exports in Japan and 40 percent of exports in France and the United Kingdom. In the United States the figure drops to approximately 10 percent.[18] The United States does not offer mixed credits or other concessionary lines of credit except in isolated instances.[19]

*Whether or not to maintain the grain embargo against the USSR might have turned out to be the most delicate problem faced by the Reagan Administration in its first year in office. There were compelling arguments in either direction and the decision was a difficult one.

C. Antiboycott legislation has caused difficulties for U.S. exporters in part because three different departments (Commerce, Treasury, and Justice) apply three separate laws dealing with U.S. government efforts to prevent boycotts by Arab countries of firms dealing with Israel.[20] As a result, many American multinational companies are sourcing their exports to the Arab world from Europe rather than from the United States.

D. Since penal sanctions are applied against violators of the Foreign Corrupt Practices Act of 1977, many exporters have chosen to forego a sale abroad rather than risk having a commission deemed a bribe, or risk making payments to facilitate customs clearance or docking privileges not otherwise obtainable. The Department of Justice has been reluctant to issue regulations to make clear just when the act applies. Congress might consider amending the statute to make it a disclosure requirement rather than a penal statute. This would have two advantages: (1) other countries would be encouraged to adopt similar legislation, and (2) fear of disclosure would discourage requests for compensation from foreign public officials.*

E. The application of antitrust laws outside the United States also affects the competitiveness of U.S. companies. Congress has recently taken up legislation to clarify the application of U.S. antitrust laws abroad in the face of the Justice Department's reluctance to issue any clear regulations to guide U.S. business transactions outside the country. Such legislation, one hopes, will allow trading companies operating abroad to represent a number of competing U.S. businesses in a given industry so that their products may be promoted and financed abroad on an industry, rather than an individual company, basis.† In addition, there may be legislation passed allowing U.S. concerns to engage in joint research efforts, perhaps even with some governmental funding. The development of new types of automobile engines might be one such example of industry-wide research.

The analogy here is to Japan, who has given government financial support to joint research efforts in the microprocessing field. Many other interesting antitrust questions will be raised in the future in the chemical and petrochemical industries, since joint ventures can be expected in-

*The SEC announced towards the end of the Carter Administration that it would not prosecute if business review procedures of the Department of Justice had been followed. In February 1980, the Justice Department was directed by the President to establish this review procedure. Much more needs to be done in this area to help U.S. business compete.

†This legislation, initiated by Senator Adlai Stevenson, passed the Senate 77 to 0 in September, 1980, but failed to get to a vote in the House. It was passed again by the Senate in 1981, and has the strong support of the Administration.

creasingly in OPEC countries between state-owned companies from the OPEC nations and U.S. chemical or petrochemical firms. What are the consequences of one or more sovereign countries agreeing to sell feedstocks to such joint ventures at below market cost? Businessmen will long remember Gulf Oil's role in the uranium cartel, a cartel in which the other members were sovereign states that established the rules for sovereign and private-firm participants alike. Is a nation acting in its sovereign or commercial capacity when it allocates and prices its natural resources? What will be the political consequences if the United States decides to attack a major oil supplier for alleged violations of U.S. antitrust laws in the petrochemical field? It would be appropriate for Congress to consider these questions, particularly as more and more production in international trade tends to come from state-owned concerns.

F. Under two acts of Congress, the Arms Export Control Act and the Foreign Assistance Act of 1961, controls were established over military sales outside the United States that have had a tendency to reduce U.S. arms sales.

G. There are a number of laws that restrict exports for "national security" reasons, because nuclear exports are involved, or because they relate to fuels and chemicals in short supply. With respect to the export of "sensitive" products, under the Mutual Defense Assistance Control Act of 1951 and the Export Administration Act of 1969 five departments of the Executive Branch headed by Commerce and including State, Treasury, Defense, and Energy apply the laws and regulations. Each department is also entitled to veto a transaction. With respect to controls over nuclear exports, as provided in the Atomic Energy Act of 1954 and now the Nuclear Non-Proliferation Act of 1978, controls have been applied so that the U.S. share of the world market of nuclear exports plunged from 100 percent in 1972 to 17 percent in 1977.[21] As a result of the Three Mile Island incident, government agencies having jurisdiction over such exports are even more reluctant than before to approve nuclear plant exports. Rules on nuclear fuels are even stricter than for the plants themselves, as was noted earlier. With respect to fuels and chemicals in short supply, there is special legislation applying a quota system that is contained in the Export Administration Act of 1969 and the Trans-Alaskan Pipeline Authorization Act of 1973.

H. Legislation adopted by Congress to halt terrorism was applied by President Carter, particularly in the case of Libya. A recent instance was the blockage of the sale of Boeing 747s to Libya even though the planes were fully paid for and the United States had a balance-of-trade deficit with Libya amounting to $4.6 billion in 1978.*

I. In terms of transportation, an additional disincentive to exports may be found in the legislative requirement that exports financed by Eximbank be shipped in U.S. vessels unless the Maritime Administration specifically waives this provision.

J. The United States needs tax legislation that will favor the exporter, as many other countries do. The Domestic International Sales Corporation program is patently insufficient to give U.S. business the same advantages available to the French or the Japanese, for instance.[22] Additionally, Americans working abroad should be subject to taxation under the laws of the country where they reside and not under U.S. law as at present. The United States is the only industrialized country in the world that applies its income tax laws on the basis of citizenship, instead of residence, with the result that our engineers and businessmen (or their companies) are penalized for working abroad. As we saw in our examination of the construction industry, it is the home country that benefits from the activities abroad of its citizens. United States citizens should thus be encouraged to undertake work abroad as an integral part of U.S. export policy.

The Carter Administration became increasingly aware of the necessity to do something about at least some of the disincentives outlined. Pursuant to the requirement of Section 1110(a) of the Trade Agreements Act of 1979, the President, on September 9, 1980, sent to the Congress a report on export promotion and on elimination of disincentives. This may turn out to be an important first step in reducing export disincentives and aiding the restoration of U.S. trade competitiveness. It is expected that the Reagan Administration will actively pursue this effort of removing disincentives to exports.

6. Review of immigration laws and concepts to encourage "upgrading" of workers

One of the most difficult problems faced by the United States in its attempts at reindustrialization is its approach to its own immigration laws.

* In April, 1981, Boeing received government permission to ship 747s and 727s to Iraq, a nation accused of aiding terrorists. State Department refusal to allow shipment in 1980 was due to opposition from Senator Richard Stone (Florida) on the Senate Foreign Relations Committee, who faced a difficult reelection campaign.

In Japan, the individual counts for little. The very ideograph for the word "individualism" means someone unable to get along with his fellow man. The system is based upon the submission of the individual to the goals of the nation, the constant striving for a consensus. Does it work well? For Japan yes, because it has been the essence of the Japanese character for hundreds of years. In the Soviet Union a very different society has been developed, built entirely upon privileges for those who are deemed to contribute the most to the dictated goals established by the state. In West Germany, in part because of the sheer vitality of the population, in part because of the respect that has always existed for the concept of taking instruction from those "expected to lead," we again find a highly structured society. Japan and the Soviet Union are countries where minority groups are either second-class citizens or tolerated only as limited-time residents.

In France, while the concept of individual expression is very deeply rooted, there exists a "mandarinate" system based on the elevation of the individual in society to leadership in the state who is capable of passing successive examinations in both scientific and cultural subjects. Again, it is both an individualistic and elitist society based on recognizing that the educated man should have the right to make rules for others in the society to follow, whether in government or business. Since the early days of the monarchy, France has always been a highly structured state with a bureaucracy based on educational merit tending to run all aspects of society whether government, business, legal institutions, or whatever. Members of the bureaucracy are highly educated, responsible, and authoritarian.

This is, incidentally, one of the reasons why the Francophile states of Africa have tended to develop faster than other countries on that continent. The French system of education has been passed on with the gradual substitution of blacks for whites, but the same concept of government by a highly organized system of well-educated technocrats making the day to day business and government decisions has remained. (Unfortunately, in Francophile Africa there has not been the same development of technical high schools as in France, where technicians are trained to handle the machines required by an industrialized society. The result has been an increased bureaucracy but few mechanics, and hence here, too, a decline in development has resulted.)

Compare these concepts with the United States, where we like to pretend that government does not interfere with our daily lives, and where our educational system prides itself on its diversity. Everything is questioned; the individual is entitled to study whatever he wishes and to do whatever he wants without the slightest concern for the goals of the society of which he is a part. Government continues to function, not so much because of the quality of those who administer it, but because of a system established through a process of ever-increasing legislation and regulation. During the period when this vast continent remained to be explored, conquered, and developed, there was little government in the United States. Now that that structure has become a necessity, can we continue to act as if our own Siberias remain to be developed in the future? Frontier societies are individualistic and generous to others coming in. Phrases such as "melting pot," "out of many we have made a whole," etc., represented deeply ingrained thinking that was common to an underpopulated country waiting to be developed.

But can an unstructured, classless, open-door society continue in the United States without adversely affecting the wish for an improved standard of living for its present population? Instead of a policy of making a whole out of many peoples, our politicians are now stressing the opposite, enhancing the differences rather than the similarities, urging each group within our society to find its own roots, its own culture, its own way of doing things. Education is being restructured in the same way: "If you will not learn English, we will teach you in Spanish." We have been engaged in a seemingly directed attempt at reducing the demands that society makes on the individual, whether in education, in work performance, in service to the state, in respect for its institutions, or in acceptance of the primary rule that society if it is to survive must command the respect of the citizens who comprise it.

Is it acting responsibly under these circumstances to continue to absorb millions of immigrants, both legal and illegal, when our social structure is so fractured from constant attack, both from within and without? At the moment there is essentially no control over illegal immigration in the United States. Had we not better do as other countries have and reduce immigration until we are ready to absorb new groups of people with different cultures, relying on a system of temporary work permits to satisfy the seasonal needs of the agricultural or business cycle? Are the unions wise in building their power on the weight of numbers, rather than concentrating along with management on justifying higher wages through increased productivity? Society in the United States is at a crossroads. Its immigration policy may well determine whether we shall continue to raise our standard of living through increased productivity or gradually reduce it to the level of the masses of people that seek to enter our country.

7. The government should do more to speed up "advances" in knowledge

We have seen how medical research was advanced by wartime grants and how commercial aircraft development came from the funding of military aircraft development. Today the United States is falling behind in research. The government should be doing much more than it has to spur the research effort.*

First, the government should decide from time to time, as it did in the past, that certain research efforts are essential for national security reasons. New technologies in space are but one example. Already, the Soviet Union may be far ahead of us in developing antisatellite satellites. Development of laser beams for use on satellites is another obvious example. Expanded research funding for defense purposes should be given the highest priority by government.

At the business level, in order to motivate both innovation and more research effort, why not allow tax credits rather than simple deductions for certain research projects? Why not, as President Carter suggested in the case of automobiles, have government grants for research projects related to energy conservation, to the development of new fuels, or to new ways of using existing fuels more efficiently? What about expanding research through grants for coal gasification as a high-priority program?†

Finally, we need to examine the advisability of revising our U.S. patent system to give the researcher more incentive to produce new products. Perhaps we should have special trial judges to hear patent disputes who have first qualified as patent attorneys. Patents are a delicate matter where government funding is involved. The government automatically derives half the benefits of the exploitation of new technology through

*Government has a duty to maintain the nation's scientific base at all levels of education. Quite apart from international commercial competitiveness, failure here would mean risking eventually military security.

†There are three basic levels of research: pure or fundamental research, application, and product development. Government's effort works best in funding the first stage, sometimes the second, but never the third, which private industry is much better equipped to do itself. A good example of the first is government funding of pure atomic research, carried on at the Brookhaven Laboratory and managed by seven universities.

application of the tax system. Furthermore, since the government selects for its funding that which is determined to be important for national security or other national interests, the payoff to government comes from the development of the product itself. Its interest is to push the research effort and disseminate new knowledge quickly so that the country derives maximum benefits from the resulting invention and as rapidly as possible.

To spur innovation further, the researcher should be given the patent even where there is government funding, and development should be accelerated, unless national security forbids it, through exploitation by the private sector. Why should government exploit inventions beyond national security needs, since the private sector does it quicker and better? Why not use an auction system to license government-funded patented inventions?

8. Efforts to promote education and training, better health, mobility of the workforce, and economic efficiency; the role of government in salvaging inefficient enterprises to maintain employment in a given industry should be discouraged

An interesting paradox has developed in the United States. In 1978, for instance, the economy added 3.6 million new jobs, yet the gross national product increased by only a nominal 4 percent.[23] The difference was made up in declining productivity. Now, the maintenance of full employment is a clear national goal.[24] Increasing productivity, however, must also be a national goal.* These aims need not be contradictory. It is quite wrong to think that business has been able to increase its hiring in the past few years only because of lagging productivity. If machine tools permit men to accomplish more, the additional workers who would have been employed to do the same job may be released to take on other jobs. It means that if the system is to work satisfactorily there must be additional flexibility so that employment can be maintained.

In Japan, we saw that the guarantee of lifetime employment in the larger companies gives the workers greater loyalty to their companies because it is only if the company prospers that their jobs are safe. It also gives the company the right to employ their workers where the company

* The Council of Economic Advisers should move vigorously under Humphrey-Hawkins to review the impact of existing policies on productivity and economic progress and to coordinate and provide leadership in developing a coherent set of policy proposals to promote these objectives.

thinks they are best suited since the company must continue their employ. Loyalty and flexibility are built into the system. Because of guaranteed employment, the large companies subcontract wherever possible so that changes in the business cycle can be met through more subcontracting in good times and less when the cycle turns downward. In other countries, West Germany, France, and Switzerland, for instance, flexibility is arrived at through licensing of foreign workers who take temporary jobs within the country when the production cycle is rising.

It is clear the United States needs to develop similar flexibility to meet changes in the business cycle. Perhaps Congress should consider requiring a guarantee of employment in companies that have reached a certain size in sales or employment. Would this not be a better deterrent to the growth of business conglomerates than the present antitrust laws that were never meant to apply to size as such? As mentioned earlier, additional flexibility might be found through changes in the immigration laws. There are other ways of achieving the flexibility required. Certainly, the government might make a much greater and better-designed effort to train displaced workers. It has always seemed that if the government has a national interest in greater productivity, then it must also have a national interest in the training and development of the work force.

In France, business has been motivated through tax credits to make a much greater effort to train workers, particularly young people and women who are entering the work force for the first time.[25] This compares favorably with the Comprehensive Employment and Training Act in the United States. For the federal government to give funds to states and municipalities for youth training when the result is that youths are paid to come in once a week for their check is a great misuse of a necessary program. The minimum-wage law should not apply to youths being trained for permanent employment or those under a certain age. The private sector must be motivated to train those coming into the labor market, because it is only by doing a job that one can learn that job. Outside of funding technical schools to train new job entrants, private industry must do much more than it has. To accomplish this worthwhile end, government must both encourage and motivate business in this direction.

Geographical mobility has always, in every country, been a puzzle. In western Canada there is a shortage of labor just as there is in many parts of the western United States. In Nova Scotia and Appalachia, the opposite is true, yet people are reluctant to move to those areas where there is available employment. A similar situation exists in Europe. Can the government effectively aid persons in finding available jobs? Surely, as was said earlier, the government might call on panels of senior business executives and academics familiar with high-technology developments in industry in the United States, or in other industrialized societies, to advise on what technological developments might become the seed of future industries, to be perhaps financed through special research grants.

Similarly, where, as in the automobile industry today, a common technological problem is perceived that requires a capital-intensive answer, it would seem advisable for the government to participate along with industry in the necessary funding, just as it does in the case of space technology. In West Germany, for example, the government provides 50 to 95 percent of the research and development funds for those private sector companies that need help developing products judged to be important to the economy as a whole. Can this be done without abusing the funding process? Of course. We rely on our Defense Department, under the supervision of Congress, to spend wisely for national security product development. Why not a similar funding effort for research on new products or industries where there is a high national interest? We have noted how successfully the Japanese have done this in semi-conductors and the computer industry.

There is, of course, a vast difference, both in concept and in application between the government's funding of a portion of the cost of technological developments deemed to be important to the nation as a whole and the government's contributing capital funds to rescue a private-sector company that has been mismanaged over a long period of time. A bailout, such as occurred in the case of Chrysler, appears highly questionable.* What business does the government have in rescuing the stockholders or the bankers of a private company? Employment would not have been lost at Chrysler to the extent that it is now being reduced even with the government's loan guarantees. Either Volkswagen or Mitsubishi, or both, would have taken over the plants, other than those where tanks or other national defense products were being manufactured, and this production could have been continued under separate U.S. ownership and management.

There is no need, as has been suggested, for a new government-run

*Contrary to what is thought, Japanese industrial policy allows businesses to fail. In 1978, for example, the number of Japanese bankruptcies was more than twice that in the United States, a much larger economy. When Mazda faced bankruptcy in the late 1970s, both management and workers took deep cuts in salary to reestablish the company's competitiveness without government support.

Reconstruction Finance Corporation to protect inefficient managements making unsatisfactory products.* Such ideas are generally advanced for the protection of bankers rather than employees. If private industry is entitled to government funding, it has given up its rights to independence and must accept the government's interference (ostensibly to protect employment) on every important management decision.

9. The role of the government in encouraging the better use of resources.

The government's role in helping to fund the development of new technologies that will result in the creation of new industries has been discussed. Development of new sources of energy is a case in point. The country cannot function without energy. Hence, government, business, and the public must accept that it becomes the highest national priority to solve what is no longer a political problem (indeed it cannot be permitted to remain so) but an urgent economic problem, fully as important as national defense itself.

Perhaps other solutions might be better than those proposed to date. Seen from ten years in the future, however, it will make little difference that another solution might have been quicker, or less costly. The important consideration is to find a consensus, proceed with all diligence with a program already too many years overdue, and ignore criticisms or cost differentials, that, in the final analysis, must be minimal. Since there is no reasonable alternative, any errors in the program have to be irrelevant.

10. The role of management and labor

The days of Servan-Schreiber's *The American Challenge* have long since passed. It was in the 1950s that Europe and Japan sought to explain superior American productivity in terms of the quality of American managers. And in truth, the American management system, with its global marketing strategy and its educational backup in such institutions as the Harvard Business School, appeared to have found the definitive method by which economic growth could be achieved in an atmosphere of mu-

* Protectionism itself is one of the greatest disincentives to business development and competitiveness because it destroys private initiative and the necessity for a greater research effort. As soon as European governments funded the development of computer hardware in individual countries, the private competitive effort ceased, and the industry withered. The Japanese designed their government effort on the lesson of Europe.

tual government-business confidence and labor cooperation. In the United States we invented the method; others were to model their business strategies after ours. The only problem was that we ceased to innovate or even apply our own system, while the Germans, the Japanese, and the French took our business management ideas, adapted them to their own needs, and applied them in a much broader concept of national interest in a global economy.

Where did we go wrong, and how should management thinking adapt to the 1980s? The first step, obviously, is to raise our sights from business interest to national interest, and from consideration of a domestic market to a worldwide market. Just as the rest of the business world learned from us thirty years ago, we now need to learn from other countries, and adapt to our needs what other countries are now doing, much better than we.

Perhaps where we became too complacent was in the area of labor-management relations. In Europe, in particular, management has had to focus much more on employee relations because labor unions, in many countries, have been so politicized and class antagonisms have grown so fierce that they have often prevented cooperation between employer and employee. If a labor union affiliated with a Communist party and representing workers nationwide calls a strike for political reasons, the only defense of the individual company's management is to make the employees see that their own economic interest is being sacrificed for political ends.* This situation has given management an enormous incentive to make its employees more conscious of their stake in the company's future and their own participation in it. The development of co-determination in West Germany and economic participation in France comes, to a large degree, from the politicization of the labor union movement in Europe and management's answer to it. In Japan, because of the guaranteed employment concept, the situation has not been the same. There the employee necessarily has a vested interest in the economic progress of the employer. If hard times force the employer to let him go, the system of guaranteed employment in other firms makes it more difficult for him to get a job elsewhere, regardless of his skills. How have these European developments worked out in practice? In West Germany, despite strong

* The extent to which workers will demand a role for an association of their choice to prevent exploitation by the employer—in this case the state—is shown by the recent strikes in shipbuilding plants in Poland. Politicization of labor unions in Europe is increasingly being fought by the workers, whether in Western or Eastern Europe. This phenomenon can be expected to continue and to grow.

management reservations at the beginning, results have been very positive on the whole. Management has been surprised to learn that workers will exert themselves to increase productivity and profits because they now are participating directly in the management process and thus understand the necessity for profits to pay for modernization of facilities.

From the workers' standpoint, it has given them a feeling that they are no longer just workers in a plant, but part of a system in which they share responsibility and profit participation. For co-determination will not succeed if it does not lead either to a system of business based on sharing results or a system of employee share-purchase plans that gives workers an economic interest in the financial results of the plant.

In France, employee participation in benefits has gone further, also with excellent results. It is not generally known that Charles de Gaulle's third program in France (after strengthening the executive branch and extricating France from its colonies) was the revitalization of the capitalist system so that workers would directly participate in the results of the enterprise where they worked. The so-called "Plan Vallon" was finally passed under his successor and has done more to reduce the power of the Communist labor unions than any step ever taken. To the surprise of most workers who saw the plan as one more attempt to raise worker productivity for management's benefit, the workers in participating plants are now receiving cash bonuses from their company based on the year's results. The government's participation is to fund a portion of the cost through tax credits.

In time, the system in both France and West Germany will tend to spread much further, unless changes in the political system force an abandonment of economic motivation for labor. Workers (along with management, lenders, and stockholders) will then increasingly participate in the results of the enterprise through both cash bonuses and stock purchase plans. We saw how in the United States, in part as a result of SEC actions, faceless institutions now control an increasing share in companies. In Europe, on the other hand, we are beginning to see the opposite taking place at long last, with governments and banks being gradually replaced by management, individuals, and plant workers as owners of individual businesses. As a result, the capitalist system is being increasingly reinvigorated from below in Western Europe. We need to encourage the same movement in the United States.

In recent years, however, there have been some hopeful signs in management-employee relationships in the United States. At IBM, for many years, foremen have been trained to consider their role as one of teacher rather than enforcer of productivity norms. This is similar to the role of the *meister* or teacher in a German plant. The Japanese, of course, are ahead of everyone in creating within the plant a spirit of cooperation and individual development among the different categories of employees. At General Motors, largely through the efforts of its director of Organizational Research and Development, the company and the United Auto Workers have made great strides in eliminating worker-management friction in individual plants. Today there are more than 100 "quality circles" at GM plants around the country—committees of employees meeting with management's support to discuss operating problems and morale issues.

This is one instance of a U.S. company successfully establishing a system similar to the Japanese *ringis,* which have worked so well there. A comparison of labor relations at GM's Tarrytown plant with Ford's recently closed plant at Mahwah clearly indicates how important it is for management to constantly strive to better worker-management relations at the individual plant level.[26] Given the education of the average worker in an automobile plant, it seems obvious that the worker who is performing a monotonous job must be given a feeling of participation in plant decisions affecting his work to hold his interest. There are, of course, other reasons why Mahwah failed and Tarrytown is succeeding. The important factor to note, however, is that much more needs to be done in the United States both to further automate routine work and to increase worker participation in plant decisions affecting methods of work.

Businessmen in the United States have always taken great pride in their understanding of marketing techniques. Yet automobile executives, some of whom were paid as much as $1 million a year to understand marketing, have recently proved that they did not have the remotest idea of what the customer wanted by way of a car. Nor is this an isolated case history. In Europe and Japan this could not have happened. The Japanese, in particular, send missions constantly to all parts of the globe studying and reporting back on what products are desired. This, of course, is one of the reasons why the trading company system works so well.

In contrast, in the United States, friction tends to develop in almost every company between those whose responsibility is marketing and those in charge of production. In West Germany marketing opportunities are often obtained in international trade by the banks, since the relationship between manufacturing companies and their bankers is very close. In France it is apt to be government trading missions (again the role of government in business). The United States has relied for too long on having a presence abroad rather than on making a marketing effort by the parent company. Others are now practicing in our place the art of international marketing that we developed some thirty years ago.

What about innovation? We saw how too many corporations in the United States have extended the life cycle of their products by failing to innovate more quickly. Increasingly in Europe and Japan, perhaps because corporate funds are scarcer, management is more interested in abandoning outdated products or outmoded systems than in worrying about how to coordinate research for the development of future products. American management needs to accelerate product obsolescence where necessary to maintain technological competitiveness. It is one of the secrets of our successful aircraft industry, which declares a plane obsolete and subject to modification as soon as it comes into production.

In financial practice, many businesses in Europe have a tendency to develop two budgets, one for the short range—the operating budget—and one for the long range—the budget for future products, which, while only a fraction of the operating budget, will make it possible to program adequately the investment cycle for new products.

Perhaps the greatest difference between top management in the United States and other industrialized countries comes from the manner in which the executive conceives of his role in society. In the United States, in recent years, the heads of large companies appear to have lost the position they once held in the public mind. The appearance of the senior management of the major oil companies before Congress in 1976 certainly did nothing to reassure the public of their concern for the national interest. The press no longer appears interested in their views of the future. Administrations do not seek out their advice. Is this change in attitude towards big business and its leaders deserved?

In Europe and in Japan the focus appears to be changing in the other direction. Why? The answer is not hard to find. The U.S. business leader no longer sees himself as the spokesman for his country. Outside the United States, managers tend to see themselves as a national asset and as spokesmen for the country in the accomplishment of its national goals. Since they are considered national leaders, they tend to act accordingly. In Japan, for example, business leaders constantly talk about what is required in the national interest, not what is required by Japanese business, much less their own industry. Leaders of business in the United States should raise their sights equally high. For, under current world political and economic conditions, businessmen have a real role to play in stimulating changes in the structure of our society. Unless they believe it and act on it, why should society not judge them harshly?

If the media and the public perceive business leaders quite differently today than heretofore, what about union leaders? The labor movement in the United States is today perceived quite differently than in the past. In the first place, as wages in nonunionized industries are fully equivalent to those in highly organized industries, the pressure to join a union to be treated fairly by management has declined. Just as businesses have tended to grow more and more into large monolithic and relatively inefficient institutions, labor unions have tended as they have grown to be run by leaders who surround themselves with technical experts but have relatively little to do with the rank-and-file member, his aspirations, or grievances. As a result, the leaders tend in public to concentrate on the adversary relationship between labor and management, rather than on the necessity of combining their efforts so companies can do a more productive job and workers can also earn a larger share of the profits.

At Davos, Switzerland, at the annual Management Forum in 1978, the active heads of the labor federations of West Germany, Great Britain, and the United States held a discussion about labor relations within their respective countries. The German speaker refreshingly pointed out that in his opinion business, in order to remain competitive, had to increase its profits so that it could continuously replace its plant and equipment. German labor unions, he said, believed that profits were essential to business success. They believed in helping business achieve these profits by mutual cooperation. But they also believed in worker participation in earnings if, as a result, there was increased productivity and hence increased profits. The other speakers spoke only of labor's insistence not to be taken advantage of by management.

There are many intelligent and dedicated persons in the labor movement in the United States. But there is a desperate need for the old adversary relationship between management and labor to be replaced by a realization that only a new spirit of cooperation will close our current productivity gap. It is only by so doing that labor can earn wage increases without adding to the current inflation. In 1961, President Kennedy was surprised by the labor unions' positive response to his proposal for investment credits. Today labor's support is needed if the revitalization of the country's economic base is to go forward.

Conclusion

A few years ago, I gave a seminar to the senior executives of a European multinational company at a former monastery in eastern France. The participants came from West Germany, France, Spain, and Brazil. After the first day of discussions, I asked the participants their response to the positions I had espoused. "It seems to us you are too American," was the response of one participant. "You seem to consider that the principal function of a business is to make a profit. In Europe we would put that fourth. The first is, are you producing the goods which you should be producing in the national interest; the second, are you employing the maximum number of people that the enterprise is capable of supporting within its need for modernization; thirdly, are your employees developing themselves in the business to the extent required to feel they are fulfilling their expectations; then, after that comes the importance of profits." I replied that without continuity of the business made possible by profits, all the other three goals became unlikely. Nevertheless, the thought persists that the European perception that evening may have been the correct one.

There is today in the United States a clear need to change the direction of our thinking on the relationship among government, business, and labor, and on the implementation of national goals. There has been much discussion in this book about what is happening in Japan, West Germany, and France and how these countries, in adapting U.S. concepts of management to suit their more clearly perceived national goals, are making greater headway today than we are in achieving these goals.

It is no use pretending, as some U.S. political leaders do, that government will go away and that if this can be made to happen the old innovative spirit of business will return. It will not happen. The role of the government is to create a climate in which individuals in society may function in their own most creative way. The government must motivate and encourage private business to achieve national economic goals delineated and even funded by the government, but it must not directly perform these functions itself, unless no alternative is possible. For if it does, it will bureaucratize and strangle the innovation that it is trying to achieve. The steps suggested here for adoption by the government are all directed at setting national goals and creating the climate to achieve them. Undoubtedly, wiser heads will have other and perhaps better programs to suggest. In our thinking we can surely learn from the Japanese as they have learned from us, without adopting their system, which would be quite inappropriate to our way of doing things.[27]

If our perception of our national goals can be heightened and government functions accordingly reduced, then we can concentrate our efforts to establishing a very different relationship than we have at present between management and labor, and between government and business.

A number of references have been drawn to the experience of other countries and a number of recommendations made in this regard. Business leaders in the United States must regain their prior position of leadership within the country because their role is essential to economic growth, increased employment, and to the maintenance of our standard of living. But management must broaden its thinking and raise its sights to the level of national goals if it is to earn the confidence and respect of the community. If this can be done, then the workforce and the leaders of labor unions will respond, and we may begin that shift from confrontation to cooperation, that is so long overdue.

If we are going to provide the innovative thinking that may solve the many problems the world faces, we need to be more humble, more respectful of the aspirations of others, less sure of our own answers and much more willing to listen.* This applies whether we find ourselves in the government, in the academic world, in business, in a labor union, in finance, or in the media.

* Above all, we need to avoid depending upon quick answers based on past historical perspective founded upon the experience of pre-war Britain and the writings of Keynes. As one noted scholar, Harry Johnson, has written: "All in all, it is difficult to avoid the conclusion that Britain has paid a heavy long-run price for the transient glory of the Keynesian Revolution, in terms both of the corruption of standards of scientific work in economics and encouragement to the indulgence of the belief of the political process that economic policy can transcend the laws of economics with the aid of sufficient economic cleverness, in the sense of being able to satisfy all demands for security of economic tenure without inflation or balance-of-payments problems, or less obvious sacrifice of efficiency and economic growth potentialities."[28]

11
Conclusions

> If a freely elected government makes a simple plan clear, free people can immediately adjust to it. Businessmen could plan investments, working people could plan savings, shopkeepers plan inventories, and farmers plan their fields.
>
> JEAN MONNET

A book on the role of the United States in international trade, if it is to have any practical value, must explain the effect of such trade on the position of the United States in the world economy and how this position can be maintained or enhanced.

There is a definite relationship between the decline of the United States in trade and the rise in inflation in the United States and throughout the world, the decline in U.S. economic growth, and the reduced value of the dollar all during the past twenty years. They are all part of the same phenomenon. It will be the purpose of this final chapter to show this linkage and explain what steps might be taken to reestablish the competitive economic position of the United States, without which it cannot exercise a position of leadership in a highly competitive world.

What preliminary conclusions can be drawn from the discussion in previous chapters? In chapters 1 and 2, the U.S. position in international trade in manufactured goods was shown to have declined steadily over the past thirty years. The factors bringing about this decline were examined. It occurred through successive administrations and without regard to party affiliation or philosophy of government.

In chapter 2, I expressed the belief that this decline need not continue. Interestingly enough, in the Japanese language, the same ideograph signifies both "opportunity" and "disaster." Given the sharp focus of our trade deficits—by product (i.e., energy) and by geographical area (i.e., Japan and Canada)—there would appear to be clearly indicated solutions to the restoration of our trade balance. We need, for example, to make a much greater effort in the energy area, including an immediate halt to price subsidization that distorts both our view of the problem and the efforts to arrive at a solution. In chapter 3, I indicated in detail just how we might accelerate the reduction in our bill for imported oil. This effort alone can reestablish the trade balance.

We need to maintain pressure on the Japanese to open their own domestic market to American products. Why should we continue to allow Japanese automobiles to be sold in the United States while the Japanese effectively keep out our semiconductors and computers, in order to favor the establishment of a new domestic industry? The case history of Motorola alone shows how difficult it is for American manufacturers to penetrate the Japanese market. We have indicated the importance of developing in our relationship with Canada—and also with Mexico—policies that will lead to greater regional trade.

In chapters 4, 5 and 6, we examined, in turn, the monetary system that controls the means of payment used in international trade, the international banking system established by private banks to finance transactions in international trade, and the role of international institutions such as the World Bank in extending credit for trade to the developing countries.

In these chapters we explored the monetary roots of the world economic crisis. The key points may be summarized briefly as follows:

1. Inflation is not caused simply by recurrent budget deficits. In large part the responsibility must rest with the Federal Reserve's policy of constantly adding to the money supply to accommodate the failure of successive administrations either to raise taxes or to lower expenditures in order to reduce or eliminate federal budgetary deficits. Monetary accommodation has thus been substituted in the United States for fiscal responsibility. During the Vietnam War, the Federal Reserve accommodated President Johnson's reluctance to pay for the war through tax increases; in 1970, the new chairman accommodated President Nixon's fear of corporate bankruptcies; during the Carter Administration, the Federal Reserve again adopted an easy money policy to accommodate the President's vast new social programs. In President Carter's term alone the federal budget increased from $401.9 billion (actual) in 1977 to $739.3 billion (proposed) in 1982, an increase of 84 percent in a single presidential term.

2. United States inflation cannot help but be exported as other countries increase their own currency in circulation in order to prevent further

increases in the value of their currencies relative to the dollar and thereby hurt their trade.

3. The resort to floating exchange rates has allowed governments to adjust the international impact of their domestic social policies and budget deficits by exchange-rate manipulation or interest-rate increases rather than by sound domestic budgetary policies. This was the principal error of the Carter Administration's economic policies. The result, a "liquidity" glut, increased inflation everywhere, and global economic dislocation.

4. The Eurocurrency system has been of great help in recycling the international redistribution of wealth brought about by the OPEC cartel but cannot be relied upon to handle increased payments to OPEC for oil either from the industrialized countries or from those developing countries that are rapidly achieving industrialized-country status (and hence need more energy).

5. The World Bank group and the other MDBs are playing important roles in financing international trade but should restrict their activities to continuing infrastructure projects. It is not the function of the World Bank to engage in balance-of-payments financings or oil exploration. The IMF, which *does* finance temporary balance-of-payments disequilibriums, needs additional sources of funds to help certain countries, particularly those developing countries achieving industrialization, adjust to the higher prices of oil. It would appear particularly important at the present time for the MDBs to avoid financing industrial projects to the detriment of agricultural development, especially in the poorer countries that cannot afford to import food and must depend upon local produce to feed their people.

6. Despite the monetary dislocations of the past few years, the role of the dollar as the key currency in international trade has not decreased but grown. We can say that the world is effectively today on a paper-dollar standard, with the quantity of such paper continuously increasing.

If the Reagan Administration continues its pressure on the Federal Reserve to stop increasing the money supply, then the rate of inflation worldwide will begin to decline and the dollar will become more valuable. No doubt business dislocations will occur, and a much greater effort will have to be made by American business firms to stay competitive in the export of their products.

In chapter 7 we examined the changing "rules of the game" established by the principal trading nations to govern their trade relationships. We showed the sophisticated means by which certain industrialized nations, notably Japan, have kept imports out while making every effort to increase their own exports. It can be expected in the future that competition for exports will continue to grow, not only among the industrialized countries but also between the mature industrialized nations and the intermediate developing countries (the NICs) such as Brazil, Mexico, Taiwan, and South Korea.

In chapters 8 and 9 we analyzed new factors on the scene since the end of World War II: the developing countries and the state economies of the Communist world. These new entrants in international trade have raised several important questions for U.S. authorities. Should American companies be discouraged by government action from establishing plants in, or transferring technology to, developing countries seeking to manufacture such products as steel or textiles that are already in surplus in the industrialized countries? To what extent should American companies supply technical products or know-how to the Soviet bloc, or to the People's Republic of China, particularly where these products may have military applications or increase the capacity of these countries for military action? If we permit technology transfers, what categories of products should we include—oil technology and drilling equipment? computers? electronics? telecommunications equipment? transportation technology? even agricultural products?

I would argue that the government should exercise the greatest possible restraint in restricting exports, whether for national security reasons or because products made abroad as a result of the transfer of U.S. technology might later be exported to this country. The United States is no longer, except in a very few areas, the leader in technology. The result of preventing an export from the United States, for fear of its effect on domestic employment, is to discourage innovation and better technology in favor of protecting the inefficient and outdated. If, as Samuel Johnson pointed out, patriotism is the last refuge of the scoundrel, then protectionism is the last refuge of noncompetitive business.

Finally, chapter 10 discussed in detail the decline in U.S. productivity over the past twenty years, a decline brought about by a change of attitude toward the work ethic, a tendencey to focus on the quality of life rather than individual or national accomplishment. This has been accelerated in recent years by greatly increased government regulations and controls. Much like the British, we have been living off the wealth and effort of past generations. As someone has said, we are akin to the third generation of a successful entrepreneur, engaged in leisure and good works, while using the power and the money of our forebears.

This brings us to the synthesis to be drawn from the analysis made in the first ten chapters of this book. A good manager, in developing his corporate strategy, relies on his analysis of his company's strengths and weaknesses. Nations can do the same to similar advantage.

Our economic strengths in the United States are enormous. We have to list only a few: abundant natural resources, a well-developed infrastructure, transportation, electrical power, manufacturing facilities (although too often old), agricultural development, communications network, educational institutions, as well as an extraordinarily developed capital market to channel savings into business investment, highly innovative technology-oriented new industries in electronics and telecommunications that make it possible to modernize and develop almost any industry, an excellent banking system organized to service industry worldwide, a high cash flow from earnings on foreign investments and services rendered abroad, and a general freedom from the kind of government constraints that countries with weakened currencies are obliged to adopt—exchange controls, restrictions on foreign investment, nationalization of industry. Above all, we have avoided class conflict, although deep and growing ethnic divisions have aspects of social and cultural conflict.

If our strengths are most impressive, the weaknesses discussed in this book are also growing. Among the more noteworthy of these, measured in terms of the attitude of government, business, and the general public, are the following:

From the standpoint of government

1. An attitude, until recently, of disinterest with respect to the value of our currency;
2. A lack of interest in strengthening the world's monetary system;
3. An inadequate response to trade barriers imposed by others;
4. A failure to enact a clear national export policy;
5. No clear immigration policy;
6. Growing disincentives to export;
7. A failure to revise the tax system to favor exports;
8. An inability to control budgetary deficits, thereby adding to inflation;
9. Continuous increase in the burden of social programs;
10. A lack of understanding about the sad condition of our manufacturing plants.

From the standpoint of business

1. Little appreciation of the need for exports because of the size of the domestic market;
2. The substitution of investments abroad for a policy of marketing *from* the United States;
3. Reduced research and development budgets in all but a few growth industries;
4. Inadequate training programs for executives marketing U.S. products abroad, together with a failure to develop foreign language skills.

From the standpoint of the public generally

1. A continuing adversary spirit of confrontation rather than cooperation between various segments of society: e.g., business versus government, management versus labor;
2. A distrust of businessmen, particularly of the executives of multinational corporations;
3. A distrust of politicians, whether those in the administration or in Congress;
4. An acceptance of inflation as a way of life, which has converted the United States into a nation of borrowers rather than savers;
5. A lack of understanding about the extent to which exports mean jobs. It has been pointed out that for each $1 billion worth of exports, an additional 40,000 jobs are secured, but there appears to be no public appreciation of this; increasingly, job security has become a right the government is expected to guarantee.

The strengths we have listed above are real; the weaknesses are principally attitudinal and therefore subject to change, given the will to do so.

From all this it appears that much of the world's economic problems come from our failure to understand the linkage between international trade, economic growth, inflation, and the value of our currency. This concluding analysis will therefore focus on how inextricably interrelated these four factors really are.

All Americans express themselves in favor of continued strong economic growth as well as a reduced rate of inflation. But how many of us have considered how exports and a strong currency can affect the rates of economic growth and of inflation?

A strong dollar means increased investment from abroad. Over the past thirty years, as we saw in chapter 4, the outflow of dollars has steadily increased. This has brought about the growth in the Eurodollar market that we noted in chapter 5. Now we need to do whatever is possible to repatriate this flow of dollars from abroad, particularly in view of the billions we now must spend to solve our energy problem as outlined in chapter 3, and to bring about the second U.S. industrial revolution, which we spoke about in chapter 10.

There are many reasons why OPEC dollar surpluses would tend to be invested in the United States: political stability, the ability to move funds freely in and out, the flexibility of our capital markets. Investors, however, are noticeably reluctant to bring their money to the United States when government officials make clear (as they did in 1977–78) their disinterest in maintaining the value of our currency or when they confiscate foreign holdings, as was done in the case of Iran. There is an attitudinal change to be made here; we need to actively encourage capital inflow. Already, since the 1980 election, confidence that the new administration will adopt consistent policies and a strong currency has resulted in capital flows toward the United States.

The movement of capital back to the United States will bring about reduced inflation at home by increasing production. It will also increase jobs for Americans, since increases in production—the so-called supply-side economics we hear so much about these days—adds to the supply of goods and services and thus tends to match demand for these goods, making it more difficult for producers and sellers to raise prices. Through the enactment of credit controls in March, 1980, the administration brutally slowed demand. How much better it might have been if government policy over the past few years had been directed at increasing the production of goods.

A strong currency also tends to reduce inflation by reducing the dollar cost of imported goods, thereby maintaining competitive pricing of domestic products. The answer to the steel industry's plight in the United States is not to prevent the importation of foreign steel that may come in at more attractive prices but to make the U.S. steel industry more competitive so that it can meet those prices. This means changes in management outlook and a vast new input of capital.

Perhaps the best point to make about the importance of maintaining a strong currency is that it will bring about an increase in domestic productivity to maintain America's competitive edge. Given American inventiveness and the flexibility of our capital markets, I would argue that it is possible for American industry, even in steel and textiles, to remain competitive without government restrictions on imports. The same is true of the automobile industry. To hasten the modernization of an industry through government credits or funding is one thing; to prevent the American public from buying fuel-efficient imported cars of consistent quality and dependability at attractive prices is quite another.

If a strong currency is helpful to both economic growth and diminished inflation, what about a national policy to increase exports? The first result of increased exports would, of course, be a tendency for the dollar to increase in value. In March, 1980, the Federal Reserve attempted to maintain the value of the dollar by raising interest rates. Although such a move may have been unavoidable by the time it was taken, it is, in the long run, a poor way to protect the value of the dollar.

The right answer would be to have adopted an effective means to promote exports in 1977, if not earlier. Now, unfortunately, the Reagan Administration is reducing the lending capacity of the Export-Import Bank. By this decision, American exporters will be denied the same financing support foreign competitors receive from their governments. The director of the Office of Management and Budget has indicated that the Bank needs no support because it only plays a role in 2 percent of total exports. This is an inaccurate assumption. The Bank's financing is not needed for high-technology products or those otherwise unavailable from elsewhere because financing is not a factor in these transactions, nor is it in most sales to other industrialized countries, or to countries like Saudi Arabia or Libya, which can pay cash. In the Third World, however, the fastest-growing market for U.S. products, a substantial portion of U.S. sales of manufactured products receive some support from the Bank.

So long as other countries give the same or better financing terms, the Bank has a vital role in U.S. exports, particularly where the goods would otherwise be sold by American companies with overseas plants in countries where favorable financing is made available to exporters. If competitive financing cannot be obtained from the United States, American multinationals will simply source from other countries, where government financing for the importer is available. Almost all U.S. production except aircraft can be sourced by American multinationals from outside the United States so financing is increasingly the key to the sale. Yet the Export-Import Bank has been criticized for financing U.S. aircraft sales which must be competitive with the goverment-owned Airbus consortium. Unless the present policy is changed, American aircraft too may have to be manufactured outside the country in order to obtain government financing for export sales.

As has been noted, if a country's exports increase, the value of its currency is maintained. But inflation is also thereby reduced through the increased value of the currency, which reduces the cost of competitive imports. For the United States, increased exports will, without sacrificing currency values, permit the country to increase its imports of those raw materials on which U.S. industry is increasingly dependent, and, because the dollar is strong, reduce the price. Thus, increased exports benefit not only the United States but also our trading partners—particularly the developing countries—which depend upon the export of raw materials for their own gradual development.

We need not dwell on the importance of continued economic growth to the United States. As noted earlier, government policy in the last year of the Carter Administration was mistaken in trying to slow the economy to curb inflation. Although recession reduces demand it also reduces production and increases unemployment, leaving, at the same time, fewer dollars chasing fewer goods. Growth reduces inflation by increasing production and hence the supply of goods. It also increases exports by reducing prices through more efficient use of plant capacity, and it stimulates innovation by creating a positive economic climate. Growth is essential both to increased employment and productivity.

It seems clear that the United States must have a truly meaningful national export policy if it is to maintain the value of its currency, reestablish a growth economy, reduce its rate of inflation, and regain its position as a leader of the free world. Our government has tended to focus on these factors individually, rather than collectively. It has been shown that they are inexorably woven together.

Some years ago Nikolai Lenin prophetically stated: "The best way to destroy the capitalist system is to debauch the currency. By a continuing process of inflation, government can confiscate, secretly and unobserved, an important part of the wealth of its citizens."

While this need not happen, mistaken policies of the past twenty years make it all the more important that every effort now be made to maintain the value of the currency, to reduce inflation, and to restore economic growth. The phenomenon known as *stagflation*—inflation combined with a sluggish economy and no growth—is caused by the inability of governments in industrialized countries to make the difficult choices required to halt inflation.

As long as governments continue to fund social programs through budgetary deficits financed through increases in the money supply, inflation will continue unabated. Massive transfer payments create no new wealth within an economy, but only redistribute wealth already created. And herein lies the problem. For while transfer payments increase demand, they create no compensating increase in the supply of goods and services to offset this new demand, building upward pressure on prices. Unless such transfer payments occur simultaneously with increases in productivity, inflation is an inevitable consequence. To continue needed social programs and not drive up prices we must increase the investment necessary for greater productivity. In the United States in particular, the nation's industrial plants need to be modernized so that the same number of workers can produce more goods, and hence at reduced prices. This is what is meant by supply-side economics, and why the concept has merit.

It should not need saying that the problem of stagflation is not an American problem alone. In 1980, in the European Community, for example, the external trade deficit increased to $61 billion, 86 percent above the 1979 level, and very much higher than the 1978 deficit of $5.7 billion.[1]

What is then to be done? Can a country have real growth in its economy with inflation? Brazil has proved over the past fifteen years that this is possible. But it is thought that you cannot fight inflation except by reducing growth, causing rising unemployment, raising interest rates, and in this manner adding to budgetary deficits. That has been, as we saw in chapter 4, the experience of the Thatcher government in Britain.

As a result of the recent election in France bringing François Mitterrand and the socialists to power with a clear majority for the first time in twenty-three years, we will now be able to observe the economic effect of totally different philosophies of government in two principal Western countries: the United States and France. In the United States, the Reagan Administration has begun to reverse fifty years of increased Federal Government expenditures and controls; in France, the government is headed in the directly opposite direction with an even greater role for government, more nationalization of industry, more central planning and control, and expanded social programs. There are many differences, of course, between the two countries: France is probably today the wealthiest country in the world, with very little debt and enormous assets. Perhaps this is why the French public believes it can afford a mandate to government to increase social programs. In the United States we have the greatest government debt in the history of the world, a rising deficit from years of overspending by government, and are now making an effort to regain control over government expenditures. As French government spending increases under projected government social programs, France will necessarily become more inflation-prone, with higher costs of manufacture, less emphasis on high technolgoy, and in due course less competitiveness in international trade.

A better approach for the United States in 1981 should be to structure the economy to spur production regardless of the budgetary effect. In this way the economy can build up enough momentum to absorb new employees, produce more, begin to lower prices, and set in motion a new cycle of economic growth.

In such an effort, exports can play a most significant role. The surest way to insure that they do is to adopt without delay a strong, clear, national export policy.

Everything that has been said in this book is directed toward an understanding that if the United States is to regain its productive strength it must encourage not only the investment of its citizens' savings, but those of other lands as well, particularly of OPEC countries like Saudi Arabia, Kuwait, and the Emirates, which cannot use anywhere near the totality of the funds they have acquired through increases in the price of oil. If the world is to grow in productive capacity sufficient to meet the needs of a constantly increasing population, it must produce much more, not less. This process should be started in the United States by encouraging domestic savings and investment and by making foreign investment as welcome in 1981 as it was in 1881. In 1932, Roosevelt spurred the country on hard times through deficit spending. Over a span of nearly fifty years, most of it good times, his successors continued this deficit spending, thereby multiplying the federal budget by 100, from $7 billion per annum to $700 billion and managing to create a national debt of almost $1 trillion.

To deal with the situation we now have, we must encourage the return of foreign claims against the country by making investment in the United States very attractive. We need to deemphasize the current effort to redistribute our existing wealth, which generations of Americans earned through their creativity and hard work, and instead, rekindle that spark once called Yankee ingenuity by allowing those who create wealth to reinvest a fair share of the results of their efforts so that the economy as a whole may continue to grow. In every generation, in every country, there have been men who create and reinvest, others who manage, still others who prefer to live their lives in other ways.

It is only through the creation of new assets that the standard of living of all Americans will again begin to grow. Faced with the indebtedness that this generation of Americans has created for the next, we have little time in which to start creating the new capital base within this country that will be needed to satisfy the future needs of our people, as well as to amortize the debt created by our past profligacy.

Glossary

A

ADB	Asian Development Bank
ADF	Asian Development Fund (soft-loan window of the Asian Development Bank)
ADR	American Depository Receipts
AEC	Atomic Energy Commission (U.S.)
AFDB	African Development Bank
AFDF	African Development Fund (soft-loan window of the African Development Bank)
AFL-CIO	American Federation of Labor and Congress of Industrial Organizations
AGA	American Gas Association
AID	Agency for International Development (U.S.)
ASME	American Society of Mechanical Engineers
ASP	American Selling Price

B

BIS	Bank for International Settlements
BLS	Bureau of Labor Statistics (U.S.)

C

CACEX	Foreign Trade Department, Bank of Brazil
CAP	Common Agricultural Policy
CDX	Plywood quality standard, usually applicable in the U.S.
CEIB	Central European International Bank, Ltd., a Hungarian international banking institution headquartered in Hungary, belonging 34% to the Central Bank of Hungary and 66% divided among 4 Western European banks and 2 Japanese banks
CEQ	Council on Environmental Quality
CETA	Comprehensive Employment and Training Act
CIA	Central Intelligence Agency (U.S.)
CIF	Cost, Insurance, Freight
CMEA	Council for Mutual Economic Assistance (USSR, Bulgaria, Czech-

	oslovakia, East Germany, Hungary, Poland, Romania and Cuba (but not Yugoslavia)
COCOM	Consulting Group Coordinating Committee (created by the United States, its European allies, and Japan to coordinate export control policies)
COMECON	Economic group organized by the Soviet Union and its allies as a counterpart to the European Economic Community. Members are: Bulgaria, Czechoslovakia, East Germany, Hungary, Poland, Romania, USSR plus Cuba, Mongolia, and Vietnam
CRS	Congressional Research Service

D

DOC	Department of Commerce (U.S.)
DOE	Department of Energy (U.S.)

E

EC(EEC)	European Economic Community, created by the Treaty of Rome in 1958. Includes West Germany, France, Italy, Belgium, The Netherlands, Luxembourg, United Kingdon, Ireland, and very recently Greece
EDF	Electricité de France
EMS	European Monetary System
ENI	Ente Nazionale Idrocarburi (Italy)
EOR	Enhanced oil recovery
EPA	Environmental Protection Agency (U.S.)

F

FAS	Freight aboard ship
FASB	Financial Accounting Standards Board
FDA	Food and Drug Administration (U.S.)
FDI	Foreign Direct Investment
FOB	Freight on board
FSO	Fund for Special Operations (soft loan window of InterAmerican Development Bank)

G

GAO	Government Accounting Office (U.S.)
GATT	General Agreement on Tariffs and Trade
GDP	Gross Domestic Product
GNP	Gross National Product
GOSPLAN	Soviet State Planning Commission (USSR)

I

IBEC	International Bank for Economic Cooperation (USSR and its allies)
IBRD	International Bank for Reconstruction and Development
ICM	Imposto de Cireulacao de Mercadorias (Brazil)
IDB	InterAmerican Development Bank
IET	Interest Equalization Tax
IFC	International Finance Corporation
IFI	International financing institution
ILO	International Labor Organization
IMF	International Monetary Fund
IPI	Imposto Sobre Productos Industrializadas (Brazil)
IRS	Internal Revenue Service (U.S.)

J

JEC	Joint Economic Committee (U.S. Congress)
JETL	Japan Electrical Testing Laboratory

K

KOTPA	Korean Promotion Corporation (South Korea)

L

LAFTA	Latin American Free Trade Association
LDC	Less Developed Country
LIBOR	London interbank offer rate

M

MAIBL	Midland and International Banks (a consortium of banks engaged in international trade headed by Midland Bank of London)
MDB	Multinational development bank
MFN	Most Favored Nation
MIT	Massachusetts Institute of Technology (U.S.)
MITI	Ministry for International Trade and Investment (Japan)
MTN	Multinational Trade Negotiations

N

NIC	Newly Industrialized Country
NNPA	Nuclear Non-Proliferation ACT

NRC	Nuclear Regulatory Commission (U.S.)
NTT	Nippon Telephone and Telegraph (Japan)

O

OAS	Organization of American States
OECD	Organization for Economic Cooperation and Development
OPEC	Organization of Petroleum Exporting Countries
OSHA	Occupational Safety and Health Administration (U.S.)

P

PDCI	Parti Démocratique de la Côte d'Ivoire (Ivory Coast)
PIRF	Petroleum Industry Research Foundation
PRC	Peoples' Republic of China
PRI	Partido Revolucionario Institutional (Mexico)
PROEXPO	Export Promotion Fund (Colombia)

R

R & D	Research and Development
RDB	Regional Development Banks

S

SASOL	South Africa Coal, Oil and Gas, Limited (project in Sasol, South Africa)
SDR	Special Drawing Rights
SEC	Securities and Exchange Commission (U.S.)
SEV	Swiss Elektrotechnisher Verein (Switzerland)
SHC	Sherman H. Clark Associates
SPR	Strategic Petroleum Reserve

T

TASS	The official news agency of the Soviet Union
TVA	Value added tax (France)
TVA	Tennessee Valley Authority (U.S.

U

UAW	United Auto Workers (U.S.)
UBAF	Union de Banques Arabes et Françaises (a consortium of Arab and European banks based in Paris)
UNCTAD	United Nations Commission on Trade and Development
UNIDO	United Nations Industrial Development Organization

USGS	U.S. Geological Survey
USTR	United States Trade Representative
UTE	Union Technique de l'Electricité (France)

V

VLSI	Very large scale integration (referring to high-density memory circuits)

W

WAES	Workshop on Alternative Strategies
WCARRD	World Conference on Agrarian Reform and Rural Development
WIN	Whip Inflation Now

Appendix 1. U.S. balance of payments (in millions of dollars)

Line #	*1970*	*1971*	*1972*	*1973*
1. Merchandise Trade Balance	2,603	−2,260	−6,416	911
2. Exports	42,469	43,319	49,381	71,410
3. Imports	−39,866	−45,579	−55,797	−70,499
4. Military Transactions, net	−3,354	−2,893	−3,420	−2,070
5 Travel & Transportation, net	−2,038	−2,345	−3,063	−3,158
6. Investment Income, net (7 + 8 + 9)	7,877	9,079	10,152	14,457
7. U.S. Direct Investment abroad	9,926	11,086	13,064	19,055
8. Other Investment	3,578	3,547	3,815	5,266
9. Foreign investments in the U.S.	−5,627	−5,554	−6,727	−9,864
10. Other Services, net	533	686	806	880
11. Balance on goods & services (1 + 4 + 5 + 6 + 10)	5,621	2,267	−1,941	11,020
12. Unilateral transfers (13 + 14 + 15)	−3,294	−3,702	−3,854	−3,881
13. Private remittances & other transfers	−1,096	−1,117	−1,109	−1,250
14. U.S. Government pensions & other transfers	−1,736	−2,043	−2,173	−1,938
15. U.S. Government grants of goods & services (excluding military)	−462	−542	−572	−693
16. Balance on Current Account (11 + 12)	2,327	−1,435	−5,795	7,139
17. Long-Term Capital, net (18 + 19)	−5,816	−8,628	−5,323	−8,847
18. U.S. Government capital flows other than foreign official reserves agencies	−1,589	−1,884	−1,568	−2,644
19. Private Capital flows, net (20 + 21 + 22 + 23 + 24 + 25)	−4,227	−6,744	−3,755	−6,203
20. U.S. Direct Investment abroad	−7,589	−7,617	−7,747	−11,353
21. Foreign direct investment in the U.S.	1,464	367	949	2,800
22. Foreign securities	−1,076	−1,113	−618	−671
23. U.S. securities other than Treasury issues	2,189	2,289	4,507	4,041
24. Other, reported by U.S. banks	259	−886	−1,197	−922
25. Other, reported by U.S. nonbanking concerns	526	216	351	−98
26. Short-Term capital net (27 + 28 + 29 + 30)	−6,551	−10,105	1,816	−1,822
27. Claims reported by U.S. banks	−1,122	−2,368	−2,199	−5,047
28. Claims reported by U.S. nonbanking concerns	−10	−1,061	−811	−1,987
29. Liabilities reported by U.S. commercial banks	−6,321	−6,661	4,605	4,475
30. Liabilities reported by other foreigners	902	−15	221	737
31. Balance on capital account (17 + 26)	−12,367	−18,733	−3,507	−10,669
32. Errors and Omissions	−216	−9,777	−1,879	−2,654
33. Allocation of Special Drawing Rights	867	717	710	—
34. Official reserves transactions balance (16 + 31 + 32 + 33)	−9,389	−29,230	−10,471	−6,184
35. U.S. official reserve assets, net	2,481	2,439	−4	158
36. Foreign official assets in the U.S., net	6,908	26,879	10,475	6,026

Source: U.S. Department of Commerce/Bureau of Economic Analysis, Survey of Current Business

[a] Preliminary figures for 1980 and subject to wide fluctuation.
[b] After 1977 the separation of bank claims and liabilities according to length of maturity was discontinued by the U.S. Department of Commerce. For the purposes of this table, all claims and liabilities were assumed to be short-term from 1978 to 1980.
[c] The data source did not disaggregate some of the services accounts for 1980 because they were preliminary numbers. However, they are included in line 10 as part of other services.
[d] For 1980 lines 13 and 14 were reported together. Data source did not separate public transfers from private transfers.
[e] After 1978 the division of claims and liabilities of nonbanking concerns according to length of maturity was discontinued by the U.S. Department of Commerce. In 1979 and 1980, they were assumed to be short-term.

1974	*1975*	*1976*	*1977*	*1978*	*1979*	*1980*[a]
−5,343	9,047	−9,306	−31,503	−33,759	−29,386	−27,354
98,306	107,088	114,745	120,186	142,054	182,068	221,781
−103,649	−98,041	−124,051	−151,689	−175,813	−221,454	−249,135
−1,653	−746	559	1,628	886	−1,275	N/A[c]
−3,184	−2,792	−2,558	−3,323	−3,188	−2,695	N/A[c]
18,413	16,043	19,213	21,540	25,281	37,996	32,535
22,227	20,138	22,530	23,874	29,940	42,857	37,068
8,430	8,756	10,287	12,506	17,807	29,305	38,961
−12,244	−12,851	−13,604	−14,841	−22,466	−34,166	−43,494
1,076	1,342	1,473	1,536	1,577	320	1,896[c]
9,309	22,894	9,381	−10,122	−9,203	4,960	7,077
−7,186	−4,613	−4,997	−4,605	−5,055	−5,066	−6,958
−1,017	−906	−917	−859	−798	−955	N/A
−5,475	−2,894	−3,146	−2,775	−3,171	−1,187	−2,452[d]
−694	−813	−934	−971	−1,086	−3,524	−4,506
2,123	18,281	4,384	−14,727	−14,258	−706	119
−6,443	−18,866	−19,807	−16,073	−11,781	−15,260	−10,551
366	−3,474	−4,214	−3,693	−4,644	−3,783	−5,111
−6,809	−15,392	−15,593	−12,380	−7,137	−11,477	−5,440
−9,052	−14,244	−11,949	−12,898	−16,345	−24,319	−20,592
4,760	2,603	4,347	3,728	7,897	9,713	8,204
−1,854	−6,247	−8,885	−5,460	−3,450	−4,643	−3,188
378	2,503	1,284	2,713	2,811	2,942	7,443
−477	−47	652	156	2,197[b]	4,830	2,693
−564	40	−1,042	−619	−247	N/A[e]	N/A[e]
−3,138	−11,345	−10,079	−5,178	−19,338	6,463	−35,921
−18,333	−11,175	−19,006	−10,676	−33,631[b]	−25,868	−46,608
−2,747	−991	−2,254	−1,841	−3,800	−2,029	N/A
16,008	908	10,759	6,346	16,259[b]	32,668	10,687
1,934	−87	422	993	1,834	1,692	N/A
−9,581	−30,211	−29,886	−21,251	−31,119	−8,797	−46,472
−1,620	5,753	10,367	−880	11,354	23,765	37,177
—	—				1,139	1,152
−9,079	−6,178	−15,135	−36,858	−34,023	15,401	8,024
−1,467	−849	−2,558	−375	730	−1,133	−8,155
10,546	7,027	17,693	37,233	33,293	−14,268	16,179

Appendix 2. U.S. merchandise trade (in millions of dollars)

	1970	*1972*	*1974*	*1976*	*1978*	*1980*
EXPORTS						
Foods, Feeds, Beverages	5,874	7,504	18,638	19,830	25,156	35,519
Industrial supplies and materials	13,795	13,966	30,129	32,116	39,246	71,523
Capital Goods	14,659	16,914	30,878	39,112	46,470	73,422
Automotive Vehicles	3,870	5,485	8,625	12,100	15,584	16,822
Consumer Goods	2,798	3,583	6,399	8,022	10,418	16,449
IMPORTS						
Foods, Feeds, Beverages	6,147	7,258	10,568	11,546	15,397	18,127
Industrial supplies and materials	15,343	20,958	54,428	64,332	84,854	134,499
Fuels and Lubricants	3,168	5,101	27,488	36,975	45,648	83,913
Capital Goods	3,978	5,919	9,819	12,282	19,243	30,204
Automotive Vehicles	5,515	8,685	12,028	16,169	24,214	27,062
Consumer Goods	7,403	11,104	14,380	17,165	28,943	34,445

Source: United States Department of Commerce

Notes

Chapter 1

1. Richard M. Nixon, "Challenge of Peace," speech given August 15, 1971, text in *The Washington Post,* August 16, 1971, A14.

Chapter 2

1. "Agreement Concerning Automotive Parts Between the Government of the United States and the Government of Canada," signed January 16, 1965, (17 U.S.T. 1372 TIAS 6093); *see* also *Automotive Products Trade Act of 1965* P.L. 89–283; 79 STAT. 1016, approved October 21, 1965.

Chapter 3

1. Federal Energy Administration, *The Economic Impact of the Oil Embargo on the American Economy* (Washington, D.C.: Government Printing Office, 1974), p. 6.
2. Estimate of Herman T. Franssen, reported in "U.S. Seen Relying Heavily on Arab Oil, *Oil and Gas Journal,* January 5, 1976, p. 55.
3. *Detailed Fact Sheet, The President's Energy Program* (Washington, D.C.: Government Printing Office, April 20, 1977), p. 1.
4. Executive Office of the President, *The National Energy Plan* (Washington, D.C.: Government Printing Office, April 29, 1977), p. 5.
5. For an interesting discussion of the "least-cost" energy strategy based on minimizing consumer cost, *see* Roger W. Sant, *Gas Energy Review,* 8 (October, 1979), p. 1–8.
6. Dale W. Jorgenson and Edward A. Hudson, "Energy Policy and U.S. Economic Growth," *American Economic Review,* 68 (May, 1978), pp. 118–30.
7. *Petroleum Intelligence Weekly,* February 25, 1980, p. 3.
8. Herman Franssen, *Energy: An Uncertain Future,* prepared at the request of the Committee on Energy & Natural Resources (Washington, D.C.: Government Printing Office, December 1978), p. 74.
9. Michael Halbouty, "The U.S. is Not Drilled Out," *The Wall Street Journal,* December 27, 1979, p. 10.
10. M. E. Shields, *Summary of the Second Workshop on Western Hemisphere Energy* (McLean, Virginia: The Mitre Corporation, September, 1979), p. 16.
11. "Newsletter," *Oil & Gas Journal,* December 24, 1979, p. 3.
12. Sam H. Schurr, Project Director, *Energy in America's Future: The Choices*

Before Us, a study prepared for Resources for the Future, National Energy Strategies Project (Baltimore: The Johns Hopkins University Press, 1979), p. 233.

13. U.S. General Accounting Office, *Analysis of Current Trends in U.S. Petroleum and Natural Gas Production,* Report to the Congress (Washington, D.C.: Government Printing Office, December 7, 1979), p. 50.
14. Ibid., p. ii.
15. Robert Stobaugh and Dan Yergin, eds., *Energy Future,* Report of the Energy Project at the Harvard Business School (New York: Random House, 1979), p. 42.
16. Note 13 above, p. 15.
17. *See* Charles W. Kadlic and Arthur B. Laffer, "Does Oil Decontrol Mean Lower Prices?" *The New York Times,* September 2, 1979. This article shows that three times in the mid-seventies the government removed restraints on oil. The price of oil did not rise but stabilized, or declined. The only effect of the Windfall Profits Tax would be to increase U.S. dependence on foreign oil in both the short and long term.
18. Ibid., p. 32.
19. *Petroleum Economist,* March, 1980, p. 105.
20. *Oil and Gas Journal,* March 17, 1980, p. 59.
21. Note 13 above, p. iii.
22. An interesting analysis of the Carter Administration's policy is contained in Jude Wininski, "The Political Economy in Perspective: Energy Overview," *H. C. Wainwright & Co., Economics* (Boston, July 23, 1979), pp. 1–11.
23. Statement of Gordon J. MacDonald, at *Third Workshop on Western Hemisphere Energy* (McLean, Virginia: The Mitre Corporation, December 3, 1979); also, Gordon J. MacDonald, *Future of Natural Gas,* McLean, Virginia: The Mitre Corporation, May, 1979.
24. *Gas Energy Review,* 7 (May, 1979), pp. 1–4.
25. *Gas Energy Review,* 8 (January, 1980), pp. 4–7.
26. "It will take drilling so-called 'superwells' located below 15,000 feet. The drilling of 250 superwells by 1990 is feasible," says Robert Heffner III of GHK Companies in Oklahoma City, "Each one can produce the equivalent of 1 million barrels a year. In fact, the interesting comparison is that 10 superwells produce as much energy as six nuclear plants. And this source of energy is here, waiting to be tapped. Many of these superwells could be in operation as early as 1985." Interview with Robert Heffner, "The Resurgence of Natural Gas in Oklahoma," (unpublished translation of an article published in *L'Economie,* January 28, 1980), p. 2.
27. *Fact Book: Synthetic Pipeline Gas from Coal,* American Gas Association, September, 1979.
28. For an in-depth view, see Florencio Acosta, *The Role of Oil in the Mexican Development Plans,* Mexican Embassy, June 12, 1979.
29. *Energy Analysis, Survey of Actual 1979 Oil Offsets and Potential Offsets in the first half of 1980,* American Gas Association, December 21, 1979.
30. George H. Lawrence, *Future Developments in the Natural Gas Industry,* statement before the National Oil and Gas Policy and Regulation Institute, January 22, 1981.

31. Ibid.
32. For an interesting discussion of the vacillation of U.S. nuclear policy, *see* Lawrence Franko, "U.S. Regulation of the Spread of Nuclear Technologies Through Supplier Power: Lever or Boomerang," *Law & Policy in International Business,* 10, (1978), p. 1181.
33. Ibid., p. 1203.
34. Amory B. Lovins, "Energy Strategy: The Road Not Taken?" *Foreign Affairs,* 55 (October, 1976), p. 74.
35. P. W. McCracken, et al., Industry Energy Center, Dow Chemical Co., et al., *Report to NSF* PB 243,824 (Springfield, Va.: Natural Technical Information Service, June, 1975).
36. Ibid.
37. Note 34 above, pp. 65–96.

Chapter 4

1. Gerald M. Meier, *Problems of a World Monetary Order* (New York: Oxford University Press, 1974), pp. 6–7.
2. For further information, *see* Derek H. Aldcraft, *From Versailles to Wall Street: The International Economy in the 1920's* (Berkeley: University of California Press, 1977).
3. Gunnar Myrdal, *An International Economy* (New York: Harper & Brothers, 1956), p. 72.
4. Charles N. Henning, William Pigott, and Robert Haney Scott, *International Financial Management* (McGraw Hill, 1978), p. 87, from Albert C. Whitaker, *Foreign Exchange,* Second Edition (New York: Appleton, 1933), p. 157.
5. For a greater discussion of this subject *see* Harry G. Johnson, "Money, Balance-of-Payments Theory, and the International Monetary Problem," *Essays in International Finance,* No. 124 (Princeton, New Jersey: Princeton University Press, November, 1977); and *see* note 4 above, pp. 14–17.
6. Johnson, note 5 above, p. 15.
7. Article IV, International Monetary Fund Articles of Agreement, 1944.
8. These four principles are effectively summarized by Meier, note 1 above, p. 8, who notes that they are treated in greater detail by W. Scamwell, *International Monetary Policy* (1961), pp. 154–70; Brian Tew, *The Evolution of the International Monetary System, 1945–77,* Halsted (1979), Horsefield, ed., *The International Monetary Fund 1945–65, Vol. II: Analysis* (1969), pp. 454–67.
9. Note 1 above, p. 37.
10. Robert Triffin, *Gold and the Dollar Crisis* (New Haven: Yale University Press, 1960), treated this matter with great foresight and perception.
11. Sidney E. Rolfe and James Burtle, *The Great Wheel: The World Monetary System* (New York: Quadrangle, 1973) p. 86, from U.S. Congress, Joint Economic Committee, *Guidelines for Improving the International Monetary System* (Washington, D.C.: Government Printing Office, 1963).
12. Walter Heller, *New Dimensions of Political Economy—The Godkin Lecture*

at Harvard University (Cambridge, Mass.): Harvard University Press, 1966), pp. 2–3.

13. Richard J. Whalen, "Defending the Dollar—The Crisis of Confusion," *Washington Review of Strategic and International Studies,* 1 (July, 1978), p. 39.
14. Charles A. Coombs, "Treasury and Federal Reserve Foreign Exchange Operations" (16th Joint Interim Report, October, 1968–March, 1969) *Federal Reserve Bulletin,* 55 (Washington, D.C.: Government Printing Office, March, 1969), p. 210.
15. Richard M. Nixon, "Challenge of Peace," speech given August 15, 1971, text in *Washington Post,* p. A14.
16. Charles A. Coombs, "Treasury and Federal Reserve Foreign Exchange Operations," (21st Joint Interim Report, March–September, 1972), *Federal Reserve Bulletin 58* (September, 1972), p. 757.
17. Charles A. Coombs, "Treasury and Federal Reserve Foreign Exchange Operations," (23rd Joint Interim Report, March–July, 1973), *Federal Reserve Bulletin, 59* (September, 1973), p. 623.
18. Ibid.
19. Ibid.
20. Charles A. Coombs, "Treasury and Federal Reserve Foreign Exchange Operations," (24th Joint Interim Report, August, 1973–January, 1974), *Federal Reserve Bulletin,* 60 (March, 1974), p. 192.
21. Charles A. Coombs, "Treasury and Federal Reserve Foreign Exchange Operations," (25th Joint Interim Report, February–July, 1974), *Federal Reserve Bulletin,* 60 (September, 1974), p. 636.
22. Ibid., p. 638.
23. Ibid.
24. Ibid., p. 281.
25. Note 13 above, p. 36.
26. Note 13 above, p. 37.
27. Note 13 above.
28. Note 13 above, p. 38.
29. Art Pine, "U.S. to Intervene in Money Markets; Interest Rates Up," *Washington Post,* November 2, 1978, p. A1.
30. Ibid.
31. Edward M. Bernstein, *EMB* Report #78/180, 1978, p. 2.
32. Jacques R. Artus and Andrew D. Crockett, "Floating Exchange Rates and the Need for Surveillance," *Essays in International Finance,* No. 127 (May, 1978), pp. 1–2.
33. Harry G. Johnson, "We're Going to Have to Live with Bretton Woods, *Money Management* (March/April, 1972), pp. 30–31.
34. Peter Korteweg, "Exchange-Rate Policy, Monetary Policy, and Real Exchange-Rate Variability," *Essays in International Finance,* No. 140 (Princeton, New Jersey: Princeton University Press, December, 1980), p. 5.

Chapter 5

1. Edward J. Frydl, "The Debate over Regulating the Eurocurrency Markets—Federal Reserve Bank of New York," *Quarterly Report* (Winter 1979–80), p. 11.
2. U.S. Congress, House, Committee on Banking, Finance and Urban Affairs, Subcommittee on Domestic Monetary Policy and Subcommittee on International Trade, Investment and Monetary Policy, hearings on *The Eurocurrency Market Control Act of 1979,* 96th Cong., 1st sess., June 26 and 27 and July 12, 1979.
3. Testimony of Henry C. Wallich, Board of Governors of the Federal Reserve System, at hearings referred to in Note 2 above, p. 186.

Chapter 6

1. U.S. Congress, Senate, Committee on Banking, Housing and Urban Affairs, Subcommittee on International Finance, *U.S. Export Policy,* 96th Cong., 1st sess., February, 1979, p. 31.
2. U.S. Congress, House, Committee on Banking, Finance and Urban Affairs, Subcommittee on International Development Institutions and Finance, *Fiscal Year 1980 Prospective, International Financial Institutions' Authorization Request,* 95th Cong., 2nd sess., *hearings* December 7 and 8, 1978, p. 23.
3. Mahbub ul Haq, "The Third World and the International Economic Order, Pamphlet #22, Overseas Development Council, (Washington, D.C., September, 1976), p. 40.
4. *World Bank Annual Report, 1978* (Washington, D.C., 1978), p. 1.
5. Note 2 above, p. 26.
6. U.S. Congress, House, Committee on Banking, Finance and Urban Affairs, Subcommittee on International Development Institutions and Finance, *U.S. Participation in Multilateral Development Institutions,* 95th cong., 2nd sess., *hearings* February 28–May 18, 1978, p. 54.
7. U.S. Congressional Budget Office, *International Financial Institutions: Background and Budget Options for Fiscal Year 1978* (Washington, D.C.: General Printing Office: March, 1977), p. 7.
8. Ibid., p. 8.
9. Ibid., p. 15.
10. Ibid., p. 22.
11. U.S. Congress, House and Senate, *International Financial Institutions, U.S. Participation Increase,* October 3, 1977, PL 95-118, Stat. 1071, Sec. 901.
12. *Congressional Quarterly,* Weekly Report, June 17, 1978, pp. 1532–34.
13. For details *see,* U.S. Congress, House, Committee on Appropriations, *International Financial Institutions,* a report by the Surveys and Investigations Staff, 96th Cong., 1st sess., March, 1979, pp. 143–50.
14. "It's The World Bank, Not the American One," *The Economist* (London), April 22, 1978, pp. 19–20.
15. World Bank, *Summary Procedures of the 1977 Annual Meeting of the Board of Governors* (Washington, D.C., 1977).

16. U.S. Congress, House, Committee on Banking, Finance and Urban Affairs, Subcommittee on International Development Institutions and Finance, *hearings,* 96th Cong., 1st sess., March 21 and April 24, 1979, p. 182.
17. Ibid., p. 465.
18. Lewis James, "Why Clarence Long is Fighting the World Bank," *Euromoney,* (London) April, 1978, p. 62–65.
19. *See,* for example, note 3 above.
20. U.S. Congress, House of Representatives, Committee on Appropriations, Subcommittee on Foreign Operations, 96th Cong., 1st sess., hearings, "Foreign Assistance and Related Programs," March 27, 1979, p. 373.
21. Ibid.
22. Ibid.
23. Richard Barovick, "Development Banks: Contract Strategy," *Business America,* April 23, 1979, pp. 10–12.
24. E. Friedman and R. Goodman, "Prospects for Oil and Gas Production in the Developing World," *Finance and Development,* June, 1979, pp. 7–10.
25. Ibid., p. 9.
26. Ibid.
27. "A Program to Accelerate Petroleum Production in the Developing Countries," Memorandum of President Robert S. McNamara of the International Bank for Reconstruction and Development, dated November 30, 1978.
28. For an excellent analysis of the role of the IMF, *see,* U.S. Congress, Senate, Committee on Banking, Housing and Urban Affairs, Subcommittee on International Finance, Statement of Anthony M. Solomon, president of the Federal Reserve Bank of New York, 95th Cong., 2nd sess., April 15, 1978. Solomon discusses, in detail, quotas and the effect of the 1979 OPEC price increases on LDC needs for IMF assistance.
29. "Lending for 'Structural Adjustment'," Memorandum of President Robert S. McNamara of the International Bank for Reconstruction and Development, dated February 5, 1980.

Chapter 7

1. "The Rise in Protectionism," Pamphlet #24, International Monetary Fund (Washington, D.C., 1978), p. 1.
2. U.S. Tariff Commission, study on *Trade Barriers,* vol. 1 (General Printing Office, Washinton, D.C., 1974), p. 10.
3. Ibid., vol. 4, p. 1.
4. Article XI;1 of the GATT, as contained in Gerald M. Meier, *Problems of Trade Policy* (New York: Oxford University Press, 1973), p. 95.
5. Ibid., Articles XII:2, XVIII:9, p. 95.
6. Ibid., Article XVIII:9, p. 95.
7. Ibid., Article XI:2, p. 95.
8. U.S. Tariff Commission, study on *Trade Barriers,* vol. 4, p. 10.
9. Ibid., vol. 1 pp. 11–12.
10. Ibid., p. 12.
11. Ibid., p. 12.

12. Ibid., p. 15.
13. Ibid., vol. 5, p. 37.
14. Ibid., p. 37.
15. Ibid., p. 40.
16. Ibid., p. 101.
17. Ibid., p. 101.
18. Ibid., vol. 1, p. 18.
19. Ibid. p. 18.
20. Ibid., p. 18.
21. Ibid., pp. 18–19.
22. Ibid., vol. 4., p. 70.
23. Ibid., vol. 1, p. 19.
24. Ibid., vol. 6, p. 179.
25. Ibid., vol. 1, p. 20.
26. Ibid., p. 20.
27. Department of Commerce, *Business America,* April 23, 1979, p. 3.
28. Ibid., p. 5.
29. Ibid., p. 6.
30. Ibid., p. 6.

Chapter 8

1. World Bank, *World Development Report* (Washington, D.C., August, 1980), p. 112.
2. Martin C. Needler, *Politics and Society in Mexico* (Albuquerque: University of New Mexico Press; 1971), pp. 106–10.
3. *African Research Bulletin,* August 15–September 14, 1980, p. 6544.
4. *Financial Times* (London), September 30, 1980, p. XLII, M.L.
5. *Financial Times,* September 29, 1980, p. XVII, I.R.
6. Alex Rondos, *West Africa,* October 13, 1980.
7. Note 1 above.
8. William G. Tyler, *Advanced Developing Countries as Export Competitors in Third World Markets: The Brazilian Experience* (Washington, D.C.: The Center for Strategic and International Studies, Georgetown University, June, 1980), p. 19.
9. Ibid., p. 49.
10. Ibid., p. 51.
11. "Korea—The Miracle on the Han River," supplement, *Euromoney* (London) April, 1977.
12. K. T. Li, *The Experience of Dynamic Economic Growth on Taiwan* (Taiwan: Mei Ya Publications, Inc., 1976), p. 234.
13. Note 1 above, p. 154.
14. Note 12 above, pp. 447–48.

Chapter 9

1. Zygmunt Nagorski, Jr., *The Psychology of East-West Trade* (New York: Mason & Lipscomb, 1974), pp. xvii–xxv.
2. George F. Keenan, "East-West Trade," in *American Foreign Economic Policy,* Benjamin J. Cohen, ed. (New York: Harper and Row, 1968), pp. 290–92.
3. Note 2 above, Jay H. Cert, "We Should Do More Business with The Communists," p. 306.
4. "Doing Business with the USSR," *Business International* Research Report 71–2 (Geneva, Switzerland: Business International S.A., November, 1971), pp. 11–13.
5. U.S. Department of State, *Foreign Economic Trends and Their Implications for the United States, U.S.S.R.* (Washington, D.C.: Government Printing Office, February, 1979), p. 4.
6. Ibid., p. 2.
7. *Commerce America,* July 31, 1978, p. 22.
8. Note 5 above, p. 4.
9. Ibid.
10. Mark E. Miller, "The Role of Western Technology in Soviet Strategy," *ORBIS,* 22 (Fall, 1978), p. 545.
11. *Business Week,* November 3, 1980, p. 45.
12. Note 10 above.
13. Note 10 above, p. 547, n. 31.
14. David K. Shipler, "The Soviet Bloc: Dependence and Independence," Part 1, "Western Influence Growing in East Europe," *The New York Times,* May 14, 1979, pp. A1, A12.
15. Irene Lange and James S. Elliot, "U.S. Role in East-West Trade," *Journal of International Business Studies,* 8 (Fall/Winter 1977), p. 7.
16. Radoslav Selucky, "East-West Economic Relations: The Eastern European Policy Perspective," in *Changing Perspectives in East-West Commerce,* Carl H. McMillan, ed. (Lexington, Mass: Lexington Books, 1974), p. 7.
17. U.S. Department of State, as released by the Department of Commerce, *Foreign Economic Trends and Their Implications for the United States: Yugoslavia* (Washington, D.C.: Government Printing Office, August, 1978), p. 5.
18. *The Economist* (London), January 31, 1981, pp. 61–2.
19. Note 1 above, p. 87.
20. Note 1 above, p. 87.
21. The Conference Board, "East-West Trade, The Lessons from Experience" (New York: 1971), p. 22.
22. Mordechai E. Kreinim, *International Economics, A Policy Approach* (New York: Harcourt, Brace, Jovanovich, 1975), p. 369.
23. *Eastwest Markets,* September 20, 1976, pp. 8–69.
24. Richard Portes, "East Europe's Debt to the West: Interdependence is a Two-Way Street," Foreign Affairs, 55 (July, 1977), p. 752.
25. *Business Week,* December 16, 1981, p. 66; The Commerce Department, International Trade Administration, prepares summaries of trade statistics un-

der the caption *U.S. Trade Status with Communist Countries.* It also provides information on CMEA hard-currency debt levels. *See,* ITA East-West Trade Policy Staff Papers dated September 18, 1979; January, 1980; July, 1980; July 7, 1980; September, 1980.

26. U.S. Congress, Joint Economic Committee, Joan Parpart Zoeter, "East Europe: The Growing Hard Currency Debt in East Europe," in *East European Economics Post Helsinki,* vol. 1, 95th Cong., 2nd sess., p. 1352.
27. U.S. Department of Commerce, *Trading with the USSR* (Washington, D.C.: Government Printing Office, July, 1977), p. 7.
28. U.S. Department of State, *Soviets Reject Trade Agreement,* Press Conference (Washington, D.C.: Government Printing Office, January 14, 1975), p. 1.
29. P.L. 93–618, 88 Stat. 1978 (January 3, 1975).
30. Ibid., Title IV, Subsection (c).
31. The Atlantic Council Committee on East-West Trade, *East-West Trade: Managing Encounter and Accommodation* (Boulder: Westview Press, 1977), pp. 103–4.
32. Note 4 above, p. 41.
33. U.S. Congress, House and Senate, *Export Control Act of 1949,* February 26, 1949, P.L. 86–111, Stat, 548, et equ., (1965).
34. U.S. Congress, House and Senate, *Export Administration Act of 1969,* P.L. 91–184.
35. James Henry Giffen, *The Legal and Practical Aspects of Trade with the Soviet Union* (New York: Praeger, 1971), pp. 36–37.
36. Johnathan B. Bingham and Victor C. Johnson, "A Rational Approach to Export Controls," *Foreign Affairs,* 57 (Spring, 1979), p. 905.
37. Ibid.
38. Herbert E. Meyer, "Helping the Soviet Union to Avoid an Energy Crisis," *Fortune,* January 29, 1979, pp. 90–95. Mr. Meyer points out that various short-term Soviet solutions to aid production, such as early water injection, have cut drastically into the USSR's ability to substantially increase oil production.
39. David K. Shipler, "The Soviet Bloc: Dependence and Independence," Part 3, "In Soviet Bloc, Economics is Key to Unity," *The New York Times,* May 16, 1979, pp. A1, A11.
40. Note 38 above, p. 93.
41. Note 26 above, Carl H. McMillan, "East-West Industrial Cooperation," in *East European Economics Post-Helsinki,* p. 1265.
42. Note 5 above, p. 9.
43. Note 26 above, Pompillur Verzariu and Jay Burgess, "The Development of Joint Economic and Industrial Cooperation in East-West Trade," in *East European Economics Post-Helsinki,* pp. 1225–42.
44. Note 26 above, Matheson, McCarthy and Flanders, "Countertrade Practices in Eastern Europe," in *East European Economics Post-Helsinki,* p. 1278.
45. Nasrollah S. Fatemi, Gail W. Williams, and Thibaut de Saint Phalle, *Multinational Corporations* (New York: A. S. Barnes and Company, 1975), p. 244.
46. Note 21 above, p. 31.

47. Daniel Yergin, in a 1977 article in *Foreign Affairs,* concluded: "For it would have to be a bold Western firm that would want to commit itself to take the manufactured products of a Soviet enterprise for sale on the world market over a period of years—given the questions about quality control, flexibility and responsiveness to changing demands," "Politics and Soviet Trade," 55 (April, 1977), p. 537.
48. *Commerce America,* June 19, 1978, p. 3.
49. Ibid., p. 4.
50. Ibid.
51. *The Socialist Federal Republic of Yugoslavia* (Belgrade: The Federal Committee for Information, 1976), p. 51.
52. Ibid., p. 50.
53. Note 26 above, Laura D'Andrea-Tyson, "The Yugoslav Economy in the 1970's: A Survey of Recent Developments and Future Prospects," in *East European Economics Post-Helsinki,* p. 942.
54. Note 17 above, p. 4.
55. U.S. Department of State, *Background Notes, Yugoslavia* (Washington, D.C.: Government Printing Office, February, 1978), p. 6.
56. Note 17 above, p. 5.
57. Richard H. Solomon, "Thinking through the China Problem," *Foreign Affairs,* 56 (January 19, 1981), p. 39.
58. *Business Week,* January 19, 1981, p. 39.
59. Kenneth Lieberthal, "A Second Revolution," *Fortune,* October 23, 1978, p. 100.
60. Kenneth Lieberthal, *Chinese Politics in 1978; Modernization and the Ghost of Mao* (New York: China Council of the Asia Society, November 30, 1978), p. 7.
61. *The China Business Review,* 6 (March–April, 1979), p. 4.
62. Note 60 above, p. 4.
63. U.S. Congress, Joint Economic Committee, Martha Avery and William Clarke, "The Sino-American Commercial Relationship" in *Chinese Economy Post-Mao,* Joint Economic Committee Report, vol. 1, 95th Cong., 2nd sess. November, 1978, p. 7481.
64. Howard Turk, *Memorandum: People's Republic of China,* Export-Import Bank of the United States (Washington, D.C., January 15, 1979), p. 1.
65. Note 63 above, Robert F. Dernberger and David Fasenfest, "China's Post-Mao Economic Future," in *Chinese Economy Post-Mao,* p. 10.
66. *Business Week,* January 19, 1981, p. 43.
67. *Business Week,* June 4, 1979, p. 80.
68. *Industry Week,* January 8, 1979, p. 17.
69. *The Economist,* April 7, 1979, p. 112.
70. U.S. Department of Commerce, International Trade Administration, *Doing Business with China* (Washington, D.C.: Government Printing Office, 1980), p. 14.
71. Randall H. Hardy, *China's Oil Future: A Case of Modest Expectations* (Boulder: Westview Press, 1978), p. xvi.
72. Note 63 above, Nai-Ruenn Chen, "Economic Modernization in Post-Mao

China: Policies, Problems, and Prospects," in *Chinese Economy Post-Mao,* p. 190.

Chapter 10

1. Mark Perlman, "One Man's Baedeker to Productivity Growth Discussions," *Contemporary Economic Problems,* (Washington, D.C.: American Enterprise Institute, 1979), p. 82.
2. U.S. Congress, House and Senate, Joint Economic Committee, *Hearings* on Productivity, 96th Cong., 1st sess., June 5 and 6, 1979.
3. *Business Week,* August 13, 1979, p. 54–9.
4. Leonard Silk, "Seekings Ways The U.S. Can Spur Research by Industry," *The New York Times,* March 30, 1978, p. D5.
5. Dan Morgan, "French Radial Tires: Case History of Technology," *Washington Post,* March 9, 1979, p. A18.
6. U.S. Congress, House, Committee on Foreign Affairs, Subcommittee on International Policy and Trade, *U.S. International Competitiveness: The Aerospace Industry,* Testimony of Dr. Stephen Piper, Office of the U.S. Trade Representative, 97th Cong., 1st Sess., March 19, 1981.
7. "Robots Change The Rules," *The Economist* (London), April 19, 1980, pp. 93–4.
8. Speech by Joseph D. Williams, President of Warner-Lambert Co., at National Wholesale Druggists' Association, Honolulu, Hawaii, December 21, 1979, regarding Productivity Council for the health care industry.
9. Jack Behrman and Raymond Mikesell, "The Impact of U.S. Foreign Direct Investment on U.S. Export Competitiveness in Third World Markets," *Significant Issues Series,* Vol. 2, No. 1 (Washington, D.C.: Center for Strategic and International Studies, Georgetown University, 1980).
10. Don Ediger, "A Threat to the U.S. Lead in Atomic Power," *Business Week,* August 27, 1979, p. 58.
11. For a carefully reasoned article on the inconsistencies of the U.S. government's position over the years on nuclear energy, *see* Dr. Lawrence Franko, "U.S. Regulation of the Spread of Nuclear Technologies Through Supplier Power: Lever or Boomerang?" *Law and Policy in International Business* 10, 1978, pp. 1181–1204.
12. For an interesting discussion of competition among countries for contracts in the Middle East, *see* "U.S. 'Arrogance' Costs Firms Billions in Lost Jobs," *Engineering News Record,* November 29, 1979, pp. 26–37.
13. Ibid., p. 29.
14. Norman B. Ture and Kenneth B. Sanden, "The Effects of Tax Policy on Capital Formation," (New York: Financial Executive Research Foundation, 1977), p. 71.
15. Ibid.
16. The effect is analyzed in Robert E. Murry, "Productivity Problems in Western Surface Coal Mining," *Mining Congress Journal* August 1980, p. 43–48.
17. For additional discussion of regulatory disincentives, *see* Robert A. Flemmang, "U.S. Programs That Impede U.S. Export Competitiveness: The Reg-

ulatory Environment," *Significant Issues Series,* Vol II, No. 3 (Washington, D.C.: Center for Strategic and International Studies, Georgetown University, 1980).

18. Competitiveness Report to The Congress filed by the Export-Import Bank of the United States, January 1980. *Congressional Record,* House of Representatives, April 15, 1980, H-2523–2525.
19. Ibid.
20. 1976 Tax Reform Act PL 94–455 stat 1520; 1977 Amendment to the Export-Import Bank Act of 1945 PL 95–143 stat 1210; 1890 Sherman Act. sec 17.
21. Note 10 above.
22. A full discussion of the tax incentive to export question is contained in Thibaut de Saint Phalle, "The Masochism of American Trade: GATT and the Tokyo Round," *The Washington Quarterly,* 2 (Summer, 1979), pp. 23–33.
23. Steven Rattner, "Productivity Lag Causes Worry," *The New York Times,* May 8, 1979, p. D1.
24. Humphrey-Hawkins Full Employment and Balanced Growth Act of 1978.
25. "Paris Bourse is Booming, As Tax Rebate Pushed French Bourgeoisie to Buy Stocks," *The Wall Street Journal,* June 4, 1980, p. 18.
26. An interesting discussion is found in Peter Behr, "Automotive Primer: A Tale of Two Cities," *Washington Post,* June 1, 1980, p. F1, F6.
27. Jorgenson and Nishimizu, *U.S. and Japanese Economic Growth, 1952–1974,* p. 724. Also, Ezra F. Vogel, author of *Japan as Number One,* speech at Harvard Conference on Productivity, April 1980: "The United States is in the process of being surpassed by Japan as a modern industrial power, and this creates serious consequences America is not confronting . . . Unless we put our house in order, our problems aggregated together could not only lead to a lower standard of living, but to a divided America, as each group changes etc.
28. Harry G. Johnson, "Keynes and British Economics," in *Essays on John Maynard Keynes* (Cambridge, England: Cambridge University Press, 1975), p. 122.

Conclusions

1. *Bank Credit Analyst,* Vol. 19, No. 7, April 1981, pp. 6–7.

Bibliography

Bibliography, Chapter 1

Books

Barnet, Richard J. and Ronald E. Muller. *Global Reach, The Power of the Multinational Corporations.* New York: 1974.

Bergsten, C. Fred, Thomas Horst and Theodore H. Moran. *American Multinationals and American Interests.* Washington, D.C., 1978.

Fatemi, Nasrollah S., Thibaut de Saint Phalle and Grace M. Keeffe. *The Dollar Crisis.* Rutherford, New Jersey: 1963.

Fellner, William, Fritz Machlup, Robert Triffin, et al. *Maintaining and Restoring Balance in International Payments.* Princeton: 1966.

Gilpin, Robert. *U.S. Power and the Multinational Corporation.* New York: 1975.

Haberler, Gottfried. *Money in the International Economy, A Study in Balance-of-Payments Adjustment, International Liquidity, and Exchange Rates.* Cambridge: 1965.

Haberler, Gottfried and Thomas D. Willett. *A Strategy for U.S. Balance of Payments Policy.* Washington, D.C., 1971.

Haberler, Gottfried and Thomas D. Willett. *U.S. Balance of Payments Policy and the International Monetary System.* Washington, D.C., 1973.

Kahn, Herman. *World Economic Development 1979 and Beyond.* Boulder: 1979.

International Monetary Fund. *The Monetary Approach to the Balance of Payments.* Washington, D.C., 1977.

Organization for Economic Cooperation and Development. *Balances of Payment of OECD Countries 1960–1977.* Paris: January, 1979.

The World Bank. *World Development Report, 1980.* Washington, D.C., August, 1980.

Magazines

"The LDCs' Big New Role in The Dollar's Future." *Business Week.* May 5, 1980.

Zombanakis, Minos A. "How to Handle the Payments Deficits." *Business Week.* April 7, 1980.

Journals

Booper, Peter and John Norton. "Summary Measures of the Dollar's Foreign Exchange Value." *Federal Reserve Bulletin* 64. October, 1978.

Clarke, Stephen V. O. "Perspective on the United States External Position Since World War II." Federal Reserve Bank of New York, *Quarterly Review* 5. Summer, 1980.

Fieleke, Norman S. "What is the Balance of Payments?" Federal Reserve Bank of Boston, *New England Economic Review*. July, 1976.

Miles, Marc A. "The Effects of Devaluation on the Trade Balance and the Balance of Payments: Some New Results." *Journal of Political Economy* 87. June, 1979.

Salop, Joanne and Erich Spitaller. "Why Does the Current Account Matter?" *IMF Staff Papers* 27. March, 1980.

Monographs

Aliber, Robert J. "Choices for the Dollar (Costs and Benefits of Possible Approaches to the Balance-of-Payments Problem)." *National Planning Association Pamphlet* No. 127. Washington, D.C. May, 1969.

Allen, Polly R. and Peter B. Kenen. "Balance of Payments, Exchange Rates, and Economic Policy." *Essays in International Finance* No. 19. Princeton: April, 1979.

Behrman, Jack N. and Raymond F. Mikesell. "The Impact of U.S. Foreign Direct Investment on U.S. Export Competitiveness in Third World Markets." Georgetown University Center for Strategic and International Studies *Significant Issues Series II*. Washington, D.C., 1980.

Behrman, Jack N. and Raymond F. Mikesell. "Some Patterns in the Rise of the Multinational Enterprise." University of North Carolina *Research Paper* No. 19. Chapel Hill: March, 1969.

Dunn, Robert M., Jr. "Exchange Rates, Payments Adjustment and OPEC: Why Oil Deficits Persist." *Essays in International Finance* No. 137. Princeton: December, 1979.

Stern, Robert M., Charles F. Schwartz, Robert Triffin and Edward M. Bernstein. "The Presentation of the U.S. Balance of Payments: A Symposium." *Essays in International Finance*. No. 123. Princeton: August, 1977.

Stobaugh, Robert B., Piero Telesio and Jose de la Torre. "The Effect of U.S. Foreign Direct Investment in Manufacturing on the U.S. Balance of Payments, U.S. Employment and Changes in Skill Composition of Employment." Center for Multinational Studies, *Occasional Paper* No. 4. Washington, D.C., 1973.

Triffin, Robert. "Balance of Payments and the Foreign Investment Position of the United States." *Essays in International Finance* No. 55. Princeton: 1966.

Triffin, Robert, Charles F. Schwartz, Robert M. Stern, Edward M. Berstein and Walter Ledered. "The Presentation of the U.S. Balance of Payments: A Symposium." *Essays in International Finance* No. 123. Princeton: August, 1977.

Business Publications

Business International Corporation. *The Effects of U.S. Corporate Foreign Investment 1960–1972*. New York: January, 1974.

Polk, Judd, Irene W. Meister and Lawrence A. Veit. *U.S. Production Abroad and the Balance of Payments: A Survey of Corporate Investment Experience.* National Industrial Conference Board Special Study. New York: 1966.

Unpublished

Haberler, Gottfried and Fritz Machlup, et al. "International Payments Problems." A Symposium Sponsored by the American Enterprise Institute. Washington, D.C., September 23 and 24, 1965.

Bibliography, Chapter 2

Books

Heck, Harold J. *International Trade.* New York: 1972.

National Association of Manufacturers. *U.S. Stake in World Trade and Investment, The Role of the Multinational Corporation.* New York: 1973.

Weil, Gordon L. *American Trade Policy: A New Round.* New York: 1975.

Journals

Aharoni, Yair. "The State Owned Enterprise as a Competitor in International Markets." *The Colombia Journal of World Business* 15. Spring 1980.

Cook, Gary M. and Robert F. Williamson Jr. "Improving U.S. Policymaking in International Trade." *The Colombia Journal of World Business* 14. Spring 1979.

Magazines

"Closing the Trade Gap Could Take Ten Years." *Fortune.* July 14, 1980.

Bibliography, Chapter 3

Books

Askin, A. Bradley. *How Energy Affects the Economy.* Lexington: 1978.

International Energy Agency. *Energy Conservation in Industry in IEA Countries.* Paris: September, 1979.

Lilienthal, David E. *Atomic Energy: A New Start.* New York: 1980.

Mangone, Gerald J. ed. *Energy Policies of the World.* New York: 1977.

Massachusetts Institute of Technology. *Coal, Bridge to the Future.* Boston: 1979.

Organization for Economic Cooperation and Development. *Energy Prospects to 1985.* (Report by the Secretary General) Paris: 1974.

Research and Policy Committee of the Committee for Economic Development. *International Economic Consequences of High-Priced Energy.* Washington, D.C., September, 1975.

Research and Policy Committee of the Committee for Economic Development. *Helping Insure Our Energy Future—A Program for Developing Synthetic Fuel Plants Now.* Washington, D.C. July, 1979.

Stobaugh, Robert and Daniel Yergin, eds. *Energy Future.* New York: 1979.

The World Bank. *Energy in Developing Countries.* Washington, D.C., August, 1980.

van der Linde, Peter and Naomi A. Hintze. *Time Bomb—LNG: The Truth About Our Newest and Most Dangerous Energy Source.* New York: 1978.

Magazines

Cameron, Juan. "Washington's Ill-Starred Efforts to Stash Crude." *Fortune*. September 8, 1980.

Holt, Donald D. "How Amoco Finds All That Oil." *Fortune*. September 8, 1980.

Nulty, Peter. "The Tortuous Road to Synfuels." *Fortune*. September 8, 1980.

"Oil Greases the Skids of the World Economy." *Fortune*. August 11, 1980.

Uttal, Bro. "Life is Getting Scary in the Oil Markets." *Fortune*. January 28, 1980.

Velocci, Tony. "Energy: Elusive Solutions." *Nation's Business*. August, 1980.

Velocci, Tony. "How Bright is Sunpower's Future?" *Nation's Business*. November, 1980.

Journals

Benard, Andre. "World Oil and Cold Reality." *Harvard Business Review* 58. November/December 1980.

Dovring, Folke. "Export or Burn? American Grain and the Energy Equations." *Illinois Business Review* 37. May 1980.

Dovring, Folke. "Transportation Fuels Inflation." *Illinois Business Review* 38. February, 1981.

Fieleke, Norman S. "Trade with the Oil-Exporters: A Five-Year Perspective." *New England Economic Review*. July/August 1979.

Galli, Anton. "The Foreign Trade of the OPEC States." *Intereconomics* 14. November/December 1979.

International Energy Agency. *Annual Report on Energy Research, Development and Demonstration—Activities of the IEA 1979–1980*. Paris: 1980.

International Energy Agency. "Energy Policies and Programmes of the IEA Countries." *1979 Review of National Programs*. Paris: 1980.

International Energy Agency. "Energy Research, Development and Demonstration in the IEA Countries." *1979 Review of National Programs*. Paris: 1980.

International Energy Agency. "Outlook for the Eighties." *Summary of 1979 Review of Energy Policies and Programmes of IEA Countries*. Paris: 1980.

Levy, Walter J. "Oil and the Decline of the West." *Foreign Affairs* 58. Summer 1980.

Mohnfeld, Jochen H. "Changing Patterns of Trade." *Petroleum Economist* XLVII. August, 1980.

Mohnfeld, Jochen H. "Structural Changes in World Crude Oil Trade." *Intereconomics* 15. January/February 1980.

Nye, Joseph S., Jr. "Energy Nightmares." *Foreign Policy* 40. Fall 1980.

Oethme, Wolfgang. "Energy for the Future." *Intereconomics* 15. September/October 1980.

Scott, Bruce R. "OPEC, The American Scapegoat." *Harvard Business Review* 59. January/February 1981.

Segal, Jeffrey. "World Natural Gas Survey." *Petroleum Economist* XLVII. August, 1980.

Stock, Francine. "Alternative Energy—Power From the Sea." *Petroleum Economist* XLVII. August, 1980.

Business Publications

Exxon Corporation. *World Energy Outlook*. December, 1979.

Exxon Corporation. "Synthetic Fuels: The Processes, Problems and Potential." *The Lamp*. Summer 1980.

Exxon Corporation. *Energy Outlook—1980–2000*. December, 1979.

U.S. Government Documents & Publications

Cooper, Richard N. "Energy in a Global Perspective: Putting to Rest Three Myths." *Department of State Bulletin* 80. Washington, D.C. July, 1980.

Department of Energy. Office of International Affairs. *The Role of Foreign Governments in the Energy Industries*. Washington, D.C. October, 1977.

U.S. Congress. House. Committee on Science and Technology. Subcommittee on Investigations and Oversight and the Subcommittee on Science Research and Technology. *U.S./Mexico Relations and Potentials Regarding Energy, Immigration, Scientific Cooperation and Technology Transfer*. Washington, D.C., 96th Congress, 1st Session. July, 1979.

Bibliography, Chapter 4

Books

Cline, W. R. *International Monetary Reform and the Developing Countries*. Washington, D.C., 1978.

Corden, W. M. *Inflation, Exchange Rates and the World Economy*. Oxford: 1977.

Corden, W. M. *Trade Policy and Economic Welfare*. Oxford: 1977.

Danbusch, Rudrzir and Stanley Fisher. *Macroeconomics*. New York: 1977.

Haberler, Gottfried, Jacob Dreyer and Thomas D. Willett, eds. *Flexible Exchange Rates and the International Monetary System*. Washington, D.C. 1978.

Heller, Walter. *New Dimensions of Political Economy*. Cambridge: 1966.

Helpman, Elhaman and Assaf Razin. *A Theory of International Trade Under Uncertainty*. New York: 1978.

Holbik, Karel ed. *Monetary Policy in Twelve Industrial Countries*. Boston: 1973.

Laffer, Arthur B. "The Phenomenon of World-Wide Inflation." in American Enterprise Institute, *The Phenomenon of World-Wide Inflation*. Washington, D.C., 1975.

Meade, James E. *The Balance of Payments*. London: 1951.

Solomon, Robert. *The International Monetary System, 1945–1976*. New York: 1977.

The World Bank. *Prospects for Developing Countries 1978–1985*. Washington, D.C., 1977.

Triffin, Robert. *Gold and the Dollar Crisis*. New Haven: 1960.

Triffin, Robert. *The World Money Maze*. New Haven: 1966.

Trezise, Philip H. ed. *The European Monetary System: Its Promise and Prospects*. Washington, D.C., April, 1979.

Williamson, John H. *The Failure of World Monetary Reform, 1971–4*.

Magazines

Davenport, John A. "A Testing Time for Monetarism." *Fortune*. October 6, 1980.

Hilliard, Brian. "The Fed Comes Close to Success in Controlling the Money Supply." *Euromoney* 12. December, 1980.

Whalen, Richard J. "Negotiable Instruments." *Harper's* 260. March 1980.

Journals

Balbach, Anatol B. and David H. Resler. "Eurodollars and the U.S. Money Supply." Federal Reserve Bank of St. Louis *Review* 62. June/July 1980.

Bazdavich, Michael. "Money, Inflation and Causality in the United States 1959–79." Federal Reserve Bank of San Francisco *Economic Review*. Spring 1980.

Bhaqwat, Avinash. "International Monetary Stability—Challenges and Response." *Finance and Development* 17. December, 1980.

Blackhurst, Richard and Jan Tumlir. "International Trade is a System of Floating Exchange Rates." *Intereconomics* 15. December, 1980.

Board of Governors, Federal Reserve System. "Monetary Policy Report to Congress." *Federal Reserve Bulletin* 66. July, 1980.

Bond, Marion. "Exchange Rates, Inflation and the Vicious Circle." *Finance & Development* 17. March, 1980.

Cheng, Hang-Shen. "Exchange Rate Policies and Inflation: Theory and Evidence." Federal Reserve Bank of San Francisco *Economic Review*. Fall 1979.

Eastburn, David P. "Current Monetary Dilemmas: How Effective is Orthodoxy in an Unorthodox World?" Federal Reserve Bank of Philadelphia *Business Review*. November/December 1979.

Greenwald, Carol S. "Tight Money Won't Work." *Harvard Business Review* 58. March/April 1980.

Guffey, Roger. "Conduct of U.S. Monetary Policy: Recent Problems and Issues." Federal Reserve Bank of Kansas City *Economic Review*. December, 1979.

Joshi, V. R. "Exchange Rates, International Liquidity and Economic Development." *The World Economy* 2. May, 1979.

Judd, John P. and John L. Scadding. "Conducting Effective Monetary Policy: The Role of Operating Investments." Federal Reserve Bank of San Francisco *Economic Review*. Fall 1979.

Keran, Michael and Stephen Zeldes. "Effects of Monetary Disturbances on Exchange Rates, Inflation and Interest Rates." Federal Reserve Bank of San Francisco *Economic Review*. Spring, 1980.

Mayer, Martin. "U.S. Must Assume Responsibility for the Monetary System." *Financier* IV, June, 1980.

"Monetary Policy and Open Market Operations in 1979." Federal Reserve Bank of New York *Quarterly Review* 5. Summer, 1980.

Pigott, Charles. "Expectations, Money, and the Forecasting of Inflation." Federal Reserve Bank of San Francisco *Economic Review*. Spring, 1980.

Poole, William. "Current Issues in Monetary Control." Federal Reserve Bank of Richmond *Economic Review* 66. July/August, 1980.

Prakken, Joel L. "The Exchange Rate and Domestic Inflation." Federal Reserve Bank of New York *Quarterly Review* 4. Summer, 1979.

The Atlantic Council. "International Monetary System in Transition." *The Atlantic Community Quarterly* 18. Fall, 1980.

Volcker, Paul A. "Recent Developments in Monetary Policy." *Federal Reserve Bulletin* 66. December, 1980.

Wallich, Henry C. "The World Monetary System After Postponement of the Substitution Account." *Intereconomics* 15. July/August, 1980.

Whalen, Richard J. "Defending the Dollar—The Crisis of Confusion." *Washington Review of Strategic and International Studies* 1. July, 1978.

Withroop, Adrian. "Managed Floating and the Independence of Interest Rates." Federal Reserve Bank of San Francisco *Economic Review*. Summer, 1980.

Monographs

Artus, Jacques R. and Andrew D. Crockett. "Floating Exchange Rates and the Need for Surveillance." *Essays in International Finance* No. 127. Princeton: May, 1978.

Chrystal, K. Alec. "International Money and the Future of the SDR." *Essays in International Finance,* No. 128. Princeton: June, 1978.

de Vries, Tom, "On the Meaning and Future of the European Monetary System." *Essays in International Finance* No. 138. Princeton: Sept. 1980.

Dunn, Robert M., Jr. "Exchange Rates, Payments Adjustment, and OPEC: Why Oil Deficits Persist." *Essays in International Finance* No. 137. Princeton: December: 1979.

Emminger, Otmar. "The D-Mark in the Conflict Between Internal and External Equilibrium, 1948–75." *Essays in International Finance* No. 122. Princeton: June, 1977.

Johnson, Harry G. "Money, Balance-of-Payments-Theory and the International Monetary Problem." *Essays in International Finance.* No. 124. Princeton: November, 1977.

Kindleberger, Charles P. "Government and International Trade." *Essays in International Finance* No. 129. Princeton: July, 1978.

Lal, Deepak. "A Liberal International Economic Order: The International Monetary System and Economic Development." *Essays in International Finance* No. 139. Princeton: October, 1980.

Machlup, Fritz. "Plans for Reform of the International Monetary System." *Special Papers in International Finance* No. 3. Princeton: 1964.

Organization for Economic Cooperation and Development. "Monetary Targets and Inflation Control." *OECD Monetary Studies Series.* 1979.

The Atlantic Council. "The Floating Rate System—The Search for Balance and Stability." The Atlantic Council *Policy Papers.* September, 1978.

Tosini, Paula A. "Leaning Against the Wind: A Standard for Managed Floating." *Essays in International Finance* No. 126. Princeton: December, 1977.

Triffin, Robert. "The Evolution of the International Monetary System: Historical Reappraisal and Future Perspectives." *Princeton Studies in International Finance* No. 12. Princeton: 1964.

Whitman, Marina v. N. "Sustaining the International Economic System: Issues for U.S. Policy." *Essays in International Finance* No. 121. Princeton: June, 1977.

Bibliography, Chapter 5

Books

Aliber, Robert Z. *Exchange Risk and Corporate International Finance.* New York: 1978.

Bell, Geoffrey. *The Eurodollar Market and the International Financial System.* New York: 1973.

Chase Manhattan Bank. *Euro-Dollar Financing, A Guide for Multinational Companies.* New York: 1974.

Dreyer, Jacob S., Gottfried Harberler and Thomas D. Willett (eds.). *Exchange Rate Flexibility.* Washington, D.C., 1978.

Einzig, Paul. *The Euro-Dollar System: Practice and Theory of International Interest Rates.* London: 1973.

Fatemi, Nasrollah S., Thibaut de Saint Phalle and Grace M. Keefe. *The Dollar Crisis.* Rutherford, N.J.: 1963.

Friedrich, Klaus. *The Eurodollar System.* New York: 1968.

Katz, Samuel I. (ed.). *U.S.-European Monetary Relations.* Washington, D.C., 1979.

Levich, Richard M. and Charles G. Whilborg (eds.). *Exchange Risk and Exposure: Current Developments in International Financial Management.* Lexington: 1980.

Little, Jane Sneddon. *Euro-Dollars: The Money Market Gypsies.* New York: 1975.

McKinnon, Ronald I. *Money in International Exchange.* New York: 1979.

Prochnow, Herbert V. (ed.). *The Eurodollar.* Madison: 1970.

Stem, Carl H., John H. Makin and Denis E. Logue. *Eurocurrencies and the International Monetary System.* Washington, D.C. 1976.

Magazines

Coussement, Andre M. "Why the Bond Market Should Open Up for Developing Countries." *Euromoney.* August, 1980.

Meadows, Edward. "How the Euromarket Fends Off Global Financial Disaster." *Fortune* 100. September 24, 1979.

"Newcomers Rush to the Euromarket Loophole." *Business Week.* April 28, 1980.

Journals

"Arabs Intend to By-Pass the Eurocurrency Markets." *International Currency Review* 12. March/April 1980.

Friedman, Milton. "The Eurodollar Market: Some First Principles." *Morgan Guaranty Survey.* October, 1969.

Frydl, Edward J. "The Debate Over Regulating the Eurocurrency Markets." Federal Reserve of New York, *Quarterly Review* 4. Winter 79/80.

Giddy, Ian H. "Measuring the World Foreign Exchange Market." *The Columbia Journal of World Business* XIV. Winter, 1979.

Klopstock, Fred H. "Money Creation in the Euro-Dollar Market—A Note on Professor Friedman's Views." Federal Reserve Bank of New York, *Monthly Review* 52. January, 1970.

Kvasnika, Joseph C. "Eurodollars—An Important Source of Funds for American Banks." Federal Reserve Bank of Chicago, *Business Conditions.* June, 1969.

Little, Jane Sneddon. "The Euro-Dollar Market: Its Nature and Impact." *New England Economic Review.* May/June 1969.

Little, Jane Sneddon. "The Impact of the Eurodollar Market on the Effectiveness of Monetary Policy in the U.S. and Abroad." Federal Reserve Bank of Boston, *New England Economic Review.* January/February 1979.

Machlup, Fritz. "Euro-Dollar Creation: A Mystery Story." Banca Nazionale del Lavoro, *Quarterly Review* 94. September, 1970.

Niehans, Jurg and John Hewson. "The Eurodollar Market and Monetary Theory." *Journal of Money, Credit and Banking* 8. February, 1976.

Ossola, Rinaldo. "The Vulnerability of the International Financial System: International Lending and Liquidity Risk." Banca Nazionale del Lavoro, *Quarterly Review* 134. September, 1980.

Samuelson, Robert J. "Money Makes the World Go Round—But What if it Can't Anymore?" *National Journal.* September 27, 1980.

U.S. Government Publications

Karlik, John. "Some Questions and Brief Answers About the Euro-Dollar Market." U.S. Congress. House and Senate. Joint Economic Committee. Staff Study. 95th Congress, 1st Session. February 7, 1977.

U.S. Congress. House. Committee on Banking, Finance and Urban Affairs. Subcommittee on Domestic Monetary Policy and the Subcommittee on International Trade, Investment and Monetary Policy. *Hearings.* "The Eurocurrency Market Control Act of 1979." 96th Congress. 1st Session. June 26, 27 and July 12, 1979.

Monographs

Mayer, Helmut. "Credit and Liquidity Creation in the International Banking Sector." *BIS Economic Papers.* No. 1. November, 1979.

McKinnon, Ronald I. "The Eurocurrency Market." *Essays in International Finance.* No. 125. Princeton University. December, 1977.

Swoboda, Alexander K. "The Euro-Dollar Market: An Interpretation." *Essays in International Finance.* No. 64. Princeton University. Princeton: 1968.

Unpublished

Sterling, J. F., Jr. *A New Look at International Lending by American Banks.* (manuscript) 1980.

Volcker, Paul A. "The Recycling Problem Revisited." Speech before the Graduate School of Business Administration. New York University. March 1, 1980.

Bibliography, Chapter 6

Books

Cody, John Helen Hughes and David Wall (eds.). *Policies for Industrial Progress in Developing Countries,* New York: 1980.

Dell Sidney. *The Inter-American Development Bank: A Study in Development Financing.* New York: 1972.

Dewitt, R Peter, Jr. *The Inter-American Development Bank and Political Influence.* New York: 1977.

Hurni, Bettina S. *The Lending Policy of the World Bank in the 1970's: Analysis and Evaluation.* Boulder: 1980.

Lewis, John P. and Ishan Kapur (eds.). *The World Bank Group, Multilateral Aid, and the 1970's.* Lexington: 1973.

White, John. *Regional Development Banks. The Asian, African and Inter-American Development Banks.* New York: 1972.

Magazines

Hughey Ann. "Is the World Bank Biting Off More Than it Can Chew?" *Forbes.* May 26, 1980.

"International Banking Survey." *The Economist.* March 22, 1981.

"Latin American's Neighborhood Bank. " *The Economist.* July 5, 1980.

Journals

Dale, William B. "The Critical but Elusive Relationship Between Adjustment and Economic Growth." *Finance and Development* 13. September 1977.

Davies Derek. "Learning to Live with Debt." *Far Eastern Economic Review.* 96. June 10, 1977.

de Larosiere, Jacques. "Toward a Solution of International Economic Problems." *Finance and Development* 16. September 1979.

de Vries, Margaret Garritsen. "The Evolution of the International Monetary Fund and How it Relates to the Developing Countries." *International Development Review* 19. September 1977.

Friedmann, Efrain and Raymond Goodman. "Prospects for Oil and Gas Production in the Developing World." *Finance and Development* 16. June 1979. pp. 7–10. Taken From, *A Program to Accelerate Petroleum Production in the Developing Countries.* The World Bank. 1979.

Fromen, Stephen F. "Why the IMF is Increasing its Role in Recycling." *Euromoney* 13. January 1981.

Goodman, Raymond. "Managing the Demand for Energy in the Developing World." *Finance and Development* 17. December 1980.

Gruder, Monica. "Currents of Chance." *Finance and Development* 17. December 1980.

Guitan, Manuel. "Fund Conditionality and the International Adjustment Process: The Earlier Period 1950–1970." *Finance and Development* 17. December 1980.

Hornstein, Roger A. "Cofinancing of Bank and IDA Projects." *Finance and Development* 17. September 1980.

Hurni, Bettina. "The 'New Style' Lending Policy of the World Bank." *Journal of World Trade Law* 13. November/December 1979.

James, Lewis. "Clausen Will Help Those Who Help Themselves." *Euromoney* 12. December 1980.

Payer, Cheryl. "Commercial Banks and the IMF: An Uneasy Alliance." *Multinational Monitor* 1. April 1980.

Ping, Ho Kwon. "End of the McNamara Era." *Far Eastern Economic Review* 109. September 19, 1980.

Ruding, H. O. "Lenders Ought to Consult the IMF." *Euromoney* 12. February 1980.

Schmidt, Wilson E. "Rethinking the Multilateral Development Banks." Policy Review 10. Fall 1970.

Waelbroeck Jean L. and John A. Holsen. "The Less Developed Countries and the International Monetary Mechanism." *The American Economic Review. Papers and Proceedings* 66. May 1976.

Wright, E. Peter. "World Bank Lending for Structural Adjustment. *Finance & Development* l7. September 1980.

Monographs

Leeds, Roger S. "Co-financing for Development: Why Not More?" Overseas Development Council *Conference Paper* #29. April 1980.

Mahbub, Haq. "The Third World and the International Economic Order." Overseas Development Council *Conference Paper* #22. September 1976.

Southard, Frank A., Jr. "The Evolution of the International Monetary Fund." *Essays in International Finance.* #135. Princeton University. Princeton: December 1979.

U.S. Government Publications

U.S. Congress. Congressional Budget Office. "International Financial Institutions: Backgrounds and Budget Options for the Fiscal Year 1978." Budget Issue Paper. Washington, D.C. March 1977.

U.S. Congress. House. Committee on Banking, Finance and Urban Affairs. Subcommittee on International Development Institutions and Finance. *Hearings.* "International Development Association Sixth Replenishment and African Development Bank Membership." 96th Congress, 2nd Session. March 26–April 16, 1980.

U.S. Congress. House. Committee on Banking, Finance and Urban Affairs. Subcommittee on International Development Institutions and Finance. *Hearings.* "U.S. Participation in Multilateral Development Institutions." 95th Congress, 2nd Session. Hearings held February 28–May 18, 1978.

U.S. Congress. Senate. Committee on Banking, Housing and Urban Affairs. Subcommittee on International Finance. *Hearings.* "International Monetary Fund and Related Legislation." 96th Congress, 2nd Session. March 3l–April 16, 1980.

U.S. Congress. Senate. Committee on Governmental Affairs. Committee Print.

U.S. Participation in the Multilateral Development Banks. 96th Congress, 1st Session. 1979.

Business & Non-Profit Publications

International Bank for Reconstruction and Development. *Energy in the Developing Countries.* Washington, D.C. August 1980.

International Bank for Reconstruction and Development. *World Bank Annual Report, 1980.* Washington, D.C. 1980.

International Bank for Reconstruction and Development. World Development Report 1980. Washington, D.C. August 1980.

"LDC Prospects and the Role of the IMF." Morgan Guaranty Trust Company of New York, *World Financial Markets.* September 1980. pp. 1–15.

Unpublished

McNamara, Robert S. "A Program to Accelerate Petroleum Production in the Developing Countries." *Memorandum.* International Bank for Reconstruction and Development. February 5, 1980.

McNamara, Robert S. "Lending for 'Structural Adjustment.' " *Memorandum.* International Bank for Reconstruction and Development. February 5, 1980.

Bibliography, Chapter 7

Books

Cline, William R. *Trand Negotiations in the Tokyo Round.* Washington, D.C. 1978.

Hillman, Jimmye S. *Non-Tariff Agricultural Trade Barriers.* Lincoln: 1978.

Hindley, Brian. "Voluntary Export Restraints and Article XIX of the General Agreement on Tariffs and Trade." in *Current Issues in Commercial Policy and Diplomacy.* John Black and Brian Hindley eds. New York: 1980. pp. 52–72.

Kostecki, M.M. *East-West Trade and the GATT System. New York: 1979.*

Meier, Gerald M. Problems of Trade Policy. London and New York: 1973.

Row, Michael. *The Role of Tariff Quotas in Commercial Policy.* London: 1979.

Journals

Balassa, Bela. "The Tokyo Round and the Developing Countries." *Journal of World Trade Law* 14. March/April 1980.

Bates, Michael S. "The Voluntary Quota System for Regulating Steel Imports." *Virginia Journal of International Law* 14. Fall 1973.

Berger, Robert G. "Preferential Trade Treatment for Less Developed Countries: Implications of the Tokyo Round." *Harvard International Law Journal* 20. Fall 1979.

Grzybowski, Kazimierz. "Socialist Countries in GATT. *American Journal of Comparative Law.* Fall 1980.

Horsch, Richard A. "Eliminating Nontariff Barriers to International Trade: The MTN Agreement on Government Procurement." *New York University International Law and Politics* 12. Fall 1979.

Mayrzedt, Hans. "Unstable Exchange Rates and Trade Policy: An Impetus for Reforming GATT." 14. September–October 1979.

Olechowski, Andrzej and Gary Sampson. "Current Trade Restrictions in the EEC, the United States and Japan." *Journal of World Trade Law* 14. May/June 1980.

Page, Sheila A. "The Increased Use of Trade Controls by the Industrial Countries." *Intereconomics* 15. May/June 1980.

Rode, Reinard. "The U.S. Trade Policy Towards the EC in the Tokyo Round." *Intereconomics* 14. September/October 1979.

Samuelson, Robert J. "The Trade Game's New Rules—Will Everybody Play by Them?" *National Journal* 2. April 21, 1979.

Smith, Malcolm D. H. "Voluntary Export Quotas and U.S. Trade Policy—A New Nontariff Barrier." *Law and Policy in International Business* 5. Winter 1973.

von Dewitz, Wedige. "The Multi-Lateral GATT Negotiations." *Intereconomics* 14. July/August 1979.

Walter, Ingo. "Protection Industries in Trouble—The Case of Iron and Steel." *World Economy* 2. London: May 1979.

U.S. Government Publications

Morkre, Morris E. and David G. Tarr. "The Effects of Restrictions on United States Imports: Five Case Studies and Theory." United States Federal Trade Commission, *Bureau of Economics Staff Report.* June 1980.

Perey, Larenzo L. (ed.). *Trade Policies Toward Developing Countries: The Multinational Trade Negotiations.* Agency for International Development. Washington, D.C. 1978.

U.S. Congress. Senate. Committee on Finance. Subcommittee on International Trade. *Hearings.* "Implementation of the Multilateral Trade Negotiations." 96th Congress, 1st Session. February 21–22, 1979.

U.S. Tariff Commission. *Trade Barriers.* Washington, D.C. 1974.

Monographs

Blackhurst, Richard. "Trade Liberalization, Protectionism and Interdependence." *GATT Studies in International Trade* No. 5. Geneva: November 1977.

Business Publications

"New Focus on International Services." *Morgan Guaranty Survey.* May 1980. pp. 10-12.

Bibliography, Chapter 8

Books

Burns, E. Bradford *et. al. Latin America—A Concise Interpretive History.* Prentice-Hall, Inc., N.J. 1977. (Especially Chapters 5 and 6).

Diejamaoh, Victor P. *Economic Development in Nigeria—Its Problems, Challenges, and Prospects.* Princeton: 1965.

El Fathaly, Omar I., Monte Palmer and Richard Charckerian. Political Development and Bureaucracy in Libya. Lexington: 1977.

Erb, Guy F. and Valeriana Kallab (eds.). *Beyond Dependency: The Developing World Speaks Out.* Washington, D.C. September 1975.

Germides, Dimitri (ed.). *Transfer of Technology by Multinational Corporations.* Paris: 1977.

Grassholtz, Jean. *Politics in the Philippines.* Boston and Toronto: 1964.

Hanson, Simon Gabriel. *Economic Development in Latin America—An Introduction to the Economic Problems of Latin America.* Washinton, D.C. 1951.

Hollis, Chenery, *et. al. Patterns of Development,* 1950–1970. London: 1975.

Li, K. T. *The Experience of Dynamic Economic Growth on Taiwan.* Taipei: 1976.

Needler, Martin C. *Politics and Society in Mexico.* Albuquerque: 1971.

Organization for Economic Cooperation and Development. *Choice and Adoption of Technology in Developing Countries: An Overview of Major Policy Issues.* (See especially Chapter III.).

Ramesh, Jairam and Charles Weiss, Jr. (eds.). Mobilizing Technology for World Development. New York: 1979. (Especially Chapter 6).

Robinson, Austin. *Appropriate Technologies for Third World Development.* New York: 1979.

Thorbecke, Erick (ed.). *The Role of Agriculture in Economic Development: A Conferences of the Universities*—National Bureau Committee for Economic Research. New York: 1969.

Todaro, Michael P. *Economic Development in the Third World: An Introduction to Problems and Policies in a Global Perspective.* London: 1977.

Wade, Larry L. *Economic Development of South Korea: The Political Economy of Success.* New York: 1978.

Wraith, Ronald and Edgar Simpkins. *Corruption in Developing Countries.* London: 1963.

Yen, Chia-Kan. *Economic Development in Taiwan.* Jamaica, New York: 1970.

Magazines

"Vigorous LDCs." *Time.* September 25, 1978.

"When Poor Countries Turn the Tables in World Trade." *U.S. News and World Report* 85. October 16, 1978.

Journals

Altbach, P. "Education, Dependency and Neocolonialism." *The Education Digest* 43. April 1978.

Brecher, Charles and Vladimir Pucik. "The Banks in the U.S. Economy: The Japanese Example." *The Columbia Journal of World Business* 15. Spring 1980.

Casanova, P. Gonzalez. "Economic Development of Mexico." *Scientific American* 243. September 1980.

Diaz-Alejandro, Carlos F. "International Markets for LDCs—The Old and the New." *American Economic Review* 68. May 1978.

Hicks, Norman L. "Is There A Tradeoff Between Growth and Basic Needs?" *Finance & Development* 17. June 1980.

Lees, Francis A. and Maximo Eng. "Developing Countries Access to the International Capital Markets." *The Columbia Journal of World Business* 14. Fall 1979.

Tarapore, Sarah S. "Financing Technology Transfer to Developing Countries." *International Development Review.* 16. February 1974.

Wood, G. M. *et. al.* "Animals as an Energy Source in the Third World Agriculture." *Science* 208. May 9, 1980.

Newspapers

"Developing Countries Seek Technological Aid at U.N. Conference. *The Washington Post.* August 25, 1979. A–22.

"Mexico Liberalizes Rules for Campaign." *The New York Times.* May 6 1979. p. 7.

U.N. Unit Reports on the Third-World Food Shortage." *The Washington Post.* November 11, 1979. A–24.

Monographs

Outters-Jaeger, Ingelies. "The Development Impact of Barter in Developing Countries." Synthesis Report. Organization for Economic Cooperation and Development. Paris: 1979.

Stewart, Frances. "International Technology Transfer: Issues and Policy Options." The World Bank, *Staff Working Paper* 344. July 1979.

Tyler, William G. "Advanced Developing Countries as Export Competitors: The Brazilian Experience." The Center for Strategic and International Studies *Significant Issues Series* 2, 8. June 1980.

U.S. Government Publications

Executive Office of the President. United States Trade Representative. *A Preface to Trade.* Washington D.C. 1980.

Business and Other Publications

Hans, Bent. Rand Corporation. *Economic Development in Egypt.* Santa Monica: 1969.

The World Bank. *World Development Report*. Washington D.C. August 1980.

Unpublished

Prospects for the Least-Developed Countries in the Eighties. Report of Seminar held at the OECD Development Centre. Paris: December 12 and 13 1979.

Interdependence and Development. Seminar of the 15 years of activity of the OECD Development Centre. Paris: December 12 and 13, 1978.

Bibliography Chapter 9

Books

Fatemi, Nasrollah S., Gail W. Williams, and Thibaut de Saint Phalle. *Multinational Corporations.* New York: 1975.

Griffen, James Henry. *The Legal and Practical Aspects of Trade With the Soviet Union.* New York: 1971.

Hardy, Randall H. *China's Oil Future: A Case of Modest Expectations.* Boulder: 1978.

Kreinin, Mordechai E. *International Economics, A Policy Approach.* New York: 1975.

Nagarski, Zygmunt, Jr. *The Psychology of East-West Trade.* New York: 1974.

The Atlantic Council, Committee for East-West Trade. *East-West Trade: Managing Encounter and Accommodation.* Boulder: 1977.

Magazines

"Lending to Communist Nations." *Time.* December 1, 1980.

Meyer, Herbert E. "China's Inscrutable Paper Play." *Fortune.* October 6, 1980. (Chinese paper shopping spree).

Meyer, Herbert E. "Helping the Soviet Union to Avoid an Energy Crisis." *Fortune.* January 29, 1979.

"New Threat to China's Economy: Inflation." *Business Week.* January 19, 1981.

Ringwald, George. "Why Japan is Scrapping Sanctions Against Russia." *Business Week.* December 22, 1980.

"Slackening Pace of Soviet Output." *Business Week.* November 3, 1980.

"The Hidden Hazards in a China Grain Pact." *Business Week.* October 27, 1980.

Journals

Bingham, Jonathan B. and Victor C. Johnson. "A Rational Approach to Export Controls." *Foreign Affairs* 57. Spring 1979.

Chasin, Joseph B. and Eugene D. Jaffee. "Industrial Buyer Attitude Toward Goods Made in Eastern Europe." *The Columbia Journal of World Business* 14. Summer 1979.

Hasse, Rolf. "What is 'Normal' East-West Trade?" *Intereconomics* 15. March/April 1980.

Lange, Irene and James S. Elleat. "U.S. Role in East-West Trade." *Journal of International Business Studies* 8. Fall/Winter 1977.

Miller, Mark E. "The Role of Western Technology in Soviet Strategy." *ORBIS* 22. Fall 1978.

Solomon, Richard H. "Thinking Through the China Problem." *Foreign Affairs* 56. January 1978.

Yergin, Daniel. "Politics and Soviet Trade." *Foreign Affairs* 55. April 1977.

Yu, Nin. "Petroleum Exploration in the Peoples' Republic of China." *World Oil.* September 1980.

Newspapers

Shipler, David K. "The Soviet Block: Dependence and Independence." *The New York Times.* May 14, 1979. p. A-10.

U.S. Government Publications

Department of Commerce. "Trading With the USSR." *Overseas Business Reports.* Washington, D.C. July 1977.

Department of Commerce. International Trade Administration. *Doing Business with China.* Washington, D.C. November 1980.

Department of State. *Foreign Economic Trends and their Implications for the United States: USSR.* February 1979.

Department of State. *Foreign Economic Trends and Their Implications for the United States:* Yugoslavia. (Released by the Department of Commerce). Washington, D.C. August 1978.

U.S. Congress. House and Senate. Joint Economic Committee. Committee Print. *East European Economies Post-Helsinki.* 95th Congress, 1st Session. 1977. (Compendium of papers submitted to the Joint Economic Committee).

Business Publications

Business International, S.A. "Doing Business with the USSR." *Business International.* Geneva: 1971.

The Conference Board, Inc. "East-West Trade, The Lessons from Experience." *The Conference Board.* New York: 1971.

Unpublished

Department of State. Press Conference. *Soviets Reject Trade Agreement.* January 14, 1975.

Lieberthal, Kenneth. "Chinese Politics in 1978: Modernization and the Ghost of Mao." *Address.* China Council of the Asia Society. New York: November 30, 1978.

Bibliography, Chapter 10

Books

Denison, Edward F. and William K. Chung. *How Japan's Economy Grew So Fast: The Sources of Postwar Expansion.* Washington. 1976.

Hill, Christopher T. and James M. Utterback. *Technological Innovation for a Dynamic Economy.* Boston: October 1979.

Johnson, Harry A. "Keynes and British Economics." in *Essays on John Maynard Keynes.* Cambridge: 1975.

Kendrick, John W. *Understanding Productivity: An Introduction to the Dynamics of Productivity Change.* Baltimore: 1975.

Kendrick, John W. and Elliot Grossner. *Productivity Trends in the United States.* Baltimore: 1979.

Perlman, Mark. "One Man's Baedeker to Productivity Growth Discussions." in *Contemporary Economic Problems.* American Enterprise Institute. Washington, D.C. 1979.

Ture, Norman B. and Kenneth B. Sanden. *Effects of Tax Policy on Capital Formation.* New York: 1977.

Vogel, Ezra F. *Japan as Number One: Lessons for America.* Cambridge: 1979.

Magazines

"American Productivity Crisis: Special Report." *Newsweek.* September, 1980.

Bryant, William C. "Productivity: Only Real Cure for Inflation." *U.S. News and World Report.* March 12, 1979.

Business Week. August 27, 1979.

"Curing Ailing Industries." *Time.* July 14, 1980.

"Productivity Pinch." *Time.* August 27, 1979.

"Robots Change the Rules." *The Economist.* April 19, 1980.

"The Death of Equities." *Business Week.* August 13, 1979.

"The Reindustrialization of America." *Business Week.* Special Issue. June 30, 1980.

"U.S. Output—How it Stacks Up Against Other Nations." *U.S. News and World Report.* April 28, 1980.

Journals

Bennett, Paul. "American Productivity Growth: Perspectives on the Slowdown." Federal Reserve Bank of New York. *Quarterly Review* 4. Autumn 1979.

Daly, Keith and Arthur Neff. "Productivity and Unit Labor Costs in Eleven Industrial Countries 1977." *Monthly Labor Review* 101. November 1978.

de Saint Phalle, Thibaut. "The Masochism of American Trade: GATT and the Tokyo Round." *The Washington Quarterly* 2. Summer 1979.

Franko, Lawrence. "U.S. Regulation of the Spread of Nuclear Technologies Through Supplier Power: Lever or Boomerang?" *Law and Policy in International Business* 10. Fall 1978.

Hannon, Timothy. "The Productivity Perplex: A Concern for the Supply Side—Labor Productivity Trends 1948–1978." Federal Reserve Bank of Philadelphia, *Business Review.* March/April 1980.

"International Competition: U.S. Arrogance Costs Firms Billions in Lost Jobs." *Engineering News Record.* November 29, 1979.

Kirtschner, Ronald W., Jerome A. Monk and John Norswothy. "Productivity Slowdown and the Outlook to 1985." *Monthly Labor Review* 100. May 1977.

Lipper, Kenneth. "American Competitive Position in International Commerce Jeopardized." *Journal of Commerce.* April 30, 1980.

"Productivity and Unit Labor Cost Comparisons for Selected Countries." *Capital Goods Review.* March 1980.

"Puzzling Drop in Productivity in Terms of National Income per Person Employed." *Challenge.* May/June 1979.

Saito, Katine A. "Labor Productivity in Major Corporations." *Oriental Economist* 48. May 1980.

"Savings Levels and Productivity Growth: Comparative Trends in Major Industrial Countries, 1960–1977." *Capital Goods Review.* April 1980.

Tatom, John A. "The Productivity Problem." Federal Reserve Bank of St. Louis, *Review.* September 1979.

Weinberg, Edgar. "Defining the Game and the Players." *IEEE Spectrum.* October 1978.

Wyss, Al. "Declining Rate of Productivity Threatens Economy." *Journal of Commerce.* December 26, 1979.

Newspapers

Behr, Peter. "Automotive Primer: A Tale of Two Cities." *The Washington Post.* June 1, 1980. p. F-1, F-6.

Drucker, Peter. "Learning from Foreign Management." *The Wall Street Journal.* June 4, 1980. p. 24.

Feaver, Douglas. "Imported Subway Cars Roll." *The Washington Post.* February 24, 1980.

Morgan, Dan. "French Radial Tires: Case History of Technology." *The Washington Post.* March 9, 1979. p. A-18.

"Paris Bourse is Booming as Tax Rebate Pushes French Bourgeoisie to Buy Stocks." *The Wall Street Journal.* June 4, 1980. p. 18.

"Productivity Lag Causes Worry." *The New York Times.* May 8, 1979.

Monographs

Behrman, Jack and Raymond Mikesell. "The Impact of U.S. Foreign Direct Investment on U.S. Export Competitiveness." Center for Strategic and International Studies, *Significant Issues* Series 2, No. 1. 1980.

U.S. Government Publications

Department of Labor. Bureau of Labor Statistics. *Productivity Indexes for Selected Countries 1978.* Bulletin #2002. Washington, D.C. 1979.

Executive Office. Report of the President to Congress on the Trade Agreements Act of 1979. September 9, 1980.

Presidential Commission on International Trade and Investment Policy. "United States International Economic Policy in an Interdependent World." Report Submitted to the President. Washington, D.C. July 1971.

"Study of U.S. Competitiveness." Study of Export Trade Policy as Mandated in Section 1110 of the Trade Agreements Act of 1979. Sumbitted to the Economic Trade Policy Analysis Subcommittee of the Trade Policy Staff Committee. July 15, 1980.

U.S. Congress. House. *Congressional Record.* "Competitiveness Report to the United States Congress." Submitted by the Export Import Bank of the United States. January 1980. H-2523-2525. April 15, 1980.

U.S. Congress. House and Senate. House Ways and Means Committee. Joint Committee on Taxation. Committee Print. *Tax Policy and Capital Formation.* April 1977.

U.S. Congress. House and Senate. Joint Economic Committee. *Hearings* on Productivity. (Especially Testimony of Joji Arai). 96th Congress, 1st Session. June 5 and 6th, 1979.

U.S. Congress. House and Senate. Joint Economic Committee. *Hearings.* Special Study on Economic Change, Part II. 95th Congress, 2nd Session. June 8, 9, 13 and 14, 1978.

U.S. Congress. House and Senate. Joint Economic Committee. *Hearings.* "U.S.–Japanese Trade Relations." October 10, 1979. (96th Cong. 1st Session.)

U.S. Congress. House and Senate. Joint Economic Committee. Staff Study. *Achieving Social and Economic Balance.* June 1980.

U.S. Congress. House and Senate. Joint Economic Committee. Staff Study. *Productivity and Inflation.* Washington, D.C. April 24, 1980.

U.S. Congress. House and Senate. Joint Economic Committee. Staff Study. *Productivity in the Federal Government.* May 31, 1979.

U.S. Congress. Senate. Committee on Banking, Housing and Urban Affairs. Subcommittee on International Finance. Hearings. (Held Jointly with the Committee of Commerce, Science and Transportation. Subcommittee on Science, Technology and Space.) 95th Congress, 2nd Session. May 16, 1978.

United States–Japan Trade. Report by the Comptroller General of the United States. September 21, 1979.

Business Publications

"Behind the Slump in the Productivity Growth, United States, 1948–1978." *Morgan Guaranty Survey.* November 1978. pp. 7–11.

"Investment and the Growth Productivity." *Morgan Guaranty Survey.* September 1979. pp. 10–15.

The New York Stock Exchange. *Building a Better Future—Economic Choices* for the 1980's. December 1979.

The New York Stock Exchange, Office of Economic Research. *Reaching a Higher Standard of Living.* 1979.

Unpublished

Hefner, Robert A. III. "Inflation, Productivity and the Inferno of Red Tape." Address to Harriman Campus, Columbia University. Harriman, New York: March 22, 1980.

Kilmarx, Robert. Director of Business and Defense Studies, Center for Strategic and International Studies. "Declining U.S. Export Competitiveness." Address, CSIS. October 16, 1979.

Williams, Joseph D. Address Regarding Productivity Council for the Health Care Industry. Given at National Wholesale Druggists' Association. Honolulu: December 21, 1979.

Index

See glossary for definitions of abbreviations and acronyms.